Russia's Invasion of Ukraine

Paul J. J. Welfens

Russia's Invasion of Ukraine

Economic Challenges, Embargo Issues, and
a New Global Economic Order

Paul J. J. Welfens
European Institute for International Economic
Relations (EIIW)/Schumpeter School of Business
and Economics
University of Wuppertal
Wuppertal, Germany

ISBN 978-3-031-19137-4   ISBN 978-3-031-19138-1   (eBook)
https://doi.org/10.1007/978-3-031-19138-1

Cover image credit: Anton Petrus/Getty Images

This Palgrave Macmillan imprint is published by the registered company Springer Nature
Switzerland AG.
The registered company address is: Gewerbestrasse 11, 6330 Cham, Switzerland

PREFACE

Russia's invasion of Ukraine on February 24, 2022, was a turning point for Europe and the global economy. This latest phase of the war of aggression against Ukraine (after the 2014 invasion and annexation of Crimea) represents a breach of international political trust by President Vladimir Putin by way of an attack on Ukraine and its 44 million inhabitants, an invasion that was quickly followed by the uncovering of potential war crimes. Within six weeks of the 2022 invasion, around five million Ukrainians had already fled abroad, fleeing destruction, suffering, and death. Russia has not succeeded in achieving the expected quick victory over Ukraine, as communicated to his domestic audience by President Putin, nor has his rather strange expectation that Russia's troops would be welcomed as liberators by the people of Ukraine materialized. In addition to the military aspects of the Russo-Ukrainian war, a new international economic war has also broken out in the context of the massive Western-led sanctions as well as Russian counter-sanctions.

The economic debate and analysis concerning what economic sanctions would be optimal when it comes to the energy sector—concerning oil and gas—has been somewhat controversial in Germany and many other European Union (EU) member countries as well as in the US, the UK, and indeed elsewhere. Particularly in Germany and the EU, as well as in the US, issues surrounding an energy import embargo are critically discussed with regard to Russia. In the media, it is repeatedly pointed out that EU energy imports from Russia are largely financing its war expenditures. What at first thus sounds like a plausible view to hold, it is not really convincing on closer examination. What would be the effects of a gas import boycott by the EU or a conceivable EU import tariff on Russian gas exports to the EU? If Germany or the EU as a bloc were to be affected by gas embargo decisions taken in Russia—concerning exports—or taken within the EU itself concerning Russian imports—which would result in gas shortages for households and industry, how would one cope with the problems of a short-term gas shortage or stark gas price increases? The oil import embargo announced in June 2022 by the EU will be largely ineffectual, as Russia will be able to sell oil no longer sold in Europe to customers elsewhere, such as in Asia.

If, for example, one wanted to significantly reduce the use of gas in electricity generation, one would have to counter the problem of a gas shortage by using more coal in electricity generation. However, this would lead to a strong increase in CO_2 emissions in the EU energy sector, which should actually be prevented in view of the EU's goal of achieving climate neutrality by 2050. The Russo-Ukrainian war thus brings many problems, including an important one for the entire world—beyond the conceivable threat of war: namely, that the goal of climate neutrality is now much more difficult to achieve than before. This means that, in a broader sense, the costs of war are very high not only for Ukraine and Russia but also for the entire global economy. Yet if these war costs—broadly defined—are indeed so high, if there are indeed global effects, why—from the point of view of intelligence services and the scientific field—was the potential for a full-blown war between Ukraine and Russia not taken much more seriously much earlier? Why was the war not prevented—or to put it bluntly: who are the culprits in this war?

Among the interesting insights of this book is not only a much broader view of the Russo-Ukrainian war than is usually the case in the publications that have appeared so far. Rather, there are also additional insights offered herein, which are, however, sometimes of a peculiar nature: for example, for just €18, one could have read the French book by Michel Eltchaninoff, a professor of philosophy, in 2015, which provided fundamental and disturbing information on the development of Vladimir Putin's ideology. Incidentally, the author of these lines was astonished to find out in the course of researching this book—as presumably will the vast majority of the readership of this book be—that state visits by Russia leaders to the UK only take place every 129 years; and that this was apparently considered quite sufficient in London and Moscow. There was evidence of some willingness for improvement from the British side as Prime Minister Cameron visited Moscow in 2011, but this thawing of diplomatic relations already had cooled noticeably by 2014 when President Putin decided to occupy parts of Ukraine in early 2014. Putin apparently did not fully understand just how much was at state when he ordered Russian forces into Ukraine that year.

The international economic effects of the war include a massive increase in oil prices—and in their slipstream, an increase in inflation—as well as a significant slowdown in economic growth in both developed and emerging economies. Russia's economic output is expected to collapse by more than 10% in the medium term, with significant braking effects also on the economies of Central Asian countries via reduced trade and reduced guest worker remittances from Russia to these countries.

The scope of analysis of the Russo-Ukrainian war is often much too narrow. Since May 2022, however, it has been understood that the effects of this war will not only affect energy market developments; it is also about Ukraine's wheat exports and indeed Russia's wheat exports, with Russian President Putin being able to impose de facto export barriers on both countries. The EU has announced that in the event of restrictions on Ukraine's wheat exports via its Black Sea ports, it will help Ukraine to increase truck and rail-based exports to the West; however, the very long lines of trucks which were visible in Ukraine at its western borders in May 2022 showed little evidence of unbureaucratic, rapid EU measures to support Ukraine.

The West, which was already marked by increased inflation in 2021—caused in part by broken international supply chains (think, for example, of the container ship *Ever Given*, which became stuck and blocked the Suez Canal for a week)—is, in mid-2022, facing inflation rates in almost double digits in the context of the Russo-Ukrainian war. Firstly, disrupted international supply chains are again playing a role here, as China's zero-COVID policy in the case of Shanghai and other cities facing lockdowns cripples some of the world's largest ports for weeks, as well as key manufacturing facilities in China. Added to this, this time because of the war, are rising energy prices and rising international grain prices. Here, Russia's belligerence and its foreign economic policy may contribute to a serious inflation problem in many countries across the West, and not only there. There is some danger of a wage-price-wage spiral, but this can be temporary if monetary policy and income policy work together sensibly. The fact that unemployment rates are temporarily falling in EU countries and in the US is due to a new Phillips curve phenomenon: unexpectedly high inflation rates cause the real wage rate of those in work to fall. Vladimir

Putin may hope that political unrest will emerge in the West and that this will weaken support for Ukraine in the medium term. However, it is also understood in the capitals of the EU that the fall of Ukraine is likely to critically increase Russia's propensity for military aggression against other Eastern European countries.

Russia's invasion of eastern and southern Ukraine brought some initial Russian success, with invading forces ultimately occupying Mariupol, Ukraine's second most important port city, four months after the invasion, which was launched on February 24, 2022. The military approach that appeared designed to cut Ukraine off from the Sea of Azov appears to be partially successful. Russia's military is far from occupying Ukraine more broadly; however; the full capture of the Donbas region appears possible.

One key issue concerns the question of whether Western policies could have helped avoiding Putin's shift toward a much more aggressive foreign policy stance after 2005. The extent of Western ignorance and, arguably dangerous, early policy developments in terms of the West's relationship with Russia are rather unsurprising, if one would note, for example, that official visits of the Russian head of state to London occur only every 129 years. This is, with a hint of cynicism, an allusion to Putin's state visit to the UK in 2003. Moreover, Russia has a structural advantage as a large country—its sheer size makes it almost impossible to attack with any prospect of success (Napoleon and Hitler were among those leaders who had to learn this lesson the hard way). However, geographic size is also a structural disadvantage when it comes to the choice of form of government: developing such a large country as a democracy is conceivable, but the lack of foreign travel—as a consequence of size—is a disadvantage in the political debate for achieving democracy in a country with 144 million inhabitants.

If you live in the Netherlands, for example, you could have reached dozens of democracies at a reasonable price after a maximum of a six-hour flight. If you fly six hours within Russia, you are still in Russia, unless you have flown north-south. Nevertheless, after 1991, new travel opportunities emerged for only the top 20 million or so, those who could travel to Athens, Paris, Berlin, London, or Lisbon; thanks also to the emergence of low-cost airlines flying from Russia and from EU countries. These almost 15% of the Russian population were able to visit Western countries (but the time spent in the West was apparently too short to win a large majority of the Russian population over to Western ideas).

The countries reached by Russian travelers are not exactly examples of democracies either, apart from Turkey, a fragile Lebanon, and Israel. Moreover, the populist promises of any autocracy—that it will provide prosperity and stability as well as preserve conservative traditions—may sound attractive in a country that classifies its own development as relatively stable and that, for example, suffered the transition to a market economy in a democratic system in 1998 in the form of a shocking economic collapse. This was before broad democracy-friendly privatization had been achieved—as had been achieved to some extent in Poland, the Czech Republic, and the Slovak Republic, as well as Bulgaria by 1997. While based at the University of Potsdam, I indeed led a project team on a research project (financed by the Alfred Krupp von Bohlen And Halbach Foundation, Essen) in which we tried to develop some key insights for a consistent Russian transformation policy in core fields whereby colleagues from the Leontief Center in St. Petersburg and from the Higher School of Economics in Moscow also participated. However, our presentations and publications, including a 2004 book in the Russian language, which I coedited along with Evgeny Gavrilenkov—*Infrastructure, Investment and Economic Integration: Perspectives on Eastern Europe and Russia* (original title: *Infrastruktura, investicji i ekonomiceskaja integracja. Perspektivy Vostocnoj Evropy i Rosiii*), University Publishing House/GU VSchE, Gosudarstviennyj Universitet Vysschaja Schkola Ekonomiki, Moscow— had only a limited effect on the political and economic debate in Moscow; much in contrast to a similar transformation project in Poland (with colleagues from Hertford College at the University of Oxford), we found it quite difficult to gain access to the managers of leading Russian companies. Later at two conferences in St. Petersburg, which involved representatives from ministries of the Russian government, I occasionally had the impression that the self-proclaimed big power status of the new Russia resulted in a certain resistance to benefiting from Western and Eastern European experiences in terms of key policy reform elements and the broad range of available transformation experiences.

There was also little in the way of broad privatization achieved in Ukraine or Hungary; Ukraine, like Russia in 1998/1999, realized an oligarchic privatization, which means a very strong concentration of wealth in the hands of very few. In Hungary, there was only weak domestic entrepreneurship in many sectors as Hungary had initially organized the privatization of the economy in a kind of large-scale tender for foreign multinationals as major investors.

In the Balkans, Russia retained some of its old influence in certain countries; Serbia is one such important partner—not only since the Kosovo War—which at the same time also strives to develop economically in the direction of the EU. All of these changes were considered relatively uninteresting by the Trump administration in the US from 2016 till 2020—the judgment had been reached that the US was uninterested in Ukraine. The West will see in the 2021 withdrawal from Afghanistan an ignominious exit that was managed only slightly better militarily speaking than Russia's own withdrawal from Afghanistan in 1989. The instability of the partial Western occupation of Afghanistan was followed by the victory of the militarily and technologically inferior Taliban, which is not easy for either Russia or the US to understand as military superpowers.

Russia certainly understood the US withdrawal from Afghanistan as a sign of military weakness; moreover, President Putin's support for Syrian autocrat Bashar Al-Assad ensured that he was able to hold on to power in 2020/2021, leaving his opponents—supported by the West—losing out; in the mix, there was also the Islamic State terrorist group, whose birth was attributed by the political leadership in Russia to the seemingly chaotic US-led intervention in Iraq. Thus, 2022 seemed to present a good opportunity for Putin to lead the "fraternal" people of Ukraine (or, in imperial Russian terminology, "Little Russia") back to the Russian "family".

Putin came to the view that Ukraine actually belonged to Russia over the course of about a decade—with an ideology constructed around the works of just a few Russian philosophers. Thus, from Putin's point of view, the use of the Russian military to intervene to recover Ukraine was a relatively attractive prospect—the philosopher Ivan Ilyin had warned against Ukraine's "separation" from Russia early on—leading to his announcement that this intervention would happen under the headings of the liberation of Ukraine and in support of Ukrainian democracy.

In 2014, the Russian intervention in and occupation of Crimea seemed to succeed as a master-stroke facing relatively little resistance, and Putin's argument that Crimea had always been part of Russia—politically and culturally—did not seem to be easily dismissed; especially since a democratic majority in a regional referendum likely yielded a majority in favor of the annexation of Crimea by Russia. For Putin, the annexation of Crimea increased the temptation to achieve further "successes" with his military. The resulting Russo-Ukrainian war of 2022, which came partly as a surprise from the perspective of the West, is a turning point and threatens to destroy the established global economic order; one can note, that several regional specialists on Ukraine and Russia had pointed out the risk of Russian military aggression from about 2007 on. The stakes in this conflict are naturally high for Ukraine and Russia, but also for Germany and the EU, respectively, not to mention the US and China.

The following economic analysis focuses on trade and economic relations between the EU and Russia. The question of possible EU energy import embargos—with a focus on oil and gas supplies from Russia—concern important sectoral and macroeconomic aspects: with worldwide economic effects, which were controversially discussed in the first half of 2022, especially in Germany and the EU as well as in the US. Important questions about the effects of large refugee flows from Ukraine toward Eastern and Western Europe are addressed; aspects of integration and migration, as well as problems of a possible enlargement of the EU to admit Ukraine as a member, are also in focus. Are Germany and other EU countries, as well as the UK and the US, providing enough humanitarian, financial, and military support to Ukraine? A controversial debate, which also arose in this regard in the first half of 2022, is critically reflected upon before the final chapter illuminates perspectives for a new world order after the Russo-Ukrainian war. Questions regarding New Political Economy perspectives of the world economy are raised herein also with a view to developments in the next decade(s).

Even if, by nature, only a scenario analysis can be carried out on some important points, it cannot be overlooked that there are serious dangers, which can be identified: the existing system of a rules-based international order in conjunction with effective international organizations could go under. But the "political club" of the BRICS countries—Brazil, Russia, India, China, and South Africa—is also facing new kinds of tensions. In a historic departure from the export policy of the Soviet Union, Russia is using its energy export policy as a political weapon, which may strengthen Moscow's position in the short term, but will cast doubt on the country's reliability internationally for many years to come. That some EU policymakers seem to want to see energy import sanctions imposed against Russia as a means of weakening Russia's war financing is, moreover, mainly wishful thinking when one takes a closer look at global adjustment processes. At the same time, it should be noted that Russia is no longer a constitutional state, as the important principle of proportionality of punishments no longer applies: anyone who calls Putin's invasion of Ukraine a "war" risks being sentenced to several years in prison.

De-globalization and chaos in many parts of the world—with and without military conflicts—are conceivable as a negative outcome. Even if such a negative scenario can be avoided, there are critical and difficult questions to be answered, namely how to first achieve some economic stabilization after a peace settlement, and what reforms are essential for a globally influential and cooperative "West+". Here, "West+" refers to the expansion of the OECD group of countries to include certain G20 countries, such as India and Brazil; whether the West will be able and willing to maintain the previous high expansion dynamics in terms of economic relations with China and Russia after an eventual peace agreement between Ukraine and Russia is an open question. Globalization is likely to become more selective, whereby the US and the EU—within the framework of the new EU-US Trade and Technology Council (TTC)—have been focusing on increased cooperation in the security-relevant area of information and communication technologies since 2021—even before the start of the Russo-Ukrainian war of 2022. From a Western perspective, there are arguments that global supply chains should be organized more flexibly and thus autocratic supplier countries in particular should be given less political power; autocratic power structures are often linked to state-owned enterprises.

The EU faces a particular challenge, as the question of an enlargement to admit Ukraine as a member will arise. Such an enlargement would be contentious with regard to the question of the order of candidate countries. There are numerous candidate countries, including Turkey and countries in the Western Balkans, which are quasi ahead of Ukraine in terms of time spent in the accession process. It is hard to see that the latter, in turn, would readily want to claim in a special way that it indeed fulfills the Copenhagen Criteria required for EU accession and that, moreover, the existing EU countries could easily cope with Ukraine's accession without any significant problems. A rapid accession of Ukraine to the EU could in turn bring serious problems for the EU, namely the next BREXIT-type event; or even several such cases. The accession of Ukraine, with about 40 million people, to the EU could in turn give rise to considerable distributional conflicts within the EU, where Western EU member states and also some Eastern EU member states are then unlikely to receive any EU funding (in 1993, Ukraine still had 52 million inhabitants—and its population is still declining). Moreover, Germany will play a special role, which will also amount to a military strengthening of Germany; whether this will contribute to stability in Europe in the long run remains to be seen.

The European Commission has a special function in the upcoming EU enlargements; of course, also in terms of the accession negotiations with Ukraine, which the Commission has already visibly supported in May and June 2022. It is strange, however, that the EU's statistics agency, Eurostat, of all places has been listing the population figures for Ukraine excluding the population of Crimea and the dispute regions in the Donbas since 2015, thus showing a lower population figure for Ukraine than, for example, the World Bank. The latter shows 44.6 million for 2018, but Eurostat, as the statistical office of the EU, shows 42.3 million as the population of Ukraine in 2018 (Demographic Statistics for the European Neighbourhood Policy—East Countries, 2019 edition, Brussels: there is a reference to a structural break in 2014, which probably relates to Russia's annexation of Crimea and involvement in the separatist regions of Donetsk and Luhansk). The population of countries plays an important role, among other things, in weighted votes at the European Council and Council of Ministers; and, of course, how the EU or the World Bank determines Ukraine's population is also a political question. It is hoped that the unresolved conflict in Crimea can be resolved diplomatically.

A serious and significant challenge for the West is to build better relations in the longer term, especially with China and Russia. That the democracies of the West will have problems building good relations with an autocratically ruled China and an autocratic, or even totalitarian, Russia will not be seen as surprising. Failure to develop peaceful cooperative relations—initially with a focus on economics—could result in a series of dangerous new international conflicts in the twenty-first century, conflicts that may be difficult to control.

As for the challenge between the West and Russia, one can point, by way of example, to the UK-Russia relationship between 1991 and 2021, which deteriorated almost continuously through various phases after 1991: Partly because Russia had developed a less than realistic foreign policy vis-à-vis the UK; but in part also because London has made relatively little effort to build better relations with Russia over time. Apart from joint counter-piracy efforts in Asia—a problem in the wake of the 1997/1998 Asian Crisis—London and Moscow have developed a few cooperative projects.

From the perspective of EU countries, a new period of uncertainty has emerged since 2016. Firstly, a populist president, Donald Trump, came to power in the US. Secondly, the opportunities economic globalization via trade and direct investment have presumably reached a limit after three decades—the risk of de-globalization and also regional disintegration, see BREXIT and questions about further EU exits, is visible on the horizon. Thirdly, the question arises as to whether the EU will succeed in shaping or stabilizing the EU integration process in a meaningful way—if the EU should stumble into a series of unstable new integration projects after the Russo-Ukrainian war, it will gradually disintegrate, meaning next to the already destabilized US would be a destabilized EU and a disintegration of the UK would likely follow. The decline of the West—with its three pillars of sustainable democracy, the rule of law, and a stable (for the most part) economy—would then be threatened.

A global policy toward achieving climate neutrality by the middle of the century would then be an illusion. A successful policy aimed at reaching climate neutrality by 2050 would certainly require all G20 countries, including Russia. The latter, under Putin, has become a country where the president may complain, in part rightly, about NATO (the North Atlantic Treaty Organization) eastward expansion, but where this president, above all, clearly exaggerates the threat to Russia posed by NATO—right down to the outlandish claim on May 9, 2022, at the Victory Day military parade in Moscow that NATO had planned to militarily conquer the Crimea region annexed by Russia in 2014.

Russia's invasion of Ukraine stemmed from a military and political calculation that counted on a quick military victory for Russia and the removal of the legitimate government in Ukraine—with its replacement by Russia-friendly politicians. This plan had already visibly failed by early May 2022. The political legacy of President Mikhail Gorbachev—with positive perspectives for democracy, a market economy and the rule of law—for Russia could not be preserved (I met Gorbachev twice myself, once in Boston and once in Linz, Austria—both times after Gorbachev's term in office was already over; my first scientific encounter with Eastern Europe—in socialist times—occurred at a 1982 workshop of young scientists in Warsaw and the result of a follow-up workshop was the publication some years later of the book *Innovationsdynamik im Systemvergleich* [transl. PJJW: Innovation Dynamics in Comparative Systems] (1988), edited together with Leszek Balcerowicz; in Russian, I contributed to a conference volume "Russia's Economy: Transformation Experience of the 1990s and Development Perspectives" after a workshop in Moscow and further books on transformation issues appeared in English).

In the 1980s, when the socialist system of the Soviet Union and other socialist countries began to experience a crisis, Russia's position vis-à-vis the West had improved in one aspect in foreign trade: namely, in the share of oil and gas in Western energy imports. Here, Russia was able to benefit economically from the politically deteriorating relationship between the EU and US, on one hand, and the primarily Middle Eastern countries in OPEC (Organization of the Petroleum Exporting Countries).

Under Gorbachev, Russia's relations with the West improved temporarily. After President Yeltsin took over from President Gorbachev, it took until 2003 for *his* successor, Vladimir Putin, to visit the UK. This was the first visit of a Russian head of state to London since 1874, and it is obvious that both London and Moscow had made little effort in the matter of state visits even as early as the period from 1875 till 1917. The Second World War brought some meetings between British and Russian leaders outside the UK (i.e., Yalta, Potsdam) and after 1997, there were meetings at a G8 level for a few years—this rapprochement was already frozen again in 2014 when Russia occupied Crimea. This tenuous UK-Russia relationship was no serious substitute for bilateral relations between a leading Western country and Russia.

That Putin saw the majority in favor of BREXIT in the June 2016 referendum in the UK as a personal success—the result of his policy of interference and destabilization via the role of Russian oligarchs (often with dual citizenship and a visible inclination to strengthen with donations the Conservative Party of David Cameron, Theresa May and Boris Johnson as party chairpersons and heads of government, respectively)—is obvious: publicly, Putin pointed out with regard to the British political debate that the democratic result of the BREXIT referendum demanded that a BREXIT indeed be carried out. Economically speaking, this amounted to a visible weakening of the UK and to new political conflicts within the UK, as well as economically to a weakening of the EU.

Russia's strongest integration into the international system came in 2012, when it became a member of the World Trade Organization (WTO). However, by 2016 with the election of the populist Donald Trump, the WTO was already on the US administration's hit list. In 2020, the WTO was no longer able to fulfill its mandate as the US had blocked the election of judges to the WTO's Appellate Body—undermining its role in the field of dispute settlement.

With the election of President Joe Biden, a temporary phase of policy normalization came about in the US and a quasi-recovery of the WTO was achieved; but the Biden administration also sought success in renewed bilateralism: instead of clearly focusing on patient WTO reforms, a new US-EU institution was founded in the form of the transatlantic Trade and Technology Council (TTC),which seeks to create a kind of substitute forum to the WTO for leading democracies and technology-relevant economic sectors in 2021/2022, with little visible political energy. From a US perspective, dissatisfaction with many international organizations, from the UN to the WTO to the World Bank, results from the fact that undemocratic countries also participate in such bodies and authoritarian countries not infrequently—think of Russia or China—prevent meaningful solutions to problems through approaches that were reasonable from the Western point of view. At the UN, a vote on the Russo-Ukrainian war produced a clear majority of countries on the side of the US. However, the countries that abstained—including India and China—represented almost half of the world's population.

The West, first and foremost the US, reacted promptly to the invasion with harsh sanctions against the Russian economy and state—to be more exact against Russia's leadership and elites. The EU had launched six packages of sanctions by mid-June 2022. Massive increases in oil and gas prices have, at times, increased inflationary pressure in developed and developing countries, weakening the recovery in member countries of the Organisation for Economic Co-operation and Development (OECD) in the medium term—and this at a time of economic stress in the wake of the Corona recession. In the following analysis, the focus is indeed substantially on the economic aspects or effects of the Russo-Ukrainian war. The present study has been written against the backdrop of an often emotionalized debate in the EU and the US due to the horrific images of war reaching every television, newspaper, computer, and smartphone; in many cases, there were loud calls for an immediate energy import boycott of European countries against Russia in the spring of 2022, and statements supportive of the supply of heavy weapons to Ukraine were also audible in the parliaments of several EU countries.

Above all, there were many examples in the political debates in Europe of people imploring Germany, in particular, to become more involved as a leading country in the sanctions. An energy import embargo was often called for on the grounds that this would significantly weaken Russia's financial base, which it uses to wage the war against Ukraine; it was said that without a boycott against Russia, the EU would effectively be indirectly financing the war against Ukraine. However, this view is not really tenable from an economic perspective.

The economic effects of the Russo-Ukrainian war also concern trade, direct investment and guest worker remittances in Europe and worldwide. There have been significant changes in oil and gas prices and, in addition, a broad transatlantic debate began on the issue of a possible EU energy import embargo targeting Russia and the associated economic effects such an embargo would bring. Finally, the challenge of large movements of refugees and aid, primarily from the OECD group of countries, to Ukraine and the Ukrainian people, respectively, has been addressed—with some potentially very misleading claims regarding the latter from the Kiel Institute for the World Economy. The Bachmann et al. study on the question of a German embargo against Russia, which underestimates the risk of a recession in Europe due to certain methodological weaknesses, is also not a very appropriate contribution with which to try and understand the economic challenges. More precisely, carefully considered and sensible strategies need to be implemented: Different approaches are called for with regard to the EU's import of gas and oil from Russia. Putin's war of aggression must be contained and rebuffed—also through a strengthened EU capable of swift and decisive action. In this context, however, a hasty enlargement of the EU, that is, the expedited accession of Ukraine, is questionable. Attempts to push through such an accession, albeit well-meaning, could sow the seeds of the next BREXIT-type scenario. In the end, the big question facing policymakers is how to bring about a new, stable and humanitarian world order with good prospects for achieving climate neutrality—not by permanently excluding Russia from the global community, but by integrating the country better only after comprehensive political reforms.

The question of what a sensible sanctions strategy against Russia should look like is indeed complicated; the aim is obviously to persuade President Putin to engage in peace negotiations with Kyiv as soon as possible and, more broadly, to reduce Russia's propensity and capability to wage war (in Ukraine or elsewhere). It would make little sense to implement what would in effect be simply a symbolic sanctions policy. Considerable political pressure has been building in this direction in Germany since the invasion, with the argument that if Russia's energy exports were reduced, the country would slacken its war effort. This is hardly realistic. Nor can a sanctions policy be simply about inflicting maximum damage on the Russian economy as a whole—for example, with the effect of plunging Russia's economy into a serious recession, which could last several years.

Germany experienced a three-year recession in the early 1930s in which real national income fell by a total of 16%—the result was a complete political destabilization and the massive radicalization, which ultimately brought the Nazis to power in 1933. Germany should have learned a few things from its own history, impulses for further political radicalization in Russia are not in Europe's interests; however, it will also be difficult to hold those Russian politicians who bear responsibility for the attack on Ukraine and who broke international law accountable. The prospect of a trial at the International Criminal Court in The Hague, however, should be a real risk for both President Lukashenko of Belarus, who has arbitrarily imprisoned thousands of opposition figures and allowed his country to be used as a staging point for the invasion of Ukraine, and President Putin.

Instead of leading Russia successfully and peacefully into a period of stable economic expansion, President Putin has launched a war of aggression against Ukraine in violation of international law—without any comprehensible justification. In doing so, Putin has effectively removed Russia from the world economy; and, if China naively continues to uncritically support Russia, China could also experience almost the same economic crisis as Russia under Vladimir Putin. An obvious lack of competent advisors has led the Russian leader to a dangerous impasse.

From an economic perspective, a debate on the meaningful options vis-à-vis a Western sanctions strategy against Russia developed over the spring of 2022. Particularly in Germany and the EU, but also in the US, questions about further possible sanctions against Russia were discussed on the basis of a study by Bachmann et al. concerning a German energy import boycott against Russia. However, there were already other studies in March 2022, which estimated Germany's loss of real income due to such a boycott to be significantly higher than the estimated effects in the analysis by Bachmann et al. which only arrived at a decline in gross domestic product of 0.5–3%. In Germany and the EU, a gas import boycott against Russia would have a particularly severe impact on the chemical, steel/metal, construction, and food sectors. There could also be significant negative effects on jobs in other sectors via supply chains. A sharp increase in the price of oil or gasoline will also have a dampening effect on automobile production, which is an important economic activity in many EU countries.

The idea of an EU import tariff on Russia's gas exports as a sanctions measure, as proposed by Ricardo Hausmann and Daniel Gros, also does not really work: It is assumed (by Gros) that Gazprom, as Russia's export company for gas, behaves as a profit-maximizing monopolist, which is rather implausible in the context of the Russo-Ukrainian war. Rather, the majority state-owned Gazprom is likely to follow the Kremlin's policy line and adopt its goals even if it were to mean lower profits; in any case, a duopoly model is more appropriate with regard to the EU gas market than a Gazprom monopoly model. In a duopoly, unlike in a monopoly case, government revenues from an EU gas import tax on Russian gas can hardly be expected to be sufficient to compensate consumers and the wider public for the disadvantages of a tariff—that is, in the case of increased gas prices—through increased transfers. Nevertheless, under certain circumstances, a gas import duty may be useful as part of sanctions against Russia.

Incidentally, it is apparently not widely appreciated that an energy import boycott by the EU countries against Russia would have the consequence that Germany and France, for example, would have to supply oil and gas to Eastern European EU member states in addition to coping with their own national economic problems as part of the EU's solidarity obligations in the event of a crisis. In the case of doubt, it would also be required that the EU countries, and presumably the UK, would also feel an obligation to supply gas to Ukraine. Its own leader, President Zelenskyy, defends his country's interests and is apparently trying in this context to involve NATO in the Russo-Ukrainian war in various ways—even if this entails the risk of a third world war between NATO countries and Russia.

It is debatable how much an energy import embargo by Germany or the EU will weaken Russia's economic growth; and whether such an embargo will be able to significantly reduce President Putin's willingness to continue the war, or whether Russia's ability to wage war in the future can be significantly restricted in this way. There is little doubt that Russia will be able to sell its oil (possibly no longer able to sell it in the West) at a discount in Asia. In the event of a Western gas import boycott against Russia or a Russian gas export boycott, there will also be a surplus supply of gas from Russia; surplus gas tends to be difficult to sell in the short term, as pipelines dominate gas exports and the gas transportation capacity of many pipelines is fully expended. The West's financial sanctions against Russia are likely to have a harsher effect, although they also appear questionable in some respects. The problem of a cyberwar between Russia and OECD (or NATO) countries should not be underestimated as an additional disruptive dimension. It should not be assumed that the West would impose sanctions against Russia without counter-sanctions coming from Moscow. Even without an energy import boycott by EU countries,

Russia's economy will shrink significantly in the medium term; by a good 10% in 2022 alone, and the recession will continue in subsequent years.

An economic collapse in Russia would likely have only a minor impact on Russia's propensity for war in Ukraine initially; in any case, it will lead to economic destabilization effects in other Central Asian countries—two countries recorded an inflow of guest worker remittances from Russia in 2021 that accounted for more than 15% of their respective national incomes. Rising unemployment in Russia will certainly affect migrant workers from Central Asian countries, and the prosperity and import opportunities of these countries will decrease. Border disputes that already exist between some Central Asian countries—and which have even resulted in military clashes in recent years—could intensify in a phase of weakened economic development, with Russia temporarily dropping out as the previous regional power and guarantor or order; the EU has no presence in the region to speak of; at most, Turkey could expand its role as an influential power and try to maintain order in the region. Western economic sanctions against Russia thus certainly have an impact not only on Russia, and its government, but also on many countries around the world.

Since Russia and Ukraine are both leading exporters of wheat and important raw materials, the Russo-Ukrainian war could also lead to significant problems in the production of industrial goods in OECD countries as well as to massive price increases and more hunger in developing countries. An important task of the International Monetary Fund (IMF), the World Bank and the United Nations Food and Agriculture Organization (FAO) is to have a dampening effect here by employing aid funds. The IMF will also continue to monitor its policies toward Ukraine and Russia. I myself was invited by the IMF to an expert meeting in Washington, DC, in 1998 during the Russian financial crisis—also called the Ruble crisis. The discussion among the experts at that time was no doubt helpful in some regards. The 1998 Russian financial crisis was, paradoxically, partly caused by the outlandish advice from the IMF for Russia to fix the Ruble exchange rate against the US dollar. This was a clear contradiction to the standard economic approach in the theory of optimal currency areas, according to which a country like Russia—with a dominance of a few goods in its exports (in this case, energy exports)—should have flexible exchange rates.

At the Washington, DC, IMF expert meeting on Russia in 1998, which was chaired by Stanley Fischer, I was able to refer to a wide range of transformation and Russia-focused analysis at the research institute of which I am president, namely the European Institute for International Economic Relations (*Europäisches Institut für internationale Wirtschaftsbeziehungen* or EIIW); I referred, moreover, to the issue that there was no representative from the Bank of Finland's Institute for Emerging Economies sitting at the table, although the analyses of the Bank of Finland's Russia experts were considered to be at the cutting edge of research on the Russian economy at the time.

One might hope that the competence of the IMF teams in 2022 is appropriately high in the context of the Russo-Ukrainian conflict. In Germany and beyond, a very public dispute emerged in the wake of the Russian invasion concerning the competence of Western, and especially German, policy with respect to Russia in the decades before 2022. Quite a few moderators and presenters in televised news and current affairs discussion programs present the situation in such a way that one could and should always have known that Russia would indeed one day take military action against Ukraine; and that the German (and Western European) formula of change through rapprochement—specifically: "change through trade"—corresponded to a misjudgment. However, in the past decades, those same media commentators and presenters have themselves hardly ever asked critical questions about Germany's Russia policy, with the possible exception of the Nord Stream 2 gas pipeline project.

Second, the idea that a greater trade intensity between countries is conducive to peace is indeed an old view that can be traced all the way back to the British economist David Ricardo in the nineteenth century. Unfortunately, economic history has often shown that increased trade is only one condition for peace; otherwise, for example, there would have been no Balkan wars following the breakup of Yugoslavia. For Germany and other EU countries, the Kosovo War in 1999 brought the first recent turning point in terms of large refugee flows. Bodo Hombach, former head of the Chancellor's Office under Chancellor Gerhard Schröder, pointed out in a lecture in Washington some years ago that Germany's participation in the Kosovo War was motivated by the fear of an uncontrollable wave of refugees emanating from the Balkans toward Germany, which would have been expected in the case of a continued and extended rule by Serbian President Slobodan Milošević, who had engaged in violent oppression against Kosovars and Bosnians.

Massive refugee movements from Ukraine have occurred in spring 2022 and, in economic terms, this means a macroeconomic demand stimulus for the countries of refuge—above all Poland and other Eastern

European EU countries, but also Germany, Italy, and France—and, of course, problems associated with finding accommodation, which may result in price increases on the real estate market in the short term. In the medium term, when some of the refugees are integrated into the respective labor markets, there will also be a positive growth effect. Some EU countries have made large commitments for refugees from Ukraine: with Poland and several other eastern European EU countries plus Germany and Italy being leading countries in this context. Taking a closer, comparative look at aid commitments for Ukraine—relative to the real income of donor countries—shows interesting (and rather different) rankings; there is an IfW-Kiel-ranking, which ignores the expenditures on refugees, and an alternative EIIW-ranking, which includes expenditures for Ukrainian refugees

Many EU countries have responded to Russia's attack on Ukraine by increasing defense spending. Higher defense spending is a positive demand driver in OECD countries. At the same time, it should be borne in mind that the significant number and types of Western sanctions measures and Russian countermeasures amount to a significant weakening of global economic integration.

There will be strongly negative economic effects of the Russo-Ukrainian war. The weakening of the Western economic recovery and the increase in defense spending in Germany and other Western countries will increase the government budget deficit ratio. However, some Western countries are unlikely to see real interest rates rise—for example, the US, the UK, Germany, and France are considered to be "safe havens" from the perspective of international investors. In view of inflationary pressures, the central banks of the US, the UK, and the Eurozone would actually have to raise central bank interest rates significantly in 2022, but due to the economic weakness in the OECD countries, some central banks will postpone such measures. It remains to be seen whether this will give rise to serious stagflation risks in the medium term.

The world economic order could change fundamentally if the Russo-Ukrainian war cannot be ended relatively quickly and Russia's role as an active member of important international organizations restored. This latter process is likely to take about a decade. However, if China and Russia were to move closer together politically and militarily, and a continued or further weakening of international organizations could not be avoided, then the disintegration of the current international rules-based economic order would be imminent. For countries with a strong international position in terms of trade and capital flows, such as Germany, the UK, the Netherlands, Belgium, and Switzerland, this would be a structural deterioration and a threat to long-term prosperity. In the longer term, there is the threat of an increased militarization of international economic relations.

The study builds upon earlier analyses of economic system transformation in Russia, Poland, Hungary and other Eastern European countries—including a project that was carried out during the Gorbachev era, whereby the project team also included researchers from St. Petersburg (Leontief Institute) and Kharkiv University. In view of the Russo-Ukrainian war, the system transformation has only been partially successful, and the question of how to secure prosperity, international economic cooperation, and peace in Europe in the long term is an ongoing challenge. The German and Eurozone economies face significant structural adjustments after 2022/2023, and the global economy faces increased inflationary pressures, tendencies toward de-globalization and slower economic growth, and deteriorating cooperation in international climate policy. The corona crisis in Europe and the global economy has not yet really been overcome, as the Russo-Ukrainian conflict has led to significant price shocks in many regions of the world economy and is likely to continue to weigh on financial markets for several years; increased risk in industrialized countries will be reflected in increased fluctuations on the stock markets, among others effects.

The post-war reconstruction of Ukraine will be a particular challenge for Western countries. EU integration is likely to intensify, but at the same time, it will become more complicated as economic heterogeneity in the EU will increase with the probable acceleration of EU enlargement round to include some Western Balkan countries. This will make it more difficult to find a political consensus. This would also hold in the case of an enlargement of the EU to admit Ukraine as a member; a hasty and ill-conceived EU enlargement in the east is likely to lead to the next BREXIT case. Thus far, the EU has not drawn the real and necessary conclusions from the BREXIT debacle.

It will remain a difficult task for the EU to secure good relations with Russia and China and to restore security across Europe. The economic debates and the main aspects highlighted here are manifold, the effects of the Russo-Ukrainian war are global and fundamentally affect the dynamics of globalization. In the medium term, we can expect at least a temporary de-globalization of the economy and the influence of international organizations is likely to decline—a worrying perspective in a phase of an increased tendency toward international conflict. There will be a whole range of decisions to be made in the context of the Russo-Ukrainian war in Europe, the US, Asia, and Africa, and the analytical findings presented herein are of fundamental importance in many areas. Of course, the present study can only work through a limited field of problems. Yet the interconnectedness of the issues highlighted as well as the research methodology used on important topics should hopefully provide readers with a quality of analysis that should have lasting appeal and the warnings presented and policy options of a new kind recommended should be useful.

In the first year of war, it is fundamentally impossible to make any detailed forecasts on the further dynamics of the war itself. However, major economic dangers and risks, as well as serious challenges to and changes in the world order, can nevertheless be foreseen. In fact, the relatively limited Russo-Ukrainian war is leading to global problems and weighty changes in foreign, economic, and cooperation policies, among other areas. Critical economic questions that have been raised in the West since this war began with regard to Russia are also being raised to some extent with regard to China, which has positioned itself as a political ally of Russia. The new global order is likely to be less characterized by globalization and international worldwide cooperation; and here lies considerable risk not only for prosperity and stability in the industrialized countries and worldwide, but also for global climate protection policy. The latter can only be successfully implemented by way of cooperation between the West, Russia, and China as well as other important groups of countries. Cooperation is likely to become much more difficult for a few years; and a foreseeable reduction in global technology trade—and presumably less direct investment relative to global income—will also make it more difficult to achieve climate neutrality by 2050 either more quickly or indeed optimally through increased global innovation dynamics. For now, the major international challenge is the terrible war in Ukraine - and how to end it.

One of the peculiar findings of the analysis presented herein is that the fields of science and politics in the West have not really picked up certain relevant and timely studies in the matter of Russia and Putin's own ideological framework, respectively. In 2015, the French philosopher Michel Eltchaninoff published a very insightful book, which was also published in German a year later; but which appeared in English only in 2018. The English edition of the book *Inside the Mind of Vladimir Putin* (Hurst &

Co. Publishers) was cited very rarely in the following three years—although, one should note that one such citation was by a US military analyst in her publication. Unfortunately, the latter author, misunderstanding Eltchaninoff's analysis, concluded that Russian further military aggression against Ukraine was not to be expected. One can only wonder to what extent the study by Eltchaninoff was taken up in time—or at all—by Western intelligence services and politicians. Incidentally, the media coverage of Ukraine and related issues is sometimes strangely erroneous (even the World Bank published a press release on April 10, 2022, that, for example, reported the sum of guest worker remittances from Russia to Kyrgyzstan and Tajikistan to be twice as high as they actually were). The fact that on certain news broadcasts on German television in March 2022, reporters also repeatedly confused millions and billions of Euro in terms of EU military aid is, by the way, worrying in terms of the quality of journalism on a very important topic; it is also downright dangerous with regard to a potential escalation in terms of an EU-Russia conflict.

In the end, the big question facing policymakers is how to bring about a new, stable and humanitarian world order with good prospects for achieving climate neutrality—not by permanently excluding Russia from the global community, but by integrating the country better only after comprehensive political reforms.

Looking at the four economic fields of an aging society, ICT expansion (ICT stands for information and communication technology), economic inequality and globalization (trade and direct investment), and relating them to the Russo-Ukrainian war, important perspectives emerge for Russia, China, the EU (plus the UK), and Ukraine as well as Japan and China. Depending on the outcome of the Russo-Ukrainian conflict, two alternative scenarios emerge here—an increase in nominal interest rates in the medium term and real interest rates in the long term. The Russo-Ukrainian war causes an international slowdown in economic development, which for China brings a dampening effect in real growth and a lower inflation rate than in the US and the Eurozone plus UK.

In the UK, the Johnson government will push for the UK's agreement with the EU over Northern Ireland (the Northern Ireland Protocol) to be effectively terminated in the slipstream of the Russo-Ukrainian war. However, according to Speaker Nancy Pelosi, the US will reject such a move—there can be no US-UK free trade agreement, she said, if the UK would, in doing so, also effectively undermine the Good Friday Agreement, which brought peace to Northern Ireland (and in which the US played a part in negotiations). The British strategic approach after BREXIT, namely that of a "Global Britain" with more trade after leaving the EU, would then be neutralized. It will also hardly be feasible because the US has only partially given full support to the World Trade Organization under the Biden administration; difficulties with reforms of the aforementioned organization have led the Biden administration to tackle international trade issues more via, for example, the new US-EU institution Trade and Technology Council in 2021/2022, which means a BREXIT-related disadvantage for the UK.

Ukraine will push for quick EU membership after a peace deal with Russia, but one could advise the EU against rushing an accession, as the risks of the next "BREXIT" would then be relatively high, unless a really well thought-out admission strategy for Ukraine is developed on the EU side. If the next hasty enlargement of the EU to the east should only accelerate further EU disintegration, Putin would probably have achieved his goal of weakening the West in various areas after all. From the EU's point of view, US leadership should be seen with a question mark in the medium term, because the US is latently unstable politically speaking due to the enormous economic inequality in that country that could be overcome with European-style social policies, while at the same time opinion polls in the US show that the majority of the electorate rejects such social policies. Rather, a relative majority of respondents want large US firms and businesses to eliminate inequality by changing corporate wage structures: an illusory expectation in the US market economy. This, in turn, favors the resurgence of populism in the US, that is, Trumpism, along with political polarization that will hardly allow for Western leadership (on this, see my book *The Global Trump* [2019, Palgrave Macmillan]).

It is therefore up to the—already in part overstretched—EU to contribute to the stabilization of the West through clever reforms and policy projects and, in the process, ultimately also to induce the US to switch more strongly to a social market economy model as the economic order of the twenty-first century. A multi-year occupation of parts of Ukraine by Russia will create a relatively unstable situation in the middle of Europe. Overall, the present analysis shows how the terrible Russo-Ukrainian war came about—identifying political mistakes on the part of the West and certainly also on the part of Russia, as well as weaknesses in Western research on Russia are two important explanatory pillars. Incidentally, there is little reason to believe that the US market economy is inherently stable—the 2007/2008 Transatlantic Banking Crisis has already exposed enormous weaknesses in the Anglo-American model. With its democracies, however, the West has always remained capable of reform in important fields, which can make the combination of a market economy, democracy, and the rule of law an attractive prospect in the long term; perhaps one day it could even bring about a rethink in China.

I would like to thank my colleagues at the Chair of Macroeconomic Theory and Policy and at the EIIW, at the University of Wuppertal, for their support in the research process, especially Julia Bahlmann, David Hanrahan, Kaan Celebi, Alina Wilke, Tobias Zander, and Tian Xiong; as well as Christina Wiens, Rebecca Addy, and David Hanrahan for editorial assistance. I am very grateful to my colleague Werner Röger for his valuable insights and comments on the economic aspects of an EU energy import boycott; finally, I am grateful to anonymous reviewers of the draft manuscript who suggested that I consider additional aspects—I hope their feedback is now reflected in the—improved—book. The responsibility for the analysis lies solely with the author.

Wuppertal and Brussels, Germany   Paul J. J. Welfens
September 2022

CONTENTS

About the Author

Paul J. J. Welfens is a long-time researcher of Russian economic development and European integration as well as an expert on EU-US and EU-China economic relations. He has been invited as an expert to the US Senate, the IMF, the World Bank, the European Central Bank, the European Parliament, the European Commission, the German Bundestag, and the UN, as well as the InterAction Council, amongst others. He is President of the European Institute for International Economic Relations (EIIW) at the University of Wuppertal, where he also holds the Jean Monnet Chair in European Economic Integration and the Chair of Macroeconomic Theory and Policy. He is a research fellow at IZA, Bonn, and a Non-resident Senior Research Fellow at AICGS/Johns Hopkins University, Washington, DC. He was Alfred Grosser Visiting Professor at Sciences Po, Paris, in 2007/2008.

List of Figures

LIST OF TABLES

PART I

The Background to the Russo-Ukrainian War and Contextual Factors

CHAPTER 1

Beginnings of the Russo-Ukrainian War

The escalation of the Russo-Ukrainian war, which entered its current phase with an act of Russian aggression at the end of February 2022, has led to considerable arms deliveries by North Atlantic Treaty Organization (NATO) countries to Ukraine plus sanctions measures being imposed by the West, including by the European Union (EU). These include interventions in international financial flows and the ability of a considerable number of Russian banks to participate in international payments, for example, via the SWIFT network. In addition, there is a relatively comprehensive EU oil import embargo against Russia, but as of yet no EU embargo has been imposed on gas from Russia. On the other hand, by mid-2022, Russia had stopped gas deliveries to five EU member countries, and gradual cuts in the gas supply by Russia to Germany and Italy in June are probably an expression of Russian countermeasures against EU sanctions.

It is clear that Russia's 2014 invasion of Ukraine and occupation of Crimea—and the subsequent annexation of Crimea—based on a questionable referendum—has already worsened the political and, less so, the economic relations with the West over almost a decade; a limited range of sanctions on Russia has been among the consequences, while Russia's membership of the Group of Eight (G8) was also suspended. At the same time, it seemed that Russia's strategic position in the Black Sea area had improved due to full control of the ports of Crimea. The new, Russian-built Crimean Bridge (also known as the Kerch Bridge), which links

© The Author(s), under exclusive license to Springer Nature Switzerland AG 2022

P. J. J. Welfens, *Russia's Invasion of Ukraine*,
https://doi.org/10.1007/978-3-031-19138-1_1

Crimea with Russia, could become a target of the Ukrainian armed forces since Ukraine has obtained some new medium-range weapons from Western countries with which it could target the bridge from a great distance. However, if Ukraine would destroy this new bridge, it could be seen as an escalation of the war and one may presume that the US would not easily accept such an attack by the Ukrainian military. As regards the consequences of the Russian annexation of Crimea, and the Russian government's support for political and military unrest in the Donbas region, there has been an in part low-key radicalization of Russia's policy stance over time—however, Vladimir Putin's public questioning of the legitimacy of an independent Ukrainian state has apparently been the political starting point of Russia's preparation of the further invasion of Ukraine in 2022—and the international responses to that act of military aggression—which are the focal point of this book.

Overall, there is a kind of economic war being waged between the West plus Japan, the Republic of Korea as well as Australia and others on one side, and Russia on the other. The Russo-Ukrainian war itself has significant repercussions for Ukraine, which is under attack, but also for Russia. Russia's position as a major international exporter of oil, gas, wheat, and fertilizer, and Ukraine's similar role especially in terms of wheat, creates global economic effects through rising price expectations for commodities and grain, while the large number of political adversaries of Russia among industrialized countries indirectly internationalizes the conflict's impact. In Russia itself, there is probably a relatively small opposition to the war, especially among young people and intellectuals. However, President Vladimir Putin is cracking down—as he has done before—on protesters and critics. The sanctions imposed by the West make economic life more difficult for people in Russia every day. Yet in the past 40 years, Russia has also already endured a real income decline of over 10% (during the transformation crisis at the end of the Soviet Union).

For Russia, at least in the short term, the decline in energy export revenues is relatively manageable as market prices for oil and gas have risen in 2022: lower export volumes to Europe are accompanied by significantly higher energy prices. Meanwhile, the fierce military clashes in Ukraine continue. Russia's invasion of Ukraine is a shocking experience for the people of that country and brings with it an enormous amount of suffering and destruction; it also brings significant declines in exports and production. The International Monetary Fund (IMF, 2022b) estimates the decline in Ukraine's real gross domestic product (GDP) in 2022 at -35%.

This is significantly higher than the corresponding estimate for Russia, which the IMF (2022c) puts at −8.5%, while the inflation rate in Russia is expected to be a high 21% in 2022. If the war drags on, the loss of life and the economic cost will continue to rise. As recently as January 2022, the IMF growth expectation for the year was just over 2% for Russia. The economic war with the West and reduced imports from the EU, the UK, the US, and other Western countries will result in production losses in Russia and at the same time increase import prices. According to IMF estimates from June 2022, the unemployment rate is likely to be close to reaching 9% over the course of the year. These figures serve as a kind of statistical departure point as changes in the perception of Russia's economic development and output growth in the West and the world economy have arisen, including on the side of the IMF (2022d), for example.

KEY THOUGHTS ON THE ANALYTICAL FRAMEWORK

Looking at the developments in Ukraine, Russia, the EU, the UK, the US, and other Organisation for Economic Co-operation and Development (OECD) countries plus Newly Industrializing Countries (NICs; including China) from an economic perspective—and with a politico-economic view—means raising several key questions:

- What is the recent historical background to the Russo-Ukrainian war, which—at first glance—started with Russia's invasion of February 24, 2022, but which obviously has a far longer history at least back to 2013 when Russia's plans to conquer Crimea gained significant momentum followed in 2014 by Russia's invasion—partly in a covert format using unidentified military personnel, which became known as the "little green men"—of Crimea; Russia also sponsored rioting and unrest in the eastern parts of Ukraine—the Donbas region—which have a Russian-speaking majority, whereby Russian-speakers make up a minority in Ukraine as a whole. Ukraine was part of the Soviet Union until Nikita Khrushchev and the Presidium of the Supreme Soviet of the Soviet Union, respectively, transferred jurisdiction of Crimea to Khrushchev's own home republic, Ukraine, in 1954. Originally, the Russian Empire had annexed—against the will of the weakening Ottoman Empire—the Crimean Khanate in 1783. The Russo-Ukrainian war seemed in the months to be primarily a war about control over the eastern Donbas region, which Russia apparently wanted to conquer and annex as it had Crimea. However, with Ukraine receiving sophisticated Western weaponry, in August 2022, Kyiv seemed to begin a serious attempt to possibly reclaim Crimea in the south, which may be considered to be an escalation of the war in the view of the Russian government (such a view was voiced at the Davos Summit 2022 by the former US Secretary of State Henry Kissinger).

- Should or could contributions from experts, analysts, and scientists not have alarmed Western leaders much earlier than in 2021 when the US security agencies clearly anticipated that a Russian invasion in Ukraine would take place within a year or earlier? There is one book to which I will refer in this context particularly, namely the book *Inside the Mind of Vladimir Putin* by Michel Eltchaninoff, which was published in 2015 in French and in 2018 in English (and also in other languages). One might argue that no single book could have critically sharpened the West's analytical understanding of Putin's thinking on the question of Russia and Ukraine. Further research could provide a more definitive answer here; but this book indeed makes a very useful and critical contribution concerning Putin's ideological development over time and points out, among other elements, the fact that Ivan Ilyin became the preferred "new" philosopher of Putin after 2000 (several of Ilyin's books were written during the 1920s and 1930s, but many were published in Russia only in the late 1990s; and Ilyin's focus on Russia and Ukraine in a potential post-Soviet perspective is remarkable). If a US president would gift 10,000 copies of a book of his "new" preferred philosopher—a bit more than was the case in Russia under Putin to reflect the larger US population compared to Russia—to leading employees in his administration plus to managers from top companies and some personal friends, scientists, and journalists, many politicians abroad would take notice of this. The book, which Putin gave in 5000 copies to his network and friends, was hardly covered in the Western media and apparently noted only a few analysts and experts in the period 2018–2021. It is not known to this author the extent to which Western secret services considered this book in a timely fashion (historians will perhaps find out more about this in the future). It is crucial to emphasize that research on Russia and Ukraine—particularly with a focus on Russian imperialist tendencies (see, e.g., Galeotti and Bowen (2014) or Soroka and Stepniewski (2020)) and with an understanding of the strategic foreign policy goals of Russia under Putin in the second decade of the twenty-first century (e.g., Kuzio, 2020)—have pointed out that continued peaceful relations between Russia and Ukraine seem to be rather unlikely. The books of Anders Aslund (2007, 2009) and Dragneva-Lewers and Wolczuk (2015) also are crucial contributions to the broader Russia-Ukraine-EU debate where authors have emphasized successful market economy reforms in the new Russia on one hand, while a sustained democratic system could not be established on the other. One may add the loan-equity deal under President Yeltsin—he faced a very high government budget deficit and borrowed from wealthy Russians in order to greatly reduce the expected deficit, where major state-owned firms were given as collateral in the relevant loan agreements with the "oligarchs"; and when his government found it impossible to repay the loans obtained, a small group of less than 40 rich families had achieved a very profitable, silent privatization of major firms in Russia in 1995/1996: From that point on, a normal variant of a Western democracy was impossible to realize in the new Russia (it is also interesting to note that in the influential writings of German economist Walter Eucken [Eucken, 1952] on Germany and the market economy, he had emphasized the risk for democracy and competition policy if economic power would be concentrated in the hands of very few owners of the largest companies). There are several interesting and insightful publications on the recent history of Ukraine—and indeed some historical analyses too—which cover not only the important event of Ukraine's Maidan Revolution (or Euromaidan) of 2013/2014 but also other critical aspects of Russia's Ukraine policy and Russia's expansionist foreign policy (see, e.g., Wood et al., 2015; Petro, 2017; Plokhy, 2017; Shore, 2018; Wynnyckyj, 2019; Smith, 2022).

- How uncertain are leading economists about the impact of Western economic sanctions from spring 2022 on Russia and the direct impact of the Russo-Ukrainian war on Russian real gross domestic product? This question leads to a slightly modified question, namely how strong are the forecast revisions of the IMF with respect to Russia in the first six months after its invasion of Ukraine? Alternatively, one could also check for similar figures with the World Bank and other international organizations. The IMF's July 2022—revised—World Economic Outlook (IMF, 2022d) provides some interesting insights and indeed shows that the Russo-Ukrainian war (plus possibly smaller impulses from other regional/global shocks, including instabilities in worldwide delivery chains emanating from China) has had considerable national, regional, and global economic effects: In the Western world, the IMF has noted some downgrades in the previously (early April 2022) forecasted GDP figures (IMF, 2022a); not least because of the strong relative price increases of fossil fuel energy sources, which have affected the world economy—particularly in a negative way in the South of the world economy where inflation acceleration 2021/2022 was also more marked than in major OECD countries. At the same time, the July 2022 revisions of the IMF have indicated that Russia's exports of fossil fuels and other commodities have been sustained at levels better than anticipated by the IMF in its April 2022 World Economic Outlook (IMF, 2022a). In July 2022, the IMF (2022d) also indicated that uncertainty indicators for the world economy have increased in the first half of 2022 and this economic uncertainty is partly related to newly perceived military conflict risks in Europe and elsewhere, such as in Asia where China's reaction to Nancy Pelosi's visit—she is the Speaker of the US House of Representatives—in early August 2022 was rather unfriendly and clear: With military maneuvers and exercises in the waters around Taiwan and economic sanctions on agricultural exports of Taiwan. Pelosi's visit to Taiwan was apparently aimed at demonstrating in the midst of the Russo-Ukrainian war that a potential future Taiwan-China military conflict could lead to a similar US political and military support for Taiwan as was the case with Ukraine in its military conflict with Russia in 2022. While the economies of Russia and Ukraine account for circa 3% of world GDP and a bit less than 0.5% of world GDP, respectively (both figures based on purchasing power parity statistics for 2021), the international destabilization impulses from Russia and Ukraine are considerable: world market prices for oil and gas are raised by the conflict between the two countries and Russia's energy export policy pattern. With both countries being major exporters of wheat and fertilizer—and Ukraine also of corn—delivery problems due to Russia's export policy and the blocking of Ukrainian grain exports via the Black Sea (a problem that seems to have partly been solved due to successful negotiations of Turkey, Russia, Ukraine, and the United Nations in late July 2022) could affect key commodity markets and also raise grain prices in the South of the world economy to a critical extent: creating new risks of deeper poverty and hunger problems as well as new South-North migration pressure. Russia's destabilization potential in the neighboring Central Asian former Soviet republics, which have for over a decade sent many migrant workers to Russia is also considerable as a serious recession in Russia will lead to higher unemployment rates and reduced international remittances of migrant workers, which, in turn, could destabilize countries such as Turkmenistan, Azerbaijan, Uzbekistan, and Kazakhstan (which has a border with Afghanistan) plus Kyrgyzstan and Tajikistan—the latter three also with borders to China. Rosstat (2019) has indicated that legal immigrants in Russia amount to 1.7 million; however, one may presume that there also is a high number of illegal immigrants from Central Asian countries so that data on remittances abroad are rather interesting. To the extent that Russia's military and Russian mercenaries are active in parts of the Arab world and Africa, the international destabilization potential of Russia is much bigger than the share of its gross domestic product in world income indicates. Military supplier links to India and other countries come on top of this.

- Russia's 2022 invasion of Ukraine can be understood to be an element of Russian imperialism and Putin's particular policy vis-à-vis the former Soviet Republics. Soroka and Stepniewski (2020) point to Putin's Russia as seeking status at the international level and its ambition to have a clear superpower status is not least linked to at first becoming once again an influential, dominating regional power—with a focus on the former Soviet Republics. This kind of imperialism could indeed translate into an aggressive foreign policy and threats with a military intervention. From this perspective, the Russian invasion of Ukraine did come as a surprise for this strand of the literature with its emphasis on a new imperialism of Russia under Putin since about 2005.

- A special risk from the Russo-Ukrainian war concerns that nuclear power plants in Ukraine could be damaged or destroyed by military action by either side so that a new Chernobyl-type radiation propagation could affect Russia, Ukraine, the EU, or other countries—depending on wind directions relevant after a potential meltdown of one of the reactors. Analyzing such risk is beyond the scope of this study.

- In mid-2022, some key questions concerning the long-run effect of the Russo-Ukrainian war are still unclear and some scenario-based reflections thus seem to be adequate. The war is not an isolated element in shaping, for example, the role of international economic organizations. Those organizations that are relevant to maintaining a rules-based global economic system working for trade and international capital flows, including crucial foreign direct investments, have already be weakened by four years of the US Trump administration, which in particular undermined the working of the World Trade Organization (WTO). The WTO principles of non-discrimination of foreign firms and the most-favored nation (MFN) clause in tariff policy as well as a functional peaceful conflict management are crucial to maintain the current economic globalization. If the conflict in Europe and some "shadow spillovers" from the China-Taiwan conflict would bring Russia and China more close together, there will be a heightened risk that the world economy will split into two main camps; not just multipolar actors in one globally integrated region shaped by common rules such as those enshrined at the WTO and the Bank for International Settlements (the latter in the field of prudential supervision of internationally active banks). A clear perspective on the global economic order is difficult to draw, but one may identify major risks and impulses relevant for the international dynamics and there are indeed some drivers, which could replace the established system of international organizations and global cooperation (e.g., at the G20) by a different international system in which new long-term rivalries of major countries or country groups in a setting with weakened international organizations could emerge. In 2016, the then Director-General of the WTO said that the purpose of that organization with regard to its members is "to make the weak strong and the strong civilized" (Azevêdo, 2016). If the WTO and other leading organizations are weakened in a sustained manner, the expected losers in terms of power would be mainly the majority of rather small countries in the world economy.
- A new problem of some leading Western countries facing an aging society is the potential moral hazard problem concerning elderly voters once they would represent a majority of the electorate—the rationality of certain political decisions in a democracy could be weakened in a critical way as, for example, could be observed in the case of BREXIT (Welfens, 2022); and if political decision-making in

countries should become characterized by weaker rationality and consistency, both the cooperation among Western countries and their ability to jointly pursue a consistent policy in international organizations could be undermined, which, in turn, would allow new international regimes to emerge. Without going into details about BREXIT, one can clearly point out that a very large majority of economists and indeed the HM Treasury study on BREXIT by the British government in 2016 have warned about the high economic real-income losses, which would arise due to BREXIT; the order of magnitude in key simulation studies was in the range of 6 to -10%. If one does not assume that the alleged political benefits from BREXIT—for example, higher policy autonomy for the UK—outweigh the economic losses, then there is a voting paradox apparent in the British EU referendum (and referenda could play a role also in EU countries in certain cases in the future and the aging problem in countries such as Germany, Italy, and Spain is not so different from that in the UK in the long run). In the UK, a clear majority of Leave voters comprised the elderly strata of society (British Election Study, 2017; Goodwin and Heath, 2016a, 2016b) and if they voted for BREXIT in a vote of political frustration about welfare cuts in the UK in the five years after the Transatlantic Banking Crisis of 2008–2010—in the knowledge of a potentially high expected real income loss as a consequence of BREXIT—they could have a view, which basically said: If there are economic benefits from BREXIT as claimed by the Leave campaign, then all the better; if, however, the Remain campaign's warning about high economic losses indeed are accurate, we can still get compensated for those losses from the national government since we will vote at the next national election for that party, which would promise such compensation. This "elderly risky voting paradox" is a new hypothesis for aging societies in democracies in OECD countries, but if further research would come up with clear evidence to support the existence of such a paradox, the rationality of the Western world would face a new political problem, which would generate additional international policy challenges, including a weakening of the West. In the rather special context of the horrendous attack on the author Salman Rushdie in the US in August 2022, one finds in part of the press the perception that the rationality of both the West and the East—including Arab countries and Iran (or other Islamic countries with a growing religious

influence on politics and the broader society)—has been declining
(see, e.g., Abdel-Samad, 2022).

- The international perspective for a stable order and global prosperity
  plus climate neutrality will become more complex through the
  Russo-Ukrainian war and the associated politico-economic dynamics. For example, if an EU enlargement to allow the accession of
  Ukraine would not draw clear lessons from BREXIT, there would be
  a high risk that adverse macroeconomic shocks coupled with an
  asymmetric, early, laissez-faire immigration scheme for Ukrainian
  workers in some EU countries could undermine the politico-
  economic stability of the EU. From a strategic viewpoint, the major
  drivers of Western weakness are the basic politico-economic contradictions, which became visible with the election of Donald Trump as
  the president of the US (Welfens, 2019); the result being political
  polarization as a by-product of populism and renewed nationalism,
  which amounts to a critical undermining of the traditionally broad
  political consensus in the fields of foreign policy and military policy
  in the US. The current international rules-based order with a strong
  role for international organizations is in serious danger once the US
  leadership of the West should be weakened in a sustained way. An
  alternative view is that the global network of international organizations is still strong enough to fend off major challenges from China
  and Russia (Goddard, 2022). In any case, the Russian decision to
  stop cooperation on the joint International Space Station program,
  as declared in August 2022 by the Russian government, is a serious
  setback for international cooperation between the US and Russia in
  particular. At the same time, China has declared in August 2022 that
  it will stop—in the context of Nancy Pelosi's visit to Taiwan—
  Sino-US cooperation on climate change policy among other fields. If
  these are to prove lasting decisions, the international order would
  have changed in negative way whereby declining cooperation in climate change policy would make achieving global climate neutrality
  by 2050 (or 2060: the year which China's government had declared
  to be the official target year for Chinese climate neutrality) much
  more difficult.
- One key player in the G20 is the EU, but the EU has been weakened
  by BREXIT—as has the UK itself—and there is the serious question
  as to whether or not the EU27 countries and the EU, respectively,
  will be a stable, prosperous and coherent group of countries within an

efficient integration framework. It is obvious that the close cooperation, which emerged in 2022, has done so in the special context of a
common external threat, namely Russia's invasion of Ukraine. The
EU has already declared in summer 2022 that it is willing to consider
Ukraine as an EU candidate country, which is a status without a legal
meaning; rather this simply an act of political signaling for now.
Looking at BREXIT dynamics (Welfens, 2022), one can show how a
hypothetical EU-Ukraine enlargement would change the power balance within the European Council in the case of qualified majority
voting considerably (for more detail, see details of the analysis of
Kirsch [2022] in Chapter 13 and Table 13.1): The Banzhaf Index is
based on a game-theoretical approach and measures power by the
relative probability of country i in a hypothetical integration club to
be the decisive marginal country, which makes a current coalition of
loser countries j_1, $j_2...j_n$ become a majority winning coalition; here
the minimum majority requirement fixed in the EU's quasi-constitu-
tional Lisbon Treaty is, of course, crucial. As regards an EU-Ukrainian
enlargement, there are some countries which, based on the Banzhaf
value, gain power while others lose out—and some are indifferent in
a relative power perspective; and it is worthwhile to identify the main
drivers of BREXIT where immigration has been one of the clear factors. Poorly controlled high immigration from Ukraine to the EU
could create new exit risks as one may conclude from the BREXIT
analysis, including empirical findings and specific statistics in the context of labor markets and immigration dynamics in the first decade
after the first EU eastern enlargement of 2004. The UK—along with
Ireland and Sweden—waived its right to implement a possible transition regime for gradually opening up to total free labor mobility from
the new member countries and indeed it attracted a large share of the
growing emigrant numbers from the new EU members, but after the
shock of the Transatlantic Banking Crisis in 2008/2009—when the
UK was facing a massive recession—the political support for immigration from EU eastern accession countries reduced sharply (by contrast Germany, Austria, and most other EU countries had opted for a
seven-year transition period with reduced immigration from Eastern
EU accession countries). Moreover, the recession associated with a
deficit-GDP ratio of slightly above 10% in 2009 caused the British
government to strongly cut welfare spending over the course of the
next five years; moreover, central government transfers to local

authorities, which often finance essential services locally, were cut by 5% of GDP, which, in turn, led Britons to raise the question as who is to blame for the under-provision of services—and the standard answer in 2015/2016 largely was: the immigrants—a standard argument by the right-wing UKIP, but also in 2014/2015 by Prime Minister David Cameron (see Welfens, 2022: this second edition of *An Accidental BREXIT* shows these and more issues underlying BREXIT in greater detail). Whether or not Russia's policy in the years prior to BREXIT amounted to relevant interference into British politics is rather unclear (see Ellehuus, 2020; Intelligence and Security Committee of Parliament, 2020).

At the bottom line, the theoretical analysis available has been used in this study and the main empirical insights and simulation findings in key fields related to the Russo-Ukrainian war are presented. One major analytical challenge concerns, for example, the macroeconomic and politico-economic impact of a German/EU gas import boycott vis-à-vis Russia (Lan et al., 2022; see also Annex T which explains the modeling approach of these authors in greater detail) or of a Russian export boycott to key EU countries. Obviously, Russia's export behavior—selectively targeting some EU countries for a full or partial cut in gas deliveries—is difficult to anticipate, but analytical papers and various simulations can be quite useful for policymakers in Europe and Russia. In Germany, the reduced deliveries of Russian gas particularly affected Uniper—a major gas distribution company which is majority owned by the Finnish government—which had to be saved via an equity participation of the German government as Uniper had to replace contracted Russian gas deliveries which were not realized. Hence, Uniper had to buy replacement gas elsewhere at very high spot prices in the international gas market. The German government has decided that all private households using gas for heating and hot water as well as firms using gas will have to pay a general surcharge on the gas price from October 1, 2022, for covering mainly the losses of Uniper and some other gas suppliers facing similar problems as Uniper.

The German government—and its regulatory agency for networks (the *Bundesnetzagentur* or BNetzA)—has imposed a gas price increase of 2.4 Euro Cent/kWh, which is equivalent to an extra 0.8 point inflation increase in 2022; the high inflation rate in Germany of close to 8% in mid-2022 already reflects an increase of roughly 3 percentage points from the rise in the prices of fossil fuels in the first half of 2022, driven by the

Russo-Ukrainian war and rising inflation expectations—partly in the context of Western sanctions (e.g., the EU import boycott of Russian oil). There is also a political debate in Germany about prolonging the operation of the three still operational nuclear power plants, which were expected to stop energy production at the end of 2022, whereby the basic idea is to reduce the use of gas-fired power stations in the winter of 2022/2023 so that the risk of a gas shortage affecting households and industry would be reduced; it is Germany's Green Party—part of the three-party governing coalition in Germany—which has argued firmly in the public debate in summer 2022 against an extension of nuclear power generation in Germany standing for about 6% of overall power production. Given the strong increases of fossil fuel prices in Germany and other EU countries, as well as the UK, it is clear that electricity prices in European countries will also increase in 2022 and beyond. As the US gas price is only about 1/6th of the EU gas price in 2022, the output contraction from gas price increases in 2022 in the EU will be much larger than in the US.

The strongly rising inflation rates in OECD countries in 2022 have encouraged Western central banks to raise the central bank interest rate, after almost a decade, and to thus bring about a higher risk of recession in the medium term:

- If the Russo-Ukrainian war indirectly accelerates inflation rates in OECD countries and this in turn brings a rather strict anti-inflation policy of major central banks, which in turn would bring about an international recession, the impact on Russia will be negative in two key points: Imports from Russia will generally decline and relative oil and gas prices will reduce. Hence, an enhanced Russian current account surplus in 2022 could be followed by a declining surplus in the medium term; rising internal conflicts among the oligarchs in Russia may be expected in this context, particularly if Western sanctions really start to bite in the medium and long run.
- The political coherence of Western countries could be undermined if a recession should be coupled with high inflation rates for more than two or three quarters. Russia's interest in getting Western sanctions lifted could thus be facing an improved outlook in the medium term. One important international transmission channel from more volatile oil and gas markets in the world economy could be a broader destabilization of financial markets and enhanced safe haven preferences on the part of investors who would, for example, reinforce

investment positions in the US, the UK, and the Eurozone while reducing investment positions in emerging market economies. Therefore, risk premiums in the financial markets in the global South could rise considerably—some evidence of this was already visible in summer 2022 (see IMF, 2022d)—and this in turn would reduce economic growth.

The economic perspectives for Russia differ in terms of the medium term and the long run:

- Russian firms have a long history of flexible adjustments in difficult environments. The output loss and the rise in unemployment in the short term thus could be rather modest, but should increase in the medium and long term. There might be some problems with Russian output statistics in 2022—possibly not reflecting accurate real income figures, but there is a straightforward methodology to use electricity consumption figures as a proxy for real gross domestic product (on this, see a basic regression analysis and discussion in Annex S).
- A professional approach to monetary policy by the Russian Central Bank has apparently been rather successful in avoiding a high depreciation of the Ruble over the course of 2022.
- Russian consumers are likely to accept the negative economic effects of the Russo-Ukrainian war in the short and medium terms, but in the long run, shortages of high-tech consumption goods and traveling opportunities to the West could create considerable frustration among influential consumer groups.
- As regards the International Monetary Fund's July 2022 update to the World Economic Outlook (WEO), the IMF has emphasized that global output growth forecasts have been reduced for the world economy and for most OECD countries—compared to the IMF's previous WEO report of April 2022; at the same time, there were upward revisions of the inflation forecasts and downward revisions of the trade volume growth in the world economy. The output decline forecast for Russia has been revised upwards, that is instead of the 8.5% forecast in April 2022, the IMF expects in its July WEO update a decline of only about 6% in 2022; and another -3.5% in 2023 (see Table 1.1). Thus, the unemployment rate will increase in Russia, but at a smaller margin than the IMF's April forecast had suggested.

Table 1.1 Selected data for the world economy and key countries/country groups from the IMF July 2022 World Economic Outlook (WEO) Update, including size of revisions between July and April WEO, for output, inflation, and trade

	2020	2021	2022[a]	2023[a]	2022[b]	2023[b]
World output	-3.1	6.1	3.2	2.9	-0.4	-0.7
US	-3.4	5.7	2.3	1.0	-1.4	-1.3
Eurozone	-6.3	5.4	2.6	1.2	-0.2	-1.1
Germany	-4.6	2.9	1.2	0.8	-0.9	-1.9
France	-7.9	6.8	2.3	1.0	-0.6	-0.4
Italy	-9.0	6.6	3.0	0.7	0.7	-1.0
Spain	-10.8	5.1	4.0	2.0	-0.8	-1.3
UK	-9.3	7.4	3.2	0.5	-0.5	-0.7
Russia	-2.7	4.7	-6.0	-3.5	2.5	-1.2
World trade volume[c]	-7.9	10.1	4.1	3.2	-0.9	-1.2
Advanced economies	-8.8	9.1	5.3	3.2	-0.3	-1.4
Emerging market and developing economies	-6.2	11.7	2.2	3.3	-1.8	-0.9
World consumer prices	3.2	4.7	8.3	5.7	0.9	0.9
Advanced economies	0.7	3.1	6.6	3.3	0.9	0.8
Emerging market and developing economies	5.2	5.9	9.5	7.3	0.8	0.8

Notes: [a]Data for 2022 and 2023 are projections; [b]data show the difference compared to the April 2022 World Economic Outlook (WEO) projections; [c]Goods and Services

Source: IMF (2022d), Table 1, p. 7

Western sanctions are likely to bite relatively strongly in the medium term and in the long run Russia would suffer economically if the trade, investment, and technological links to OECD countries could not be restored in the context of a sustainable peace in the conflict.

The aforementioned analytical framework should be useful in helping to understand the medium- and long-run challenges arising from the Russo-Ukrainian war. Naturally, there are some caveats here since there is still considerable uncertainty and not only with respect to medium-term military developments. One might also face policy shifts in Western countries after elections or, in the context of a gas supply shortage, any political and social unrest related to this; there could also be changes in Russia's political system in the medium term, which are impossible to clearly anticipate at this point of time. There is little doubt that Western support plus support from Australia, Japan, and the Republic of Korea for Ukraine's resistance to Russian aggression will continue for many years if necessary.

Ukraine might end up—for some time—as a divided country; but as long as the existence of Ukraine can be maintained in a clear way, Russia might face serious political problems in the long run as a poor domestic economic performance cannot be compensated for by military adventures and success abroad.

The analysis presented in each chapter and in the overall book should be useful for understanding the broader conflict and its national and international short- and medium-term effects. One should also get an understanding of some of the contradictions of Western sanctions, such as the EU import boycott on Russian oil in 2022 which was imposed to cut Russia's ability to finance the war in Ukraine as emphasized by leading EU politicians. The economic analysis suggests, however, that such an approach cannot work in a world economy with globally integrated oil markets—Russian oil exports would be redirected mainly to Asian countries, which could buy an extra volume of Russian oil at a considerable price discount (say, about $20–30/barrel); the price discount was, however, from an elevated international oil price level so that Russia's export revenues increased and Russia's current account surplus bound to rise. Details on the international adjustment dynamics will be presented subsequently, but for the Western policy vis-à-vis Russia, certain called-for measures are actually counterproductive. There are also interesting legal aspects—first and foremost concerning the breach of commercial contracts by both the West and by Russia, or Putin's strategy to manipulate the international humanitarian law (Riepl, 2022)—an aspect that, however, cannot be covered in this study. Finally, the often visible economic analyses tend to focus on rather selected fields of the effects of the Russo-Ukrainian war are useful in many ways, but to combine the key insights from the various fields should give analytical benefits from the larger picture. Hence, the broader picture shown in this study could improve the quality of the international debate.

Russia is vehemently continuing its war of aggression against Ukraine in the second half of 2022, although in many cases—outside the Donbas region—it is encountering a Ukrainian army that has in part been fortified with good defensive positions; supported by arms supplies from the US, the UK, and many EU countries. In addition to military, economic, and humanitarian aid—including funding for refugees from Ukraine in many European countries and the US—the West's political support for Ukraine plays an essential role.

The logic behind the West's support for Ukraine through arms deliveries is based on the one hand on political sympathies for this country, which has shown a pro-EU orientation on the part of politics and the majority of the population for about a decade. In addition, several EU countries fear that if Ukraine is defeated in a comprehensive war against Russia, its military expansionism will lead it to take the next step westwards: toward the Baltic states, for example, with their Russian-speaking minorities.

NATO countries—and thus also the majority of the EU countries—have declared that they do not want to send NATO troops into the Russo-Ukrainian war; a major war, possibly even a nuclear war, must be avoided at all costs. Instead, the main focus is on indirect support for Ukraine and a comprehensive Western sanctions policy against Russia, which also includes freezing Russia's foreign currency held at Western central banks.

However, the EU has not sensibly exercised its sanctions policy in one important respect, as international news reports made clear on June 20, 2022: Lithuania had announced that it would no longer allow trains from Russia to Kaliningrad Oblast (the Russian exclave on the Baltic Sea formerly known as Königsberg; hereafter referred to as Kaliningrad for brevity) carrying coal, steel, and other sanctioned goods to transit through its territory, which from the Russian side is certainly seen as a massive political attack on the Russian population of Kaliningrad (see Fig. 1.1). Since one

Kaliningrad and the Baltic States

Fig. 1.1 Map of Eastern Europe showing Ukraine, Russia, the Russian exclave of Kaliningrad, the Baltic States, Poland, Belarus, and other countries. Source: Own representation; map created using Datawrapper https://www.datawrapper.de

million Russians live in the Kaliningrad, they will count on the support of their compatriots; the EU, with its undifferentiated sanctions against Russia (in this case Kaliningrad in particular) with its almost 145 million inhabitants, is creating a wave of solidarity across the Russian Federation. At the same time, the EU is creating an escalation impulse that has apparently been little thought through in advance and could drag EU and NATO countries into the war. One only has to consider the geographical location of the exclave of Kaliningrad to immediately recognize the potential for an escalation of the conflict: Kaliningrad is squeezed between Lithuania and Poland on the coast of the Baltic Sea, it was created in 1991 when the Soviet Union disintegrated, and the new Russia has continued to station substantial stocks of weapons, including missiles, in the exclave. Russian trains normally transit through Belarus and Lithuania on a main line toward Kaliningrad. Russia can make up for part of the shortfall in train deliveries to Kaliningrad by transporting more goods by ship across the Baltic Sea. Germany has pushed the EU to come up with a soft rule for intra-Russian trade concerning the Kaliningrad exclave in June and the European Commission seemed to be able to almost solve the conflict; but a new problem emerged in August 2022 when the only Lithuanian bank processing transactions with Russia seemed no longer to be willing to continue facilitating such business transactions such that, for example, transit payments for Russia trains going to Kaliningrad could no longer be paid (the final outcome of this conflict was unclear at the time of publication of this study).

However, Russia is unlikely to simply accept such a partial blockade of its territory and has immediately protested against the restrictions on transit transport through Lithuania. Many of the people of Kaliningrad have a pro-European outlook and it is considered a popular holiday destination for wealthy Russians from various metropolises in the summer (I myself taught for several years at the Klaus Mehnert Academy at the University of Kaliningrad as part of a cooperation project). In wartime situation, in which Putin emphasizes a kind of nationalism and solidarity, the pressure on the people of Kaliningrad to rally behind the state leadership in Moscow will increase in turn.

At the root of this new Kaliningrad conflict created by the EU, was an irresponsible move on the part of the European Commission such that the danger is present that the Russo-Ukrainian war could develop into a wider NATO-Russia war—more or less unintentionally or incited by unprofessional EU diplomatic moves. As much as Russia's aggression against

Ukraine is to be condemned, an EU sanctions policy, which does not adequately take into account the special circumstances of Kaliningrad cannot be considered sensible.

Here, the European Commission is responsible and one wonders what the European Parliament has to say about it; and why Lithuania has apparently willingly agreed to such a sanctions regime of the EU, surely knowing the potential for conflict that a rail blockade against Russia entails. Lithuania is playing as a kind of free rider in terms of security policy if it behaves in this way—with the Lithuanians seemingly agreeing to the sanctions against Russia in their present form, knowing full well what consequences this would have for transiting rail traffic. At the same time, Lithuania has invited the German Bundeswehr to station several thousand German troops in the country for its protection: The Bundeswehr is leading the NATO troop contingent in Lithuania, which thus affects Germany's security interests. A risky, ill-conceived EU sanctions policy here creates dangers for the EU, but ultimately also for the UK and the US.

In July, under pressure from Germany, the EU tried to defuse tensions over Kaliningrad, which concerns trade within the Russian Federation itself, and seemed to succeed for a while. With Lithuania indirectly threatening once again to block Russia's overland deliveries—ostensibly over the processing of financial transactions—to Kaliningrad, it is taking unreasonable steps to unnecessarily stoke the Kaliningrad conflict and accordingly the EU should act to ensure a sustainable solution to the problem. Conversely, the agreements between Turkey, Russia, Ukraine, and the United Nations to allow wheat and maize exports to depart from Ukrainian Black Sea ports by ship are a first step toward an international understanding in the Russo-Ukrainian war.

The Russo-Ukrainian war has large geographical dimensions and the case of Kaliningrad is just one particularly vivid example of the complicated geography of the conflict. The fact that Russia has reported that gas exports to the West through the Nord Stream 1 gas pipeline will have to be reduced in June 2022 due to a needed turbine compressor that has not yet returned from repair at Siemens Energy is another sign of the contradictory and ultimately self-damaging aspects to the Western sanctions policy: the turbine compressor in question was sent by Siemens Energy to Canada for servicing and an overhaul, but due to the Western sanctions on Russia, the repaired turbine cannot easily be shipped back to Russia from Montreal. This may give Russia the excuse it needs to cut back on Western gas exports. As early as the summer of 2022, in Germany and Italy, it could already be seen that a harsh winter could lead to a serious gas supply crisis; inflation rates in EU countries could rise further, industrial profits and industrial employment could fall. For the time being, employment in many OECD countries is supported by the higher inflation rates seen in 2022 and expected in 23. With real wages falling due to high inflation, it pays more to use labor from a business perspective. Yet with inflation rates at times approaching 10% in the UK and the Eurozone, households' real purchasing power declines significantly and consumer demand falls—a recessionary impulse. The latter is likely to be exacerbated in the medium term by the central banks' policy of raising interest rates, intended as an anti-inflationary policy in the US, the UK, the Eurozone, and other countries.

That the West has imposed comprehensive sanctions against Russia is, as a whole, understandable in view of its military aggression against Ukraine. However, there are some astonishing shortcomings. Even if the Russo-Ukrainian war continues for months and years, it is important to understand the causes of the war and its short-, medium- and long-term effects in essential fields; and ultimately also to consider the perspectives for a new and lasting peace in Europe.

Russia's attack on Ukraine, which was launched on February 24, 2022, ends the post-war order in Europe through an act of aggression for which Russian President Vladimir Putin is ultimately responsible. This crisis marks the end of a phase of covert alienation dynamics between Russia and the West, to which President Putin had already drawn attention in 2007 in a speech at the Munich Security Conference under the chairmanship of Horst Teltschik, which was widely considered both alienating and unco-operative in the West. Putin had classified NATO's eastward expansion as a threat to Russia and stressed that Russia would not accept a unipolar world. For his part, US Senator John McCain at the same conference warned that Russia was moving toward an authoritarian system. Fifteen years after that Munich Security Conference, Russia has realized a military invasion of Ukraine from several sides, with Belarus being the staging post for part of the deployment of Russian military forces. Wolfgang Ischinger, long-time head of the Munich Security Conference, said in a German TV interview in late March that he would have classified Putin's 2007 speech as being down to Russia's president simply having had a bad day. This level of misjudgment gives pause for thought.

However, the great contradiction between the state of war in May 2022 and Russia's own war aims in February 2022, which can be summarized under the heading of pushing back NATO influence in Northern and Eastern Europe, realizing regime change in Kyiv and the installation of a Russia-friendly new government, as well as a gain in terms of Russia's overall power and prestige (among other things, also in the context of an expected friendly welcome from large parts of the population in Ukraine "liberated" by Russian troops), can lead to confusion. In the spring of 2022, the large numbers of Ukrainians who were to cheer on the advancing Russian forces were nowhere to be seen, there was no regime change, and Russia's prestige has certainly dropped enormously worldwide. By mid-2022, Russia's military has been able to strengthen its positions in eastern and south-eastern Ukraine.

Finland's application for NATO membership in May 2022 certainly tends to represent an expansion of the NATO alliance's power, that is, precisely the opposite to what was intended by Moscow (the same applies to Sweden's application to join NATO). The fact that 5 of Russia's 80 regional governors resigned or were forced to resign in the same month can be seen as evidence of the first cracks in the political network of Putin's internal power structure. Putin's apparent expectation to conquer Ukraine quickly—and to much acclaim in many Ukrainian cities—is arguably an illusion created by his own echo chambers of intelligence and compliant subordinates. At the same time, it cannot be overlooked that Russia has options to reduce or cut off gas supplies to EU countries in the short term. By the end of May 2022, Finland—by then a new NATO candidate country—had experienced the same problems in this regard as Poland and Bulgaria had previously, while many economists had discussed the issue of a gas import embargo.

An indication of certain political differences of opinion in the corridors of power in Moscow was also shown by the public disagreement between Russia's Foreign Minister Sergei Lavrov and President Putin, who apologized in early May to Israel's head of government for Lavrov's representation that the fiercest persecutors of Jews in history have themselves been Jewish (this extraordinary claim emerged in the context of Lavrov's narrative that the government in Kyiv was essentially composed of Neo-Nazi factions). Ukraine has been ably defended by a great number of citizens, courageous and well-organized, many of whom have certainly benefited from Western support through military reconnaissance and arms supplies. After a brief period of initial political shock to the invasion itself, many Western and Eastern European governments supplied arms to Ukraine from March 2022; the shock that arose in certain EU capitals in the immediate aftermath of the Russian attack quickly gave way to a committed determination to support Ukraine's defense efforts after a short time.

Surveys carried out among young people in 2021/2022 show that there is a certain hopelessness with regard to the expectations for the future. The challenges of global warming, the corona pandemic and the Russo-Ukraine war represent a kind of overstretch of optimism: despite the many technological possibilities in the early twenty-first century, a timely international political reconciliation of interests on important issues hardly seems possible, and key global challenges such as achieving climate neutrality by 2050 and preserving peace (in the sense of the avoidance of a Third World War) may indeed be overwhelming. The positive expectation that the world's population will continue to rise until 2050, as will real average per capita income in the long term—while preserving peace—has become a minority view among the younger (now more pessimistic) generations of many countries.

Incidentally, one of the approaches of "modern politics" that endangers prosperity is the view of those, including in the German government for example, that one no longer wants to be dependent on Russia and other countries for raw materials and other goods in the future. It has been known since the time of Adam Smith and David Ricardo that the international division of labor, and thus mutual dependence via foreign trade, is an important basis for prosperity. However, interdependence on the side of foreign trade cannot replace a well thought-out regional international security architecture. Simply reducing the intensity of foreign trade makes little sense in the long term; this does not, of course, preclude a sensible diversification in the procurement of items such as raw materials, computer chips, and medicines.

The internal national consensus has also visibly weakened in some countries, among the OECD countries, this is probably true of the old world power, the US, more than any other. In Europe, EU integration is not a truly comprehensive peace project, as not somehow including the new Russia in the EU (or indeed in NATO) does not really work in a post-Cold War world—as can be seen in the Russo-Ukraine war, which to a large extent is in fact dragging EU countries into a major war in continental Europe and creating new fears of war in many EU countries; especially since one can no longer be sure in the EU that the political stability of the US is sufficiently great as to be able to fully rely on the US offer of a nuclear shield for EU members or NATO countries in the next decades.

That Russia increasingly became a threat to the West in a peculiar digital way since 2012, when mass demonstrations against Putin took place, was pointed out by Mikhail Zygar in an article in DER SPIEGEL article in May 2022 (Zygar, 2022): Since 2012, the Internet in Russia has been increasingly manipulated by trolls and bots to create an echo chamber for conservative-nationalist-militarist views (and, presumably, such trolls and bots from Russia played an important role in elections and the referendum in the UK around the BREXIT decision and in the US in the context of the 2016 and 2020 presidential elections). The Internet offers a lot of valuable information, but a strengthening of the world's democracies in the digital sphere does not happen automatically.

The Russo-Ukraine war means that there will be sharp increases in the relative prices of fossil fuel energies in the short term. This is because of the expectations of shortages in the medium-term supply of oil and gas; and in view of the discussions on an EU import energy embargo against Russia or indeed a Russian supply boycott for gas. The sharp price increases for oil and gas should be taken as an opportunity in EU countries to make increased compensation payments to private households and, if necessary, also temporary subsidy payments to some companies. Transfer payments could essentially be financed from increased revenues from CO_2 taxes and the state sale of CO_2 emission certificates. However, the increase in relative prices should be allowed to take effect in the medium and long term so that an efficient allocation of resources can be made. Apart from research funding, subsidy payments should therefore always be limited in terms of time.

Between 1991 and 2013, there were only about 15 years of partial political stability in the relationship between the West and Russia. However, from a theoretical point of view, the tendency of authoritarian systems to go to war is greater than that of democracies, and democracies almost never go to war against each other. In his article "Powerful Pacifists: Democratic States and War", Lake (1992) clearly pointed out that the demand for security or for a state can be explained with a relatively simple monopoly model. Extra economic income (i.e., economic rents), that the state or state actors can appropriate, leads to an abnormally large state—or an abnormally large military budget. This is also the result when the state itself artificially inflates external or foreign threats in the perception of its citizenry.

Indeed, this approach can clearly be seen in the new Russia, where President Putin has repeatedly referred to Western countries as aggressors against Russia: Even on May 9, 2022, the day of the military parade marking the allied victory against Nazi Germany, one could hear a concocted threat that NATO countries had planned an invasion of Crimea and that Russia's "special military operation" in Ukraine had effectively pre-empted a Western attack on the Russian Federation.

If one adopts Lake's approach, it follows that democratic states—with a lower inclination to wage war than autocracies—will come together in large defense coalitions; and then, in the event of war against an autocracy, have a greater likelihood of victory on their side. The applications for NATO membership submitted in May 2022 by Sweden—neutral for over 200 years—and by Finland, with its long border with Russia, show that Putin's attack on Ukraine was understood as signaling a significant and broad threat to their own security in northern Europe.

The West's expectation that international borders in Europe, in place since the collapse of the Soviet Union, would no longer be changed by military force had already proved too optimistic in 2014, when Russia occupied Crimea and sought to annex it to the territory of the Russian Federation following a referendum in favor of such an annexation. The question of the continuation of a Russian lease agreement for Ukrainian Crimean ports on the Black Sea had thus been settled from Russia's point of view. The Budapest Memorandum, adopted in 1994 by the US, the UK, Russia, and Ukraine—according to which Ukraine would hand over Soviet nuclear weapons stationed on its territory to Russia, while the other countries would guarantee its territorial integrity, that is, ultimately the existing Ukrainian borders—also proved to be unenforceable.

There might indeed be some historical arguments that Crimea's rightful place is as part of a greater Russia rather than as part of an independent Ukraine, so Russia's 2014 occupation of Crimea might seem on the face of things to be an acceptable, albeit forcible, correction of Ukraine's south-eastern border with Russia. The counter-argument, of course, was that Russia was seeking to simply imitate the approach of Hitler around the time of the Munich Agreement of 1938 in the context of a Franco-British soft appeasement policy, after Nazi Germany was "gifted" part of Czechoslovakia at the negotiation table in return for peace—but ultimately seized the rest of Czechoslovakia by force of arms anyway in 1939.

One can classify some developments in the relationship between Russia and the West as very strange in the run-up to the Russo-Ukraine war—in the years from 1991 to 2021—although they hardly played a major role in public perception. With the collapse of the Soviet Union and the Warsaw

Military Pact in 1991, the West witnessed a historic victory at the end of the Cold War, and the new Russia had to deal with high inflation rates and sharply declining output for several years. Mikhail Gorbachev, the reformist president, had attempted some reforms in the final phase of the Soviet Union. When the Soviet Union indeed disintegrated in 1991, the question arose as to how the West intended to integrate Russia into the "Western world system": membership in important international organizations seemed to be a reasonable partial approach. Talks between Germany, Italy, France, and the UK and the new Russia could presumably also be an important political bridging element.

Germany, grateful to Russia and Gorbachev in particular for supporting the opportunity for reunification, developed momentum for significant growth in the area of German-Russian foreign trade. France too was eager to establish broad channels of discussion with Russia's leadership and, in doing so, saw an opportunity to significantly increase the growth of its own foreign trade with Russia. President Putin also succeeded in getting a large number of major companies from France to invest in Russia. Germany, however, was historically ahead of France in terms of its investments in Russia. Putin's war in Ukraine, however, puts an end to the issue of investing in Russia for hundreds of innovative companies from the US and Western Europe for now. In May 2022, Siemens declared that after 159 years of production in Russia, it was leaving the country, an exemplary indication of how great the economic damage of the Ukraine war is for Russia.

In the UK, a fountain of democracy in Western Europe, a certain political interest in more intensive contacts with Russia's political leadership was manageable. With the British BP oil group and the Anglo-Dutch Shell oil group, there were two large energy multinationals that were prepared to enter Russia's oil and gas sector as direct investors—both multinationals also declared their intention to withdraw from Russia in May 2022. For Russian corporations and oligarchs, respectively, the UK with its liberal rule of law was an attractive investment location; London in particular offered excellent investment opportunities in the real estate sector for wealthy oligarchs from Russia. Did the UK's political relations help to anchor democracy, the rule of law, and a market economy in Russia? Under the government of Tony Blair, there was a state visit in 2003: President Putin visited London, setting a historic tone—the first official state visit since Czar Alexander II in 1874. However, it would remain Putin's only such visit to the UK, exemplifying a negative approach. There must be something wrong in the policy of the West (in this case, the UK in particular) and Russia, if official state visits between two such important countries should only take place every 129 years. At least there was a visible improvement in Anglo-Russian relations as Prime Minister David Cameron visited Moscow in 2011, but with the invasion of Crimea in 2014, Putin decided to abruptly end the short-term improvement of the British Russian economic relations.

In the winter of 2013/2014, major political unrest erupted in Kyiv when President Yanukovych—relatively Russia-friendly—refused to sign the finalized trade agreement (Association Agreement) with the EU. Large protests erupted in Kyiv's Maidan Square, with the president using force against the demonstrators. Yanukovych then had to flee to Russia, and a more pro-Western government subsequently came to power, which President Putin saw as a political defeat and challenge. Putin probably believed that Russia, Belarus, and Ukraine continued to represent a historical, natural community of states. This view may have been shared by the population in parts of eastern Ukraine, but apparently not in the other regions of Ukraine. Putin's response to the change in the balance of power in Kyiv was the occupation and annexation of Crimea in 2014, and presumably Russia's government gradually moved toward plans for an occupation of Ukraine in subsequent years. With Ukraine, as with other ex-Soviet republics, Russia can exploit political connections to Russian minorities, whose targeted settlement often took place in Soviet times, so that Moscow would have a solid reason to intervene politically in the republics of the former Soviet Union if necessary. With the collapse of the Soviet Union in 1991, this Soviet legacy remained as a potential factor of contention in the former Soviet republics (one can certainly be critical of the fact that in the Baltic states, the governments only issued "foreigners' passports" to Russians who had been living in the country for decades, which certainly made the integration of Russian residents more difficult).

President Putin was able to bring about some measure of stabilization of the Russian economy within a few years of taking office. Under President Boris Yeltsin, Russia had experienced a serious economic crisis in 1998. The US and Western countries had to some extent—and perhaps unsurprisingly—exploited the economic weakening of the new Russia in the serious economic crisis of 1998. It is a paradox that the IMF with its strange support for Russia's desire to fix the Ruble exchange rate in the years before the crisis in fact contributed to this crisis. One may note that the optimum currency area literature would not give any argument why Russia—with a dominant energy exporting sector—should adopt a fixed exchange rate.

After Putin came to power in 1999 as the new Russian president, after Boris Yeltsin, a decade of economic consolidation started, but the rule of law remained weak and the dominance of the oil and gas sector as major sources for Russia's government facilitated modernization approaches in the energy sector while many other sectors, including education, health and parts of manufacturing industry, witnessed only relatively modest productivity gains. Scientific cooperation of Russian universities with universities in the EU remained rather weak and there was only a limited intellectual debate between Western Europe (and groups of leading intellectuals from eastern European EU countries) and the civil society in Russia.

It is remarkable that forgotten Russian philosophers from the nineteenth and early twentieth centuries instead became influential in political groups in St. Petersburg and Moscow: with Ivan Ilyin (born in 1883, he died in exile in Switzerland in 1954) as an important philosopher whose books could be published in Russian only after 1991 and who often was quoted in major speeches of President Putin. In 2003, 2004, and 2005, Putin cited Ilyin's writings in his speeches to Russia's upper house, the Federation Council (Eltchaninoff, 2016).

Ilyin had been a Russian nationalist who had opposed the October Revolution of 1917 and had advocated in his publications a specific Russian and Slavic nationalism, emphasis on the Orthodox religion as a basis of Russian values as well as the idea that Ukraine was part and parcel of Russia; and that the West sooner or later could push in a future post-Soviet setting for disintegration and a political divorce between Russia and Ukraine. This ideology of Putin as well as other philosophical influences have been identified early on by Michel Eltchaninoff (in French as "Dans la tête de Vladimir Poutine", Eltchaninoff, 2015; German edition, Eltchaninoff, 2016, expanded further edition in Eltchaninoff, 2022; English edition "Inside the Mind of Vladimir Putin", Eltchaninoff, 2018).

It seems that not many leading Western politicians were aware of the ideological basis of Putin, which includes other philosophers as well and whose political aggressiveness vis-à-vis Ukraine was growing after 2012—with Ukraine considered by Putin to be a country that was politically manipulated by the US and some of its Western political allies. Unfortunately, the international dissemination of Eltchaninoff's knowledge and analysis were very modest in 2018–2022, given the English edition of the book has been cited barely 25 times since 2018 in all languages as determined by a Google Scholar search (see Appendix).

For the people of Ukraine, the war unleashed in 2022 by Russia is indeed a disaster. The US and the EU have little ability to directly oppose Russia's aggression, and EU countries are poorly positioned in terms of energy security. This is especially true for Germany, which buys nearly 60% of its natural gas from Russia, along with 50% of its coal, and which had not even begun to build any liquefied natural gas (LNG) offloading terminals that could provide flexibility in the international sourcing of natural gas by 2022.

The German government's decision at the end of February—announced in Chancellor Scholz's speech to the Bundestag on February 27, 2022—to build two such stations is a step in the right direction. In this speech, Scholz also emphasized for the first time the achievement and even surpassing of the 2% target for defense spending; for 2022, this would amount to around €30 billion in additional spending on the defense budget of €47 billion, which would represent an enormous and hardly efficiently realizable sudden increase in the budget item.

In addition, Chancellor Scholz had also announced defensive arms deliveries to Ukraine—a departure from the long-standing principle of not supplying arms to warzones. This change was attributed to Russia's massive violation of international law with its war of aggression on Ukraine, and because Ukraine was in a defensive situation. Russia's president justified the war by pointing out that he wanted to protect the Russians living in Ukraine from genocide, to "de-nazify" the government in Kyiv, and to prevent NATO from expanding eastward into Ukraine. Moreover, in a publication in 2021, Putin had invoked a historical connection between Russia and Ukraine and even denied Ukrainian statehood (on the history of Ukraine and Russia, see Kappeler, 2022; for some historical reflections of the president himself, see Putin, 2021).

As regards the short-term international economic effects of the Russo-Ukrainian war, the IMF (2022a) has presented revised forecasts in the spring World Economic Outlook of April 2022: according to the IMF simulations, the growth rates of real output in the Eurozone have declined considerably for 2022 and 2023; for example, to 2.8% in 2022 and 2.3% in 2023. This then is the baseline, which has to be considered for the case of a potential EU energy import embargo vis-à-vis Russia.

Looking at the frequency of Google searches in the US and Germany for the words war, Russia, inflation, recession, and gasoline price from April 1, 2017, to early April 2022, it appears that the public in Germany (Fig. 1.2) quickly became more concerned about the Russo-Ukrainian war in March 2022 than Internet users in the US (Fig. 1.3). At the same time, one can see that no major recessionary fears had yet arisen in either the US or Germany by the end of March; however, more frequent concerns about inflation was apparent in both countries. Search queries about the price of gasoline developed in parallel with concerns about the war itself. With regard to Russia, public interest rose in both countries—one can say in the US and in the Eurozone/Germany. Inflation concerns in the US were more pronounced in 2021 than in Germany, if you look at the corresponding Google trend development in the two countries.

Insofar as the relative price of gasoline influences demand for cars or car production, a negative impulse can be expected in March 2022 for the automotive industry, which is economically important to Germany and some other EU countries; this, in turn, is likely to dampen the economic upswing in Germany and the Eurozone. Since more gasoline-efficient cars will be in greater demand as gasoline prices rise, the German and EU auto industry can expect advantages in the export business—notably to US

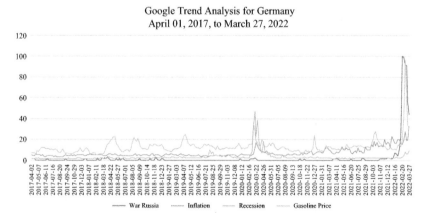

Google Trend Analysis for Germany
April 01, 2017, to March 27, 2022

Fig. 1.2 Google trend analysis for Germany: "War Russia", "Inflation", "Recession", and "Gasoline price". Note: Weekly data are in whole numbers; lowest value "<1". Source: Own representation; data from Google Trends (https://www.google.com/trends)

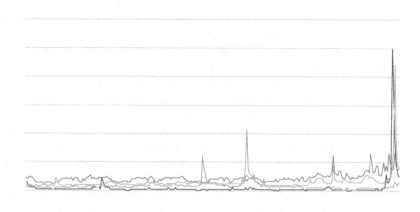

Fig. 1.3 Google trend analysis for the US: "War Russia", "Inflation", "Recession", and "gasoline price". Note: Weekly data are in whole numbers; lowest value "<1". Source: Own representation; data from Google Trends (https://www.google.com/trends)

sales markets, where relatively large and, in some cases, particularly gasoline-thirsty vehicles are still driven. However, in the US—and the EU—leading electric car producers may have a competitive advantage in a situation with rising relative prices of gasoline and diesel. With Russia's war of aggression against Ukraine, economic developments will become gloomier in the medium term, especially in EU countries.

The sanctions imposed by the West against Russia in March 2022 go far beyond the economic sanctions and measures realized in 2014 in the context of Russia's annexation of Crimea—at that time, Russia had taken visible countermeasures against the EU with import restrictions on agricultural products. Western industrialized countries from the OECD region have varying degrees of dependence on Russia's economy as an export destination when looking at value-added exports to Russia as a share of national income or as a percentage of value-added in 2018: For the majority of European industrialized countries, it was about 1–3% of value-added (OECD, 2022), with Germany—a relatively large EU country—recording just under 1%. At first glance, therefore, there is no critically high export dependence on Russia from the perspective of most OECD countries.

However, it is not only from a German perspective that the Russo-Ukrainian war poses expropriation risks in Russia and new loss risks for production in Eastern European EU countries. For example, there are steel companies operating plants in Poland and other EU accession countries from Eastern Europe, which source inputs from Russia or Ukraine. The war between the two countries could thus cause major disruptions to supply chains affecting Eastern European EU countries or even Western industrialized countries in some sectors.

Commodity Exports from Russia and Ukraine

In the context of the Russo-Ukrainian war, strong attention has to be paid to the export side of both Russia and Ukraine, as in some fields, high magnitudes or significant global market shares in commodities can be observed: Critical in many cases in the short term if one thinks of supply disruptions or conceivable Russian steps toward a selective export boycott against Western countries, Japan, Australia, and some others. For example, Russia and Ukraine represent a global market share of about 30% for wheat, 20% for corn, fertilizer, and natural gas, and 11% for oil.

Russia is also a major exporter of palladium (needed for exhaust catalysts in cars) and nickel, which is often used in steel production. Russia and Ukraine are both major suppliers of argon and neon—necessary in chip production—and titanium, which is used in aircraft construction, among other things. In addition, both countries are characterized by large (by international standards) uranium deposits. Since the start of the war in Ukraine on February 24, 2022, the prices of the aforementioned products have risen considerably; in the case of crude oil, however, after a steep rise before mid-March, prices have fallen again slightly (this is shown by data from Refinitiv and the OECD, 2022). In 2022, the oil price could fluctuate around the $100 per barrel mark (see Fig. 1.4).

The Biden administration in the US, where mid-term elections to the US Congress are due to take place in November 2022 and where a high inflation rate was observed in the first half of 2022, also driven by significantly higher oil prices, released parts of the national Strategic Petroleum Reserve in the spring of the year as a quasi-anti-inflationary measure. In the event of a gas embargo on Russian natural gas, however, the oil price could rise even

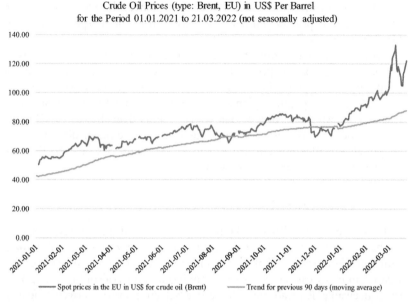

Crude Oil Prices (type: Brent, EU) in US$ Per Barrel
for the Period 01.01.2021 to 21.03.2022 (not seasonally adjusted)

⸺ Spot prices in the EU in US$ for crude oil (Brent)   ⸺ Trend for previous 90 days (moving average)

Fig. 1.4 Changes in crude oil prices on a daily basis, from January 1, 2021, to March 21, 2022. Source: Own presentation and calculations; data from Federal Reserve Economic Data (as of 2022)

further. Considerable energy price and food price increases have already occurred in the run-up to the Russo-Ukrainian war during 2021, but this war is providing further inflationary impetus in the Western industrialized countries. With inflation rates above 5% recorded in many Eurozone countries in March 2022, there is a threat of sharper disputes in wage negotiations in the medium term: Increased wage cost pressures could bring a return to economies of the kind of problems experienced in the 1970s in Western industrialized countries and in Japan in the context of the two Organization of the Petroleum Exporting Countries (OPEC) oil price shocks.

The inflation rate is expected to rise to 7–9% in the medium term in the Eurozone and the US, whereby inflationary pressure had already started in 2021. It will take until spring 2022 for the Federal Reserve in the US to react to the inflationary pressure and implement the first interest rate hikes. In the Eurozone, such central bank measures are only planned by the ECB for the quarters after mid-2022. In the UK, the Bank of England began an anti-inflation policy in spring 2022 and the British government also sought to mobilize financial resources with a special tax on extra profits, for example, in the energy sector, which could be used on the expenditure side for higher transfer payments to households. Similar measures have been taken in Italy and Greece.

As for the collapse in output in the event of a German energy import boycott—or a supply embargo on energy exports against Germany—the expected drop in income is higher than in the case of the OPEC price shocks in the 1970s. At that time, there were recessions with a decline in real national income (and GDP) of just over 2%. Energy price shocks in the context of the Russo-Ukrainian war, however, have a smaller economic drag than in the 1970s, since the energy intensity of production in OECD countries in 2020 is less than half that seen in the 1970s.

The income fluctuations of the 1970s and the following decades are shown in Fig. 1.5. The OPEC price shocks of the 1970s are clear, and

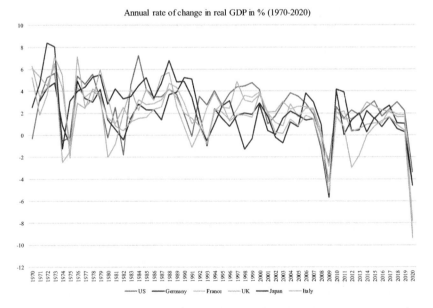

Annual rate of change in real GDP in % (1970-2020)

US   Germany   France   UK   Japan   Italy

Fig. 1.5 Business cycles from 1970 to 2020 in the US, Germany, France, Italy, the UK, and Japan—percentage of annual rate of change in real GDP. Source: EIIW presentation; data from the World Bank (World Development Indicators, as of 2022)

these brought major new EU suppliers into play in energy markets in the subsequent decade with North Sea oil from the UK, Dutch gas, and gas from Norway. In addition to these new market players, the Soviet Union became an increasingly active exporter of oil and gas. Following the severe economic downturns of the decade from circa 1973–1982, major western OECD countries then experienced an economic slump in 1992/1993. This was followed in 1997 by the Asian Crisis, which then also brought a relatively sharp drop in growth in Japan—and also in Russia in 1998. Russia was hit by transmission effects from the member countries of the Association of Southeast Asian Nations (ASEAN) which faced high currency devaluations and at the same time high foreign debt and thus huge public finance problems when a severe recession occurred in 1997—starting from Thailand and a massive devaluation of the Thai Baht—and Indonesia's still large net oil exports in 1997. Indonesia's rising oil exports were supposed to help stabilize the state and its revenues, but with falling world market prices the effect was insufficient; in addition, there was the Asian economic crisis, which caused demand for oil in Asia to shrink sharply—and thus also depressed prices—and as Mexico, as a major oil exporter, also relied on more oil exports, the world oil price fell even more in 1997/1998. In these conditions, the situation for Russia's state budget suddenly became critical, especially since here, too, a strong devaluation of the Ruble was now imminent in the face of falling oil export prices, which (as in Thailand) increased the burden of foreign debt for the state and firms. At times, the oil price sank below $10 per barrel.

In 2008/2009, the Transatlantic Banking Crisis resulted from an under-regulation of banks in the US, the UK, and some other EU countries. This strange under-regulation of banks, combined with inadequate risk pricing on the markets in the US and Western Europe, ensured that banks took on far too much risk, especially in real estate markets—with a paradoxical development of the risk premium in the US, among other places, where risk premiums (as the difference between the bond rate for AAA-rated corporate bonds and the US government bond rate) fell in a peculiar manner in the period from 2003 till 2006 during the phase of a late economic upswing.

Only quantitative easing, a new type of vigorous monetary policy, which involved the large-scale purchases of long-term government bonds by central banks, succeeded in stabilizing the Western OECD countries in an environment of already very low interest and inflation rates. However, abnormally low nominal and real interest rates (whereby the real interest rate is measured as the nominal interest rate minus the inflation rate) now resulted, with quantitative easing being implemented first by the US Federal Reserve, then by the Bank of England and finally by the European Central Bank.

Unexpectedly, this policy was continued for a relatively long period of time in various countries. One of the reasons for this was the unforeseen global corona shock in 2020/2021 which had triggered a severe global economic slump. However, the economic upswing that set in during the second half of 2021 was then already accompanied by a significant increase in inflation rates and oil or gas prices in important Western industrialized countries; inflationary effects were probably also exacerbated by global supply chain disruptions—even in the spring of 2022, when a radical corona lockdown policy undertaken by China's government virtually shut down the trade, export, and import center of Shanghai, which at the time was affected by only a few hundred coronavirus infections, for weeks because of a stringent containment policy. A significant increase in relative oil and gas prices did not really act as a strong disruptive impulse in the Western industrialized countries—simply because, compared to the 1970s, the energy intensity of production had more than halved.

On March 23, 2022, President Putin declared that Russia's energy exports to what he termed "unfriendly countries" must in the future be paid for in Russian Rubles, which is a strategic move in the international economic conflict between the West, Japan, Australia, and others against Russia. If Russia enforces invoicing in Rubles, part of the sanctions against Russia and its central bank will be undermined. Since Russia's supply contracts usually specify euros and US dollars as the currency of payment, Western countries plus Japan and the G7, respectively, have rejected a move to Ruble-denominated payments. Russia then declared in late March that it would implement a gas supply boycott if payment for gas supplies was not made in Rubles. The outcome of this conflict over the invoicing of Russian supplies is likely to be decided only after a few months; if Russia wanted to suddenly stop its gas exports to EU countries, this will cause a loss of revenue and also considerable reorganization efforts in the Russian gas production and transport sectors as well as at Russian power plants. By mid-2022, Russia had imposed a gas supply boycott against Poland, Bulgaria, Finland, the Netherlands, and Denmark, as well as Shell.

Table 1.2 shows that many countries face considerable dependency pressures with regard to fossil energy supplies from Russia. Table 1.2 shows particular dependencies on the part of Lithuania, Hungary, Slovakia,

Table 1.2   Share of fossil energy imports from Russia in domestic energy consumption of selected countries, 2019

Ranking of countries by level of dependence	Country	Dependence on imported fossil energy from Russia
1	Lithuania	121.2%
2	Hungary	76.3%
3	Slovakia	68.5%
4	Netherlands	65.6%
5	Finland	50.4%
6	Bulgaria	40.4%
7	Greece	37.5%
8	Poland	36.7%
9	Latvia	35.5%
10	Belgium	30.5%
11	Germany	28.9%
12	Italy	28.1%
22	France	9.7%
25	UK	8.7%
26	Spain	7.2%
27	Japan	7.1%
34	US	1.2%

Note: The indicator is composed of the sum of Russian imports of coal, oil, and natural gas in relation to domestic energy consumption. The figure can be greater than 100% if more was imported than consumed (transit transactions, if applicable). Since not all figures from 2020 are available, 2019 was chosen as the starting point for the purpose of completeness

Source: IEA (2022), available online at https://www.iea.org/reports/reliance-on-russian-fossil-fuels-data-explorer (last accessed March 30, 2022)

and the Netherlands, where more than 60% of fossil energy comes from Russia. Among the major EU countries, Germany and Italy are relatively dependent: with Russian shares of around 28% in 2019. With a Russian share of just 1.2%, the US has been virtually independent of supplies from Russia for fossil energy, facilitating the US oil, gas, and coal import boycott against Russia in mid-March; the UK, with a share of 8.7%, has also announced a UK energy import embargo for the end of 2022 at the same time. The overall significant dependency differences evident from country to country on a case-by-case basis are unlikely to facilitate a unified Western front for action in the area of energy trade disputes with Russia.

Financial markets—here the share prices of important countries—have reacted to the Russo-Ukrainian war. Even before the outbreak of war in 2022, share price developments in the UK were already relatively weak (due to BREXIT). However, in March 2022, the EuroStoxx index declined significantly and approached the weaker UK short performance. Interestingly, China's leading stock index also recorded a significant decline in the initial months of the conflict (Fig. 1.6).

On March 30, 2022, Germany's Council of Economic Experts published an updated economic forecast (German Council of Economic Experts, 2022): with expected values for real economic growth in 2022 and 2023 that were significantly lower than the values forecasted in the annual report of Fall 2021; the revision of the growth rate for 2022 is -2.8 percentage points, and the growth rate is expected to be just below 2%. The Council of Economic Experts does not assume that there will be an energy import boycott against Russia or a Russian energy export embargo. In such a case, the downward revisions to the growth forecast values for

Fig. 1.6 Selected share price developments, 2019–22 (daily values): Germany, the US, Eurozone, the UK, Japan, China. *Note: This chart shows the performance of the world's major stock indices from January 4, 2019, to March 29, 2022 (January 4, 2019=100).* Source: Own calculations; data from investing.com, onvista.de

Germany and the Eurozone would be significantly higher than the revision to the forecast values for gross domestic product shown in the chart compared with the forecast values of fall 2021. The expected international trade disruptions due to the Russo-Ukrainian war are only partially included in the Council of Economic Experts' analysis.

The following analysis first addresses the turn-of-the-century perspective in the Russo-Ukrainian war context, with cyber-attacks being a relatively new aspect of the conflict; in addition, bilateral perspectives on German-Russia trade and multilateral perspectives are examined. This is followed by a look at fundamental energy issues for Europe and the West, followed by the question of the extent to which a German energy import boycott against Russia—or an EU embargo—makes sense or what effects can be expected here. Then the focus is directed to the possibility of a Russian supply boycott. This is followed by an analysis of Asia and of the global effects of an EU energy boycott against Russia, as well as a broader analysis of EU-China-Russia perspectives. Finally, refugee and immigration issues are addressed, as well as selected scenario aspects and perspectives for a new global economic order. Overall, the Russo-Ukrainian war leads to global position shifts in the longer term; the decline in German real income is incidentally estimated at around -6% in the case of an energy import boycott against Russia, which is higher in percentage terms than the decline in real GDP in Russia as a result of the boycott (a sanction in which one harms oneself more than the addressee of the sanction should be carefully reconsidered).

LITERATURE

Abdel-Samad, H. (2022). Es gibt unzählige Rushdies in der Welt [transl. PJJW: There Are Numerous Rushdies in the World], Neue Zürcher Zeitung, August 14th 2022/International Edition. Retrieved August 18, 2022, from https://www.nzz.ch/feuilleton/es-gibt-unzaehlige-rushdies-in-der-welt-sie-leben-gefaehrlich-ld.1697890

Åslund, A. (2007). *Russia's Capitalist Revolution: Why Market Reform Succeeded and Democracy Failed.* Peterson Institute for International Economics.

Åslund, A. (2009). *How Ukraine Became a Market Economy and Democracy.* Peterson Institute for International Economics.

Azevêdo, R. (2016). DG Azevêdo pays tribute to Luzius Wasescha, speech on 23 November 2016. Retrieved August 18, 2022, from https://www.wto.org/english/news_e/spra_e/spra147_e.htm

British Election Study. (2017). Brexit Britain: British Election Study Insights from the post-EU Referendum Wave of the BES Internet Panel, British Election Study Wave 9. Retrieved August 18, 2022, from https://www.britishelectionstudy. com/bes-resources/brexit-britain-british-election-study-insights-from-the-post-eu-referendum-wave-of-the-bes-internet-panel/#.Yv4hVd9CRPY-imperialism-racism-and-war/

Dragneva-Lewers, R., & Wolczuk, K. (2015). *Ukraine Between the EU and Russia: The Integration Challenge*. Palgrave Macmillan.

Ellehuus, D. (2020). Did Russia Influence Brexit?, Centre for Strategic and International Studies, published 21 July 2020. Retrieved August 18, 2022, from https://www.csis.org/blogs/brexit-bits-bobs-and-blogs/did-russia-influence-brexit

Eltchaninoff, M. (2015). *Dans la tête de Vladimir Poutine*. ActesSud.

Eltchaninoff, M. (2016). *In Putins Kopf. Die Philosophie eines Lupenreinen Demokraten*. Klett-Cotta.

Eltchaninoff, M. (2018). *Inside the Mind of Vladimir Putin*. Hurst & Co Publishers.

Eltchaninoff, M. (2022). *In Putins Kopf: Logik und Willkür eines Autokraten*. Tropen.

Eucken, W. (1952). *Grundsätze der Wirtschaftspolitik*. UTB.

Galeotti, M., & Bowen, A. S. (2014). Putin's Empire of the Mind, Foreign Policy, June

German Council of Economic Experts. (2022). Updated Economic Outlook 2022 and 2023, published 30th March 2022. Retrieved May 24, 2022, from https://www.sachverstaendigenrat-wirtschaft.de/fileadmin/dateiablage/ Konjunkturprognosen/2022/KJ2022_CompleteVersion.pdf

Goddard, S. (2022). The Outsiders: How the International System Can Still Check China and Russia, Foreign Affairs, 28/2022 https://www.foreignaf-fairs.com/articles/ukraine/2022-04-06/china-russia-ukraine-international-system-outsiders

Goodwin, M., & Heath, O. (2016a). The 2016 Referendum, Brexit and the Left Behind: An Aggregate-level Analysis of the Result. *Political Quarterly, 87*(3), 323–332. https://doi.org/10.1111/1467-923X.12285

Goodwin, M., & Heath, O. (2016b). Brexit Vote Explained: Poverty, Low Skills and Lack of Opportunities, Joseph Rowntree Foundation. Retrieved August 18, 2022, from https://www.jrf.org.uk/report/brexit-vote-explained-poverty-low-skills-and-lack-opportunities

IEA. (2022). Reliance on Russian Fossil Fuels Data Explorer, International Energy Agency: Paris. Retrieved March 30, 2022, from https://www.iea.org/reports/ reliance-on-russian-fossil-fuels-data-explorer

IMF. (2022a). World Economic Outlook. War Sets Back Global Recovery, April 2022, International Monetary Fund, Washington DC

IMF. (2022b). Ukraine At A Glance, International Monetary Fund, Washington DC. Retrieved June 22, 2022, from https://www.imf.org/en/Countries/UKR#ataglance

IMF. (2022c). Russian Federation At A Glance, International Monetary Fund, Washington DC. Retrieved June 22, 2022, from https://www.imf.org/en/Countries/RUS#ataglance

IMF. (2022d). *World Economic Outlook,* July 2022 Update. International Monetary Fund, Washington DC.

Intelligence and Security Committee of Parliament. (2020). Russia Report, published 21 July 2020. Retrieved August 18, 2022, from https://isc.independent.gov.uk/wp-content/uploads/2021/01/20200721_HC632_CCS001_CCS1019402408-001_ISC_Russia_Report_Web_Accessible.pdf

Kappeler, A. (2022). *Unequal Brothers. Russians and Ukrainians from the Middle Ages to the present* (2nd ed.). Beck.

Kirsch, W. (2022). The Distribution of Power within the EU: Perspectives on a Ukrainian Accession and a Turkish Accession. *International Economics and Economic Policy, 19*(2), 1. https://doi.org/10.1007/s10368-022-00541-w

Kuzio, T. (2020). Crisis in Russian Studies? Nationalism (Imperialism), Racism and War, E-International Relations. Retrieved August 18, 2022, from https://www.e-ir.info/publication/crisis-in-russian-studies-nationalism

Lake, D. (1992). Powerful Pacifists: Democratic States and War. *The American Political Science Review, 86*(1), 24–37. https://doi.org/10.2307/1964013

Lan, T., Sher, G., & Zhou, J. (2022). The Economic Impacts on Germany of a Potential Russian Gas Shutoff. IMF Working Paper No.WP/22/144. Washington DC

OECD. (2022). *OECD Economic Outlook, Interim Report. Economic and Social Impacts and Policy Implications of the War in Ukraine.* Organisation for Economic Cooperation and Development. https://doi.org/10.1787/4181d61b-en

Petro, N. (2017). *Ukraine in Crisis.* Routledge.

Plokhy, S. (2017). *The Gates of Europe: A History of Ukraine.* Basic Books.

Putin, V. (2021). On the Historical Unity of Russians and Ukrainians, article published July 12, 2021. Retrieved May 24, 2022, from http://en.kremlin.ru/events/president/news/66181

Riepl, M. (2022). *Contributions to International Humanitarian Law. A Contrastive Analysis of Russia's Historical Role and its Current Practice.* Nomos.

Rosstat. (2019). Current Statistical Survey, 2019/2 (103), Moscow.

Shore, M. (2018). *The Ukrainian Night: An Intimate History of Revolution.* Yale University Press.

Smith, C. M. (2022). *Ukraine's Revolt, Russia's Revenge.* Brookings Institution Press.

Soroka, G., & Stepniewski, T. (2020). Russian Foreign Policy Towards the "Near Abroad", Soroka, G. and Stepniewski, T. (Eds.) in Journal of Soviet and post-Soviet Politics and Society, Vol. 6, No. 2. pp. 3-12

Welfens, P. J. J. (2019). *The Global Trump—Structural US Populism and Economic Conflicts with Europe and Asia.* Palgrave Macmillan. https://doi.org/10.1007/978-3-030-21784-6

Welfens, P. J. J. (2022). *An Accidental BREXIT*, 2nd Enlarged Edition. Palgrave Macmillan (forthcoming).

Wood, E. A., Pomeranz, W. E., Merry, E. W., & Trudolyubov, M. (2015). *Roots of Russia's War in Ukraine.* Woodrow Wilson Center Press / Columbia University Press.

Wynnyckyj, M. (2019). *Ukraine's Maidan, Russia's War: A Chronicle and Analysis of the Revolution of Dignity.* Columbia University Press.

Zygar, M. (2022). Wie der Atomkrieg in Russlandpopulärwurde [transl. PJJW: How nuclear war became popular in Russia], Der Spiegel, 14 May 2022. Retrieved May 24, 2022, from https://www.spiegel.de/ausland/wladimir-putin-wie-der-atomkrieg-in-russland-populaer-wurde-kolumne-von-mikhail-zygar-a-e8e0eb6d-d247-4609-892a-15a8d39be19e

CHAPTER 2

Turning Points in the Russo-Ukrainian War

The following analysis first addresses the "turning point" perspective in the context of Russia and Ukraine, with cyber warfare in particular being a relatively new aspect of the current conflict; in addition, bilateral perspectives on German-Russian trade and multilateral perspectives are examined. This is followed by a look at fundamental energy issues for Europe and the West and by the question of the extent to which a German energy import boycott against Russia—or an EU embargo—makes sense or what effects could be expected here. The focus is subsequently directed to the possibility of a Russian supply boycott. This is followed by an analysis of Asia and of the global effects of an EU energy boycott against Russia, as well as a broader analysis of EU-China-Russia. Finally, refugee and immigration issues are addressed, as well as selected scenario aspects and perspectives for a new global economic order. Overall, the Russo-Ukrainian war leads to global position shifts in the longer term; the decline in German real income is incidentally estimated at around -6% in the case of an energy import boycott against Russia, which is higher in percentage terms than the decline in real GDP in Russia as a result of the boycott (a sanction in which one harms oneself more than the intended target of the sanction measures should be carefully reconsidered).

For three decades, most EU countries and the US assumed that military force would no longer be used to change international borders in Europe, that war was not a means of implementing policy, and that economic and political relations with Russia would develop well in the long

© The Author(s), under exclusive license to Springer Nature Switzerland AG 2022
P. J. J. Welfens, *Russia's Invasion of Ukraine*,
https://doi.org/10.1007/978-3-031-19138-1_2

term (apart from certain periods of political disruption over time). With the war in Ukraine in 2022, this view has proved unrealistic, and the peace dividend realized by many OECD countries since the end of the Cold War in 1991 in the form of low defense spending relative to national income—often less than 1.5%—is no longer tenable. It appears that most NATO countries, as well as neutral European countries (such as Finland, Sweden, Austria, and—de facto—Ireland), will see a significant increase in defense spending after 2021, as conventional military deterrence is now prominent on the political agenda.

The Russo-Ukrainian war marked a European and international turning point, and within a few short weeks the West—plus Japan and Australia and others—discussed and, in some cases, quickly decided on a number of common approaches in important policy issues. These included coordinated economic sanctions measures against Russia. However, some issues remain open on the policy agenda for the time being, and this also applies to economic policy countermeasures against economic dampening and inflation boosting impulses in the context of the current war (e.g., whether US and ECB monetary policy will opt for further interest rate hikes in quick succession has been considered doubtful since the war began, despite increased inflationary pressures). The quickly decided upon questions in the West concerned:

- An increase in defense spending and the redeployment of NATO troops to Eastern European NATO member countries
- Decisions on economic sanctions against Russia
- Policy steps to strengthen the political unity of the West
- First steps to reduce energy imports from Russia; questions of a short-term total energy import boycott against Russia were discussed in this context as late as March 2022 with regard to Germany and the EU (the boycott study of Bachmann et al. (2022) played a role)
- Policy measures for the reception of Ukrainian refugees
- Humanitarian aid for Ukraine
- In the case of some countries, also military indirect support—mainly defensive weapons deliveries and the sharing of military intelligence findings—to Ukraine

The Russo-Ukrainian war, however, raises anew a whole series of further, globally relevant questions—many also with a crucial economic focus—in a broader view. Precise information on the relevant military, economic, and political issues is required, but at times such information was dangerously scarce. Clear information in the media is obviously important in the context of ongoing international crises. Nonetheless, there were a number of significant misinformation stories on German television in March 2022: Anne Gellinek, ZDF's Brussels bureau chief, repeatedly confused millions and billions and wrongly magnified the EU's aid to Ukraine by a factor of 1000 with her false billion-dollar claims about concerning military aid(the mistake is obviously less noticeable to the audience than if a journalist claimed on TV that a person X was caught by a radar system in a car driving at 80,000 km/hour in the inner city, whereas the correct figure should be 80 km/hour). On March 26, 2020, the ARD broadcast a commercial for the next evening's Anne Will current affairs program—featuring Chancellor Olaf Scholz—and also addressed Germany's military aid, showing the unloading of a tank from an aircraft as a background clip. However, Germany's government had explicitly stated that it would not supply tanks to Ukraine. Such misinformation from public television sources is unacceptable and risks being shown in translation to viewers on Russian television stations: As evidence of egregious interference by Germany or the West in the Russo-Ukrainian war. In Germany at least, public television, with its special obligation to inform viewers, is apparently occasionally plagued by serious quality issues in its reporting.

Within weeks of the Russian invasion of Ukraine, the question of an energy import boycott against Russia arose in the West, a question that was then positively decided on the US side in mid-March with a view to the US. However, American energy imports from Russia are much lower compared to those of Germany and the EU. In fact, for the US, the move away from Russia as an energy supplier quickly led to other significant changes in US foreign policy. The Biden administration established contacts with Venezuela, which had previously been economically sanctioned for many years—due to its own statist, authoritarian government—for the purpose of encouraging an increase in oil production and Venezuelan oil exports to the US, and a broader new beginning was also attempted with the old adversary Iran.

In March 2022, the Biden administration attempted to initiate a thaw in relations with Iran—a producer of oil and natural gas—and recommitted to reaching a new multilateral nuclear agreement with that country, which in turn Russia apparently sought to prevent. In a series of steps, the West imposed comprehensive sanctions on Russia, primarily directed against the country's economic strength and its international economic relations. The EU and the US intensified the sanctions imposed since Russia's annexation of Crimea in 2014.

One sanction imposed by the US on Russia that is not easy to understand is that US citizens will be prohibited from accepting interest and dividend payments from Russia as of May 24, 2022 (after the Bucha massacre in Ukraine—committed by Russian soldiers—become known, the Biden administration even brought the critical date forward to April 6). In this way, the US is driving those Russian companies that have issued bonds internationally—including in the US—toward an artificial insolvency; moreover, certain Russian government bonds could then no longer be serviced, which is likely to plunge Russia into bankruptcy. A massive conflict between the US and Russia is apparently brewing here. In any case, the question arises as to whether the West can credibly present its traditional emphasis on a triad of institutional qualities, namely the combination of democracy, a market economy, and the rule of law, if the US imposes sanctions of this kind against Russia. No legal assessment is presented here. However, what the Biden administration is pursuing as a policy here seems strange, discriminatory and risky.

Germany, for its part, whose federal government suspended the commissioning of the so-called Nord Stream 2 natural gas pipeline at the end of February 2022 (the contract for Nord Stream 2 was signed by Germany in 2015, just one year after Russia's annexation of Crimea), was still stepping up its search for alternative energy trading partners in mid-March: Qatar will apparently play a significant role in the medium term, as newly reached agreements between Qatar and Germany suggest: as a result of the Russo-Ukrainian war, Economics and Climate Minister Robert Habeck saw himself faced with the task of securing new gas supplier countries in particular and significantly diversifying gas imports internationally overall. The German government wants to see three floating new LNG terminals in operation as early as 2022/2023, so that liquefied natural gas could be available to Germany in significant quantities within a year; this would require at least two floating LNG terminals to come on stream and the US to provide high levels of LNG supplies to Germany. Despite the war in Ukraine, it is probably safe to assume that Russian natural gas will continue to reach EU countries through Ukraine as a transit country in 2022.

The new long-term cooperation agreement between Germany and Qatar—a country that has been criticized by the EU for many years in terms of weak human rights—is strategically important for Germany: While Qatar's share of the world's gas reserves is estimated at 13%, Russia's share will be 19.9% in 2020 (BP, 2021). With its share of the world's natural gas reserves, Iran is almost as important as Russia (see Table 2.1).

Table 2.1 Top 15 leading countries in natural gas reserves as of end of 2020

Ranking	Country	Share of world natural gas reserves (%)
1	Russia	19.88
2	Iran	17.07
3	Qatar	13.11
4	Turkmenistan	7.23
5	US	6.71
6	China	4.47
7	Venezuela	3.33
8	Saudi Arabia	3.20
9	UAE	3.16
10	Nigeria	2.91
11	Iraq	1.88
12	Azerbaijan	1.33
13	Australia	1.27
14	Canada	1.25
15	Algeria	1.21
Total		88.01

Source: Own representation; data from BP Statistical Review of World Energy July 2021 (2021)

The top five gas exporting countries (see Table 2.2 for 2017) were Russia, Qatar, Norway, the US, and Canada, with Russia's market share at 18%, the US standing for 8%, and Canada at 7%. In Europe, the Netherlands represents a major gas exporter with a global market share of 4.4%. However, gas production is actually expected to decline significantly from 2022.

Due to the Russo-Ukraine war, the German government would like to become largely independent of Russia's gas supplies as quickly as possible. In March 2022, the federal minister of the economy referred to the target date of mid-2024, which can be seen as diplomatically clumsy insofar as this provides Russia's government with information important relevant for its own policy countermeasures and thus indirectly weakens the West at the international negotiating table.

Russia's invasion of Ukraine is not entirely unexpected. The author Anne Applebaum has pointed to the possibility of war between Russia and Ukraine in her Polish book *Wybór*. US intelligence agencies also apparently largely correctly assessed Russia's war plans—the Biden administration warned even during the Winter Olympics that Russia was indeed planning an invasion of Ukraine.

Russia's attack on Ukraine may be attributed to the peculiar views of Putin, in particular the idea that Ukraine historically belonged to Russia as a

Table 2.2   Top 15 natural gas exporters (in volume), estimated 2017

Ranking	Country	Natural gas exports (in million cubic meters), 2017	Share of world[a]
	World[a]	1,166,342	100.00%
1	Russia	210,200	18.02%
2	Qatar	126,500	10.85%
3	Norway	120,200	10.31%
4	US	89,700	7.69%
5	Canada	83,960	7.20%
6	Australia	67,960	5.83%
7	Algeria	53,880	4.62%
8	Netherlands	51,250	4.39%
9	Malaysia	38,230	3.28%
10	Turkmenistan	38,140	3.27%
11	Germany	34,610	2.97%
12	Indonesia	29,780	2.55%
13	Nigeria	27,210	2.33%
14	Trinidad and Tobago	15,490	1.33%
15	Bolivia	15,460	1.33%
Total		1,002,570	85.96%

Source: Own calculations (IV); data from The World Factbook (CIA, 2022)

[a]World is here calculated as the sum of the 215 countries included in the dataset; 56 countries have natural gas exports greater than zero

"brother" nation, a view that would have led to the expectation of a friendly reception for Russian troops in large parts of Ukraine, which, however, was out of the question in March 2022. Putin's view of Russian security interests apparently also played a role in the war against Ukraine; specifically, Russia had vehemently opposed Ukraine's NATO membership diplomatically for over two decades, serious prospects of accession to NATO had first been offered by the US in 2008. It should be noted here that the enshrinement on the part of the Parliament of Ukraine on February 7, 2019, of an "orientation of Ukraine toward membership in the EU and NATO" can be seen as strange. This cannot be a justification for Russia's war against Ukraine. Yet one can only wonder who in the West at a high political level said anything critical of this unusual—and politically frivolous—constitutional clause being adopted in Ukraine at the time (apparently nobody).

Also in 2019, Ukraine's parliament passed new legislation on languages, with a three-year transition period until March 2022, that effectively restricted Russian as a language in the print media (Russian newspapers would have to print the same circulation in Ukrainian as in Russian, which is a quite odd and economically inefficient condition) and its use in government offices. These were less than friendly political gestures toward some eight million or so people in Ukraine who predominantly use Russian as their everyday language. This not only created new tensions in Ukraine, but also with Russia's government. The OSCE (the Organization for Security and Co-operation in Europe) and the Council of Europe had already criticized the non-permanent language legislation introduced in Ukraine's parliament in previous years to restrict the use of Russian, among other languages. Even according to the EU's own standards, discrimination against a linguistic minority should be viewed critically here; one thinks, for example, of regulations on bilingual populations in South Tyrol, where Italian and German are both considered official languages in the law courts, among other examples.

Anchoring the NATO clause in Ukraine's constitution could probably be understood as a provocation in a one-sided view on the part of Russia's government, since a contradiction with earlier promises made by the West seems to be visible here: With the end of the Soviet Union, according to the words of the then German Foreign Minister Genscher, no expansion of NATO in Eastern Europe was planned; the then NATO Secretary General Wörner had also made similar statements in Brussels on May 19, 1990. However, it is not unknown whether Russia sought any contractual assurances from NATO in the 1990s on the basis of Genscher's or Wörner's comments. The 1997/1998 Russian economic crisis, moreover, left Russia's international position looking weak for several years. After all, NATO undertook to maintain military personnel in new Eastern European member states only for a short time—for a maximum of six months—and in limited numbers (in accordance with the NATO-Russia Founding Act).

Under Russian President Yeltsin, the successor of President Gorbachev, privatization in an "oligarchic model" was born out of acute need for state financing: About three dozen families came into possession of the largest part of hitherto state-owned companies. In 1997, President Yeltsin agreed to the NATO-Russia Founding Act, according to which Russia would not oppose NATO's eastward expansion—Yeltsin had argued against NATO's eastward expansion for years—while at the same time NATO pledged not to station nuclear weapons in Eastern European NATO member states. The treaty partners wanted to recognize the territorial inviolability of countries. In addition, cooperation was to be intensified within the framework of the Organisation for Security and Co-operation in Europe (OSCE) and a new institution, the NATO-Russia Council, which was to help resolve disagreements between Russia and NATO member states. Poland, Hungary, and the Czech Republic subsequently joined NATO in 1997.

Putin, an assertive and effective Moscow official, came to power after Yeltsin's resignation and achieved large majorities in subsequent elections; however, in the context of elections that were rarely fair, as political competition was massively suppressed. Putin's economic model has seen the Russian economy fall behind that of democratic Ukraine in real growth terms after 2016—thus, Ukraine also appears to be a political-economic challenge for Putin. It should be noted that in polls on Putin's popularity, he suffered significant losses during periods of weak economic growth; after the occupation of Crimea, which Putin hailed as an historic, integral part of Russia, the Russian president recorded particularly high approval ratings in polls.

While the government of Russia claims that the war against Ukraine is necessary because of the need to prevent genocide in the eastern Donbas region—in the context of the "civil war" in Ukraine—because chemical and biological weapons laboratories are operating in Ukraine, and because a government comprised of neo-Nazis should be deposed, the reality is apparently very different: Even if the state TV media keeps repeating the propaganda to justify the "special military operation" in Ukraine. Contradictions were evident in Russia itself on March 14 from a protest on the first TV channel's main news program: there are cracks even in the state media, which are tightly controlled by the president and the government. Journalist Marina Ovsyannikova, who held up an anti-war poster behind the news anchor on that TV channel, also apologized in a video on the Internet for supporting Kremlin propaganda for years. This apparently shows that in Russia, there was no clear majority of the population in favor of the war in Ukraine. The younger generation, which frequently informs itself on the Internet, is probably largely opposed to Russia's war. Since the occupation of Crimea, Russia has recorded an annual emigration of about 300,000 citizens, and in the spring of 2022, the number of Russian emigrants has increased significantly.

In the three decades since the end of the Cold War, Europe has failed to build a stable security partnership. Russia was the eighth country to be admitted to the G7 in 1998—but was then excluded from the G8 after the annexation of Crimea. NATO's admission of numerous Eastern European states after 1991 is seen in the West as an expression of these states' sovereignty. However, as NATO moved closer to Russia, Ukraine's military status became increasingly conflictual. It was known to NATO countries that NATO membership for Ukraine was likely to be politically and militarily provocative for Russia (in 2008, the US had offered the prospect of NATO membership to Ukraine—following the Russia-Georgia war—but Germany and France had opposed it at the time). Between 2008 and 2021, NATO countries, Ukraine, and Russia failed to reach binding agreements on the Ukraine military issue; for many years, the three actors apparently did not sufficiently push this issue diplomatically. Beyond military issues, there are also important economic and political aspects to developments in Ukraine and Russia and to Russia's war of aggression against Ukraine.

For a long time, Ukraine did not show a better economic development than Russia. However, the support of the International Monetary Fund (IMF) and particularly of the German government—with a long-term project to improve Ukraine's economic development via government consulting, implemented first mainly by the DIW, then by Berlin Economics—certainly led to the expectation that Ukraine could achieve higher growth rates than Russia in the medium term in the course of institutional reforms and the reduction of corruption as well as a pacification of the conflict in eastern Ukraine. In any case, Ukraine presents a challenge to Putin the autocratic leader of Russia: Ukraine as a democracy and a market economy as well as a constitutional state with the rule of law—gradually evolving—tends to challenge the autocratic model in Russia. Whether there would have been a meaningful option prior to 2022 for Ukraine as a neutral country in the middle of Europe is unclear. In principle, neutrality is more likely to be a realistic option for small countries than for larger ones, to which Ukraine could be counted in terms of area and, to some extent, population (44 million in 2021).

The war in Ukraine could become a significant burden on the export dynamics of Eastern European exports of Germany and the EU. The Committee on Eastern European Economic Relations (2022) announced on its website on February 10 with a view to 2021 and the war in Ukraine, respectively:

With strong growth of almost 20 percent in exports and imports, German trade with Eastern Europe marked a new all-time high in 2021, with total sales exceeding the half-trillion euro mark for the first time. "German companies and their partners in the region are doing a fantastic job in the face of continuing corona restrictions", commented Oliver Hermes, Chairman of the Committee on Eastern European Economic Relations, on the record figures. "We all benefit from a close-meshed network of business connections and supply relationships with our eastern EU neighbors, as well as with important partner countries such as Russia, Ukraine and Kazakhstan. That the fruits of this labor are now once again being put at risk by unresolved political conflicts is completely irresponsible", Hermes said. "We don't need war planning and protectionist measures, but new prospects for intensifying our cooperation".

As far as the economic weights of Russia and Ukraine are concerned, in dollar terms, Russia's national income in 2020 was slightly higher than that of Spain. However, in terms of purchasing power parity—which allows a meaningful international comparison of economic performance—Russia's economic weight is about twice that of Spain. Ukraine's national income in dollar terms is about one-tenth as large as Russia's, the latter having 145 million inhabitants (as opposed to Ukraine's 44 million), so the average per capita income in Russia is higher than in Ukraine (about 2.7 times in 2020). In purchasing power parity terms, the gap narrows, but the magnitude is similar—Russian national income is about 8 times that of Ukraine, and per capita income is about 2.3 times (World Bank/WDI, 2022). From 2016, was real growth in Ukraine for a number of years higher than in Russia (see Fig. 2.1). Due to the Russo-Ukrainian war, production will decline significantly in 2022; in Ukraine due to war-related destruction and the flight of refugees and capital, in Russia due to international economic sanctions and the emigration of many, relatively young, professionals—many have taken advantage of opportunities to

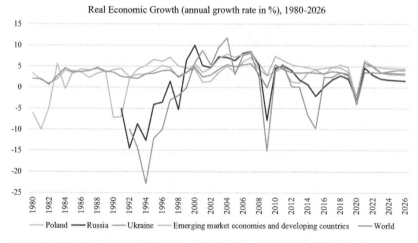

Fig. 2.1   Real economic growth (annual growth rate in percent): Emerging market economies and developing countries, world, Ukraine, Russia, Poland. Source: International Monetary Fund (World Economic Outlook, as of October 2021)

emigrate to Finland, for example; in some cases, probably also to avoid conscription into the military in Russia. At the end of March, the St. Petersburg-Helsinki rail connection will be discontinued. The emigration of Russian citizens, which has amounted to 300,000 per year since 2014, will thus decrease massively. Under Putin, Russia changed in spring 2022 into a country whose repressive regime is approaching that of the former Soviet Union. Since the end of March 2022, there is no independent media left in Russia and the penalties for demonstrating against the war have been made even more draconian.

The West, together with Japan, the Republic of Korea, and Singapore, largely blocked Russia's major banks from the international financial markets in February 2022 by excluding them from the SWIFT system. The sanctions were initially chosen on the part of EU countries—including Germany—so that trade in oil and gas from Russia could continue. However, in mid-March, the EU countries and the US also discussed cutting such imports from Russia or suspending them altogether for a certain period of time. Russia, for its part, announced on March 7 that it was also considering plans to stop filling the long-used natural gas pipeline to EU countries with gas, which would have been seen as a Russian gas boycott of EU countries as a countermeasure to Western sanctions. At a special summit in Versailles in March 2022, the EU decided that it would not follow the US, that is, it would not implement an immediate import boycott of coal, natural gas, and oil against Russia. On the part of the EU, there have been several rounds of sanctions against Russia; on March 14, a ban on investments in Russia's energy sector was presented by the EU as part of the fourth sanctions package. At the same time, the US is increasing pressure on China not to help circumvent Western sanctions against Russia by supplying Chinese goods to Russia. A fifth package of sanctions was agreed by the EU at the beginning of April. In March—as the US imposed its energy embargo on Russian imports—the UK had also already announced that it intended to end energy imports from Russia by the end of 2022.

The suspension of international transactions for cardholders from Russia by the leading US card-payment service providers Visa and Mastercard at the beginning of March and the announcement by the leading Russian airline on March 6, 2022, that it would no longer operate international flights (due to the closure of the airspace of many industrialized countries to aircraft from Russia and the risk for Aeroflot that aircraft leased abroad could be confiscated if they land outside Russia as part of Western sanctions) make it clear to many citizens that Russia has become internationally isolated as a result of the war in Ukraine. It remains to be seen to what extent this will be received as important information by the older majority of the population in Russia with regard to Russia's TV-based war propaganda—which gives a different picture of the Russian invasion of Ukraine than independent media (e.g., in the EU, Switzerland, Norway, the UK, and the US). The younger segments of the population, many of whom could access digital social media information during the first two weeks of Russia's war of aggression against Ukraine, seem to have a critical view of Russia's invasion of Ukraine.

In the first weeks of the war, Russia's leadership emphasized, among other war aims, the goals of achieving the demilitarization and denazification of Ukraine; while there are right-wing neo-Nazi undercurrents in parts of Ukrainian society (see Cohen [2018] and commentary in Annex C), they represent only a small minority of Ukrainians. Using them as a justification for a war of aggression against Ukraine comes across as a far-fetched justification.

Russia's invasion of Ukraine and occupation of the country is likely to mean a new Cold War in Europe. Germany's export industry will face temporary problems in connection with the Western sanctions against Russia, and exports to Russia are likely to fall significantly; especially in the high-tech sector. The value of imports from Russia will rise significantly on a temporary basis as oil and gas prices worldwide will increase in the short term: Oil, gas, and metals are Russia's main exports. As far as gas prices for private households in Germany in January 2022 were concerned, the price was 80% above the 2008 price level; this will then be compounded in subsequent months by further price increase effects resulting—in a broader sense—from the Russo-Ukrainian war. The inflation rate in Germany and the Eurozone is expected to reach 7% in 2022, which will lower real wages in the short term and therefore increase companies' demand for labor—new jobs could be created here, but only temporarily.

The West will increase its military spending in both the short and medium terms, which could help stabilize overall economic demand. The German government's decision to set aside a special fund of €100 billion for the Bundeswehr creates a basis for Germany to finance significantly higher defense spending in the medium term. Whether this will succeed in mitigating the Bundeswehr's weaknesses in terms of procurement efficiency remains to be seen.

If Italy increased its military expenditure ratio from 1.6% to 2% in parallel with the rise in the German and Spanish military expenditure ratios from 1.4% to 2% each, this would result in a fiscal expansion effect of initially around 0.3% of GDP for the EU27. However, imports from the US account for a considerable share of increased military spending, so that the fiscal expenditure multiplier and thus the expansion effect on EU national income remain relatively low.

In addition to production in Ukraine, its exports will also decline in 2022 due to the war. German and Western European companies that procure inputs from Ukraine—for example in the automotive industry—will experience production disruption as a result. However, this is only likely to have a temporary negative impact on production in Western Europe. Russia's massive attack on the important Ukrainian export port city of Mariupol will significantly worsen the export opportunities for Ukraine's economy.

Like the US, the UK, and Switzerland, Germany is likely to benefit from falling interest rates on government bonds, as demand for "safe havens" or financial products rises in times of international crisis; this effect should be seen separately from inflation-related impulses to raise interest rates. The reduction in interest rates in Western countries stimulates investment, at least in some sectors. However, it cannot be ruled out that a decline in production in energy-intensive sectors, for example, will ultimately have a dampening effect on the economy as a whole. Additional spending on the government side could, in the short term, result from refugees from Ukraine; in the medium term, these people will make a positive contribution to production in Germany or the EU (and other countries) once they are integrated into the respective labor markets. In the short term, the refugee flows could lead to an expansion of the shadow economy in the host countries.

Since Ukrainian refugees in Germany, as in many EU countries, receive a quasi-automatic multi-year residence and work permit because of the war situation, many refugees or workers from Ukraine are also likely to come increasingly to Germany in the medium term—in the areas of construction and care workers in the domestic sector, as well as in a few other sectors as far as numerically significant numbers of workers are concerned. Even before the Russo-Ukrainian war, there were significant numbers of workers from Ukraine in the EU: Especially in Poland, where about three-quarters (or 1.4 million people) of the mobile Ukrainian workforce flowed. A large share of the immigrants and refugees from Ukraine is well-educated and highly skilled, whereby especially younger workers possess professional digital competences.

Cyber Warfare and Digital Combat via the Internet

Several months before Russia's war of aggression, the US—or Ukraine—had apparently communicated with well-informed intelligence sources on the policy orientation of Russia's President Putin. According to a March 9 *Financial Times* report (Tett, 2022), the US sent experts in cyber warfare with the goal of protecting critical Ukrainian infrastructure from Russian Internet-based attacks. Ukraine had increasingly been the target of Russian cyber-attacks since 2014—in 2015, a cyber-attack on Ukraine's power grid resulted in the city of Kyiv being without power for several hours. This US assistance likely significantly bolstered defense capabilities in the early weeks of the war in Ukraine, and the *Financial Times* article reports that unofficial US assistance in the fight against computer viruses in Ukraine were helpful, as was, for example, special support measures that Microsoft took—steps that the US government then recommended be transferred also to NATO partner countries.

A February 28 blog post from Microsoft President Brad Smith (Smith, 2022) said that just hours before Russia's attack on Ukraine, Microsoft's Threat Intelligence Center had detected a new wave of offensive and destructive cyber-attacks against digital infrastructure. Microsoft immediately contacted the government of Ukraine and provided guidance for countering these cyber-attacks—a Microsoft engagement that has also continued. There had also been indications of attempts at data theft from Ukrainian government agencies. The president of Microsoft also stated his concern that recent cyber-attacks had been noted against Ukrainian civilian digital targets, with this affecting the financial sector, the agricultural sector, emergency services, humanitarian aid engagements, and the energy sector, as well as private businesses. Microsoft was cooperating in this field with NATO services and also with US authorities in Washington, DC.

Ukrainian President Zelenskyy repeatedly addressed the people of Russia, as well as Russian soldiers in the Ukrainian war, with speeches in the Russian language during the first weeks of the war. He also delivered speeches, digitally relayed from Kyiv, to the parliaments of Canada, the US, Germany, France, Italy, Denmark, Israel, and Japan, among others. This outreach strengthens international political support for Ukraine in the war against Russia.

Russia's government and President Putin, in turn, have censored radio and TV stations in Russia, which are critical of the Kremlin, as well as Internet services from the West (such as Facebook and Twitter). For the younger generation in Russia, such behavior by the state leadership is likely seen as tantamount to a Kremlin admission of guilt in the matter of the Ukraine war, which, in view of Russia's attack, may officially only be referred to in Russian society as a "special military operation" in Ukraine. With this attack against Ukraine, the prospects for growing Germany-Russia trade are certainly significantly worsened for many years to come.

LEADING OECD DONOR COUNTRIES: A CONFUSING DEBATE

How significant is the financial, humanitarian, and military support for the Ukrainian people? The study by Antezza et al. (2022) argues—considering these three elements of aid for Ukraine combined—that the support provided by the EU (i.e., EU27) countries for Ukraine is smaller than that of the US. This information is not true if one includes the commitment of EU member countries vis-à-vis refugees from Ukraine (Antezza et al. exclude this position deliberately, which makes no sense in economic and political terms). By the end of March 2022, Poland had accepted almost 3 million Ukrainian refugees, which—on the basis of an estimated €500 in expenditures per refugee per month—implies a commitment of €18 billion from Poland on top of the figures covered by Antezza et al; the latter have added other bilateral commitments of €2.9 billion made by EU27 member countries to the commitments of €1.4 billion from the European Commission and the European Council and €2 billion by the European Investment Bank (which sums up to €6.3 billion for the EU/EU27). As regards Germany with about 300,000 Ukrainian refugees—and an estimated €1000 in expenditures per person per month—this equates to an additional commitment of around €3 billion from Germany for 2022 which should be reflected in a "gross" EU27 commitment. Italy with an estimated 200,000 refugees would stand for an additional €2 billion expenditures. The combined implicit expenditure commitment of other EU countries roughly adds up to another €2 billion for support for Ukrainian refugees. The coverage gap by Antezza et al. amount to roughly €25 billion for the EU, which means that the figures published by the Kiel Institute for the World Economy thus seem to be misleading the public debate. Therefore, it holds that taking into account expenditures of EU member countries, the UK and the US for refugees from Ukraine as commitments, EU countries have clearly committed a much higher level of effective aid to the Ukrainian population than the US (or the UK). The respective expenditure figures for refugees by the UK and the US are much smaller than the expenditures of Germany or Italy. In Europe, Germany's support for the Ukrainian people exceeds that of the UK, France, and Italy.

Leading OECD donor countries for Ukraine are shown in Table 2.3 from the Kiel Institute for World Economics (Antezza et al., 2022); the figures are based on expenditures for humanitarian, financial, and military aid for Ukraine. The ranking of leading donor countries should, however, also take into consideration the expenditures for Ukrainian refugees—for example, €300 million per month in Germany (based on an estimated 300,000 refugees); for 2022, about €3 billion in humanitarian expenditures for refugees from Ukraine will come on top of the figures for Germany covered by the Kiel Institute for the World Economy in an approach that is biased as it does not include the expenditures for refugees in the respective OECD countries.

BILATERAL PERSPECTIVES ON GERMANY-RUSSIA TRADE

On the import side, Germany's trade with Russia is dominated by Russian metals—some of which show critically high market shares for Russian suppliers—and the supply of gas, oil, and coal. According to a statement made by the German minister of economics at the end of March 2022, Germany intends to very significantly reduce energy imports from Russia by the summer of 2024, that is, apparently through not renewing expiring supply contracts. In the case of natural gas, Germany intends to stop importing gas from Russia by mid-2024, with the exception of residual volumes. As far as Germany's dependence on imports from Russia is concerned, Russian natural gas supplies are critical for Germany; for the EU as a whole, too, Russia's share of gas imports is very substantial at 40%.

Germany's goods exports to Russia grew significantly before the Crimean crisis (in 2014) and at times represented 3.5% of total exports. In the wake of Western sanctions against Russia—and the Crimea region—and Russian counter-sanctions, Russia's share of German exports has fallen to around 2% (Ukraine's share of German goods exports was 0.4% in 2021). With Germany's goods export ratio at one-third, German exports to Russia represent slightly less than 1% of GDP. The mechanical engineering and pharmaceuticals sectors achieved above-average shares of exports to Russia, at 3.1% and 3.6%, respectively, while exports of automobiles had only a below-average share of exports to Russia; medical and pharmaceutical products recorded a significant expansion in exports to Russia in 2021 with an increase of a good 20% compared with 2013—export value €2.5 billion per year (Schrader and Laaser, 2022).

Table 2.3 Country ranking of bilateral aid commitments to Ukraine in percentage of donor country GDP, February 24, 2022—March 27, 2022

Country	Total aid (GDP) (%)
Estonia	0.7897
Poland	0.1777
Lithuania	0.0564
Slovakia	0.0499
Sweden	0.0456
US	0.0399
Czech Republic	0.0345
Croatia	0.0338
UK	0.0287
France	0.0174
Italy	0.0152
Germany	0.0141
Canada	0.0120
Finland	0.0099
Malta	0.0086
Greece	0.0080
Latvia	0.0078
Denmark	0.0071
Netherlands	0.0049
Luxembourg	0.0045
Portugal	0.0043
Hungary	0.0043
Belgium	0.0042
Austria	0.0033
Japan	0.0020
Romania	0.0018
Cyprus	0.0016
Slovenia	0.0003
Spain	0.0003
Ireland	0.0000

Note: Bilateral government-to-government commitments made to Ukraine from February 24, 2022, to March 27, 2022, collective EU aid is not allocated to individual member countries but would represent additional aid

Source: Own representation of data contained in Antezza et al. (2022), Fig. 4, p. 15

A massive slump in German-Russian trade in the context of the Ukraine war will have a negative impact on both Russia and Germany, and a corresponding decline in EU-Russia trade would certainly also bring significant economic dampening effects for Eastern European EU countries. On the gas import side, if Germany and the EU turn more toward liquefied natural gas (LNG) imports, this will lead to price increases in the energy sector, as LNG is about 10% more expensive than gas delivered via pipelines.

In the long term, Russia would probably have to intensify its foreign trade with China and other countries in Asia—as well as Africa. However, Russia would obviously still be a junior partner in this foreign trade as the Chinese economy is much larger than Russia's (a Sino-Russian ratio of about 5:1 in the medium term). The breach of trust marked by President Putin's invasion of Ukraine is likely to cloud the prospects for Germany-Russia trade for many years to come.

Moreover, if Germany and the EU actually stopped importing any gas from Russia in a few years, Ukraine would no longer receive any income from pipeline transit fees. Russia will only be able to sell gas surpluses to other countries and regions of the world at a considerable discount. Such price reductions could thus certainly lead to a certain dependence of these countries supplied by Russia on the energy side.

INTERNATIONAL PERSPECTIVES

War between Ukraine and Russia represents a watershed moment in international relations. In general, trust in the reliability of national borders and international law is being undermined here, at least temporarily, and the propensity for conflict in many parts of the world is likely to increase. On March 12, 2022, one Russian TV station's program featured experts discussing the possibility of Russian military occupying the Baltic countries and parts of Poland and even Sweden.

A few hours before Russia's attack on Ukraine, Ukraine decoupled its power grid from Russia's, a move which was actually designed—with parallel new connection to the European grid—as a longer-term project until 2023, with test phases due in winter and summer 2022, respectively, and a very first test phase on February 24. On that day, the day of the launch of Russia's invasion, Ukraine requested an emergency interconnection with the European grid (European Network of Transmission System Operators for Electricity/ENTSO-E). This interconnection did indeed take place and deprived Russia of the ability to control Ukraine's power grid (Sabadus, 2022).

An important international role will be played by China's leadership, which may see the Russian attack on Ukraine as an encouraging signal to step up its own attempts to seize power in Taiwan. This will also create new uncertainty in Asia, the growth engine of the global economy, along with the EU/UK and the US. This will weaken investment in the EU and Asia. China could find political support for Russia's war policy extremely costly, as it will certainly face sanctions from the US and presumably also the EU if Russia receives significant aid; China's trade volume with the US and EU is about ten times that of Sino-Russian trade. Incidentally, China's stock markets had plummeted significantly in mid-March; a slowdown in growth due to the Russo-Ukrainian war will reduce China's exports and thus its national income, and probably also prevent it from achieving the growth targets set by the Chinese Communist Party.

The countries of the EU will want to join forces more strongly than before, both economically and militarily, in order to better protect themselves against further Russian aggression. Germany, France, and Italy are likely to play a leading role here. Russia's cyber-attacks on institutions in Ukraine is a warning for EU countries that more attention must be paid to the issue of digital defense. National budgets, like the EU budget, will have to be increased in the medium term, and industry should also be given incentives to invest more in IT security. The question of a significant increase in the EU budget is likely to arise soon: from the current 1% of the EU's national income to around 2%, with joint defense spending becoming part of a higher EU budget.

In Germany, the short- and medium-term losers of the Russo-Ukrainian war include the automotive, chemical, and mechanical engineering industries, for which Russia was an important sales market for many years. A slump in share prices is to be expected in Russia on the one hand, but also in the Western industrialized countries on the other. A few days after the start of the war, Russia closed its stock exchange—apparently in order to avoid having to report massive price reductions in the context of Western sanctions and the war; a reopening for—only—30 stocks took place four weeks after the start of the war. The stock market value of the shares halved as a result of Russia's attack on Ukraine.

Falling (real) stock market prices were also seen in Germany, France, and other EU countries in March 2022. Economic growth will then be dampened via reduced investment growth. In Germany, the planned 2022 shutdown of the last three nuclear power plants should be reviewed. There is too little reserve capacity in the German electricity market, especially as higher gas prices are making some gas-fired power plants uneconomical. The Green Party's federal economy minister will have to make some difficult decisions. A rapid phase-out of coal-fired power generation, which is desirable from a climate policy perspective, will also not be possible if oil and gas prices rise significantly.

The US announced on March 9, 2022, that it would stop purchasing gas and oil from Russia. It should be noted that the US has been a net exporter of gas since 2017. It remains to be seen whether major EU countries will want to do without Russian gas and oil in 2022. Gas storage in Germany was only about 25% full as of mid-March 2022, which is less than in previous years. A new law on the part of the German government for 2022 will bring new requirements for the minimum filling of gas storage facilities in the fall, whereby good progress was achieved in the early period with gas storage capacities filling quickly.

Economic sanctions against Russia can have little effect in the short term; but at least stock trading in Moscow must be suspended in the short term. Russia's occupation of Ukraine will create a kind of East Germany or GDR 2.0 in Ukraine, because millions of Ukrainians will want to leave the country and Russia will only be able to counter this with a tough border regime. As little as the GDR could exist in the long run, a Russian occupation of Ukraine is also unlikely to be feasible in the long run. Time is not on Russia's side, but rather helping the West. Incidentally, high oil and gas prices are a drag on China's economic growth, as they are on Japan and other countries in Asia. The economic interests of the vast majority of countries in the world ultimately demand stability, peace, and prosperity. Putin's Russia, with its military aggression in Ukraine, has not only destroyed peace in Europe and diminished Russia's reputation, it will also face a broad political defensive front internationally.

The alliance between the US and the EU will probably be strengthened, and NATO's role enhanced. It was probably foreseeable that the long-standing NATO expansion in the direction of Eastern Europe would give rise to increased fears or feelings of being threatened in Russia. However, this cannot seriously justify Russia's invasion of Ukraine. With regard to the Baltic EU countries of Estonia, Latvia, and Lithuania—each with Russian minorities—no Russian invasion is to be expected, but Russia will seek to exercise its power more strongly in Europe after the invasion of Ukraine. Russian attempts to destabilize various countries in Eastern Europe can certainly be expected. All of these perspectives present negative prospects for Germany's export expectations and the opportunities to invest profitably in Eastern European countries.

At the UN Security Council, the resolution introduced by the US against Russia's war of aggression against Ukraine on February 25, 2022, received a clear majority, with one vote against from Russia and abstentions from China, India, and the United Arab Emirates. From the abstentions, one can discern some disapproval of Russia's actions, but at the same time narrow economic or military-political interests in terms of the bilateral relationship with Russia. On March 2, 2022, the United Nations General Assembly adopted the Ukraine resolution with 141 votes in favor, which contained a condemnation of Russia's invasion of Ukraine. From

Russia's side, only four small countries, namely Belarus, Eritrea, Syria and North Korea, voted against, a further 35 abstained, including China, India, and Pakistan.

If the OECD countries, that is, essentially the US, the EU plus Japan and the Republic of Korea, put Russia massively on the defensive by imposing economic sanctions, this will make Russia under Putin a political actor that is no longer calculable and will cause Russia to intensify its relations with China massively in the long term—whereby Russia would be weaker politically if it embraces China. Russia's eastern regions—with low population density—could see increasing numbers of Chinese seep into them over many years until they become an important minority "politically looked after" by China. Then Russia's eastern regions could become a kind of Ukraine 2 with Chinese claims, which could lead to a major international war.

In the longer term, the sanctions regime of the West could also lead to Russia's exclusion from important international organizations. Particularly important in the economic sphere are the International Monetary Fund, where Russia's membership was not yet an issue in March 2022. In addition, the World Trade Organization, the Bank for International Settlements, and other organizations with economic, political, or legal relevance. On the subject of human rights in Europe, the Council of Europe is particularly important.

On March 11, US President Biden declared that Russia would lose the benefits of the most-favored nation (MFN) clause in the World Trade Organization, with the US, Japan, Canada, and the EU taking this step in parallel to make Russian exports more difficult (this is ultimately about tariff increases on Russia's export products). The principles of the most-favored nation clause and equal treatment of foreigners, which are important at the World Trade Organization, have thus been massively weakened with regard to Russia. Russia's government in turn intends to give special national treatment to companies from "unfriendly countries" and thus discriminate against them. In addition, on the same day there was the news report that Russia is to be excluded from the Bank for International Settlements; this institution is important for the cooperation of central banks at the international level and also for agreements on rules in international banking and thus for the stability of the global financial system. The exclusion of Russia from the Bank for International Settlements seems a premature step of Western sanctions tightening against Russia; after all, there will then be hardly any reasonable options left with regard to an ultimately finite sanctions list against Russia. Russia's exclusion is also likely to be considered at the EBRD—the European Bank for Reconstruction and Development (particularly important for Eastern Europe)—in London.

The fact that the US has revoked the most-favored nation clause vis-à-vis Russia can only be justified to some extent. At the World Trade Organization (WTO), the specifications for exceptions to the GATT rules (GATT was the predecessor organization of the WTO) are described as follows in Article 21 for the protection of national security interests (Research Services of the German Bundestag, 2019):

Nothing in this Agreement shall prevent a Party from,

1. *refusing to provide information the disclosure of which they consider to be contrary to their essential security interests;*
2. *take such measures as it considers necessary to protect its essential security interests*

   (i)   with respect to fissile materials or the raw materials from which they are produced;
   (ii) in trade in arms, munitions and war material and in trade in other goods and materials intended directly or indirectly for the supply of armed forces;
   (iii) in time of war or other serious crisis in international relations;

3. *take measures pursuant to its obligations under the Charter of the United Nations for the maintenance of international peace and security.*

The US—like EU countries or countries in Asia, for example—could point out that the Russo-Ukrainian war is a serious crisis in international relations. The US could also argue that the sanctions measure against Russia is ultimately intended to preserve peace and international security.

Russia resigned its membership in the Council of Europe (with 47 states as members) on March 16, 2022—after 26 years of membership—after being suspended. The decision of the members, excluding Russia, to suspend Russia was unanimous. Russia's exclusion is, however, not necessarily wise. This is because it means that the country, or rather the jurisprudence there, is no longer subject to review by the European Court of Human Rights. This tends to weaken the protection of defendants in Russia, and the reintroduction of the death penalty in Russia has thus become conceivable. Moreover, Russia had announced on several occasions that it intends to withdraw from the Council of Europe.

On March 16, 2022, the International Court of Justice in The Hague issued a ruling that Russia must immediately cease hostilities in Ukraine.

On February 26, Ukraine had presented a case before the Court that there was a dispute with Russia over the interpretation, application, and fulfillment of the Convention Against Genocide. Russia had alleged that Ukraine was committing genocide against the population in the breakaway governmental districts of Luhansk and Donetsk, which were under the control of Russian-backed fighters: This was one of the reasons put forward by Russia's government as a justification for the war of aggression against Ukraine.

Russia's war of aggression has apparently largely isolated the country internationally. It is obvious that Russia's invasion of Ukraine must be answered with clear economic sanctions on the part of OECD countries. Wise cooperation and well-thought through approaches on the part of the US, the EU, and other countries here are indispensable.

Excluding Russia entirely from the SWIFT agreement, which is important for international payments, should probably be one of the last sanction options, as this threatens to damage international trust in the Brussels-based organization in the long term; SWIFT is a processing system of international payments, which will certainly damage global economic integration—in West and East as well as North and South. The sanction of cutting off large Russian banks—decided at the end of February 2022—puts these banks under massive pressure when it comes to international business.

Whether freezing Russian currency balances with Western central banks is a sensible policy move is open to doubt. With a view to stable international currency relations, it is not a good idea to actively involve the central banks of the Western world in foreign and sanctions policy, and there are also legal problems relating to the seizure of the currency assets of another country. Russia's reliance on its currency reserves to wage war against Ukraine can only be assumed in the medium and long term.

Russia itself holds foreign exchange reserves at the central bank of its own country, while foreign exchange reserves of around €300 billion are held by the central banks of France and Germany, among others. The foreign currency reserves held abroad by Russia probably account for almost one-fifth of Russia's total reserves. If the West emphasizes democracy, freedom, peace, market economy, and the rule of law with good reasons, it should act accordingly when choosing means of sanctions. If Russia is deprived of access to its foreign currency reserves held abroad, the West should not be surprised if Russia no longer services government bonds held abroad in the medium term, or only offers Rubles for interest payments and redemptions.

LITERATURE

Antezza, A., et al. (2022). Which countries help Ukraine and how? Introducing the Ukraine Support Tracker, Kiel Working Paper No. 2218 April 2022, Kiel Institute for the World Economy.

Bachmann, R. et al. (2022). What if? The economic effects for Germany of a stop of energy imports from Russia, ECONtribute Policy Brief Nr. 028. Retrieved May 24, 2022, from https://www.econtribute.de/RePEc/ajk/ajkpbs/ECONtribute_PB_028_2022.pdf

BP. (2021). *Statistical review of world energy.*

CIA. (2022). The World Fact Book. https://www.cia.gov/the-world-factbook/field/natural-gas/

Cohen, J. (2018). Ukraine's Neo-Nazi Problem, published by Reuters on March 19, 2018. Retrieved May 24, 2022, from https://www.reuters.com/article/us-cohen-ukraine-commentary-idUSKBN1GV2TY

Committee on Eastern European Economic Relations. (2022). NeuerRekordimOsthandel—Habe Billion geknackt [transl. PJJW: New Record in Eastern Trade—Half a Trillion Cracked, dated February 10, 2022. Retrieved March 30, 2022, from https://www.ost-ausschuss.de/de/neuer-rekord-im-osthandel-halbe-billion-geknackt

Research Services of the German Bundestag. (Wissenschaftliche Dienste, 2019). Zur Geltendmachung nationaler Sicherheitsinteressen beim Aufbau des 5G-Netzes, Berlin, online. Retrieved March 30, 2022, from https://www.bundestag.de/resource/blob/657800/a839ff5d440a7fa626c9c165ca6b636b/WD-2-079-19-pdf-data.pdf

Sabadus, A. (2022). Bold Ukrainians Defy Putin's invasion and join European electricity grid, Atlantic Council. Retrieved March 30, 2022, from https://www.atlanticcouncil.org/blogs/ukrainealert/bold-ukrainans-defy-putins-invasion

Schrader, K., & Laaser, C.-F. (2022). Germany's trade with Russia and the war in Ukraine: What is at stake?, Kiel Policy Brief 163, Kiel Institute for the World Economy.

Smith, B. (2022). Digital Technology and the War in Ukraine, blog from Brad Smith, President and Vice-Chair, published 28th February 2022. Retrieved March 30, 2022, from https://blogs.microsoft.com/on-the-issues/2022/02/28/ukraine-russia-digital

Tett, G. (2022). What Google knows about the future of war, Financial Times Magazine, published 9th March 2022. https://www.ft.com/content/344ce524-dc50-4a77-9757-0fde985baca2

World Bank/WDI. (2022). GDP per capita, PPP, Current International $, Russia Federation and Ukraine, World Development Indicators Database. Retrieved May 24, 2022, from https://data.worldbank.org/indicator/NY.GDP.PCAP.PP.CD?locations=RU-UA-and-join-european-electricity-grid/-war-cyberattacks/

CHAPTER 3

The West and Russia: Frozen Relations Between the UK and Russia for Decades

Since the collapse of the Soviet Union and the disintegration of the Warsaw Pact in 1991, the West and Russia have had three decades to develop a common security architecture in Europe, which of course would have involved not only leading European NATO member countries but also the US in corresponding negotiation processes. The Russo-Ukrainian war shows that attempts in this direction have tragically failed. US-Russia relations are particularly important because the old Cold War adversaries now faced each other in a new and altered way. Since 1991, the US no longer faced the Soviet Union, but a new Russia, and there were important arms control issues, but also cooperation issues: for example, cooperation on the project of an international space station.

Incidentally, the US was active in Afghanistan until 2021, where American troops had invaded that country in the wake of the September 11, 2001, terrorist attacks, along with a number of NATO allies. The US and Russia clashed in Syria, where a resistance movement against the regime of Bashar Al-Assad had developed in the wake of the Arab Spring. The young President Assad sought Russia's support in the fight against the Islamic State, a terrorist organization that had spread across the Middle East for a number of years. The government in Moscow saw an opportunity to visibly re-establish itself as an influential power in the Middle East and gain a military port for itself with access to the Mediterranean in Syria, in addition to an air base. The Islamic State had indeed emerged largely due to US action in Iraq, itself contrary to international law. That state was

P. J. J. Welfens, *Russia's Invasion of Ukraine*, https://doi.org/10.1007/978-3-031-19138-1_3

invaded and occupied by the US under President George W. Bush, based on the false claim that the government of Saddam Hussein had obtained chemical weapons. Russia had been just as critical of the US war in Iraq as it was of NATO's alleged use of certain chemical weapons against Yugoslavia (primarily Serbia) in response to the Kosovo War in 1999, a use that was illegal under international law. US President Obama had warned against the use of chemical weapons by Syria's military—in the slipstream of Russian military advisors in Syria—and declared a case of such use to be a "red line" which would induce retaliatory actions; in reality, the use of such weapons remained without consequences from the US.

US-Russia relations had a chance for improvement under President Trump. However, the July 2018 meeting in Helsinki between US President Trump and Russia's President Putin proved unproductive. Under President Biden, US-Russia relations deteriorated again, with the Biden administration inheriting from its predecessor, the Trump administration, among other things, the issue of civil war-like clashes in Venezuela. In that country, Russia, as well as China, had sought to gain influence by propping up the populist authoritarian rulers Hugo Chávez and Nicolas Maduro through various oil purchases in a situation where the US was seeking to encourage regime change through economic sanctions. From the Russian government's perspective, the US invasion of Iraq, which gave rise to the Islamic State—a new terrorist organization—represented an ill-conceived policy that ultimately created chaos across the Middle East.

The UK under Prime Minister Tony Blair supported the US in the Iraq war, while Germany and France did not stand by the side of the US in that invasion. Together with the US, the UK and France overthrew the authoritarian ruler Muammar Gaddafi in a brief air war against Libya in 2011, which led to civil war-like conditions there in the years that followed; some other NATO countries were also active in support alongside the US, France and the UK, but not Germany. The military intervention in Libya took place with the approval of the United Nations Security Council. The result was a civil war in Libya. In addition to the US, the UK, and France, Russia and Turkey were active on one of the two sides of the civil war. An entire book could be written on Russia-US relations, especially with regard to economic aspects, which is not what is intended here. It is more interesting—and simple—to briefly describe and analyze the development of relations between the UK and the Russian Federation.

DEVELOPMENT OF THE RELATIONSHIP BETWEEN THE UK AND RUSSIA

Relations between the modern states of the UK and Russia still go back several centuries, with shared vital interests in both the First World War and the Second World War, when the common military opponent was Nazi Germany. Between these two great powers, indeed both nuclear powers, one would expect that there should be regular visits of leading politicians. Was this the case in the relationship between the UK and Russia? The visit of Russian President Vladimir Putin to London in 2003, when Tony Blair was head of government, was the first high-ranking Russian state visit to the UK—the old Western leader—since Czar Alexander II in 1874. There can be no sustainable, solid political relationship established between two globally leading countries whose heads of government or presidents want to visit each other only once every 129 years. One can certainly speak of a policy failure here, which, in view of the period after 1973 (when the UK became a member of the European Communities—later EU), also entailed negative spillover effects on other EU countries. After all, British Prime Minister Cameron visited Moscow in 2011 and made a terse statement that Britain was interested in good relations with Russia. Nevertheless, eight important years had passed without a top-level return visit. Of course, it is not certain that more intensive and earlier travel diplomacy would have done much good in the West-Russia relationship. In 2013, Russia's President Putin was aware of the significant economic ties between Russia and the UK and between Russia and Germany, France, and the EU; and yet he still ordered the occupation of Crimea in 2014.

There was likely only a brief window of opportunity then which the West and Russia could have used to develop a common security concept in Europe. Since such a concept has not been achieved, the UK and the EU27—in addition to Ukraine and Russia—face serious problems in 2022, with the whole of Europe on the brink of a new dangerous military conflict. Successive British and Russian governments over the period from 1991 to 2021 could be accused of dangerous inaction—three decades during which several top-level meetings in London and Moscow should have been expected.

The assassination of Russian defector and naturalized British citizen Alexander Litvinenko—a former Russian spy—presumably carried out by Russian government officials, has had a massive negative impact on the attitude of both the British government and the British public toward Russia. Litvinenko apparently became the victim of a poison attack on

November 1, 2006, and died three weeks later. It is interesting to read the view of the Russian Embassy in London on British-Russian relations (Embassy of the Russian Federation to the UK, 2022), where the Litvinenko case is also addressed. On its website, the Russian Embassy in London emphasizes that Russia-UK relations have deteriorated from a previous state of good relations to openly hostile relations. The UK has frozen bilateral cooperation between the UK and Russia, including the "2+2" strategic dialogue with the participation of foreign and defense ministers, the High-Level Energy Dialogue, the UK-Russia Steering Committee on Trade and Investment, and the UK-Russia Joint Committee on Science and Technology; regular meetings of foreign ministers also no longer take place. The UK is criticized for a contradictory policy stance: the UK emphasizes that the international world order should be protected, but in fact contributed to regional destabilization with its interventions in Iraq and Libya. After BREXIT, the UK emphasized "Global Britain" as a new strategic approach to economic policy, but a course of international confrontation made it seem that this approach could not be realized. Previous UK-Russia cooperation on counterterrorism, the embassy argued, had been halted by the UK, while the British portrayal of the Litvinenko case is also wrong. Only in the area of cultural exchange was the relationship still functioning.

Box 3.1 Russo-British Bilateral Relations

The Relations between Russia and the United Kingdom historically have never been simple. In recent years, our political relationship has been characterised by instability and volatility, by abrupt changes from relatively good to overt hostility. Unfortunately, this appears to reflect the general state of our relations with the historical West. Unable to give up its claim to universal truth in international affairs, London has positioned itself on the cutting edge of such complications.

Nowadays, the Russo-British relations are going through hard times. Whatever positive achievements of recent years, those have been substantially undermined by London's projection of our differences over Ukraine, Crimea and Syria onto bilateral matters.

(continued)

Box 3.1 (continued)

We have to admit that at the moment Russo-British political dialogue is non-existent. London unilaterally froze all the bilateral formats of Inter-Governmental cooperation which proved their worth: Strategic Dialogue "2+2" with participation of Foreign and Defence Ministers, High Level Energy Dialogue, the Russian-British Inter-Governmental Steering Committee on Trade and Investment, and UK-Russia Joint Committee on Science and Technology. Regular consultations between the foreign ministries have actually ceased.

The British Government engages in hostile rhetoric which makes part of British official documents. The assertions are not brand new, but the main common point behind them is the irresponsible and groundless nature of accusations against Russia. The idea of protection of world order sounds particularly cynical from the British Prime Minister. It is enough to recall the aggressive actions of the United Kingdom in Iraq and Libya which have led not to strengthening of the international law, but to numerous casualties and sufferings of millions of people and destabilisation of whole regions. At the same time London shows fundamental incomprehension of current processes in the world and of the essence of the very UN Charter-based international legal order that the United Kingdom is vowing to protect.

The British society is currently not going through its finest hour due to the ongoing process of exiting the EU and internal splits. It is understandable that an external enemy is direly needed to distract public attention for which role Russia has been chosen. It is deeply regrettable, especially now that the United Kingdom, considering its ambition to turn into a "Global Britain", would benefit from multi-directional, pragmatic and efficient foreign policy. Such an approach would give UK extra opportunities on the emerging markets as well as strengthen its global standing through the development of dialogue with other countries. The path of confrontation chosen by London is unlikely to contribute to the achievement of these goals.

(continued)

Box 3.1   (continued)

The Britain's support of the EU sanctions regime against Russia, strongly criticised by the British entrepreneurs who conduct business in Russia, is not only futile, but counterproductive. Having included in the sanctions list the chairpersons of the Federal Assembly and other representatives of the Russian legislative branch, the British have made it impossible to maintain regular interparliamentary contacts.

Anti-Russian sanctions are now being imposed on our media against the background of the EU talks on "the need to counter Russian propaganda". London is not ready either to drop its sanctions as regards visas for Russian officials, introduced earlier. The British still refuse to fully restore the contacts between special services, which has been damaging for Russo-British counter-terrorism cooperation.

The Russian Investigative Committee terminated its participation in the "public inquiry" for the sole reason that the inquiry was non-transparent and the ultimate politicisation of legal action taken. These fears have been proved true.

We consider the Litvinenko case and the way it was disposed of a blatant provocation of the British authorities. The Russian side will never accept anything arrived at in secret and based on the evidence not tested in an open court of law. We view the whole situation as an attempt to put additional pressure on Russia in connection with existing differences over a number of international issues. For us it is absolutely unacceptable that the report concludes that the Russian state was in any way involved in the death of Mr Litvinenko on British soil...

Contacts in the area of cultural cooperation made a positive contribution to our overall bilateral relationship. The success in this field confirmed that the British public and cultural community is ready for a direct and unbiased dialogue despite the prevailing political conjecture. The exhibition "Russia and the Arts. The age of Tolstoy and Tchaikovsky" in the National Portrait Gallery, which has been a great success, gave the British public an opportunity to see masterpieces on loan from the State Tretyakov Gallery in Moscow. Some of them have never been shown outside Russia before.

Source: Embassy of the Russian Federation to the United Kingdom (2022)

In 2017, the British Parliament undertook a comprehensive review of UK-Russian relations (House of Commons Foreign Affairs Committee, 2017). At that time, the parliamentary report already noted that post-Cold War relations between the UK and Russia had reached a low point. However, the report also said that while there is a need to maintain relations with Russia because the country is a nuclear power, with a seat on the United Nations Security Council, significant tensions had arisen from Russia's behavior in Ukraine (since 2014) and Syria. The violation of human rights there must be investigated, also with financial sanctions being imposed against those responsible. Furthermore, the report finds that the Putin regime is widely accepted as responsible for such breaches of international norms; however, it also emphasizes that friendly contact between the peoples of the UK and Russia is both possible and indeed desirable.

The UK's position is likely to be problematic with regard to the government of Prime Minister Boris Johnson in one particular area in terms of credibility—as the Johnson government has announced that the UK intends to withdraw from the European Convention on Human Rights (the government emphasizes this goal in view of the fact that certain legal challenges by asylum seekers whose applications for asylum have been rejected would then no longer be possible).

Anglo-Russian relations have experienced only relatively brief phases of political cooperation since 1900, with the phase of military alliance with Britain—and the US—in the Second World War being important (for more on the history of Anglo-Russian political relations, see, for example, Lucas, 2009; Smith, 2012; German, 2016; David, 2018).

The fact that the UK and the new Russia at times developed strong relations and interdependencies in the energy sector—through direct investment—may have been seen as beneficial to both states. It would certainly have been even better if a sensible privatization of Russian state-owned companies could have been developed in Russia and if an intertwining of British energy companies with private Russian energy companies had developed. In any event, contradictions and complications would arise in terms of regulatory policy if, on the one side, there are only Russian state-owned companies and on the other only private energy companies in the UK. Incidentally, if Russia had wanted to avoid the problems of the so-called Dutch disease economy—with massive corruption problems in particular—then the West should have placed more emphasis on cooperation outside of the energy sector. It is surprising, to say the least, that only a few providers from the efficient British financial sector, of all countries, have appeared in Russia as direct investors; precisely in this field there would have been a starting point to give Russia impulses to develop toward a normal market economy. Against the background of the historical developments in Russia in the 1880s, however, there was a risk that a stronger, resurgent, Russia would have wanted to "push" foreign investors out of the country once again after a few decades. The question of the commitment to a basic market economy framework in Russia has not been asked enough by the West—nor by international organizations such as the European Bank for Reconstruction and Development (EBRD) in London or the International Monetary Fund. If one had seriously wanted to transform a post-socialist economy with massive corruption structures into a market economy with the rule of law and democracy, this question would have had to be tactfully posed. Here, one can only wonder about what role the EBRD in particular has played in London over the past few decades— not really a positive one, it seems, in view of the realities in 2022 Russia. Moreover, questions about the attitudes of ordinary citizens—for example via the World Values Survey—were not asked enough with a corresponding focus; research in this direction was not initiated to a sufficient extent by the EBRD among others.

LITERATURE

David, M. (2018). UK-Russia relations: Poisoned chalice or silver linings? *Palgrave Communications, 4,* 113. https://doi.org/10.1057/s41599-018-0168-7

Embassy of the Russian Federation to the United Kingdom of Great Britain and Northern Ireland. (2022). Russo-British Bilateral Relations. Retrieved May 24, 2022, from https://www.rusemb.org.uk/ruuk/

German, T. (2016). UK–Russia relations and the Brexit debate: Advancing integration or mutual mistrust? *Global Affairs, 2*(5), 503–511. https://doi.org/1 0.1080/23340460.2017.1286944

House of Commons Foreign Affairs Committee. (2017). The United Kingdom's relations with Russia, Seventh Report of Session 2016–2017. https://publications.parliament.uk/pa/cm201617/cmselect/cmfaff/120/120.pdf

Lucas, E. (2009). *The new cold war: How the Kremlin Menaces both Russia and the West.* Bloomsbury Publishing Plc.

Smith, B. (2012). UK relations with Russia, International Affairs and Defence Section, House of Commons Library, SNIA/6449, published 24th October 2012. Retrieved June 7, 2022, from https://researchbriefings.files.parliament.uk/documents/SN06449/SN06449.pdf

CHAPTER 4

Energy Perspectives

In this chapter, some key figures on important energy issues are presented. The gas import dependencies of individual countries, national oil import figures for OECD countries, and the respective dependencies on Russia are important starting points in the area of energy. Dependencies on Russia across EU countries vary widely. Portugal and Spain, for example, are hardly dependent, with Spain also having ample liquefied natural gas capacities. However, the EU lacks intra-EU pipelines in the south-north and west-east directions to make full use of these. It should also be noted that Russia has a wide range of options, against individual EU countries or the EU as a whole in terms of counter-sanctions. Some proposals for further Western sanctions can be considered questionable. Moreover, the increase in oil and gas prices leads to numerous problems as less energy-intensive production is profitable in the West and because private households face massive price increases in the medium term when they face having to pay their heating bills. Energy market shocks add to the international corona pandemic problems and supply chain disruptions.

Energy Import Issues

Looking at EU27 gas and oil imports by major supplier countries in 2020 and the first half of 2021, respectively, we see that Russia's share of gas in 2021 was still 2.9 percentage points higher than in 2020, at 46.8% (based on third-country gas imports). Norway, Algeria, the US, and Qatar

P. J. J. Welfens, *Russia's Invasion of Ukraine*, https://doi.org/10.1007/978-3-031-19138-1_4

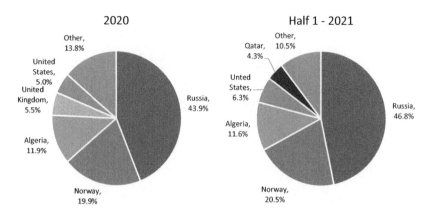

Fig. 4.1 EU gas imports from main trading partners (non-EU), 2020 and H1 2021 (share in % of trade value). Source: Own representation of data from Eurostat Database (Comext) and Eurostat estimates

followed with shares of 20.5%, 11.6%, 6.3%, and 4.3%, respectively, in 2021 (Fig. 4.1). The commissioning of the Nord Stream 2 gas pipeline to Russia would likely have increased the EU share of gas imports to over 50% from Russia. In EU competition policy, a market share of over 50% is considered a problem with regard to market dominance, and it is therefore difficult to understand why Germany, Austria, the Netherlands, and other EU countries have pushed politically in support of the Nord Stream 2 project for many years.

International diversification on the gas side requires, above all, unloading stations for liquefied natural gas in suitably equipped ports, with prices for liquefied natural gas somewhat higher than for gas from deliveries through regional pipelines. The dominance of regional pipeline deliveries for natural gas means that international price differences in individual countries or regions are much greater than for oil, where the price difference between European "North Sea oil" Brent and US oil (West Texas price) is negligible and essentially reflects only transportation costs between the US and the EU.

In the case of pipeline networks, there is also the potential for political interference with regard to transit countries, as is potentially the case with Ukraine, for example, with the old gas pipeline from Russia to Western and South-eastern Europe traversing the country, and as appears to be the case with the pan-European gas network as a widespread inefficiency problem: The regional pipeline structure is not optimal (Hubert & Cobanli, 2015).

In the EU, Bulgaria has been 100% dependent on Russia for natural gas in 2021. However, the Bulgarian government said in March 2022 that it would not renew order contracts with Gazprom. Instead, Bulgaria plans to make heavy use of gas from Azerbaijan in the future, using the Trans Adriatic Pipeline (TAP), which carries gas from Azerbaijan to Italy via Turkey. The expansion of TAP delivery capacity on a larger scale will certainly take several years.

In terms of EU oil imports from third countries, Russia accounts for 24.7% of oil imports by value in the first half of 2021—slightly lower than the 25.5% in 2020—while Norway, Kazakhstan, the US, Libya, and Nigeria recorded EU shares of 9.1%, 8.8%, 8.4%, 8.3%, and 6.8%, respectively (Fig. 4.2).

EUROSTAT (2021) provided only value ranges on EU import dependence on Russia for gas and oil in the case of individual EU countries in order to comply with the requirement of confidentiality in data publication (see Table 4.1). In the first half of 2021, for gas and oil from Russia, six countries had a share higher than 5% of total imports from third countries in terms of value for gas and oil; namely, Belgium, Germany, Spain,

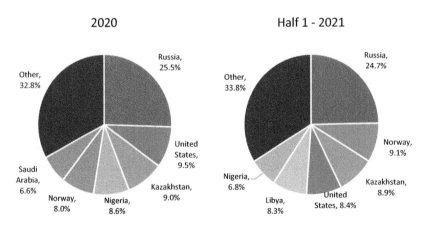

Fig. 4.2 EU oil imports from main trading partners (non-EU), 2020 and H1 2021 (share in % of trade value). Source: Own representation of data from Eurostat Database (Comext) and Eurostat estimates

Table 4.1 Russia's share in national non-EU imports of EU member states, H1 2021; share (%) of trade by value, sorted by gas share and alphabetically

	Share (%) of Russia in national Non-EU imports	
Country	Oil	Gas
Bulgaria	75–100	75–100
Finland	75–100	75–100
Slovakia	75–100	75–100
Hungary	75–100	75–100
Romania	25–50	75–100
Czech Republic	25–50	75–100
Estonia	0–25	75–100
Austria	0–25	75–100
Latvia	n.a.	75–100
Slovenia	n.a.	75–100
Poland	50–75	50–75
Germany	25–50	50–75
Sweden	0–25	50–75
Lithuania	50–75	25–50
France	0–25	25–50
Greece	0–25	25–50
Italy	0–25	25–50
Netherlands	25–50	0–25
Belgium	0–25	0–25
Ireland	0–25	0–25
Croatia	0–25	0–25
Malta	0–25	0–25
Portugal	0–25	0–25
Spain	0–25	0–25
Denmark	0–25	n.a.
Cyprus	0–25	n.a.
Luxembourg	n.a.	n.a.

Source: Eurostat database (Comext) and Eurostat estimates, EIIW presentation

France, Italy, and the Netherlands. In the case of Germany and the Netherlands, Russia accounted for more than 5% of third-country supplies by value for both oil and gas.

In the first half of 2021, the share of oil imports from Russia was more than 75% of oil imports from third countries for four EU member countries, namely Bulgaria, Slovakia, Hungary, and Finland. Ten EU member states imported over 75% of gas imports from third countries from Russia alone, namely Bulgaria, Czechia, Estonia, Latvia, Hungary, Austria,

Romania, Slovenia, Slovakia, and Finland. In each case, that is, countries with particularly high shares of Russian imports, these states are those which are relatively close to Russia.

Policy Options to Reduce Imports of Gas from Russia According to the International Energy Agency and Leopoldina

A recent analysis of natural gas imports by the International Energy Agency (IEA)with reference to the EU and Russia (IEA, 2022) and a similar study by the Leopoldina Academy (2022) on the question of the option of a significant cut to gas imports from Russia by Germany and the EU, respectively—as a protest against Russia's war of aggression against Ukraine and as a restriction of Russian war financing possibilities—are summarized next, where some inconsistencies also become apparent. Firstly, it should be noted that various EU countries are heavily dependent on imports of natural gas from Russia. Incidentally, a broad energy import boycott against Russia could also be considered from the perspective of EU countries, which would then include oil and coal in addition to gas.

The International Energy Agency (IEA, 2022) published a study on March 3, 2022, stating that EU countries could reduce their Russia gas imports by more than a third over the course of a year. Apparently, on March 8, EU Commission Vice-President Timmermans (2022) referred to important points of this study in his press presentation on EU energy policy options; Timmermans emphasized that the EU could reduce natural gas purchases from Russia by 30% in the short term, and in its text, the IEA study also refers to the EU and its energy policy, respectively, due to the European Green Deal. The aforementioned study of the International Energy Agency presents a ten-point program. The EU should

1. not conclude new gas purchase contracts with Russia, which will increase the EU's diversification opportunities in gas purchases;
2. replace Russian supply with alternative supply sources (increases in the non-Russia supply by around 30 billion m^3);
3. adopt new regulation on the minimum filling of gas storage facilities is to be adopted (this is to ensure the supply of gas next winter);
4. accelerate the implementation of new wind and solar projects (reduces gas import from Russia by 6 billion m^3);

5. maximize electricity generation through bioenergy and nuclear energy (Decreases gas imports from Russia by 13 billion m³);
6. introduce short-term tax measures to tax special profits—on the basis of the additional government revenue, poorer consumer classes could be compensated for the burden of increased energy prices;
7. accelerate the replacement of gas boilers with heat pumps (import reduction of 2 billion m³);
8. accelerate steps to increase energy efficiency in buildings and industry (import reduction of 2 billion m³ within one year);
9. encourage lower household heating use by way of a thermostat reduction of 1 degree Celsius (which would decrease gas import by 10 billion m³); and
10. intensify efforts to diversify and decarbonize more flexible power generation systems (reduce strong links between gas supply and European power security).

It is indeed worth considering in any case an extension to CO_2 allowance trading via the EU's Emissions Trading System (ETS)—following the successful Japanese example (Welfens, 2022)—to the office buildings sector; in a phase of economic dampening in the EU, it would indeed be appropriate to achieve politically targeted CO_2 reductions at minimal cost: Namely by extending CO_2 allowance trading in the EU beyond the existing energy and industry sectors; but not including the private residential rental sector (Welfens, 2022). Moreover, it is clear that the existing EU-wide coverage of industry (essentially only large-scale operations) and the energy sector by CO_2 allowance trading means that the arguably necessary mobilization of coal-fired power plants to secure desired levels of electricity production will not involve an increase in CO_2 emissions in the EU, despite a politically decreed reduction in gas purchases from Russia. If CO_2 emissions in the energy sector increase, then CO_2 reductions in industry must also increase; this is unavoidable because of the politically-mandated annual CO_2 emission reduction targets. This, in turn, is likely to be accompanied by an increase in CO_2 certificate prices and thus tends to dampen overall economic production via reduced profitability at many industrial companies.

The statement of the Leopoldina (2022) "How Russian natural gas can be replaced in the German and European energy supply" concludes that a short-term supply stop of Russian natural gas to Germany's economy can certainly be cushioned. The Leopoldina refers in particular to free landing capacities for liquefied natural gas in several EU countries; however, the problem of how additional liquefied natural gas landed elsewhere can then be transported on to Germany is not properly considered. Here, there is a lack of intra-EU pipeline capacities: especially in the south-north direction.

Various considerations of Western sanctions and a significant cut in EU energy imports as well as US imports plus UK energy imports from Russia yield interesting findings. However, Russia itself can of course work with counter-sanctions against the West in various ways, and President Putin could pre-empt a Western gas boycott with a gas supply boycott. The nationalization of subsidiaries from Western industrialized countries or OECD countries (including Japan, the Republic of Korea, Australia) is one of Russia's ways of harming foreign investors and ultimately citizens in industrialized countries: Namely, there are write-offs on investments in Russia by multinational companies with direct investments in these countries, which means reduced profits and, consequently, lower share prices in OECD countries. Anyone who has invested in the stock market directly or indirectly—for example, via a life insurance policy—will therefore realize losses.

The fact that the nationalization of foreign companies in Russia will significantly harm economic dynamics is another matter. The quality of corporate management and the dynamics of innovation will drop significantly after nationalization, which also means poorer prospects for real wage growth in Russia. Moreover, Western sanctions not only contribute to a weakening of the economy in Russia, but also the five Central Asian countries Kazakhstan, Turkmenistan, Uzbekistan, Tajikistan, and Kyrgyzstan—they are closely linked to the economy in Russia—are confronted with new economic problems. These five countries receive large remittance payments from guest workers who work in Russia; moreover, the reduction of real income in Russia means that its imports from almost all countries will decrease. The global flight of investors to safe haven countries (a typical reaction in times of international crisis) increases the devaluation pressures on the currencies of the five aforementioned countries resulting from a reduction in their exports. Currency devaluations mean increased inflation and, in particular, a sharp rise in import prices.

As far as natural gas demand in Germany is concerned, it is expected to decline by only 6–17% by 2030 (BCG, 2021; dena, 2021; Prognos et al., 2021). Natural gas could remain an important, even dominant, energy source for heat supply in the medium term and will initially be difficult to replace in industry as well; in steel production, for example, natural gas is used in the direct reduction process for a further transition phase—until green hydrogen generated on the basis of renewable energies can then be used in the long term. Beyond the heat markets, natural gas plays an important role in the electricity market, as power plants running on natural gas can be ramped up quickly; in the long term, these power plants could be operated with biogas or also with green hydrogen. In this context, it appears that at least a doubling of existing capacities will be necessary. The Federal Network Agency in Germany (BNetzA, 2021) assumes that there will be a need for expansion from 32 gigawatts to 59–88 gigawatts in 2045.

Thus far, stable gas supplies from Russia have been an important pillar of Germany's energy supply, and a conceivable (politically desired) massive cutback in gas imports from Russia raises a number of serious economic challenges; by increasingly integrating coal-fired reserve power plants into electricity production, significant quantities of natural gas could be freed up in Germany for industry and for heating purposes in private households (Fischer & Küper, 2022). It goes without saying that this would be problematic in terms of climate policy, but it would probably be acceptable on a temporary basis in the situation of a gas supply crisis.

In the case of Germany, Russia's oil and gas imports accounted for 59% of total imports in 2021 (Federal Statistical Office, 2022; see Annex A). For Russia's export revenues and also for the financing of the state budget, however, gas exports are less decisive than Russia's oil exports.

An Optimal Gas Energy Import Tariff of the EU Vis-à-Vis Russia

Several economists have suggested imposing import taxes on Russian energy deliveries to the EU and the Western world, respectively (see, e.g., Hausmann (2022) who has advocated a 90% import tariff). Daniel Gros (2022) has considered the problem in a refined theoretical framework where EU countries face a Russian monopoly exporter. What is the welfare-maximizing optimum import tariff from an EU perspective? This question is posed in an implicit three-region perspective with the EU, Russia, and Asia—where the latter represents part of world energy demand. The main findings in the analysis of Gros (2022) who uses a linear model to analyze natural gas markets—with Gazprom as Russia's monopolist exporter—are as follows:

- One-half of the import tariff will result in higher prices for EU consumers while the tariff revenue would be more than sufficient to compensate consumers for this loss.
- The EU tariff which maximizes welfare for the EU would be close to one-third of the price at which the EU would stop importing from Russia; and this would reduce Gazprom's net revenues by about half.
- If the import tariff is to be used as a sanctioning instrument to reduce revenues for Russia, the tariff should be higher—about 60%. This would cut Gazprom's revenues to one-fourth of the free trade level.

From this perspective, an EU import tariff on Russian gas would have a considerable effect on Russia's earnings from natural gas exports and would improve the EU's terms of trade. According to this conclusion, it would be adequate for EU countries to impose an import tariff on Russian gas deliveries. There are, however, two counter-arguments against an import tariff:

- Firstly, Gazprom is not really a monopoly supplier and does not maximize profits; instead Gazprom may be understood to act in line with the Russian government's goal, namely to inflict maximum damage on the EU—hence a net price reduction, price net of the tariff—should not really be expected.
- Secondly, the natural market in the EU is not so much a monopoly situation (with Gazprom as the monopoly supplier), but rather it is characterized by an oligopoly. If Gazprom's supply of gas to Germany/the EU would be reduced, the mark-up of other suppliers would increase in the medium term—for additional quantities delivered; and the other large gas suppliers might also try to adjust existing long-term contracts and the respective price in those contracts so that the gas price will indeed increase as will mark-ups, which means an economic advantage for Norway, the Netherlands, and Algeria plus the US and Qatar as major LNG producers.
- If one was to consider a duopoly model of the EU gas market in which Gazprom is the Stackelberg market leader before 2022 (whereby other firms follow Gazprom's production decision as the leading Russian gas exporter), while after spring, a supplier of liquefied natural gas (LNG), for example from the US, emerges as the new Stackelberg market leader, numerous interesting findings emerge (Roeger & Welfens, 2022): An EU import tariff on gas from

Russia leads to a price increase for gas in the EU that is equivalent to one-quarter of the import tariff and also one-quarter of the cost difference of the new LNG market leader to the old market leader, namely Gazprom. Under Gros' monopolist approach, the price increase after the imposition of a tariff is half of the tariff amount. Gazprom's sales volume falls relatively sharply (also more sharply than in the case of a gas import tariff and unchanged market leadership of Gazprom), which tends to dampen tariff revenues. Russia's current account position deteriorates due to reduced gas export revenues. This effect is nevertheless relatively small in terms of the revenue side of the Russian state budget; beyond taxes, Russia's state budget is strongly shaped by the oil sector (for details, see Yermakov & Kirova, 2017). The oil sector is about four times as important in this context as the gas sector.

An import tariff on the part of the EU imposed on natural gas from Russia would therefore ultimately be borne entirely as an additional burden by consumers and in part by industry using natural gas; the proposals of Hausmann/Gros for a gas import tariff therefore do not make sense. An approach that considers a market characterized by a duopoly would seem to be more appropriate.

Also, one may add with respect to the Gros approach that the benefits for the EU could clearly be reduced if the Russian government would adopt countervailing import tariffs on EU exports or would react with, for example, a wave of cyber-attacks against EU governments, firms, and other institutions. Russia would, of course, run the risk of facing digital counter-attacks by the West. There is indeed quite some risk that all this could end up in an escalation spiral, which would inflict massive economic losses on both Russia and the West, including a major recession for both Western countries and Russia.

The fact that by May 2022 Russia had terminated gas supplies to Poland, Bulgaria, and Finland appears to be illegal insofar as Russia did not terminate the gas supplies in accordance with existing contracts, but in the case of Poland and Bulgaria pointed out that both countries had not complied with the demand of President Putin that payment be made in Rubles; and, in the case of Finland, that the government in Helsinki was being punished, so to speak, for wanting to join NATO. Unilateral violations of treaties are unacceptable in international trade; Russia—and of course also the EU countries—should abide by treaties and international rules.

Part of the whole energy import embargo debate—including discussion of EU import tariffs against gas exports from Russia—ultimately stems from the fact that for over three decades following the OPEC shocks of the 1970s, EU countries increased energy imports from Russia, and Russia increased energy production and exports accordingly. However, it would have made sense for Russia to expand rather its export production in the industrial and digital services sectors back in the 1990s. Russia's government has not made much use of the possibilities of reducing its historically strong dependence on the raw materials sector, for example, by increasing exports of industrial goods and digital services; and in doing so, also reduce the problems associated with the so-called Dutch disease—including massive corruption-related challenges. In a certain sense, the West has paid too little attention to the problems of Russia's New Political Economy under Putin or to the traditional economic approach in Russia.

A Russian economy more strongly oriented toward industry, software and service exports, and innovation—if possible also with more competition and more private ownership of the means of production (and only a few large companies or oligarchs)—could also have given rise to a greatly different political system. Putin's economic model, which is very corrupt in many areas, was for many years necessarily weak in growth and little oriented toward the rule of law or the international legal system; this made it all the more tempting for the populist Putin to try to increase his domestic popularity through military adventures abroad. Such strategic considerations have apparently not been developed in Berlin, Paris, London, or Washington, DC. If such a strategic rethink had been attempted, it would certainly have met with enormous resistance in Russia—even if the West had advocated a different modernization of Russia, including financial support. The path dependency of Russia's economic development as a major exporter in the energy sector should at least be clearly seen as problematic.

Incidentally, the oil price paradox as described by Hans Werner Sinn does not necessarily apply. According to the paradox, major efforts by the West to reduce oil and gas consumption—with a view, for example, to the problem of climate protection policy—will cause the world market price to fall sharply, which will induce the poorer half of the world economy to consume even more fossil fuels that it would otherwise consume. Once you approach a critical minimum share of renewable energy in the global economy—and additional nuclear power generation if necessary—you will reach a certain point beyond which further spending on expensive exploration and fossil fuel transportation is no longer worthwhile. However, the West's sometimes ill-advised strategic economic policies at the international level are now finding an additional impetus from the Russo-Ukrainian war pushing some countries to temporarily increase the use of fossil fuels—precisely so that, for example, EU countries could largely avoid Russian gas supplies; by 2023/2024, this could largely succeed. In a new era of peace, of course, the fundamental economic logic will still speak in favor of substantial trade in energy between Russia and the EU.

With the Russo-Ukrainian war, the question quickly arose in the public debate of whether the EU countries—and of course also Germany—were not significantly financing the war through energy imports from Russia. Conversely, it was oft claimed that an energy import embargo of the EU (or Germany) against Russia could massively complicate Russia's war financing and help to end Russia's capacity to continue its war. Is this argumentation correct? Here are a few points:

- An EU energy import embargo will further increase the price of oil and gas on the world market and will help Russia to continue to generate high oil and gas export revenues by redirecting oil and gas exports from Europe to customers in, for example, Asia. It cannot be ruled out that EU countries could succeed in reducing the important oil revenues of the Russian state in particular, if, for example, oil tankers flying the flag of EU countries (e.g. Greece, Malta, Cyprus) could not be chartered for the purposes of transporting Russia's oil exports to Asia; or because the corresponding ships would no longer receive insurance policies, meaning that they could not land their cargo in many important ports in Asia. Whether or not this is politically feasible is something that negotiations between the EU countries in Brussels will essentially have to show; it can hardly be assumed that Greek oil tanker owners, for example, will easily allow themselves to be banned from engaging in a lucrative business here—but it is conceivable. The idea must be pursued further. If, however, EU countries no longer want to import oil from Russia, this does not mean that they want to do without the corresponding oil volumes altogether. Rather, the resulting shortfall would need to be replaced by higher oil and gas supplies from OPEC countries and the US for example. However, if these countries cannot simply realize increased production volumes in the short term and thus want to make the additional deliveries to Europe, these countries will reduce sales in the direction of Asia and sell instead to Europe. This will create a gap that Russia will try to close by increasing exports to Asia in the event of an EU import boycott. The West could, of course, use US pressure on countries in Asia to try to prevent Russia from selling its oil, which would no longer be marketable in the EU (or the US, the UK, and potentially elsewhere), in Asia. In such a scenario, an EU energy import boycott of Russia would turn into something like an economic world war. Part of Russia's oil and gas production will be lost in any case year after year due to a lack of Western spare parts; about 5–10% per year.

- If Russia is indeed short about 20% of its state budget revenues from reduced oil and gas exports, then the Russian government will likely tap the state's reserve fund, which in earlier years was financed from earlier high oil and gas exports. Moreover, Russia will then spur even further increased inflationary war funding, which is likely to damage President Putin's reputation; but even an inflation rate of 50–70% is no guarantee that Putin would stop the war against Ukraine. This might well hold even more true in the event of a sustained and successful Ukrainian military resistance. It is hard to imagine that the West will allow Russia to win the war against Ukraine. Following the aggressive expansionist logic of Putin's ideology, there is a very high risk that Russia will simply invade other ex-Soviet republics and possibly even enter NATO territory.

- The longer the war goes on, the greater the risk that NATO countries will be inadvertently drawn into direct involvement in the Russo-Ukrainian war. It is unlikely that Russia will be able to occupy territories in Ukraine for a long time without any significant problems. This is because support for Russia is likely to be quite low in some of the occupied areas in the Donbas region, and even in Russia itself there is unlikely to be a majority in favor of a Russian occupation of Ukraine if free speech is allowed again. Freedom of expression in Russia must be restored if Russia is to emerge as an accepted member of the world community and the G8 after a peace agreement—presumably under changed political leadership. All of this does not mean, by the way, that Ukraine's own leadership should not offer new compromises in the internal language dispute (such as recognizing Russian as a second official language in certain regions)—a source of contention, which goes back to the decade before 2014. In fact, making peace will involve accomplishing a difficult task in terms of the relationship between Russia and Ukraine, but will also like require resolving internal conflicts in Ukraine.

- When Ukraine repeatedly emphasizes how important Germany is in the EU—especially the Ukrainian Ambassador to Germany, Andriy Melnyk, who has repeatedly underlined this in public—it is clear that Ukraine is pursuing its own interests: Ukraine would like to receive as many heavy weapons as possible from Germany; to this end, Melnyk has also repeatedly invoked the memory of the Second World War and the special responsibility that Germany has from a historical point of view alone. However, one can doubt that massive German arms deliveries would represent a wise German and European policy. From Germany's perspective, it is important to seek a solid anchoring in EU policy on these issues. That the German government should suddenly follow the doubts spread in many media regarding the idea that *Wandel durch Handel,* that is, "change through trade" is not in Germany's and Europe's strategic interest is an unconvincing view (the case may be valid if one considers the question of a reasonable international diversification of oil and gas suppliers, which was no longer upheld when Russia's share of the gas market in Germany rose to over 50%. This could already be seen as a paradoxical, self-created problem on the German side in terms of antitrust law, although strangely few reservations against the critically increasing role of Russia in gas supplies were visible or audible during the years of the Grand Coalition in Berlin).

If we refer rather to the economic questions of an energy boycott by Germany or the EU—as governmental measures in the context of the Russo-Ukrainian war—the analysis will focus first and foremost on the macroeconomic implications. Beyond that, it is a matter of differentiation: whether Germany should impose a gas import embargo, for example, which would affect some important technical aspects, but above all economic issues and aspects. As far as an import duty on gas from Russia is concerned, such a duty should obviously be imposed by the EU27, since the EU is a customs union; this should not be undermined by government measures in the individual EU27 countries. An oil import boycott on the part of the EU would be a special case of Western sanctions against Russia, which should by no means be approached under the overly simplistic slogan of "we will stop financing Russia's war in Ukraine". Those who, for example, with an ill-conceived boycott policy, would significantly increase the world market price for oil or the regional gas price, could actually end up making it easier for Russia to finance the war against Ukraine. As far as the magnitude of the economic effects of an oil or gas import boycott by Germany or the EU is concerned, various analyses and studies were already available by the beginning of June 2022.

LITERATURE

BCG. (2021). Climate Paths 2.0—A Program for Climate and Germany's Future Development, report by the Boston Consulting Group for the Federation of German Industry. Retrieved March 30, 2022, from https://english.bdi.eu/publication/news/climate-paths-2-0-a-program-for-climate-and-germanys-future-development/

BNetzA. (2021). Bundesnetzagentur, 2021, Kraftwerksliste. https://www.bundesnetzagentur.de/cln_1411/DE/Sachgebiete/ElektrizitaetundGas/Unternehmen_Institutionen/Versorgungssicherheit/Erzeugungskapazitaeten/Kraftwerksliste/kraftwerksliste-node.html

dena. (2021). Dena pilot study towards climate neutrality provides a foundation for energy and climate policy for the next German government, German Energy Agency, available online (in German only). Retrieved March 30, 2022, from https://www.dena.de/fileadmin/dena/Publikationen/PDFs/2021/Abschlussbericht_dena-Leitstudie_Aufbruch_Klimaneutralitaet.pdf

EUROSTAT. (2021). Share of Russia in national extra-EU imports, 2021. Retrieved from https://ec.europa.eu/eurostat/statistics-explained/index.php?title=EU_imports_of_energy_products_-_recent_developments&oldid=577333

Federal Statistical Office. (2022). Facts on Foreign Trade with Russia, Press Release No. N 010, February 24, 2022. Retrieved March 30, 2022, from https://www.destatis.de/DE/Presse/Pressemitteilungen/2022/02/PD22_N010_51.html

Fischer, A., & Küper, M. (2022). Die Bedeutung russischer Gaslieferungen für die deutsche Energieversorgung. Untersuchung bestehender Lieferbeziehungen und Ausblick auf die weitere Entwicklung [transl. PJJW: The Role of Russian Gas Deliviers fort he Germany Energy Supply. A study of existing supply-channels and a perspective on future developments], report for the Atlantik Brücke e.V., Cologne.

Gros, D. (2022). Optimal tariff versus optimal sanction, The case of European gas imports from Russia, CEPS Policy Insights, No. 2022-12, Brussels. https://www.ceps.eu/ceps-publications/optimal-tariff-versus-optimal-sanction/

Hausmann, R. (2022). The case for a Punitive Tax on Russian Oil, Project Syndicate, dated February 26, 2022. Retrieved April 13, 2022, from https://www.project-syndicate.org/commentary/case-for-punitive-tax-on-russian-oil-by-ricardo-hausmann-2022-02

Hubert, F., & Cobanli, O. (2015). Pipeline power: A case study of strategic network investments. *Review of Network Economics, 14*(2), 75–110.

IEA. (2022a). A 10-Point Plan to Reduce the European Union's Reliance on Russian Natural Gas, International Energy Agency, Paris. Retrieved March 30, 2022, from https://www.iea.org/reports/a-10-point-plan-to-reduce-the-european-unions-reliance-on-russian-natural-gas

Leopoldina/National Academy of Sciences. (2022). How Russian natural gas can be replaced in German and European energy supply, Ad Hoc Statement, March 8, 2022, Halle. Retrieved March 30, 2022, from https://www.leopoldina.org/publikationen/detailansicht/publication/wie-sich-russisches-erdgas-in-der-deutschen-und-europaeischen-energieversorgung-ersetzen-laesst-2022/

Prognos; Öko-Institut e.V.; Wuppertal-Institut. (2021). Klimaneutrales Deutschland 2045 (Climate-neutral Germany by 2045), Wie Deutschland seine Klimaziele schon vor 2050 erreichen kann. Commissioned by Stiftung Klimaneutralität, Agora Energiewende und Agora Verkehrswende. Retrieved March 30, 2022, from https://www.agora-verkehrswende.de/veroeffentlichungen/klimaneutrales-deutschland-2045-langfassung/

Roeger, W.; Welfens, P.J.J. (2022b), EU gas import tariff under Duopoly: A contribution to the energy sanctions debate on Russia, EIIW Discussion Paper No. 314. https://eiiw.wiwi.uni-wuppertal.de/fileadmin/eiiw/Daten/Publikationen/Gelbe_Reihe/disbei314.pdf

Welfens, P. J. J. (2022). Global climate change policy. Palgrave Macmillan. https://doi.org/10.1007/978-3-030-94594-7

Yermakov, V., & Kirova, D. (2017). Gas and taxes: The Impact of Russia's tinkering with upstream gas taxes on state revenues and decline rates of legacy gas fields, Energy Insight 20, The Oxford Institute for Energy Studies, October 2017. https://www.jstor.org/stable/resrep33915

PART II

The Implications of an Energy Import or Export Boycott

CHAPTER 5

A Russian Energy Import Boycott by Germany or the EU as a Policy Option?

In a study published in March 2022, several scientists examined how a possible boycott of Russia's energy imports by Germany would affect the German economy (Bachmann et al., 2022)—according to their findings, a decline in real GDP of 0.5% to 3% is expected. Compared with the 4.5% drop in GDP in Germany in the corona recession of 2020, this initially appears to be a tolerable price to pay for an intended weakening of Russia's economy and its ability to increase military spending and continue the war of aggression against Ukraine. It should be borne in mind, however, that Russia could forestall a boycott of energy imports by Germany, for its part, by implementing a partial or complete boycott of supplies of oil, gas, coal, and grain, and that Russia, moreover, could sell quantities of oil, gas, and coal that can no longer be sold in Germany at price discounts in the rest of the world economy. Incidentally, the modeling carried out by Bachmann et al. is not really a standard macroeconomic model as it is based on growth decomposition, which is an approach not really adequate for the problem under consideration. Of particular analytical interest could be a modified DSGE macro model with trade and direct investment (Roeger & Welfens, 2021, 2022), which consistently covers complex international effects or adjustment paths. In the event of an energy import embargo, Germany's Bundesbank (2022) simulates a loss of real income of up to 5%; in addition, inflation would be 1.5 percentage points higher in 2022, and in 2023, there would be an additional inflationary push of a similar—perhaps slightly higher—magnitude.

© The Author(s), under exclusive license to Springer Nature Switzerland AG 2022
P. J. J. Welfens, *Russia's Invasion of Ukraine*,
https://doi.org/10.1007/978-3-031-19138-1_5

If the EU were to impose an oil import boycott on Russia, Russia would be able to sell its surplus oil at acceptable discounts in Asia, for example. In the case of oil, Russian price discounts are likely to be low because of the integrated global market, while high price discounts are to be expected in the case of gas, since customer countries are supplied via pipelines—and only in part via LNG ships. Pipelines from Russia to China, for example, are unlikely to have any reserve capacity to cope with surplus Russian supply in the event of an EU energy import embargo against Russia.

The largest dependencies on Russian supplies in the total energy supply in 2019 were in Lithuania, Hungary, Slovakia, and the Netherlands, with Russian shares of over 60% (OECD, 2022; see Fig. 5.1); these were followed by Finland, Austria, Greece, Poland, Latvia, Belgium, Germany, Italy—the latter two with a Russia share of about one-third—and Czechia. Denmark and Sweden, among others, are less dependent on Russian supplies and did not purchase any natural gas from Russia in 2019.

For a realistic assessment of an energy import boycott against Russia, it is important to model the adjustment reactions on the part of Russia and Germany in a meaningful way. This is not the case in the paper by Bachmann et al. as retaliatory measures by Russia and labor market reactions in Germany are not included in the authors' model. The decline in real income in Germany in the event of an energy import boycott will not be around €1000 per capita, as Bachmann et al. claim, but rather between €1500 and €2000, or a good 5% of GDP, which is higher than in the corona recession year 2020. A severe recession in Germany will have a clearly negative impact on economic development in the Netherlands, France, and Belgium—and from there will be corresponding negative repercussion effects on Germany.

The energy shortage occurring in Germany is likely to drive up the price of electricity in the medium term, with increased German replacement demand for gas from Norway, the Netherlands, Algeria, Qatar, or the US, for example, also likely to temporarily increase the price of gas and, moreover, the price of electricity throughout the EU. Other main global exporters of gas are Australia, Malaysia, and Indonesia, which, however, mainly supply the markets in Asia (Germany's gas exports, in turn, will be close to zero in the event of a Russia energy import boycott, as domestic production is consumed domestically, provided existing international supply contracts can be terminated).

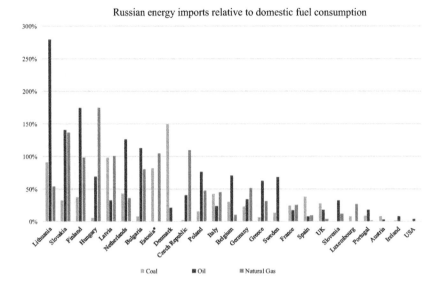

Fig. 5.1 The share of Russia in total energy import supply for selected countries, relative to domestic consumption, 2019. Note: Figures above 100% may include (a) transit volumes, (b) stocks, and/or (c) import of crude oil, its refining and subsequent oil exports. * Estonia shows negative values for oil (-4574%, set to 0% here) due to statistical processing of oil shale liquefaction processes. Due to the structure and definition of energy balances, the TES for crude oil is negative as it picks up exports but not production. This methodology is only applied for these two years, but will be extended to all time series in the forthcoming IEA statistical release. Source: Own presentation based on OECD (2022), data from IEA (2022): Reliance on Russian Fossil Fuels, online: https://www.iea.org/data-and-statistics/data-product/reliance-on-russian-fossil-fuels-in-oecd-and-eu-countries

LITERATURE

Bachmann, R. et al. (2022). What if? The Economic Effects for Germany of a Stop of Energy Imports from Russia, ECONtribute Policy Brief Nr. 028. Retrieved May 24, 2022, from https://www.econtribute.de/RePEc/ajk/ajkpbs/ECONtribute_PB_028_2022.pdf

Bundesbank. (2022). Monthly Report of the Bundesbank, full report in German only, summary in English. Retrieved May 24, 2022, from https://www.bundesbank.de/en/tasks/topics/war-against-ukraine-energy-embargo

IEA. (2022). Reliance on Russian Fossil Fuels Data Explorer, International Energy Agency: Paris. Retrieved March 30, 2022, from https://www.iea.org/reports/reliance-on-russian-fossil-fuels-data-explorer-could-significantly-weaken-german-economy-889696

OECD. (2022). *OECD economic outlook, interim report. economic and social impacts and policy implications of the war in Ukraine.* Organisation for Economic Cooperation and Development. https://doi.org/10.1787/41 81d61b-en

Roeger, W., & Welfens, P. J. J. (2021). Foreign direct investment and innovations: Transmission dynamics of persistent demand and technology shocks in a macro model, EIIW Discussion Paper No. 300. https://eiiw.wiwi.uni-wuppertal.de/fileadmin/eiiw/Daten/Publikationen/Gelbe_Reihe/disbei300.pdf

Roeger, W., & Welfens, P. J. J. (2022). The macroeconomic effects of import tariffs in a model with multinational firms and foreign direct investment. *International Economics and Economic Policy, 19*(2). https://doi.org/10.1007/s10368-022-00538-5

CHAPTER 6

A Russian Gas Supply Boycott Against Western Countries

In 2021, Russia had a world market share of 17% for gas and 13% for oil. Russia threatened a gas supply boycott in late March in response to Western countries' refusal to pay for energy imports from Russia in Rubles as demanded by President Putin. A Goldman Sachs study in early March analyzed such an eventuality—which was deemed unlikely—and produced the following main findings (under three scenarios, one being a halt to gas exports by Ukraine, another being a complete supply boycott in 2022); first, the case of a partial Russian supply boycott:

- Real income in the Eurozone will fall by 0.6% compared with the baseline scenario (excluding the supply boycott), and by 0.1% in the UK.
- In Germany, real income will fall by 0.9% due to the relatively strong dependence on gas supplies from Russia.

In the case of a complete boycott of deliveries to the Eurozone, the real income effects are:

- -2.2% decline for the Eurozone;
- -3.4% for Germany and -2.6% for Italy.

In addition, the inflation rate in the Eurozone will rise by 1.3% compared with the baseline scenario. A Russian halt in gas supplies to EU

P. J. J. Welfens, *Russia's Invasion of Ukraine*, https://doi.org/10.1007/978-3-031-19138-1_6

countries will initially affect three sectors in particular, and then indirectly *at least* one other important sector:

- the chemical industry (including fertilizer production)
- the food sector;
- the steel sector; and
- indirectly negatively affected: Automotive sector.

If steel production comes to a complete halt due to a lack of natural gas supplies in Germany, for example, then almost all automobile production in Germany will come to a standstill within a few weeks; it is not only production problems that will cause the automotive industry in Germany (or the EU automobile industry in the event of a supply boycott against the entire EU) to shrink, but also the declining demand for consumer durables, including automobiles, as unemployment rates expectedly rise. In Germany, one in six jobs in the automotive industry is linked to the automotive sector. In the event of international supply cuts, the emergency gas plan in place in Germany provides first of all for industrial companies to expect supply shortfalls for natural gas in accordance with rational economic logic; only secondarily do private households come into focus, where supply shortfalls will then lead primarily to heating problems for around one-third of households. On March 30, 2022, the first stage in the emergency plan for gas was declared in Germany for the first time. There is another warning stage—where the markets still secure the supply—and finally a third stage, where government intervention and orders manage the gas shortage politically.

It is easy to imagine that millions of private households and thousands upon thousands of companies, fearing problems with regard to heating with natural gas in winter, will buy and install electric heaters by the millions, which without government regulation in the field of electric heating could then temporarily lead to a collapse of the power grid. Even conceivable record orders for solar panel installations at private households and companies will only be realized to a small extent within a few months and, of course, only at increased prices.

Hecking et al. (2015) examined a gas supply disruption for Germany and EU countries in three scenarios early on, assuming a Russian supply boycott for three, six, and nine months, respectively. Two key findings of the study were that a three-month boycott could be faced without major problems in Europe, except for Bulgaria, Poland, Turkey, and Finland; in the case of a nine-month supply boycott, however, Germany, Italy, France, and many Eastern European countries would face significant economic problems.

As for the economic impact of a gas supply boycott of OECD countries by Russia, which can be categorized as halving Russia's world market share in gas, this would result in quite substantial price increases—with international regional differences, since gas markets are not globally integrated unlike oil markets. Hamilton (2022) has pointed out that during the OPEC price shocks of the 1970s, the decline in world oil supply was 7% in 1974 and 4% in 1979, both of which were roughly accompanied by a quadrupling of oil prices and a severe recession in the US (and many EU countries as well as Japan); Hamilton blames the recession in the US on a sharp decline in automobile demand in the wake of sharply higher crude oil prices—which significantly worsened consumer sentiment. Of course, increased spending on energy on the part of households in the short-term means that demand in many other markets declines, with an increase in the unemployment rate in the case of nominal market rigidities (inflexibilities hinder very rapid adjustments in terms of structural change). The price elasticity of gas demand in OECD countries will be lower than for oil in the short term, so that substantial price increases can be expected for both companies and consumers. In addition, most gas is supplied internationally via pipelines, so there will also be larger price differentials internationally. A strong gas price increase in the EU will allow EU companies to realize increased import shares for liquefied natural gas; for Germany, this is only a partial relief because LNG terminals are mainly found in Spain, France, and Italy and because the intra-EU gas transport infrastructure is largely lacking.

In terms of the EU as a whole, a Russian gas supply boycott could only be sensibly countered through a combination of gas demand reduction measures, on one hand, and supply increases from other countries on the other. Gas price increases in the EU will be part of the market-based adjustment processes (even if Spain and Portugal, for example, want to introduce state price caps, as emerged at the EU summit in Brussels at the end of March 2022). Complete international substitute supplies for gas from Russia, which are conceivable in principle, appear to be unrealistic (McWilliams et al., 2022):

- LNG capacity in many EU countries is limited, as are intra-EU gas export opportunities. LNG shipping capacity is limited in the short term (however, most contracts are such that the port of destination can be changed—here, wealthy EU countries could probably then also prevail in competition in a number of cases).

- In the case of international LNG exports, countries in Asia and the long-term supply contracts concluded there are important; it is hardly likely that larger LNG export volumes from Asia to the EU can be diverted in the short term, especially since the markets in Asia will continue to grow in importance in the long term.
- If rising EU LNG imports continue to drive up gas prices in the EU, this will weaken the economy via rising energy prices.
- An intra-EU distribution of additional LNG, co-organized by the European Commission, will in many cases lead to political conflicts within the EU; especially since Ukraine is also likely to have to be supplied.

Before turning one's attention to focus on the option of a broader German or EU import embargo vis-à-vis Russia, one should analyze the option of an import tariff on Russia gas.

OECD Modeling of an Energy Import Reduction and Bachmann et al. Study

The OECD XE "Organisation for Economic Co-operation and Development" (2022) as an international economic organization has simulated the effect of a general 20% energy import reduction for individual industrialized countries on the basis of the NiGEM model (aforementioned effects are not included). For a 40% energy import reduction—which would represent an energy import boycott in several EU countries—the magnitudes shown in the figure are to be doubled if real income declines, which for some countries would amount to real income falling by 2% to 4.5%. For Germany, the decline would be around 1.9%, and for Spain, Italy, and the Netherlands, the decline would be around 2.5%. The OECD model results depend to a large extent on the assumptions about short- and medium-term elasticities of substitution, which the OECD apparently sets relatively high—namely, in line with standard models, which, however, tend to focus on long-term adjustment processes (in the OECD's 2022 study, this issue is difficult to trace). The OECD simulation results on income declines in the context of a 20% energy import

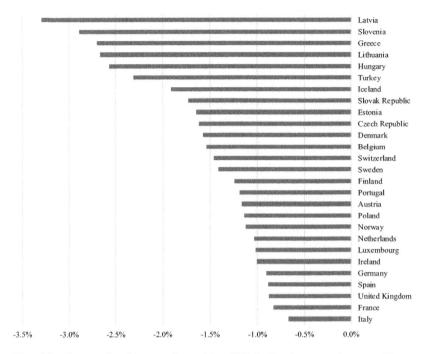

Fig. 6.1 Expected real income loss with a 20% decline in energy imports. Note: *Based on a reduction of 20% of direct and indirect imported energy inputs from fossil fuels, refined fuel products, and electricity and gas supply.* Source: Own calculations based on OECD (2022), Fig. 6. Data from OECD IOTs 2021 database

reduction are probably a much too optimistic estimate of income declines in OECD member countries (see Fig. 6.1, based on a figure from the OECD Economic Outlook, Interim Report March 2022).

The modeling used in Bachmann et al. (2022) has significant shortcomings and a total of seven weaknesses as a result of an overly narrow view of the problem, the shortcomings in terms of macroeconomic modeling (little beyond a growth decomposition approach), and a flawed model assumption for employment, can be identified:

1. It ignores the fact that Russia will take economic retaliatory measures against Germany—or the EU as a whole; increased Russian

import duties, for example, could significantly depress German exports to Russia. The real drop in income could reach around 0.1% of GDP for Germany.

2. Russia could nationalize the assets of German companies in Russia in response to a German energy import boycott. The stock of German direct investments in Russia amounts to about €20 billion, which corresponds to a good 0.5% of German real income.

3. The economic modeling employed by Bachman et al. is essentially such that domestic demand or the supply of goods is depicted as dependent on the use of energy, capital, and labor; an energy boycott is modeled in such a way that energy use decreases. However, the use of capital and labor remains unchanged, which is especially implausible in the case of labor input. If labor input declines by 3% (with real income declining by 3%), this implies an additional real income loss of about 2%. However, it can be assumed that the energy price increase associated with an energy boycott and the related electricity price increases as well as the energy shortage—for instance in the chemical industry—will lead to declining goods production and increased unemployment. IHS (2014) studied the sectoral effects of a relative electricity price increase for Germany and identified significant production declines in the chemical industry as an effect. The IHS (2014) study showed how many additional jobs depended in each of the metal production, chemical/pharmaceutical production, mechanical engineering, and automotive sectors for every 100 direct sector jobs: 190 additional jobs in the automotive sector, 178 indirect jobs in the chemical/pharmaceutical production sector, and an additional 138 and 96 jobs in the metal construction and mechanical engineering sectors, respectively. The IHS study found that Germany's major export sectors are relatively energy-intensive and that increased gas production in Germany could increase international competitiveness; and that electricity price increases in industry would reduce the competitiveness of important sectors and thus result in significant direct and indirect job losses.

4. The decline in real income considered by Bachmann et al. for one year will be accompanied by (reduced) dampening effects on economic development in Germany in subsequent years if real economic adjustment reactions in some sectors are sluggish; in the following year, the decline in real income could amount to another 0.5% to 1% (see Annex M on some key modeling aspects of the

approach of Bachmann et al.). Incidentally, Russia could stop gas exports to the majority of EU countries in response to a German energy import boycott against Russia and then also plunge Ukraine into serious winter-related problems by refusing to export gas, whereby the government of Ukraine will certainly rely on compensatory gas exports from the EU to Ukraine—a serious economic, logistical and political problem then arises here, which has apparently not been discussed at the European Commission nor the European Council by the end of March 2022. One also has to consider that Russia's output—expected to decline without a German/EU energy embargo by about 11% in 2022 (World Bank, 2022)—would further reduce in the case of a Western energy import embargo, which will have considerable negative spillover effects on real income in countries in the central Asian countries where two countries had remittances from Russia exceeding 15% of national income in 2021 (ADB, 2022); migrant workers in Russia will lose their job in many cases as a consequence of a major recession in Russia and hence remittances could fall considerably, which, in turn, undermines economic and political stability in central Asian countries. These aspects have also been neglected by Bachmann et al.

5. There will be negative repercussions of the economic slump in Germany on Germany's main trading partners, that is, the Netherlands, France, the US, and China—from which there will then be negative repercussions on Germany's export and economic development. These repercussions are likely to amount to a German real income loss of 0.3% of GDP.

6. Germany will be expected to contribute to the stabilization of Ukraine's gas and electricity supply; this means a medium-term cost of 0.1% of Germany's GDP.

7. Volatility on Euro financial markets increases—measurable by the Composite Indicator of Systemic Stress (CISS) indicator of the European Central Bank (Hollo et al., 2012; Kremer, 2016; see Fig. 6.2)—which can have a negative impact on real economic development. The CISS value in the crisis month of March 2022 was similar to that after the negative result in the UK's EU referendum in June 2016, but it was lower than in the Transatlantic Banking Crisis. If there were a gas supply freeze by Russia in the short term or a German energy import embargo from Russia, the CISS fluctua-

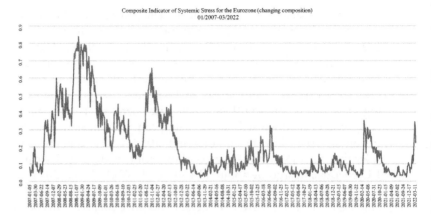

Fig. 6.2 European Central Bank's CISS indicator for financial market system stress in the Eurozone, from January 5, 2007, to March 25, 2022. Note: *Weekly index data for January 5, 2007, until March 25, 2022.* Source: ECB Statistical Data Warehouse, Composite Indicator of Systemic Stress (2022), EIIW Graph

tion indicator for Eurozone financial markets would likely rise significantly: Negative financial market impulses or declines in real income are then to be expected—among other things, due to increased risk premiums in the corporate sector—via reduced investment in the industrial and service sectors or due to an increase in friction on financial markets; these are likely to amount to around 0.5% of national income. A negative correlation between the CISS indicator value and growth risks in the Eurozone was shown by Figueres and Jarociński (2020). In the context of an updated CISS indicator concept, corona shock experiences in financial markets are included, which increases the economic relevance of the (modified and thereby daily updated) indicator.

In the updated CISS indicator concept, it can be seen from the comparison of the CISS indicators for the Eurozone and the US that the Russo-Ukrainian war has led to higher volatility in the system stress indicator for the financial markets in the Eurozone—compared with the US. Accordingly, the growth risks arising from financial market volatility in the spring of 2022 in the context of the Russo-Ukrainian war are relatively high in the Eurozone (Fig. 6.3).

New Composite Indicator of Systemic Stress (CISS) for the Eurozone (changing composition) and US, daily values from Jan 1, 2007, until March 31, 2022

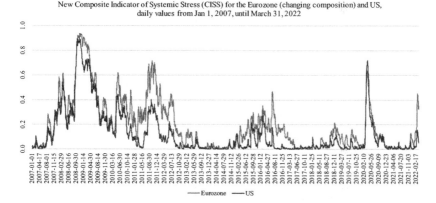

Fig. 6.3 Development of CISS in the US and the Eurozone (daily values, from January 1, 2007, to March 31, 2022). Note: *Daily index data from January 1, 2007, until March 31, 2022.* Source: ECB Statistical Data Warehouse, Composite Indicator of Systemic Stress (2022), EIIW Graph

A serious problem for Germany is that the inflation rate rose to 7.3% in March 2022. In the event of an energy import boycott by Germany (or the EU), massive further increases in energy prices could well cause the inflation rate to temporarily reach double digits. In this case, there will be temporary employment gains—in line with the logic of the Phillips curve—as real wage rates will unexpectedly fall in 2022. The state is also likely to be an inflation winner, insofar as the pension increase planned for 2022 is likely to be negative in real terms, both in western and eastern Germany.

IMK simulations (Behringer et al., 2022) with the NiGEM model show that a German import freeze of Russian energy leads to a 6% decline in real income, which is twice the worst-case value in Bachmann et al. (2022). One important question concerns the price elasticity for natural gas, which is estimated to be around -0.2 by Auffhammer and Rubin (2018): a 1% price increase leads to a 0.2% decrease in the amount of gas consumed. The IMK analysis interestingly points out that for private households that transitioned from a favorable gas supply of 6 cents/KWh after the bankruptcy of the previous supplier or provider to the standard supply of the local provider—at the increased price of about 34 cents/KWh—gas demand should have fallen to zero; this was apparently not the case. The assumption in Bachmann et al. that expansive fiscal policy (i.e., demand policy) can compensate for the shock effects of a supply disruption in the context of an energy import freeze from Russia—as it is primarily the chemical, steel production, and food production sectors that are negatively affected in production—in such a way that full employment is maintained is completely implausible. Job losses of 2–6%—as a rough calculation is a realistic scenario in the event of an energy import embargo—would mean up to two million more unemployed persons in Germany, which, in turn, would have a negative impact on overall economic demand and thus also a further decline in real GDP.

After all, Bachmann et al. (2022) consider the challenge that relatively poor households may be particularly hard hit by gasoline price increases. In this context, they suggest that the state should compensate these households via higher transfers. However, one certain challenge is known from the US in this problem context: 10% of households have no gasoline expenditures at all, while again another group of households spends more than 10% of income on gasoline (Hamilton, 2022). If one simply compensates poor households, this governmental measure would not be very well targeted.

Effects (2) to (7) in Table 6.1are not considered in the OECD study or in the study of Bachmann et al. (2022). A plausible overall effect here is considered to be a real income loss for Germany of up to -6.5%, which is equivalent to a recession shock as in the case of the Transatlantic Banking Crisis and is higher by order of magnitude than the real income decline experienced during the Corona shock year 2020. Moreover, welfare losses due to the inflation increase that occurred because of the Russo-Ukrainian war—order of magnitude 2 percentage point increase in inflation—have to be added, which will increase political discontent in Germany. This assessment is based on fundamental insights of the New Political Economy approach to the behavior of the electorate, although one has to take into account that a certain sympathy bonus for the government as Ukraine has a special effect here. The Bachmann et al. study is important for the debate on effects of an energy import boycott, but the study is clearly too optimistic with regard to the drop in income for Germany.

It is unclear what the effects will be on the real exchange rate. If one assumes that, in the event of an energy import boycott, Germany's companies will have to buy natural gas and coal on the world market at significantly higher prices, a devaluation of the Euro can be expected, which will stimulate Germany's and the wider Eurozone's exports; in other words, it

Table 6.1   Expected loss of real income in the event of a German energy import boycott against Russia (DE=Germany)

The main effects of an energy import boycott by Germany—assuming retaliatory measures by Russia	*Impact on real income in Germany (including economic international real repercussions and asset losses as % of German GDP)*
1) Economic base effect of a German energy boycott according to Bachmann et al. (2022)[a]	-0.5% to -3% (the size of the effect depends on the elasticities of substitution in goods production); -0.5% and also -1.5% income declines are unrealistic (see OECD XE "Organisation for Economic Co-operation and Development" , 2022)
2) Tariff increase by Russia	-0.1 %
3) Nationalization of many subsidiaries of German companies in Russia	-0.5 %
4) Rising unemployment, which will lead to a decline in real GDP (and national income). Moreover, in the following year, there will also be an increase in the unemployment rate	-0.3% to -2%
5) In the case of Germany: Retroactive effect of international real negative cyclical effects	-0.3%
6) Stabilization of gas and electricity supply in Ukraine	-0.1%
7) Volatility on the financial markets in the Eurozone increases; hence rise in risk premiums for companies	-0.5%
8) TOTAL EFFECT (incl. maximum)	**−3.3% to −6.5% Real income decline**

[a]*For comparison: If one takes the economic base effect according to OECD (2022): 40% decrease in energy imports = Russia boycott, this would mean, 1.9% in real gross domestic product*

Source: Own calculations and representation

will also increase real GDP. The Eurozone could also expect increased inflows of direct investment from the US, the UK, Japan, and other non-Eurozone countries in the event of a real devaluation, because, according to Froot and Stein (1991), a real devaluation brings an increase in direct investment inflows—in the context of imperfect international capital markets and essentially in the form of more international acquisitions and holdings by multinationals from abroad. However, FDI inflows in EU countries geographically close to Russia are expected to decline: for these countries, the political-military risk is increasing with a view to a possible future attack by Russia.

In favor of an appreciation of the Euro is a possible reaction in imports—excluding energy—which could fall overall as a result of the recession; at the same time, export companies are likely to try to increase their exports in the recession. The real exchange rate effect in the Eurozone could be roughly neutral. The economic costs of an energy import boycott should therefore be estimated to be at least 5–6% of national income in Germany, that is, about twice as high as calculated by Bachmann et al. and thus the expected decline in real income is actually higher than in the Corona recession of 2020.

A 6% drop in real income in Germany in one year via an energy import boycott means that there may still be a significant risk of recession in the following year. In the first year of the boycott, such a massive recession in Germany will also have a significant negative impact on the Netherlands and France, as well as Belgium and other EU countries, resulting in a negative amplification effect on the recession in Germany (via a reduction in exports to these countries). Such dynamics must be considered in a macroeconomic analysis.

A sharp multi-year decline in real incomes and rising unemployment rates regionally are likely to be reflected politically in an increase in the votes of radical parties in Germany; and this even if politicians decide to make higher transfer payments to the poorest households in conjunction with an energy import boycott against Russia. If, on top of this, there is a very strong movement of refugees from Ukraine, the increase in the vote shares of radical parties could increase even further. In any case, the conceivable political destabilization effect in the context of the Russo-Ukrainian war and conceivable measures by the German government against Russia should also be considered in the boycott debate.

Germany is not very capable of diversifying its energy imports in the short term, in particular in relation to gas imports. What has been neglected for many years cannot be implemented within a single year. Building an LNG terminal will take three years or more, and expanding the EU gas pipeline network will also take several years of construction. Ultimately, an energy import boycott by Germany against Russia would only marginally help Ukraine in its war against Russia. The claim that Germany is in fact a major financier of Russian warfare in Ukraine through energy imports from Russia sounds good; however, it does little to convince in the short term. Russia's army uses existing armaments, while the pay of and the supplies of provisions to Russia's soldiers do not require the import of goods from the West or Asia—for that, corresponding foreign currency revenues would be needed.

Weapons supplies from the West will be decisive for the outcome of the war. In the medium term, Germany and the EU can import more natural gas, especially from Norway, Algeria, the US, Qatar, and the United Arab Emirates.

For Russia, both boycott cases result in falling oil, gas, and coal prices in the rest of the world and domestically, although Russia could temporarily counter the loss of exports, sales, and revenues by increasing production rates. In fact, the net effect of international negative price and positive volume developments is likely to be negative in Russia's real income in the medium term, especially as Russia faces further share price declines in the medium term—dampening investment. The price reduction effects in Russia could be significant, as shown, for example, by the purchase of Russian gas at the beginning of February 2022 at the current market price, which had fallen by around $20/barrel below the world market price in Russia or for export to Shell. However, political pressure in the UK on this deal then prompted Shell to set aside up the special profits realized as an aid fund for Ukraine.

The EU is faced with new tasks, for example, in the form of a reduction in oil and gas imports from Russia or the expansion of pipeline networks—including from Spain to northern Europe, where it has not yet been possible to benefit from the large Spanish liquefied natural gas landing capacities. Spain accounts for about one-third of the liquefied natural gas landing capacity, but an unfinished gas pipeline to France could be completed within three to five years, for which Spain requires special EU funding (Louven, 2022).

In Germany, the storage situation in spring 2022 is a cause for concern, as the average fill level was only around 30%—with particularly low fill levels for gas storage facilities owned by Gazprom. Under Chancellor Merkel, the German government allowed Gazprom, the main gas supplier, to acquire substantial storage capacity in Germany. In doing so, the German government failed to enact reasonable regulation in the gas storage business; for example, a minimum fill level of 70% by October 1 of each calendar year.

The global economy will face an increased challenge in the politically desired path toward climate neutrality in the medium and presumably also the long term due to the price reduction in Russia and increases in the production of oil, gas, and coal considered here. As a result, the Ukraine war would not only lead to increased international military uncertainty—for example in terms of international border vulnerability—but would also have a negative global climate effect (external effect) and, in addition, world real income could also decline if the negative effects of production in Ukraine, Germany, and its main EU trading partners (the Netherlands and France as well as Belgium and Italy) were to lead to an export dampening effect outside the EU. However, such an effect may be counteracted by the relative cheapening of energy in the rest of the world economy.

A gas boycott would have a significant impact on the German economy, as not only private households would suffer in terms of temporarily increased heating costs and electricity generation from gas-fired power plants, but also the chemical industry, which uses natural gas as a basic material for many production purposes. A German or Western energy import boycott of Russia would therefore certainly also have a negative impact on exports from the chemical industry. Moreover, such a boycott would be historically quite unique and would therefore create a massive international trust problem in international trade agreements (the US effectively imposed an oil supply boycott on Japan in 1941, which Japan responded to by bombing Pearl Harbor, leading to the Americans' entry into the Second World War).

LITERATURE

ADB. (2022). Asian Development Outlook 2022, April, Asian Development Bank: Manila https://www.adb.org/sites/default/files/publication/784041/ado2022.pdf

Auffhammer, M., & Rubin, E. (2018). Natural gas priceelasticities and optimal cost recovery under consumer heterogeneity: Evidence from 300 million natural gas bills, NBER Working Paper No. w24295, National Bureau of Economic Research. https://doi.org/10.3386/w24295

Bachmann, R. et al. (2022). What if? The Economic Effects for Germany of a Stop of Energy Imports from Russia, ECONtribute Policy Brief Nr. 028. Retrieved May 24, 2022, from https://www.econtribute.de/RePEc/ajk/ajkpbs/ECONtribute_PB_028_2022.pdf.

Behringer, J. et al. (2022). Ukraine war hampers recovery after pandemic. Prognose der wirtschaftlichen Entwicklung 2022/23, IMK Report No. 174, March, Düsseldorf: IMK. Retrieved April 4, 2022, from https://www.imk-boeckler.de/fpdf/HBS-008284/p_imk_report_174_2022.pdf.

Figueres, J. M., & Jarociński, M. (2020). Vulnerable Growth in the Euro Area: Measuring the Financial Conditions. *Economics Letters, 191*(C), 1. https://doi.org/10.1016/j.econlet.2020.109126

Froot, K., & Stein, J. (1991). Exchange Rates and Foreign Direct Investments. *Quarterly Journal of Economics, 1,* 1191–1217. https://doi.org/10.2307/2937961

Hamilton, J. (2022). On Sanctions, Energy Prices and the Global Economy, Princeton Economics Webinar Presentation, March 17. Retrieved April 4, 2022, from https://bcf.princeton.edu/events/james-hamilton-on-sanctions-energy-prices-and-the-global-economy.

Hecking, H., John, C., & Weiser, F. (2015). An embargo of Russian Gas and Security of Supply in Europe. *Journal of Energy Economics, 39*(1), 63–73. https://doi.org/10.1007/s12398-014-0145-9

Hollo, D., Kremer, M., & Lo Duca, M. (2012). CISS—A Composite Indicator of Systemic Stress in the Financial System, ECB Working Paper Series, No. 1426 March 2012 https://www.ecb.europa.eu/pub/pdf/scpwps/ecbwp1426.pdf

IHS. (2014). A More Competitive Energiewende: Securing Germany's Global Competitiveness in a New Energy World. Main Report, IHS Report March 2014.

Kremer, M. (2016). Macroeconomic Effects of Financial Stress and the Role of Monetary Policy: A VAR Analysis for the Euro Area. *International Economics and Economic Policy, 13*(1), 105–138. https://doi.org/10.1007/s10368-015-0325-z

Louven, S. (2022). Gas aus Spanien soll Nordeuropa helfen—doch es fehlt eine Pipeline [transl. PJJW: Gas from Spain to help Northern Europe—but a pipeline is lacking], Handelsblatt, published 17th March 2022 available at https://www.handelsblatt.com/politik/international/ukraine-krieg-gas-aus-spanien-soll-nordeuropa-helfen-doch-es-fehlt-eine-pipeline/28173932.html   (last accessed 07.06.2022)

McWilliams, B., Sgaravatti, G., Tagliapietra, S., & Zachmann, G. (2022). Can Europe survive painlessly without Russian gas?.*Bruegel blogs.* Retrieved March 30, 2022, from https://www.bruegel.org/2022/01/can-europe-survive-painlessly-without-russian-gas.

OECD. (2022). OECD Economic Outlook, Interim Report. Economic and Social Impacts and Policy Implications of the War in Ukraine, Organisation for Economic Cooperation and Development: Paris. https://doi.org/10.1787/4181d61b-en

World Bank. (2022). Russian Invasion to Shrink Ukraine Economy by 45 Percent this Year, Presse Release, April 10th 2022, Washington DC, available online. Retrieved 24 May, 2022, from https://www.worldbank.org/en/news/press-release/2022/04/10/russian-invasion-to-shrink-ukraine-economy-by-45-percent-this-year

CHAPTER 7

Asia and the Global Effects of an EU Energy Import Boycott of Russia

In the months since February 2022, there has been a lively debate about energy import boycotts—and energy export stops on the part of Russia. Such measures have macroeconomic effects and can be analyzed, namely within the framework of asking what the effects of (disruption to) oil and gas supplies are on the respective world and regional markets and to what extent the proposed measures are suitable to significantly reduce Russia's state revenues and to dry up Russia's financial capacity to continue to wage its war against Ukraine.

If Germany—or the EU—decides to impose a comprehensive energy import boycott against Russia, it would—historically speaking—be a rather unique case of economic warfare, affecting international oil, gas, and coal markets and resulting in increased difficulties for Russia's economy in the medium term. According to certain politicians in Brussels and Berlin, the EU decision from June 2022 to gradually block the import of oil from Russia to a large extent over the course of a few months (with an exception for Hungary) is supposed to significantly weaken Russia's capabilities to finance its war. This idea, however, is a kind of vacuous economic fairy tale—the effect of this fairy tale would most likely be further gas imports from Russia, although here many EU countries are economically severely weakened; especially Germany, Italy, and some Eastern European countries. Gas exports that have so far gone to Western Europe cannot simply be diverted elsewhere by Russia due to the dominant role played by pipelines in transporting gas. The transport capacities toward

P. J. J. Welfens, *Russia's Invasion of Ukraine*, https://doi.org/10.1007/978-3-031-19138-1_7

China are largely utilized. Incidentally, revenues from the gas sector account for less than half of Russia's state revenues from the oil sector.

What does an EU oil import blockade against Russia actually achieve in view of the fact that the oil market is a highly integrated world market with a roughly uniform price in all regions of the world (this is the normal case; without the Russo-Ukrainian war). Price differentials normally reflect only differences in international transport costs (e.g., from the US to Europe via Rotterdam). If Russia can no longer sell oil to the EU27 countries and, from the end of 2022, to the UK either, then Russian oil companies will redirect their production to important markets in Asia, where—at a certain price discount—there is a corresponding demand. The two main consumer countries in this perspective are India and China. If Russia sells more oil to India, it will strengthen Russia's position in the world's largest democracy, whereby India is already largely dependent on Russia for defense equipment. Does this correspond to Western interests? Certainly not.

Of course, Russia could also sell more oil to China by ship—again at a certain discount. However, based on a high world market price of a good $100 per barrel of oil, selling the now surplus "Europe quantities" to China at a discounted price of $80 barrel of oil would still be a brilliant deal for Russia's oil companies. Of course, this, in turn, strengthens Russia's economic ties to China; this is probably not unproblematic for Russia itself in the long term, but rather positive in the short and medium term. The EU countries, on the other hand, will simply buy more crude oil from the US and OPEC instead of Russia in the medium term; if necessary, at higher prices, although we will have to wait and see how speculation on the oil and energy markets develops. There is also a particular danger that increased gas prices in Europe will drive up demand for the substitute commodity for oil (again to Russia's advantage). If the EU countries increasingly purchase oil from the US and the OPEC, then the latter will export less to Asia than they have in the past; Russia will fill this gap in Asia with its diverted "European exports". Thus, Russia will increasingly finance its war through energy exports to Asia from the point of view of its foreign exchange earnings, whereby it cannot be ruled out that Russia's foreign contribution—with declining imports of goods from Western countries and Japan plus the Republic of Korea—will even increase in the medium term. The view propagated by politicians in Brussels, Berlin, and other capitals that an EU energy import embargo will virtually deprive Russia's President Putin of financing and therefore help to end the war quickly is misleading. It is simply wishful thinking. An EU energy embargo against Russia creates international diversionary effects and, in fact, Russia's war against Ukraine will in future be financed more by countries from Asia; it is not a realistic assumption that Russia will have major budgetary problems and that the worsening financial situation will war essentially starve Russia's war machine as a result. It is more likely that Russia will face serious problems if tax revenues fall significantly due to a severe recession in the country itself. Moreover, Putin must reckon with the fact that a lack of military successes in Ukraine, combined with a severe recession and an inflation rate of over 20%, will lead to gradually growing discontent among parts of the population. However, Putin will also point out that in many Western countries, inflation rates close to 10%—and in the medium term probably a recession with many unemployed— will emerge.

As for Germany, the Finance Ministry's idea of again complying with the debt brake in 2022, of all years, and thus keeping new government debt below 0.35% of gross domestic product—the oddly narrow limit contained in Germany's constitution since the Euro Crisis—is quite problematic. Certain policymakers seem to want to take the Russo-Ukrainian war seriously—in its many economically damaging dimensions—and then at the same time pretend to celebrate a return to normal budgetary times, following the Corona pandemic shock, in 2022. Moreover, if Germany is serious about the 2% spending target for national defense, then defense spending must be increased further. Sound fiscal policy is important, but one has to be realistic about the relevant situation. Unsound promises with regard to fiscal policy do not help the German and European economy and in fact diminish the credibility of politics. Germany and the West, however, should make it a point to strengthen the credibility of Western democracies, especially in the international crisis year of 2022. The West has already lost credibility in an unexpected way over the past five to ten years because of the Trump presidency and also because of the Johnson-led British approach to BREXIT. Truth has become a very scarce commodity in US and UK politics under the influences of Donald Trump and Boris Johnson, respectively ("you don't have to say everything you know as a politician, but what you do say publicly has to be the truth", former German Chancellor Helmut Schmidt once told me during a meeting in Paris).

When private households in European countries receive their heating bills at the turn of the year 2022/2023, high additional payments will be due. What households thus have to spend on oil and gas will not be spent on the domestic goods markets. In the medium term, there is a risk of recession in the Eurozone and also in the UK and the US. This is especially true because the central banks expect further significant interest rate hikes in the medium term to break the high inflation rates.

Many countries will probably try to compensate private households somehow for the high energy prices through their state budgets; this requires increased new government borrowing. Incidentally, this may also have an impact on electricity prices, making electricity more expensive in the EU. This even applies to France with its many nuclear power plants in the summer of 2022, as due to periods of prolonged heat—probably an expression of climate change—the country is suffering from low water levels in many rivers, which are usually used to cool the nuclear power plants. Due to regional water deficits, some power plants in France had to be shut down in June 2022 and France became an importer of electricity in the EU, although France has usually been a net exporter in the EU.

As for Russia's oil, where the country stood for 13% of the world market share in 2021, the Russian government could sell volumes no longer sold in the EU elsewhere, notably to Asia—for example, China, ASEAN countries (excluding Singapore, which as the only ASEAN country, fully participated in Western sanctions against Russia as of March 2022). After the US stopped importing oil from Russia in mid-March, Russia was able to sell surplus oil to India, albeit at a good $20 per barrel discount on the world price. If Germany or the EU were to boycott oil imports, Russia would certainly be able to sell surplus oil to Asia at an even higher discount: Probably in the range of $30 to $50 per barrel. However, as long as the world market price is around $100, Russia can absorb such price reductions. A relatively cheaper oil price in Asia then means a stabilizing effect for China and the ASEAN countries as well as other emerging industrial markets in the world economy, counteracting the negative economic effects from the US, the EU, Japan, Republic of Korea, and Taiwan.

The sharp rise in oil prices on the world markets in 2022 will on the one hand stimulate oil production in the US—with some time lag—and, on the other hand, the increase in the US inflation rate due to rising energy prices will prompt the US Federal Reserve to gradually step up its policy of braking or raising interest rates. The high world market prices for oil and the increased regional gas prices—especially in Europe—are causing increased inflation rates in North America, the EU, the UK, Switzerland, Japan, the Republic of Korea, and other countries. There is a risk that the long-standing low inflation rate expectations will break from their anchor values of around 2% in the Western industrialized countries and that a wage-price-wage spiral will develop—with then significantly increased inflation rates over several years and corresponding welfare losses.

The link between higher energy prices and rising inflation rates is not necessarily inevitable, but in industrialized countries in particular, compensatory declines in the prices of other goods are hardly to be expected, since prices are not very flexible on the downside in many markets and because energy is, of course, a production factor in almost all goods and in most services. The economic significance of an oil price shock in the 2020s is less than in the 1970s—the times of OPEC price shocks (such as the OPEC oil embargo in 1973 and the revolution, which brought Ayatollah Khomeini to power in Iran in 1979, both of which led to large supply shortfalls on the world market, namely by about 7%)—because of long-term declines in energy intensity; but in terms of cost pressure effects, sharp increases in energy prices cannot be ignored in the economy as a whole.

Relatively rising oil prices will also reduce automobile sales in OECD countries and the production of the automotive industry, which was already characterized by problems in its logistics chains even before the Russo-Ukrainian war (think of the delivery problems of chips for the automotive industry). Renewable energies and thus also the production of electric cars will be stimulated by oil and gas price increases. High government subsidies for the purchase of electric cars should be reduced significantly and quickly, especially as government budgets in many EU countries and the US and Japan are likely to face increased government deficit ratios in 2022/2023. An EU energy import boycott is likely to trigger a recession in several EU countries in the medium term, especially since Russia will probably impose increased import duties or import bans on EU exports.

As the Russo-Ukrainian conflict could last for several years, a quick EU energy import boycott, together with the war in Ukraine and Putin's political breach of trust, is likely to weaken global economic expansion for many years to come. Reduced wheat supplies from Ukraine and Russia to the world market will also result in new hunger problems in many developing countries. The Russo-Ukrainian war also presents the risk of an internationalization of this war, which would have dramatic consequences for the world economy. In the economic analysis undertaken here, it is clear that, from an overall perspective, the loss of human life and the suffering caused by the war are decisive aspects in the analysis.

Distortions on the international oil and gas markets and the automotive markets, or recessionary effects in many industrialized, emerging, and developing countries, could destabilize national and international financial systems. Many oil traders came under liquidity pressures in spring 2022 because the collateral required from traders on the market for oil purchases rose significantly due to increased volatility in oil prices. Depending on the nature of any financial crisis that may emerge—with potentially strong nonlinear impulses—serious further real economic disruptive effects could emanate from banking and financial systems. This could be compounded by cyber-attacks from Russia to deliberately destabilize Western financial systems and critical infrastructure, which would not go without cyber counter-attacks on the part of Western countries. The risk of Russia and NATO countries becoming directly involved in the war would then increase.

An interesting approach to modeling the economic effects of the Russo-Ukrainian war has been presented by a group of researchers at the Vienna Institute for International Economic Studies (wiiw)—just before Russia's invasion of Ukraine. In the analysis conducted before the start of the Russo-Ukrainian war, Astrov et al. (2022a) show the effects a war between Russia against Ukraine could have, namely on Russia, Ukraine, and the EU. A distinction is made between a limited attack on Ukraine and a full-scale Russo-Ukrainian war, with correspondingly different levels of Western sanctions considered in the study. In addition to a Western energy import boycott of Russia with significant negative effects for Russia and EU countries, the exclusion of Russian banks from the SWIFT system is classified as an effective sanction by the West. Another subsequent analysis by Astrov et al. (2022b) addresses the humanitarian, economic and financial impacts of a Russo-Ukrainian war: According to this analysis, the EU will have to deal more with defense issues in the medium term; in addition, an accelerated climate-friendly transformation of energy systems is expected; finally, a weakening of broader European integration is to be expected, and membership prospects for candidate countries from the Balkans are likely to play an increased role in EU enlargement.

In the short term, price changes and higher price volatility have become visible on commodity markets in the spring of 2022. The first weeks of the actual Russo-Ukrainian war have shown that the European gas trade has been affected by the natural gas price increases that have occurred and the increased price volatility: Increased security must be provided by gas traders. Insofar as the natural gas price level—as in Italy and the EU, respectively (criticized by Prime Minister Mario Draghi)—is a kind of lead price level for electricity pricing, reforms are urgent. In the current system, electricity generation from depreciated coal-fired power plants is rewarded with special returns, which is not conducive to efficiency and innovation and which also causes unnecessary price increases for electricity in certain phases.

The high volatility of the gas price in Europe and the increased security deposits of gas traders can lead to serious liquidity problems in gas trading and ultimately to increased risks in gas supply. If natural gas imports from Russia were to be terminated in the short term—for example by Germany or by Russia—this would lead to problems in industry and presumably also in the supply of electricity in Germany. It would be possible to extend the operating lives of the remaining three nuclear power plants for a few years to secure the supply of electricity. In mid-March 2022, Belgium's government decided to set a ten-year lifetime extension for two units of the country's nuclear power plants until 2035.

LITERATURE

Astrov, V. et al. (2022a). Possible Russian invasion of Ukraine, scenarios for sanctions, and likely economic impact on Russia, Ukraine and the EU, wiiw policy notes and reports 55, February, wiiw Vienna. https://wiiw.ac.at/possible-russian-invasion-of-ukraine-scenarios-for-sanctions-and-likely-economic-impact-on-russia-ukraine-and-the-eu-dlp-6044.pdf

Astrov, V., et al. (2022b). Russia's invasion of Ukraine: Assessment of the humanitarian, economic and financial impact in the short and medium term. *International Economics and Economic Policy, 19*(2). https://doi.org/10.1007/s10368-022-00546-5

PART III

Wider Economic Challenges Arising from the Russo-Ukrainian War

CHAPTER 8

EU-China-Russia: Macroeconomic Aspects and Multinational Enterprises

China did not participate directly in sanctions against Russia during the first three months of 2022. However, significant support for Russia from China could fail to materialize in the medium term, as the negative economic effects of the Russo-Ukrainian war will have an increasingly negative impact on China. First of all, it should be noted that the Western sanctions are expected to cause Russia's GDP to fall by around 9% in 2022, which initially also means reduced exports from China to Russia; however, it is to be expected that some Chinese companies will also export more to Russia, as they will be able to replace reduced exports from the West and from Japan and the Republic of Korea to Russia. This involves technology-intensive goods on the one hand and luxury goods and automobiles on the other. In March, however, the US government—in talks with China's leadership—highlighted that the country's extensive additional deliveries to Russia will not remain without consequences on the US side; the US could, for example, impose new tariffs on China's exports to the US.

A second negative effect for China results from the sharp rise in oil and gas prices in the context of the Russo-Ukrainian war. On the one hand, this has a direct economic dampening effect on China, especially on energy-intensive sectors and companies. In the case of natural gas, it is hardly possible for China to increase energy imports from Russia in the short term. Moreover, it can be assumed that Russia will make special price concessions on oil and gas exports to China. In addition,

P. J. J. Welfens, *Russia's Invasion of Ukraine*,
https://doi.org/10.1007/978-3-031-19138-1_8

significantly higher oil and gas prices will also have a dampening effect on the economies of the western industrialized countries, Japan, the Republic of Korea, and Australia. The cyclical dampening effect that falls away from OECD countries reduces Chinese exports, thus dampening China's real income growth and employment growth.

In a conversation with the then President of the European Commission José Manuel Barroso, Putin once said that his military could be in Kyiv within two weeks if Russia wanted it to be. As of mid-March 2022, Russia's army had yet to conquer Kyiv, suggesting that Putin and other parts of Russia's political leadership have made a serious military miscalculation regarding the Russian army's Ukraine campaign. The longer the Russo-Ukrainian war continues, the higher the cost of economic destabilization in Central Asia and Eastern Europe. Such destabilization effects undermine the prospects of success for China's New Silk Road Initiative: China had indeed intended to be able to significantly increase China's exports or its overall trade volume through this initiative aimed at modernizing economic actors in Central Asia and Eastern Europe, whereby the rail transport route through Russia, among other things, is of great importance. China's influence in Europe is thus likely to diminish in the long run. Klein (2022, p. 157) wrote [transl. PJJW]:

> *as a Russian vassal state or as a divided state, Ukraine would be a frontline state in a new cold war between Russia and the West. For China, this would be the end of the New Silk Road as a logistics bridge to the EU and also the end of China's geopolitical plans to free itself from the maritime grip of the U.S.*

Whether, in an alternative scenario with Ukraine's neutral status guaranteed, China would be able to fully implement its Belt and Road Initiative with great success can be doubted; even if Ukraine were to become an EU member state. The political shock of Russia's war of aggression against Ukraine and Western sanctions against Russia, as well as Russian approaches to nationalizing foreign investors who closed their branches and production facilities in Russia for a period during the war, undermines confidence in expansion projects in Eastern Europe in parts of the rest of Europe—including Russia, of course. Some Western investors will also scale back their involvement in China or allow it to increase only slowly, as one can see in the Russo-Ukrainian war a kind of blueprint for a future Sino-Taiwan war.

If the EU reduces coal, oil, and gas imports from Russia, it will create pressure in Russia to export more to Asia. At least in the short term, a reduction in EU gas imports from Russia is unlikely to lead to increased Russian exports of natural gas to China. This is because the gas pipeline from Russia to China was apparently already at its capacity limit in the winter of 2021/2022. Building new pipeline capacity from Russia to Asia is likely to take several years.

Presumably, international trade relations will be highly politicized for years by Western countries and Japan, the Republic of Korea, Australia, and New Zealand, which amounts to new potential for conflict in the global economy. The influence of international organizations could decline, weakening the rule-based, international trading system.

EU Macroeconomic Aspects of the Russo-Ukrainian War

The Russo-Ukrainian war has a number of macroeconomic aspects. In this context, post-corona recovery dynamics in Western industrialized countries are running in the background, while in the rest of the world economy, the corona economic crisis still exists to some extent—this is largely owed to the still relatively low vaccination rates in the south of the world economy; in the case of China, also to the use of vaccines with relatively low efficiency rates: China still practices extensive regional lockdowns in the event of local outbreaks of coronavirus, which bring entire economic metropolises and even major port cities to a standstill for months at a time and disrupt global trade chains. Thus, there are corona disruptions from local lockdowns in some major Chinese cities. The Russo-Ukrainian war drama is creating new international risks in markets, an extra boost to inflation in many countries, and—in certain key countries—also leading to changes in strategic course (e.g., in Germany with a new focus toward less Russia-friendly policies):

- Increased uncertainty in the global economy; increased cost uncertainty shifts the marginal cost curve of suppliers—for risk-neutral companies—upward in a standard market model. This does not imply an inflation effect, but a one-time cost or market price increase. Since the military conflict between Russia and Ukraine could continue for many years in its current form, the upward price pressure is likely to increase for many years, including, and especially, in Russia. Russia initially faces a sharp recession in 2022/2023, accompanied by high inflation, which will lead to significant welfare losses.

- Pressure toward higher energy and raw material prices or an acceleration of inflation in Western countries: up to 9% in mid-2022 in the US, where the Federal Reserve has initiated an interest rate hike policy since the spring (a few months after a first central bank rate hike by the Bank of England in the UK). In the Eurozone, inflation was around 7% at the start of June 2022, with the European Central Bank announcing a first rate hike of 0.25% on June 9 after 11 years of a zero interest rate policy—the beginning of which reflected the fight against the 2008/2009 Transatlantic Banking Crisis: for July 2022, then further rate hikes in the fall. In this context, the ECB assumes that the core inflation rate (inflation rate excluding the influence of energy and food prices, which are considered to be particularly susceptible to fluctuations) will be 3.3% in 2022, and from a standard inflation rate of 6.8% in 2022, which is well over twice as high, the inflation rate could therefore also fall to 3.5% by 2023 (ECB, 2022). However, this is hardly realistic, unless one is counting on a quick and lasting peace agreement between Russia and Ukraine. On the contrary, there is a risk that an oil and gas import embargo by the EU—or, in a mirror image, an energy export embargo by Russia in the direction of the EU—will firstly drive energy prices up even further; in the Eurozone to around 10% at times and in the US to levels well above this mark. At the same time, the inflation rate in the spring of 2021 in the Eurozone, the US, and the UK was still in the 2–3% range, so one can speak of a surge in inflation for 2022 and also for 2023 (exacerbated by, among other factors, abnormally low grain exports from Ukraine, Russia, and India; in India, the government wants to limit the inflation rate through grain export restrictions). An unexpectedly high inflation rate in industrialized countries causes employment to rise there because the real wage rate falls unexpectedly; this means a re-application of the Phillips curve with its focus on inflation and the unemployment rate. In the medium term, however, negative growth in labor income means that there will be a further slowdown in consumption growth.
- The differences in inflation rates in Europe are considerable, with Switzerland, for example, standing for an inflation rate of 2.9% in mid-2022—with a first interest rate hike by the central bank there.

The intra-OECD inflation differentials need to be examined, with many central banks tending to follow the so-called Taylor rule in monetary policy (the central bank interest rate i' is to be set such that: $i' = r + a'$ (inflation rate minus inflation target) + a'' (real GDP minus real GDP at normal utilization); r is the real interest rate, that is, the difference between the capital market interest rate i and inflation rate, a' and a'' are positive parameters). During the prolonged zero interest rate period of 2016–2021 in many EU countries and in the UK, one could not easily apply the Taylor rule. In the UK, inflation expectations of around 10% for the end of 2022 have already led to a widespread strike by rail workers in June; presumably unions in the UK—and other OECD countries—have tended to be weakened by the spread of home office activity among the workforce: for example, many British employers in the Greater London area have responded to the multi-day rail strikes by instructing staff to engage in more home office work, meaning that the corona-related digital innovations in home office work are weakening the power of the railway workers and their union. This, in turn, suggests that workers in the UK and many other OECD countries will find it much more difficult to obtain nominal wage increases to compensate for the enormous rise in inflation rates (in technical economic terms: the short-term Phillips curves will be flatter than in the 1970s; the redistributive effects in favor of capital will probably last for several years). At the same time, in countries like Germany and France—without inflation indexation—the marginal tax burden will increase significantly with inflation, which policymakers should urgently correct, as otherwise the state share will continue to rise in a growth-hostile manner. There is therefore a medium-term stagflation risk in many OECD countries: minimal growth with high inflation rates, with central bank interest rate hikes as well as declining consumption rates contributing to minimal growth; the latter is exacerbated by the declining efficiency of the global trading system and especially the all-out economic war of the EU and other countries against Russia. In this context, the envisaged escalation of EU policy against Russia's exclave of Kaliningrad (with the eastern seaport of Kaliningrad and environs located between Lithuania and Poland) is inappropriate and risky; especially as the EU will increasingly block more goods in rail transit from Russia to Kaliningrad by the end of the year—including oil and oil product shipments bound for Kaliningrad from December

2022. There is considerable potential for escalation in Europe here, and it is to be feared that the EU has adopted its corresponding fourth sanctions package without giving much thought to the problem of transit to and from Kaliningrad. The EU countries are not at war with Russia and no sanctions package can be adopted in a critical security situation in Europe and the world without careful consideration of the details or consequences on the part of politicians. Here, there is a visible lack of responsibility and diligence (and presumably also geographical knowledge) on the part of important actors in the West. The escalation potential of the "K problem"—that is, with Kaliningrad Oblast—is considerable, the economic benefit of blocking the Kaliningrad rail transit is low, the political damage potentially very high. Russia can certainly be accused of breaking international law after it invaded Ukraine, but it cannot be the West's policy to tear down the EU-Russia transit protocols on Kaliningrad (the EU-Russia Transit Declaration of 2002). If the West were to proceed in this way, the world economy would no longer be characterized by a rules-based order, but by arbitrariness and the law of the strongest—with considerable losses in efficiency and growth in the long term for Europe and the entire world economy. What is needed is a differentiated, well thought-out sanctions strategy on the part of the West; if it should turn out that the fourth EU sanctions package (and other sanctions packages) actually did not take account of the Kaliningrad problem in Brussels, that would be a political scandal. With regard to Germany, one could see a special historical responsibility on the part of the German government to ensure that the region around the city formerly known as Königsberg does not become a dangerous bone of contention between the EU and Russia. Here, too, the question must be asked what the Foreign Office in Berlin was actually thinking and considering in terms of Kaliningrad issues in the EU sanctions packages.

- The massive increase in the German minimum wage announced by politicians in 2022—an increase of around 20%—is actually unreasonable, as it will lead to job losses or reduced working hours for some of the low-skilled workers (whether in the latter case the monthly real income will then increase would have to be examined in each individual case). In the special situation of a massive increase in inflation, however, a 20% increase in nominal wages for low-skilled workers is not that enormous, since an 8% inflation rate results in a plus of "only" 12%. Such a plus could be justified under certain economic conditions, especially if one assumes a certain monopoly power of large companies in many regions. The significant increase in real wages for the lowest wage grouping could, in turn, increase the chances of the trade unions in Germany to achieve a wage increase for all employees in the medium term that is close to compensating for inflation. However, such a positive conceivable macroeconomically enhanced real wage effect from the minimum wage increase tends to be a random effect (under no circumstances should the special economic situation in 2022 be used for a naïve general conclusion that a very high increase in the minimum wage rate remains without negative economic labor market effects). Germany's economic development will slow down over the course of 2022 due to substantial energy price increases, with medium-term gas supply problems for industry already foreseeable since June. If gas supplies from Russia are insufficient, gas prices on the free market will increase significantly—possibly doubling at the peak. Industrial production in important sectors that normally rely on gas will then drop significantly. Rising gas prices will also unsettle private households—via the additional inflation effect on the one hand and a general additional risk aspect on the other—which will depress consumer demand (then also temporarily dampen inflation slightly; with rising unemployment). A flattening of growth or a recession in Germany will have a negative economic impact on many EU partner countries and the dampened economic development in the EU partners will then have negative repercussions on Germany. Incidentally, in the event of relatively strong US interest rate hikes, the Eurozone countries could benefit from a real depreciation of the Euro in terms of net US exports; and because of the depreciation, they could also record increased direct investment inflows from abroad (with the international volume of international corporate takeovers globally dampened by the Russo-Ukrainian war), as can be seen from the relevant analysis by Froot and Stein (1991).

- The economic logic of the sharp relative increase in energy prices in 2022 will cause industrial production in all energy-intensive sectors to fall in most OECD countries—there is a parallel here with the 1970s. The federal government's insufficient gas storage and supply provision in the first half of 2022 can hardly be compensated for in the second half of the year, and in the case of a hard winter, there will certainly be serious gas supply problems in private households in 2022/2023. The use of gas in the electricity industry in particular could have been cut back quickly, and Berlin could certainly have decided to extend the lifetime of nuclear power plants for a few years. Incidentally, one can praise the German government for not responding in a knee-jerk fashion to the Bachmann et al. (2022) study, which proposed a broad energy import boycott for Germany, including a gas boycott against Russia (the study's methodological weaknesses are, incidentally, astonishing). As far as Germany's reorientation of its energy policy is concerned, this is fundamentally time-consuming and costly. There is also a certain political-economic rationality at stake in political conflict management vis-à-vis Russia. Putin's aggression toward Ukraine must be resolutely rejected politically, but one can hardly turn this into a policy of the West against the Russian people. With regard to the problem of Kaliningrad, a corresponding awareness of the issue should have been expected in Berlin, Paris, Brussels, and the Baltic states. What one sees here in reality suggests an occasionally unacceptably poor policy quality—not in the sense of EU citizenship and Europe.

- Nevertheless, investment in the Eurozone will continue to rise for some time, provided that positive economic growth is achieved in the US and Asia; in Asia, particular attention must be paid to growth not only in China but also in the ASEAN group of countries (the latter accounts for one-third of China's GDP in purchasing power parity terms). If the US Federal Reserve significantly strengthens its anti-inflation policy in the medium term, it should take at most two years before the US is in recession. In the medium term, nominal wage growth rates will indeed rise in the US and the Eurozone as well as in the UK—with relatively high wage growth in the US, as long as the unemployment rate does not climb considerably. However, inflation is likely to remain above wage growth rates for a considerable time. The real incomes of the workforce are falling temporarily; and by substantial amounts. The increased direct investment stocks of OECD countries since the 1990s have increased significantly relative to the capital stock of the respective source countries of direct investment as shown by UNCTAD figures. An order of magnitude of about 12% for the US may be cited as an example. This means that US companies will be able to exert strong influence in terms of wage negotiations with unions or the workforce; however, this will be significantly limited in some cases where the respective multinational has, for example, relied particularly heavily on high direct investment (i.e., foreign production) in China. Since the Biden administration, and in a modified form also under the Trump administration, the further expansion of foreign production in China is little supported politically in Washington, DC, production capacities in China cannot be used as a threat by management—in the event of high wage demands, production will soon be relocated abroad to a greater extent.

- If the Western central banks, including the US Federal Reserve, were to raise central bank interest rates relatively quickly in the medium term, a recession is likely to loom in 2024, especially in the US. With 2024 being a US presidential election campaign year, however, the Biden administration will try to avoid a recession at all costs. This will only be possible with a certain trade cooperation policy with China, which would benefit US exports; and strengthened transatlantic cooperation with the EU. The EU-US Trade and Technology Council, launched as part of a transatlantic cooperation agenda in 2021 (not reliant on US Senate approval), would therefore need to be positively mobilized in 2022–2024 as a source of more US-EU innovation and direct investment and growth momentum; especially in the high-tech sector. Increased transatlantic direct investment dynamics (more EU direct investment in the US, and more US direct investment in the EU) are likely to constrain the ability of unions to translate increased inflation rate expectations into rising nominal wage growth. The short-term Phillips curve for the relationship between inflation and the unemployment rate then becomes flatter: a reduction in the unemployment rate in the Eurozone tends to be associated with less inflationary pressure than in earlier decades. More detailed modeling here directs attention to an appropriately state-of-the-art DSGE model as a framework for analysis, as is available with the Roeger and Welfens model (Roeger and Welfens, 2021; 2022): only this DSGE model includes both foreign trade and direct investment in the countries' external economic links under consideration.

- In all OECD countries, increased military spending could take over the function of expansive fiscal policy, with the US defense industry experiencing a particularly strong increase in profits; above all, an increase in exports toward EU countries, with the military spending ratio in western EU countries increasing by half a percentage point in the medium term. Accordingly, in the long run, the tax ratio would have to increase, leading to a decrease in the level of per capita income in, say, Germany by about 0.5 times 0.5 = 0.25% or €110 (assumption here is that the saving function S= $s(1-t')Y$, where for the saving ratio $0<s<1$ and for the income tax rate t' is also $0<t'<1$ as a value constraint; let a usual production function $Y = K^{\beta}(AL)^{1-\beta}$, where β is usually taken to be 0.33; Y is real GDP, A is knowledge and L is labor). One could also use a simple neoclassical model to answer the question of whether a special tax is appropriate in the context of the Russo-Ukrainian war—on petroleum companies, for example. Usually, politicians may imagine that this would generate additional revenue for the state budget, which could be spent on increased transfers to poorer households, for example. If policymakers would implement such a tax policy (with a certain sectoral discrimination), but all investors from then on assume with a certain probability that there will be special political tax rates in the future, the result—via a reduction in the effective savings rate—would be a reduction in the per capita income of all in the growth model: the level of economic growth then falls. Thus, it would take a very precise and credible special tax instrument to reduce this negative effect in the long-run equilibrium level. This negative effect could be prevented, in particular, by introducing such a tax measure and using the lion's share of the additional tax revenues collected to increase the research funding rate. This main use of the additional tax revenues could then increase the trend growth rate in terms of economic growth in the long run; even if the level of the growth path drops a little in the short run, the increase in the trend growth rate will lead to a positive effect in real (inflation-adjusted) per capita income in the medium run. Incidentally, the growth prospects for the UK, the Eurozone, and the US depend above all on the development of trade relations between the West and China. In this regard, the US has pursued a less cooperative and at times aggressive trade policy since President Trump. President Biden has made only minor corrections to US trade policy: with a focus on increasing trade with the EU plus the UK as well as important trading partners in the Asia-Pacific region.

- If the US-China and EU-China trade conflicts intensify, China's GDP growth may be reduced in the medium term; it would not help China much if Russia were to supply more oil and gas at a significant price discount in US dollars. There remain heightened risks of cyber-warfare between the West and Russia in the context of the Russo-Ukrainian war, which poses a new threat of wider escalation. Incidentally, this aspect, along with the emergence of China as a global growth factor, is new when comparing the latent economic crisis dynamics in 2022 in OECD countries with the OPEC price shocks of the 1970s. Naturally, digitalization and the expansion of the digital economy are new economic factors.

- Overall, it is astonishing how strongly the initial and anticipated supply shortfall related to the relatively small global wheat export capacities of Russia and Ukraine in 2022 could already lead to strong price increases on world markets. For the medium-term development, crop yields in the US, China, Brazil, Russia, and Ukraine will be of great importance; and, of course, how long the war in Ukraine continues (including the time required for constructing new, and the reconstruction of destroyed, port capacities in Ukraine).

The Russo-Ukrainian war brings about a rise in oil and gas prices, a decline in trade of EU countries with Ukraine and Russia, and disruptions in energy-intensive sectors of certain EU countries (disruptions would strongly affect the chemicals sector, the steel sector, and the food sector in the case of a Russian export embargo for gas or an EU import embargo for gas) plus a higher volatility of asset market prices; along with a rise of the unemployment rate in case of major negative sectoral supply shocks—and a rise of the unemployment rate could translate into a recession in major EU countries. Finland as a small country—but with relatively strong trade links to Russia—is also expected to be relatively strongly exposed to the Russo-Ukrainian war (see Bank of Finland, 2022).

An expansionary fiscal policy will be a useful intervention only with respect to a demand-driven recession while sectoral supply shocks require accelerated structural change and additional efforts in innovation efforts to create new markets and rising demand. Monetary policy could deal with rising inflation pressure, but a strong rise of ECB interest rates would translate into higher real interest rates in all Eurozone countries and hence weaken economic expansion. A new recession in Italy, France, and Germany would bring a broader recession for the whole EU and negative transatlantic spillover effects. Technically, Italy's economy is facing a recession in the first two quarters of 2022. This mild recession in Italy could become much stronger if there should be a German or EU energy import embargo vis-à-vis Russia.

A strong depreciation of non-Eurozone currencies in Eastern EU countries can be expected as a consequence of the Russo-Ukrainian war. This will not only bring higher inflation to these countries but also raise foreign indebtedness for the private sector. If this brings liquidity and solvency problems for firms in key sectors, the stability of the banking sector—already facing problems of low investment and growth dynamics—could be undermined. One should also not ignore the real shock potential of adverse cyber-attacks in EU countries.

Transitorily strong increases of the inflation rate should, in the short term, bring a fall in unemployment along the economic logic of the Phillips curve: real wages are driven down by unanticipated inflation rate dynamics. However, if there is a negative energy shock to EU countries, this supply shock implies a decline of the profit rate and the real wage rate in equilibrium: In the presence of nominal rigidities in labor markets, such a real wage decline should not be expected quickly so that unemployment could rise for some time.

As regards the refugee wave from Ukraine and the effective rise of immigration numbers from Ukraine, in many EU countries, there should a positive supply-side effect in the medium term as more refugees (workers) from Ukraine will be integrated into the labor markets of host countries. To the extent that governments in major EU countries are raising military expenditures relative to national income, there will be an expansionary fiscal impulse, which, however, to a considerable extent will benefit the US, which is expected to sell fighter jets and high-tech military material to many EU countries.

Rising relative prices of wheat and corn—as a consequence of much reduced Ukrainian and Russian exports in 2022—will be a major challenge for several developing countries. The IMF and the World Bank as well as regional development banks (e.g. the Asian Development Bank and the African Development Bank) will be needed to help cushion these international price shocks. Finally, some newly industrialized countries in Asia are likely to benefit from price discounts on Russian excess oil supplies as many EU countries are cutting oil—and natural gas—imports from Russia. EU countries and the US are likely to face the challenge of helping to rebuild Ukraine after the end of the Russo-Ukrainian war. A kind of Marshall Plan for Ukraine seems to be adequate in the medium term. As long as an authoritarian or dictatorial regime is in power in Russia, Europe, and Asia, and indeed the whole world economy will face new uncertainties and risks; and more differentiated and higher risk premiums for certain countries and projects can be expected to reflect this in due time.

Among the important drivers of price and volume reactions on international markets are market participants' expectations. For example, if supply problems or cuts are expected for oil and gas from Russia, this leads to sharp price increases for oil (and to a lesser extent for gas—the latter is characterized by long supply contracts), as in March 2022. Wheat also rose sharply on the world market at the beginning of April compared with the previous year—with prices doubling. There were also large price increases in nickel at the end of March, where trading on the London Metal Exchange—in the hands of an investor from Hong Kong—was then temporarily suspended when the price more than doubled within a day.

The British Securities and Exchange Commission allowed trading to resume after an initial failed restart, and the price returned to normal in early April. It is said that a Chinese investor got into serious trouble by taking a large short position in the market (delivery of nickel then in the near future)—made in the expectation of falling nickel prices—and with the attempt to close out his position or to buy large quantities of nickel himself drove the nickel price far up; the market expectation of the Chinese major investor was wrong in that the Russo-Ukrainian war caused market prices to shoot up in the short term, especially for nickel. This is because Russia is one of the major producers and exporters of nickel. A fierce Russia-EU economic war, presumably also waged using cyber-attacks, could lead to considerable global economic destabilization overall. Russia's determination to continue the attack on Ukraine is unlikely to be broken in the short term by Western economic sanctions. Western arms deliveries to Ukraine will certainly be more relevant here.

If EU real income falls by 1%, US real income is likely to fall by around 0.2%, and that in Asia by around 0.1%. International economic problems could be exacerbated if there were to be a boycott of Russian oil, gas, and coal exports on the part of the EU as a whole and also on the part of the US in the long term; an exception would be a dampening effect of inflationary pressure in OECD countries, some of which recorded a considerable increase in inflation rates in 2021/2022 due to rising energy prices. Russia could also respond militarily to such a massive international boycott, which could include hybrid military actions such as digital disruption actions in Western industrialized countries in a first phase: with quite significant damage to critical infrastructure and production potential in some Western industrialized countries. Incidentally, in the wake of international solidarity with Ukraine since February 24, 2022, Russia itself has become a favorite target of "protest hackers" from around the world, weakening Russia's economic development, but also potentially causing domestic and international disruption to Russia's critical infrastructure. As for containing inflationary pressures in the West, it is also up to the US to lobby its political allies among OPEC countries to temporarily increase production levels.

The International Monetary Fund addressed the Russo-Ukrainian war from the leadership level, the IMF Board, on March 4 and released a statement the next day (IMF, 2022a) which includes for following excerpt:

> *The war in Ukraine is resulting in tragic loss of life and human suffering, and is also causing massive damage to Ukraine's physical infrastructure. This has led to a major exodus of more than one million refugees to neighboring countries. Unprecedentedly harsh sanctions against Russia have been announced.*

INFLATION OUTLOOK

Inflation rates in industrialized countries such as the US, the UK, and the Eurozone have risen considerably in 2021/2022 and are likely to rise further reaching around 9%, after a decade in which a range of 1–3% was more typical. The central banks of the aforementioned countries, above all the Federal Reserve in the US, have been sending a signal to fight inflation by raising central bank interest rates in 2022. This caused short-term interest rates to rise and, initially in the US, to exceed long-term interest rates. In the US, by the middle of the year, the interest rate for two-year government bonds was already one percentage point higher than that for ten-year bonds. This brings about the special phenomenon of an inverse interest rate structure, where—unlike in the normal case of a yield curve—the short-term interest rate exceeds the long-term one.

This, however, clearly clouds the yield prospects for banks as banks normally earn a part of their profits by using short-term, low-interest bank deposits to grant medium-term loans—at a higher interest rate—to commercial customers and private households. With the rise in short-term interest rates, competition for bank customers also intensifies (the banks' liquidity procurement costs rise); bank yields fall after a few quarters, as does the equity ratio—here there is a regulatory minimum ratio. As a result, banks lend less in the interest of meeting the minimum equity-to-loan ratio, which reduces investment and consumption and can soon lead to a recession. An expected international recession reduces inflationary pressure on fossil fuel energy prices.

Relatively high inflation rates—in the US in 2022 even the core inflation rate (i.e., excluding energy and food prices) was already at 5%—that deviate significantly from the 2% target will push central banks in the US, the UK, and Eurozone onto an anti-inflation course. This will dampen economic expansion. In the medium term, the unemployment rate will then rise as soon as the special effects of the rise in inflation—namely unexpected reductions in real wage cost increases that bring more jobs in the short term—are dominated by consumption dampening effects and declining investment. Consumption declines result due to households having reduced disposable income in real terms due to inflation. If the US goes into recession, it would be an international impetus for the spread of a recession in OECD countries.

Russia resumed gas supplies to Germany and certain other EU countries in July 2022, which at least temporarily dampens the rise in gas prices or fossil energy prices. In the event of a harsh winter, the high risk remains that half of the households in Germany—that is, those that heat with gas—will be sitting in unintentionally cold homes. For politicians, there is the risk of a kind of "yellow vest" protest movement emerging in Germany and other EU countries, especially since a high inflation rate and very high energy cost bills will negatively affect the majority of households.

The medium-term inflation rate is likely to decline significantly in OECD countries by 2024/2025. In the Eurozone, the resignation of the government of Mario Draghi in Italy in mid-July 2022 represents a disruptive impulse for the stability not just of Italy but also of the Eurozone as a whole. The risk premium for Italian government bonds—compared to German government bonds—has risen in this environment and could present disruptive problems for the European Central Bank and Italy in the medium term. If the ECB buys more Italian bonds, it will come under political pressure from politicians, which will damage the ECB's political independence—and weaken the Italian government's incentive to reduce the high debt ratio (more than twice the 60% ceiling in the Maastricht Treaty). Indirectly, with its decision of July 21, 2022, on a new instrument to prevent inefficiencies in the transmission of monetary policy, the Transmission Protection Instrument (TPI), the ECB is giving questionable stability impulses: possibly to preferentially buy Italian bonds or bonds of another Eurozone country if it deems the rise in interest rates on these bonds to be too high. The ECB's preconditions for the application of the TPI are not very strict. The TPI could—depending on the ECB's application practice—be an impulse for the expansion of populist parties in the EU, which tend to want to significantly increase the debt ratios of states; but this does not correspond to the stability of the Eurozone. This can be seen very critically.

Temporarily, high inflation will dampen the debt ratios of many OECD countries, while these countries—especially in Germany—are quietly increasing the tax ratio via so-called cold progression in progressive income tax (with the main focus on middle and high incomes) without any parliamentary decision. In the environment of the Russo-Ukrainian war, Germany is likely to benefit in real economic terms on the supply side of the economy through high immigration from Ukraine. The burden of large numbers of refugees from Ukraine must be borne jointly in the EU. The Russo-Ukrainian war also threatens to become a heavy burden on the EU in the medium term.

How the war can be stopped is a complicated question. Strong—and valid—emotions aside: The governments of the G20 countries are challenged to bring about a new stable, international balance of powers in Europe and worldwide in the medium term through realpolitik. The West will, if possible, defend prosperity, stability, freedom, democracy, and the rule of law nationally and internationally, and also try to secure the preconditions for a global climate protection policy, initially in the circle of the G20 countries. It would make sense to focus mainly on a globally integrated system of CO_2 emission allowance trading schemes. These systems, which the EU and a few other countries (plus California) have pioneered since 2005, ensure an efficient, secure path to climate neutrality and prevent unnecessary cost burdens that could once again drive up inflation rates and increase the number of poor and hungry people via reduced economic growth in the global economy; in other words, also bring about new conflicts in many regions.

To What Extent Is Russia's Economy Weakened by the West's Sanctions?

A paper on Russia's economic strength by University of Yale authors Sonnenfeld et al. (2022) has received some significant media attention, with the main arguments of the large group of authors, who mainly come from the field of management research (with the exception of one energy economist), being:

- Russia's economy is being very significantly damaged by Western sanctions and the withdrawal of Western multinationals from the country—around 1000 firms by mid-2022; especially as capital and skilled labor (both Western and Russian) is flowing out or leaving Russia in the context of the multinationals' withdrawal, damaging the innovation base.
- The idea of some observers and media outlets and commentators who see only minor negative economic effects in Russia in 2022 is simply wrong; especially since Russia is running a government deficit for the first time in many years, by mid-2022, the stock of foreign exchange reserves had fallen by $70 billion and, finally, monetary and fiscal policies for stabilization are not very effective.

The following points are critical of the Sonnenfeld et al. analysis from July 2022:

1. The share of oil and gas revenues in Russia's state budget is not around 60%, as the authors claim, but 40–45%.
2. It is clear that the withdrawal of Western multinationals has a negative economic impact, but direct investment stocks or subsidiaries with their real capital—physical machinery and equipment—cannot be simply or quickly withdrawn from Russia in real terms for the most part; market values and utilization rates can certainly fall, but in some sectors, they can also recover after Russian modernization efforts and even more so after the end of the war.
3. The expansion of the shadow economy in Russia is not considered at all, which will help to close some supply gaps—and should not be overlooked in an overall assessment of the situation in Russia.
4. Growing levels of corruption in the context of the expanding shadow economy are likely to become an increasing nuisance from the perspective of the wider population: Illegal shadow-economy producers and traders will seek "private legal protection" for their activities outside the official economic system by bribing actors in Russian officialdom.
5. Dysfunctional for a large country like Russia is the disruption of both national and international air traffic, partly due to the consequences of international sanctions and partly due to the dangerous lack of original spare parts for civil aircraft. However, almost all of Russia's aircraft and defense industries will suffer for some years

from the massive shortage of Western high technology –for example, computer chips—which will, however, stimulate Russia's illegal technology imports.

6. Russia is also likely to endure a difficult 2023—with increasing popular discontent (also because of the many fallen in Ukraine)—but hopefully serious peace negotiations will be reached by summer 2023 at the latest. A kind of first test for serious negotiations between Russia and Ukraine is the export agreement for grain from Ukraine agreed in July, the agreement having been brokered by Turkey. The latter has been able to increase its political influence in Europe with this important trade facilitation, which can help prevent a serious world hunger problem.

7. Whether Russia's import statistics are complete and whether or not there is a considerable phenomenon of "private imports" as unregistered imports (errors and omissions) would have to be checked, but the authors do not deal with this.

8. The decline in foreign exchange reserves by \$70–75 billion in 2022 is not a serious problem if a good \$500 billion remains; moreover, the second half of the year could well bring a temporary increase in foreign exchange reserves in the medium term due to rising nominal energy exports—of which, however, only about half is likely to be available due to the freezing of reserves by Western central banks.

9. The fact that in 2022, Russia will have a budget deficit at the central level for the first time in years is not a serious economic shock; there should be sufficient domestic demand from banks, insurance companies, and private households for Russian government bonds.

10. The Sonnenfeld et al. paper (with authors whose area of expertise is management research) is methodologically simply not up to the mark in estimating the real development of GDP in Russia and inadequate in its theoretical foundation; lacking reliable statistics, one would usually take electricity consumption, for example, as a proxy for GDP, but the authors do not do this (for a preliminary estimate using electricity consumption, see Annex S).

11. No DSGE or X-macro model is used, as can be found in the literature of Russian colleagues, among others.

12. Almost no reference is made to relevant economic literature.

Overall, the Sonnenfeld et al. paper on Russia is a methodologically weak contribution, with quite a bit of wishful thinking on the part of the authors. With a real GDP decline of almost 10% (according to the World Bank and IMF) in 2022, Russia is certainly facing a serious economic shock; the 20% expected inflation is less of a problem in the short term, while Russia's population is used to economic lean periods, at least among the older generation, for years during the Soviet Union and then in 1998/1999 in the new Russia under Yeltsin. In 1997/1998, the West did little to help stabilize Russia's economy and prevent or deal with the huge government deficit of close to 20% of GDP—certainly not the International Monetary Fund, which tended to give the wrong advice concerning a fixed exchange rate regime in the run-up to the crisis, thus worsening the scale of the crisis (when Yeltsin, in dire budgetary straits, then sold state-owned enterprises on a large scale in a privatization, which created and benefited the oligarchs, the structural basis for a democracy to thrive in Russia was largely destroyed because, from the perspective of the New Political Economy, the organization of a power quadrangle of president-military-secret service-small group of wealthy individuals controlling large corporations meant an end to the separation of powers and also gave rise to the possibility of the abolition of the rule of law by a Putin-majority Duma became easily possible). Incidentally, one can classify it as surprising—or perhaps not surprising—and misleading that Rüdiger Bachmann, a European-American economist, uncritically tweeted a recommendation of the Yale authors' study on Russia. Finally, it is of course true that the decline in manufacturing activity in Russia compared to the weak recession in the US in the first half of 2022 and a foreseeable recession in the Eurozone in 2023/2024 pose a considerable challenge to Russia's economic policy. If a peace agreement is reached in late 2022 or 2023, however, the Russian economy can also—if the right policy course is set—achieve a significant economic upswing.

One possible outcome of negotiations with Russia could be that Ukraine would end up in a partition situation similar to the division of Germany after 1945. The long-term developments in the future history of Ukraine and Russia are relatively open, although experience shows that authoritarian systems have long-term problems with political legitimacy and economic efficiency—this could then work in Ukraine's favor in the long term.

MULTINATIONAL COMPANIES WITH A VIEW TO RUSSIA

The development of Russia as a location for foreign companies (direct investments of foreign companies in Russia) and of Russia as a source country of direct investments abroad is characterized by occasionally strong fluctuations and some peculiarities. These include, since February 2022, the fact that numerous companies from Europe, North America, and Japan, as well as the Republic of Korea and Australia, have set a course toward the temporary or permanent withdrawal from Russia because of Russia's war of aggression on Ukraine. The 15 largest investors (excluding Cyprus and Bahamas, both of which arguably often stand for "carousel direct investment"—that is, money flowing from Russia, often in the context of tax avoidance or evasion, to these two countries and then from there back to Russia as direct investment) in Table 8.1 show for 2020 that there is significant cumulative direct investment from Europe and the US in Russia. Thus, at the same time, presenting an expropriation potential for Russia's government with regard to investors from European countries and the US.

With the Ukraine war, Russia is facing a tighter sanctions regime from Western countries, Japan, and other countries. In March 2022, many multinational companies from OECD countries have massively restricted or stopped their activities in Russia or even temporarily withdrawn from Russia completely. Russia's government, however, has also threatened to put Western subsidiaries in the country into bankruptcy proceedings if management personnel are withdrawn and activities are temporarily halted, or even to nationalize the assets of foreign investors from certain countries. Such a move is probably to be expected if a Western country or, for example, Japan were to impose an energy import freeze on Russia. If Russia nationalizes the assets of foreign investors, the trust of Western and Japanese investors in Russia's government, built up over 30 years, will be destroyed for many years to come.

The highest direct investment holdings are in the Netherlands, with $97.6 billion (see Table 8.1), although a significant proportion of this is likely to represent investments from other EU countries and possibly also the US and the UK. This is because the Netherlands is regarded as particularly attractive in view of tax avoidance opportunities with these countries, so foreign investors are active in Russia via intermediate investment in a holding company in the Netherlands. The Netherlands is followed by Switzerland with $31.6 billion, as well as France and Germany, followed

Table 8.1   Total net outward FDI stocks of selected OECD economies with Russia as a partner country in 2020

OECD rank	Reporting country	Partner country	Value in million US$
1	Netherlands	Russia	97,577.62
2	Switzerland	Russia	31,560.26
3	**France**	**Russia**	**23,227.39**
4	**Germany**	**Russia**	**19,613.45**
5	**UK**	**Russia**	**15,579.89**
6	Italy	Russia	14,125.82
7	**US**	**Russia**	**12,538.00**
8	Luxembourg	Russia	5770.03
9	Sweden	Russia	5677.74
10	Finland	Russia	2595.41
11	Japan	Russia	2388.82
12	Belgium	Russia	1421.03
13	Denmark	Russia	1330.73
14	Turkey	Russia	914.70
15	Poland	Russia	760.70

Source: Own presentation; data from OECD International Direct Investment Statistics Database

by the UK, Italy, and the US. A similar caveat to the Netherlands also applies to Luxembourg's direct investment holdings in Russia. Sweden, Finland, Japan, Belgium, Denmark, Turkey, and Poland complete the rankings. In the case of France, Germany, and Italy, expropriation by Russia's government could still result in asset losses for Western investors of $23.2 billion, $19.6 billion, and $14.1 billion, respectively. For the UK and the US, as source countries of direct investments in Russia, the losses would amount to $15.6 and $12.1 billion, respectively (the respective Euro amounts are about 1/10 less than the dollar figures). For Poland, almost a billion dollars is likely at stake.

Table 8.2 depicts Russia's direct investment holdings abroad showing the Netherlands in first place, recording $33.5 billion in 2020 (indirect direct investment in other countries via tax-efficient holdings is also likely to play a role). Turkey follows with $7.8 billion, followed by Germany, the US, and Spain with just over four billion dollars each. Then come Finland, Ireland, Latvia, Canada, Czechia, Estonia, Hungary, France, Italy, Lithuania, Japan, and Luxembourg. Curiously, the UK does not provide figures for direct investment stocks from Russia—a plausible order of magnitude is close to the value for the Netherlands.

Table 8.2   Total net inward FDI stocks of selected OECD economies with Russia as a partner country in 2020

OECD rank	Reporting country	Partner country	Value in million US$
1	Netherlands	Russia	33,526.81
2	Turkey	Russia	7757.29
3	Germany	Russia	4429.99
4	US	Russia	4326.00
5	Spain	Russia	4125.66
6	Finland	Russia	1937.66
7	Ireland	Russia	1844.40
8	Latvia	Russia	1838.26
9	Canada	Russia	1382.23
10	Czech Republic	Russia	993.95
11	Estonia	Russia	904.71
12	Hungary	Russia	849.14
13	France	Russia	817.28
14	Italy	Russia	677.45
15	Lithuania	Russia	351.93
21	Japan	Russia	64.93
[25–30]	UK [a]	Russia	0
33	Luxembourg	Russia	-13,313.29

Note: All resident units, immediate investor or immediate host

[a] *Non-publishable and confidential value*

Source: Own presentation; data from OECD International Direct Investment Statistics Database

Presumably, in the context of sanctions imposed by Western countries, Japan, and others, Russia's direct investments in Europe and North America will face major new hurdles in the destination countries in the future. China, as a target country for Russian investors, and Chinese multinationals in Russia are likely to play an increased role in the medium term.

It should be borne in mind that Russia's government has long been skeptical of direct investment from China, seeing prospects for heavy dependence on Chinese investors; mainly also due to fears concerning the long-term demographic problems in Russia's Far East—while there are likely to be informal limits on Chinese investors in Russia anyway (Makarov and Morozkina, 2014); the authors of the study on direct investment to and from Russia point out (p. 61) that the population of the Far East is only 6.2 million (spread over 6.2 million km², which is approximately 36% of Russia's land area), while China's three most north-eastern provinces—total area 810,000 km²—are inhabited by 110 million Chinese. Russia's important resource sector (oil, gas, coal) therefore remained practically closed to investors from China. This is because the investors from China would probably also have brought Chinese workers to Russia in considerable numbers.

Barriers were also erected by Russia in technologically demanding sectors in manufacturing—such as the automotive sector—as it was expected that companies from China could then introduce Chinese technology standards, which would be different to domestic companies with Russian standards and possibly also weaken Russian sectors complementary to such companies; or the supplier or suppliers from China could seek a market monopoly. In 2012, therefore, multinationals from the Asia-Pacific region represented only 1% of direct investment inflows into Russia. That year, however, informal restrictions on direct investment from Asia were lifted, and in 2013, the share of such direct investment increased significantly as the Russian state agreed investment projects primarily with multinationals from Japan and China. In 2014, however, direct investment from Japan decreased significantly as Japan participated in the sanctions imposed by Western countries on Russia, which annexed Crimea from Ukraine that year.

Effects of Reduced Russian Oil and Gas Exports in Russia

The systemic transformation in Russia after 1991 established elements of a market economy in many areas, but there were also considerable market power problems in many sectors, as the privatizations of large state-owned enterprises under President Yeltsin took place with little regard to efficiency and competition policy (Welfens et al., 1999). In the energy sector, Russia also has a large state-owned energy company, Gazprom, which, among other things, also operates important international pipeline networks on its own or in cooperation with others. The energy sector has been modernized since the 1990s, among other things through the participation of Western multinational energy companies in some Russian energy companies, and has remained an essential production and export sector of the Russian economy even after the transformation.

Both embargo measures on the EU's energy imports from Russia and a conceivable Russian supply boycott of gas (or gas and oil) will have effects on Russia's economy and state budget. Questions of a conceivable energy import boycott by Germany and other EU countries can therefore be raised. However, one can hardly argue that the EU is partly responsible for the Ukraine war: Since, after all, one provides Russia with high foreign exchange earnings through EU energy imports from Russia. This view is grossly flawed, as Russia's oil and gas exporters to Eastern and Western Europe will be able to export the oil and gas no longer sold to Europe in other regions of the world; the two-thirds EU oil import embargo adopted in early June 2022 implies that oil prices will increase—an advantage for Russia—and that Russian oil companies will sell more oil to Asia (the members of OPEC will sell less to Asia, but more to the EU; and the temporary oil gap in Asia will then be closed by higher Russian oil exports to Asia, which means that Russia's ability to finance war expenditures will hardly be diminished by the EU oil embargo). International financial market sanctions are more likely to affect Russia economically and lead to a decline in real income in Russia.

Assuming a combined Russian oil and gas export of 12% of Russia's national income (export revenues/gross national income), at first glance an EU energy import boycott—plus boycotts by the US and the UK—could lead to a decline in real national income in Russia of about 6%. However, this would be a double misjudgment:

- The ratio of Russia's energy exports to GDP in purchasing power parities is only about one-third as high as the above ratio based on nominal values. Nominal value-added shares, moreover, only play a role in the significance of the sectoral technical progress rate.
- If Russia could no longer sell oil and gas to Western countries, the relevant Russian companies will try to sell the initially surplus oil and gas volumes to countries in Asia and Africa at a possibly high discount compared to the—in 2022 relatively high—world market price.
- If Germany or the EU were to decide on an oil import boycott against Russia, the economic dampening effects for Russia's economy would be manageable, since surplus quantities could be sold on the world market—the oil market is globally integrated—at a relatively small price discount. Incidentally, Russia's government could respond with a gas export boycott against the EU, which would see countries such as Germany, Italy, Austria, Bulgaria, Poland, and Hungary facing short- and medium-term economic difficulties.

Accordingly, a Western energy import boycott against Russia will cause its real income to fall by around 3–4% in the short term and by 1–2% in the medium term. Instead of the recession of -9% expected in March 2022, Russia would then experience a more severe recession of a circa -12% decline in real income. This would be countered by Russian fiscal policy through an increased government spending program and, in addition, by the Central Bank of Russia through an expansionary monetary policy, so that one can expect a real income decline in the order of about 7–10% for 2022. The vast majority of the Russian population is likely to accept such a drop in income without protest, especially since TV coverage on Russia's main TV channels holds the West responsible for a deteriorating economic situation in Russia. More precise orders of magnitude for the loss of real income in Russia can only be determined with the help of a macroeconomic Russia model or in a three-country Russia-EU*-Asia model (whereby EU* would have to include the UK in addition to the 27 EU countries).

Instead of a complete energy import boycott against Russia, Western countries could also realize the increase of import duties on energy products from Russia. It is not plausible that an energy import boycott could significantly affect the financing of the state budget and thus indirectly weaken Russia's financial ability to wage war in the long term; even if, of course, adjustment problems will arise in Russia's state financing. However, the starting point for the 2021 state budget has been a budget surplus, and Russia's government could also use a special fund, co-funded by energy revenues, for defense financing for some years.

The real income decline in Ukraine could be -30% in 2022 due to the war. However, the main burden on Ukraine will be the human suffering and death and destruction caused by Russia's invasion of the country. It should be noted that in 2014—when Russia annexed Crimea—Ukraine's real income fell by 10.1% and then again by 9.8% the following year (World Bank/WDI, 2022). For 2022, the IMF (2022b) expects a 35% decline in real income for Ukraine.

The Electricity Price Shock: How to Cope with Russia's Gas Cuts in Europe

There is no easy way for the EU countries—or the UK—to cope with the declining Russian gas deliveries in the summer and early autumn of 2022: The gas price has been strongly increasing and, along with the gas price, the price of electricity has massively increased (gas price hikes were not only observed in the spot markets but also in future markets for 2023 which should be a rough indicator of future spot prices). This, in turn, reduces the profitability of many firms and will lead to an aggregate output decline. The electricity price is determined by the intersection of the demand curve and the supply curve; the latter consists—in a price-quantity diagram—of the first part of the supply curve, namely power offered at a low variable cost, which typically is nuclear power (at least in EU countries and the UK as long as liability insurance is as low as it is; for example, €2.5 billion for a nuclear power plant while the damage of the Fukushima nuclear accident brought costs of about €200 billion); the next sections of the supply curve will reflect renewable energies and then coal-fired power stations, followed by a rather steep part of the electricity supply curve, which reflects gas-fired power stations. The latter are quite flexible and can be started within minutes so that peak hours of high demand are typically characterized in this merit-order supply model by gas-fired power stations determining the electricity equilibrium price. The various types of power stations make their respective offers for an hour X, say 7 a.m. to 8 a.m. the next day.

With the Russo-Ukrainian war and the cuts of Russian gas supplies to several EU countries in summer 2002 and September—and more cuts expected for the autumn 2022 and into 2023—there is an enormous upward movement of gas spot and gas forward prices. For those hours of electricity production where gas is the marginal supply element (with a "normal" profit element for gas-fired power stations but with very high supply prices for other types of power generation), there will be rather large profits for most electricity producers, such as nuclear power, renewable energies, and coal; but those "excess profits" do not reflect monopoly power on the part of these types of power generation. Rather the steep part of the supply curve shaped by gas-fired power stations determines the electricity price so that further Russian gas export cuts drive up the gas price and thereby the electricity price—read: marginal production costs—in industrial firms and service firms in the EU countries and the UK so that cuts in electricity-intensive production will occur and hence in aggregate output (as all sectors use electricity for value-added and production, respectively). At the same time, gas price increases and electricity price increases will raise the inflation rate in the short and medium term.

The best way to cope with these problems would be to regulate electricity production in the following way—while competition authorities and regulators keep a critical eye on potential strategic supply cuts of big nuclear power firms or big coal-fired power stations, which might consider strategically cutting their own respective supply in order to make sure that gas-fired power stations are the marginal suppliers in the electricity market, which, in turn, will bring higher profits for nuclear power plants as well as coal-fired power stations (plus power stations using renewable energy):

- Government should give additional incentives to improve demand management policy in the electricity sector where more firms could sign contracts that suppliers of electricity are allowed to cut supply of electricity by a certain percentage in x hours of the day—with some pre-notification—whereby those firms would then benefit from an extra rebate on the standard industrial electricity price. This measure, designed to reduce demand during peak hours, should help to bring down the percentage of electricity generated by gas and therefore more gas would be available in households and for industry or the services sector or government.

- Secondly, government should put a price cap on gas used for power generation and reimburse gas-fired power stations for the difference of the gas market price and the gas price cap. This amounts to a subsidy for gas and would indeed increase the use of gas in the electricity sector somewhat, but the economically decisive impact would be the reduction of the electricity price, which benefits both aggregate output and employment—and contributes therefore to higher government revenues (or, in the event of a less intense recession, to a smaller reduction of the fall of government revenue than in the business-as-usual case) and also reduces the electricity bill for households. A subsidy scheme as proposed here would be particularly useful for poorer households and many small and medium enterprises and the approach would also be welfare-enhancing to the extent that real gross domestic product would increase compared to the business-as-usual case. To some extent—within an agreement of the two countries with the European Commission—such an approach has already been adopted by Portugal and Spain in summer 2022 (with an initial €40/KWh electricity cap at the beginning, followed by monthly increases of €5/KWh in Spain so that €70/KWh would be reached by end of 2022). A similar approach indeed should be adopted by all EU countries and the UK. If all EU countries would adopt a similar transitory deviation from the traditional merit-order approach in the electricity sector, economic distortions in the EU single market would be minimized.

The twin-pronged approach proposed here would be quite useful for Europe for as long as the international supply of gas is being distorted by the arbitrary cuts to Russia's gas supply.

LITERATURE

Bachmann, R. et al. (2022). What If? The Economic Effects for Germany of a Stop of Energy Imports from Russia, ECONtribute Policy Brief Nr. 028. Retrieved May 24, 2022, from https://www.econtribute.de/RePEc/ajk/ajkpbs/ECONtribute_PB_028_2022.pdf.

Bank of Finland. (2022). War in Ukraine will slow Finland's GDP growth and increase inflation, Helsinki. Retrieved April 6, 2022, from https://www.bof-bulletin.fi/en/war-in-ukraine-will-slow-finland-s-gdp-growth-and-increase-inflation.

ECB. (2022). Monetary Policy Decisions, Press Release, published 9th June 2022. Retrieved June 15, 2022, from https://www.ecb.europa.eu/press/pr/date/2022/html/ecb.mp220609~122666c272.en.html

Froot, K., & Stein, J. (1991). Exchange Rates and Foreign Direct Investments. *Quarterly Journal of Economics, 1*, 1191–1217. https://doi.org/10.2307/2937961

IMF. (2022a). IMF Staff Statement on the Economic Impact of War in Ukraine, International Monetary Fund, Washington DC. Retrieved March 30, 2022, from https://www.imf.org/en/News/Articles/2022/03/05/pr2261-imf-staff-statement-on-the-economic-impact-of-war-in-ukraine

IMF. (2022b). UkraineAt A Glance, International Monetary Fund, Washington DC. Retrieved June 22, 2022, from https://www.imf.org/en/Countries/UKR#ataglance

Klein, M. (2022). The End of the New Silk Road? *Wirtschaftsdienst, 102*(3), 157. https://doi.org/10.1007/s10273-022-3142-3

Makarov, I., & Morozkina, A. (2014). Regional Dimension of Foreign Direct Investment in Russia, Discussion Paper No. 3, Higher School of Economics, Moscow/Economic Policy Forum (EPF), Berlin.

Roeger, W., & Welfens, P. J. J. (2021). Foreign Direct Investment and Innovations: Transmission Dynamics of Persistent Demand and Technology Shocks in a Macro Model, EIIW Discussion Paper No. 300 https://eiiw.wiwi.uni-wuppertal.de/fileadmin/eiiw/Daten/Publikationen/Gelbe_Reihe/disbei300.pdf

Roeger, W., & Welfens, P. J. J. (2022). The Macroeconomic Effects of Import Tariffs in a Model with Multinational Firms and Foreign Direct Investment. *International Economics and Economic Policy, 19*(2), 1. https://doi.org/10.1007/s10368-022-00538-5

Sonnenfeld, J. et al. (2022). Business Retreats and Sanctions Are Crippling the Russian Economy, August 2022 update. Retrieved August 18, 2022, from https://papers.ssrn.com/sol3/papers.cfm?abstract_id=4167193

Welfens, P. J. J., Gloede, K., Strohe, H. G., & Wagner, D. (1999). *System Transformation in Germany and Russia. Experiences, Economic Perspectives and Policy Options.* Springer. https://doi.org/10.1007/978-3-662-13075-9

World Bank/WDI. (2022). GDP per capita, PPP, Current International $, Russia Federation and Ukraine, World Development Indicators Database. Retrieved May 24, 2022, from https://data.worldbank.org/indicator/NY.GDP.PCAP.PP.CD?locations=RU-UA

Ukrainian Refugees and Ukrainian Guest Workers in EU Countries and Their Effects on Ukraine and the EU

By the end of summer 2022, one can assume that there are up to three million Ukrainian refugees in Poland and about 500,000 Ukrainian refugees in Germany. The number of Ukrainians in Poland thus reached almost 10% of the population. At the same time, there was a great willingness on the part of private persons to help refugees from Ukraine in Poland, Germany, and many other countries in the first half of 2022. The UN Refugee Agency (UNHCR, 2022) calculated in the first half of March that already about five million people were fleeing their homes in Ukraine in 2022, which underestimates the actual number—because by March 18, the number of Ukrainian refugees had already reached about four million. The main countries of refuge were Poland (No. 1 with over 2 million), Romania, Moldova, and Hungary, which corresponded to Ukraine's western neighbors (see Table 9.1); then came the Slovakia, Russia, and Belarus. The 185,000 refugees from Ukraine listed for Russia probably originated from the Donbas region of Ukraine. In Germany, there were estimates of 250,000 Ukraine refugees at the end of March. Germany had initially not implemented official refugee registration, so there is little accurate data for February and March 2022. The flow of refugees toward the EU is likely to continue for as long as the war lasts.

The UK's involvement in taking in refugees from Ukraine is strangely below expectations. On the other hand, the UK's military support for Ukraine is probably relatively high. The fact the co-leader of the center-left SPD party in Germany suddenly announced German political

Table 9.1   Refugee movements from Ukraine, as of March 30, 2022 (total influx from Ukraine in neighboring countries)

Country	Source	Date of data	Population
Poland	Government	March 29, 2022	2,336,799
Romania	Government	March 29, 2022	608,936
Republic of Moldova	Government	March 29, 2022	387,151
Hungary	Government	March 29, 2022	364,804
Russian Federation	Government	March 29, 2022	350,632
Slovakia	Government	March 29, 2022	281,172
Belarus	Government	March 29, 2022	10,902

Note: Accumulated data in this table is higher than the total number of refugees fleeing Ukraine as it also takes into account people crossing the border between Romania and Moldova

Source: Own representation using data available from the UNHCR (2022; as of March 30)

international leadership claims as something of a novelty at the end of June 2022 can be noted with some astonishment. Germany does not have much more than the economic basis for a certain international co-leadership, the looming shadow of two world wars is a historical burden that will hardly be easily pushed aside and there is a visible lack of useful concepts and a necessary overall anchoring in the EU. Germany can have no interest in contributing to a return of the world economy to the regime of great powers as in the late nineteenth century. It is remarkable that the SPD, of all parties, is turning the tide politically with Chancellor Scholz's announcement of a €100 billion special package that will significantly strengthen Germany's defense. Presumably, positive economic effects will take effect here in the medium term, even if high imports of military equipment from the US are likely to dampen the economic multiplier effect to a certain degree. Since the Russo-Ukrainian shock will have a partially symmetrical negative economic impact on the EU countries as a whole (with differences in national fossil fuel import intensities and, of course, differences in trade impulses from Ukraine and Russia due to economic geography), it would be appropriate for the EU countries to temporarily coordinate their economic policies more closely. Germany should raise its national deficit limit from 0.35% to 0.5%, as the 0.35% was anchored unnecessarily tightly in the constitution as Germany's stability guide during the Euro Crisis; at 1.5% trend growth, a government trend deficit ratio of 0.35% of GDP amounts (in accordance with the Domar rule) to a long-term government debt ratio of 0.23%—this is obviously outlandishly low and will even then worsen the average long-term rating for the Eurozone as a whole because of an insufficient German weight in AAA bonds among total government bonds in the Eurozone: with the consequence of an increased real interest rate in the Eurozone and a reduced investment ratio, in which Germany can have no economic interest whatsoever (the proposed upper limit of 0.5% in the government deficit ratio would also bring a debt ratio of only 0.33% in the long run; if the trend growth rate falls to 1%, the long-term government debt ratio would be 0.5%, still well away from the 60% debt ratio limit of the Eurozone and EU, respectively). Intensified cooperation between Germany and France in particular would be particularly useful here, but also in the field of foreign policy and possibly also in immigration and refugee issues. In this context, it is important to anchor the strong EU cohesion, which emerged in 2022, over a longer period of time.

As far as the situation of Ukrainian refugees in the EU is concerned, they do not need to go through an individual asylum procedure in order to obtain a humanitarian residence permit, as for the first time, EU Interior Ministers on March 4, 2022, decided to approve the application of the so-called Temporary Protection Directive. Ukrainian refugees are thus granted temporary EU-wide access to medical services, work, education, and social benefits. By the end of March, the EU failed to reach agreement on national registration procedures in EU countries, citing, among other things, incompatible IT systems in those countries.

Due to the Russian war of aggression on Ukraine, there will be a large movement of people, which should then also strengthen the labor market on the supply side in the destination countries in the medium term. Since men of military age are being held back at Ukraine's borders, the international flight movement from Ukraine will initially be primarily women and children seeking to reach the EU or Western Europe—and also the US and Canada. The UNHCR projected up to 10 million Ukrainian refugees at the end of March 2022. This would be a 50% increase in global refugee numbers compared to 2017: at that time, 0.26% of the world's population were recorded as refugees, a relative decrease from 0.33% in 1990 (EBRD, 2018).

The special aspects of refugee movements can only be very briefly highlighted here, although reference can be made to some extent to the movement of people fleeing from Syria, among other countries, to the EU and especially to Germany in 2015/2016—at that time, however, the proportion of men among the refugees was initially relatively high. A small subset of refugees also came to Germany via so-called resettlement programs; authorities from Germany select refugees with high vulnerability and good integration prospects and prerequisites in a special procedure abroad (Welfens, 2021). During a visit to Moldova in March 2022, Germany's foreign minister, Annalena Baerbock, pledged that Germany would take over some of the 80,000 refugees from Ukraine in Moldova. Presumably, this will be done in a similar way to the usual resettlement procedure. Since Moldova had 2.6 million inhabitants in 2021 and will probably have 260,000 Ukrainian refugees in the country at the end of March 2022, in terms of refugees per inhabitant, this is like having 8.3 million Ukrainian refugees in Germany.

In the following, it is assumed that a significant share of Ukrainian refugees in EU countries will find their way onto the labor markets of the respective Western host countries in the longer term. A US study comparing the labor market integration of immigrants and refugees found that in the short term, the labor volume and also hourly wages of working refugees were lower than those of immigrants, but that in the long term, labor force participation and also hourly wages were higher than those of immigrants (Cortes, 2004).

As far as the effects of immigration and refugees on source and destination countries are concerned, economic migration analysis offers important insights. There is permanent emigration and circular emigration. The latter means that the guest workers return to the sending countries after some time; however, circular immigration is not a main focus in the following analysis. From the perspective of migration analysis, remittances from guest workers (or emigrants) in many sending countries represent substantial foreign exchange inflows from abroad. According to World Bank data, remittances represented over 10% relative to GDP in 29 countries around the world in 2019; this included seven EU Neighborhood Countries (broadly defined): Armenia, Georgia, Jordan, Lebanon, Moldova, Palestine, and Ukraine. Such remittances are positive for recipient households in sending countries, as disposable income is increased; there is also a kind of insurance protection, provided that these remittances are relatively high during periods of recession and crisis in sending countries. The economic importance of these remittances in relatively poor countries is further enhanced by the fact that the prices of non-tradable goods are relatively low by international standards; thus, a positive purchasing power effect in the recipient country of the remittances may need to be considered (Kapur & McHale, 2012).

Whether remittances have a positive impact on economic growth depends largely on the extent to which receiving households use them to finance consumption or investment. There are some findings suggesting that consumption and real estate financing play an important role (Chami et al., 2008). However, an econometric analysis by the International Monetary Fund (IMF, 2016) shows that, especially in countries with financing constraints for enterprises, remittances led to increased private sector investment.

By strengthening the disposable incomes of family members in the home country, remittances from migrant workers increase aggregate demand, which is allocated to non-tradable goods or many services on the one hand and to imported goods on the other. The latter leads to a deterioration of the balance of payments and therefore, with flexible exchange rates, to a depreciation; however, the execution of the initial international remittances leads to a real currency appreciation. This leads to a "Dutch disease" effect associated with increased demand for imports and reduced domestic exports, and further, slower technical progress. As a rule, the increase in aggregate demand on goods markets caused by international remittances also raises the domestic price level; the appreciation of the currency, however, makes the import of goods cheaper.

When there are substantial international remittances, they can contribute to dampening business cycles (Temprano Arroyo, 2019): Namely, when these remittances are higher in recessionary years than in economic boom years; sustained international remittances can also support better financial system development in the recipient country. Educational improvement and improved population health in recipient countries are also observable.

Moreover, remittances lead to real currency appreciation, which dampens the recipient country's net exports and thus its economic development in the medium term. Moreover, moral hazard problems arise, as the behavior of people in recipient countries may change adversely. According to the IMF (2016), a one percentage point increase in the international remittance ratio—the ratio of remittances received to the gross domestic product of the recipient country—led to a 4% real currency appreciation. This, in turn, dampens export sector growth. According to the IMF study, remittances increase the financial mobility of recipient households, which lowers the labor force participation rate and raises the "reservation wage"—the lower bound on the wage level above which an individual will offer work. In addition, there is also a moral hazard problem in that risky investment projects are more often selected in the recipient country and less is invested in existing investment projects, leading to increased differences in investment returns on the one hand, but also to increased variability in economic development on the other (see Chami et al., 2008).

Finally, it should also be borne in mind that emigration—including refugee flows—leads to a shortage of labor supply, which causes real wages to rise. A particular problem, however, is the emigration of skilled workers, which leads to a dampening effect on growth in the sending country, namely for low-skilled workers.

Emigration and flight abroad (internal refugees are a conceivable special problem) have a negative impact on state finances, since previous tax payments and social contributions are eliminated. Insofar as emigrant or refugee groups tend to relate to the younger strata of the population, the average age of the working population also deteriorates. This can lead to a slowdown in growth. To the extent that skilled workers leave the country, the growth rate of technological progress is also likely to decrease (Docquier, 2014). An analysis by the IMF (2016) showed that the growth rate of progress in Eastern European countries would have been about 2.5 percentage points higher had it not been for the outflow of skilled workers in 1995–2012. It is conceivable, moreover, that emigration provides incentives to gain better skills in sending countries (Docquier & Rapoport, 2012). The sending country can gain economically if the share of well-educated people increases and at the same time the probability of emigration is below 15–20%—then there is no critical "brain drain", that is, a loss of knowledge in society or the economy.

In the face of falling information and transportation costs, temporary or permanent emigration can cause unemployment rates to fall in sending countries, while at the same time labor shortages fall and output rises in countries with surplus demand in the labor market—demand from firms is greater than supply from domestic households (Zimmermann, 2014). Temporary migration is accompanied by problems concerning low-skilled immigrant groups who can exercise fewer rights and face worse working conditions than migrant groups who settle permanently in their host countries (European Commission, 2011; Zimmermann, 2014). The literature cited in the study by Kone and Özden (2017), moreover, shows a positive correlation between immigration and US direct investment abroad, provided that the immigrant groups represent the well-skilled: US companies will then invest more in the corresponding sending countries.

As for emigration from Ukraine before 2014, Russia was the most important destination country in the period before that, with a 43% share in Ukrainian emigration, which was estimated at about 2.5 million before the Russo-Ukrainian war. In 2017, Poland became the most popular destination country, with a share value of 39%, while Russia still stood for 26%; in addition to Poland and Russia, Italy, Czechia, Spain, Portugal, Hungary, and Germany can be considered as destination countries in 2017 (Pienkowski, 2020, pp. 11–12); in this regard, emigration toward the US is predominantly characterized by qualified people, while migration toward EU countries is characterized by workers with low and medium qualifications. As a rule, men predominate in emigration (70%); only in the case of Italy do women represent the numerically dominant group (71%).

With large refugee movements from Ukraine expected in spring 2022 in the wake of Russia's war of aggression, EU countries, as well as arguably the UK and the US, are key destination countries. By mid-March, Poland was the No. 1 destination country, with the population originating from Ukraine increasing to three million, more than doubling. Moldova, the Slovak Republic, Hungary, as well as the Czechia and Germany, were important destination countries, far behind Poland. A refugee movement is not the same as immigration, but in the medium term—over the course of a few years—refugee groups will behave partly, and probably mostly, like immigrants.

As for the economic effects in the immigrant destination countries, it is interesting to look at the effects of Ukrainian immigration before 2022. Here, a study by colleagues at the National Bank of Poland is of particular interest. Ukrainian guest workers in Poland represent just over 10% of economic growth in 2013–2018—with 1.4 million Ukrainians in Poland; this is a lower bound estimate, as the study by colleagues at the National Bank of Poland (Strzelecki et al., 2022) actually did not include a portion of working Ukrainians in the study: firstly, those who worked in Poland under short-term six- to nine-month visas and, secondly, those working in the shadow economy. Immigration from Ukraine in isolation had an annual growth effect of 0.5% in 2013–2018.

The main target countries of war refugees from Ukraine will benefit in the medium and long term from positive growth effects in the course of the integration of refugees into the respective national labor markets. Eastern European EU countries will therefore benefit disproportionately economically speaking, and to a certain extent also Germany and Italy.

Whether these refugees can actually contribute to economic convergence within the EU remains to be seen. For the countries receiving the refugees, costs will arise initially, in the first year, although a positive macroeconomic demand effect can also be expected here. It is up to the EU and the EU countries to sensibly try to influence the large refugee movements in accordance with the absorption capacity of countries and to temporarily help the main target countries financially.

If we assume three million refugees in Poland and one million refugees each in Germany, France, and Italy, then—assuming €1000 per person per week in necessary maintenance and accommodation costs—total economic demand in these three countries increases by €52 billion each within one year. For Germany, this amounts to 1.3% of national income, and for France and Italy, a good 1.5% of national income each. In Poland, maintenance and accommodation costs can be set at about half the amount as in the three largest Western European EU countries, so that in Poland national income increases by €78 billion within one year. This additional demand will strengthen aggregate demand in EU countries, whose post-corona recovery forces will thus be consolidated. In the process, the government budget deficit ratio will increase significantly on a one-off basis: In the EU as a whole by around 1% of national income.

In the second year of residence, some of the refugees will return to Ukraine, provided that peace and good reconstruction conditions prevail there. However, a significant proportion of Ukrainian refugees are likely to remain in the EU, with married women usually pushing for family reunification with their husbands. It could therefore amount to about six million refugees in the EU in the medium term after the Ukraine war, of whom just under half are likely to be able and willing to work. The labor force potential in the EU is rising; relatively quickly in Poland, where Ukrainian refugees are not expected to pose a major language comprehension problem—the same applies to the Czechia as a target country. In Germany, France, and Italy, the potential labor force is likely to rise rather slowly over time, since in many sectors refugees must first acquire sufficient language skills by attending language courses before taking up employment.

It cannot be ruled out that very strong refugee flows toward EU countries in some member states of the EU will lead to a strengthening of radical right-wing parties in particular. Here, a destabilization of Western democracies may occur as a consequence of the Russo-Ukrainian war. The economic costs of the war for Europe, including Russia, and the world economy as a whole depend on the outcome of the war in Ukraine and the duration of the armed conflict. From the perspective of the Western countries, it looks as if Russia under Putin has ultimately destroyed much of the world order that was in place after 1991. What Russia has built up over 30 years in terms of trust in many Western countries, Japan, and elsewhere has largely been lost with the war of aggression against Ukraine. It is obvious that the economic costs of the war are also quite considerable for Russia in the short term. The country is likely to fall into its worst recession since 1991. The official figures on Russia's gross domestic product will be sought to be corroborated by looking at supplementary statistics and analyses.

The West and its allies will have to discuss many important economic and political issues with China again in the future. One of the unacceptable points from the Western point of view is China's censorship of the speech at the opening ceremony of the Beijing Paralympics in March 2022: on Chinese television, some sentences were simply not translated—especially those that referred to the importance of peace.

It may be difficult for the West to quickly persuade Russia under President Putin to reach a diplomatic resolution to the Ukraine war. If China's support for Russia's political position on the Ukraine war can be significantly weakened, however, Russia's president could come under significant pressure to adapt. It seems unlikely that the West will be able to restore good economic and political relations with Putin in the longer term. If Western investors perceive China's behavior in the Ukraine conflict as being clearly pro-Russia, economic relations between the West and China will weaken considerably, as quite a few investors will view China from a political perspective in a similar way to Russia (and its war against Ukraine): In the long term, it will probably not be possible to expect more direct investment in Russia. The world economy could move toward a new Cold War, with China included. The international economic order could disintegrate as important organizations—such as the World Trade Organization—weaken.

The global economy faces an economic slowdown and higher inflation rates in 2022 and 2023 and could face a disintegration into regional blocs and a reduced effectiveness of key international economic organizations in international economic conflicts, which would dampen growth. The weakening of the international legal order should be counteracted on the part of the OECD countries, and the role of international organizations to safeguard free trade and globalization should rather be strengthened. The

US, the EU, the UK, and other countries will probably also face special challenges in helping poor developing countries, which are likely to face serious new hunger-related problems in the medium term with massively increased grain prices.

Incidentally, one result of the weakened global legal order and Russia's war of aggression against Ukraine is that the EU countries and Norway will significantly increase their respective defense spending in the medium term. As far as the purchase of military jets is concerned, the US is likely to be the main supplier country and thus experience an improvement in its trade balance as well as a medium-term appreciation of the dollar. It cannot be ruled out that the world economy will slide into a new Cold War, with the Western countries and Japan plus the Republic of Korea pitted against an autocratic Russia. China's positioning in this regard is not clear for the time being. From the German side, sales in China are 16 times higher than those of German companies in Russia, and conversely, China's exports to the US and the EU are much higher than its exports to Russia. Economic interests could encourage China to give greater weight to its relations with the EU, at least in the medium and long term.

EU countries will probably become more united politically and militarily in the medium term—without significant military contributions from the neutral member countries Ireland, Sweden, and Austria. There is no doubt that the EU, the UK, and the US, as well as other countries, will help in the reconstruction of Ukraine after the end of the war and the withdrawal of the Russian troops. A strengthening of the role of renewable energies, which is necessary from a climate policy point of view in any case, will arise in the context of the Russo-Ukrainian war in many EU countries, as well as a broader diversification in international energy purchasing. Germany can play a leading role in Europe in this respect. If the political situation in Russia improves sufficiently, the restoration of intensive trade relations with Russia can also be envisaged—an option for Western policy that will probably only emerge in the long term.

LITERATURE

Chami, R., et al. (2008). *Macroeconomic consequences of remittances.* International Monetary Fund, Occasional Paper 259, Washington, DC. https://www.imf.org/external/pubs/ft/op/259/op259.pdf

Cortes, K. E. (2004). Are refugees different from economic immigrants? Some empirical evidence on the heterogeneity of immigrant groups in the United

States? *The Review of Economics and Statistics*, *86*, 465–480. https://doi. org/10.1162/003465304323031058

Docquier, F. (2014). *The brain drain from developing countries*. IZA World of Labor: 31. Retrieved March 3, 2022, from https://doi.org/10.15185/ izawol.31

Docquier, F., & Rapoport, H. (2012). Globalization, brain drain, and development. *Journal of Economic Literature*, *50*(3), 681–730. https://doi. org/10.1257/jel.50.3.681

EBRD. (2018). *Transition report 2018–19, work in transition*. London. Retrieved March 3, 2022, from https://www.ebrd.com/documents/oce/transition-report-201819-work-in-transition.pdf

European Commission. (2011). Temporary and circular migration: Empirical evidence, current policy practice and future options in EU Member States, Publications Office, Directorate-General for Migration and Home Affairs. Retrieved March 3, 2022, from https://doi.org/10.2837/67921

IMF. (2016). *Emigration and its economic impact on Eastern Europe*. IMF Staff Discussion Note 16/07.

Kapur, D., & McHale, J. (2012). Economic effects of emigration on sending countries. In M. Rosenblum & D. J. Tichenor (Eds.), *Oxford handbook of the politics of international migration* (pp. 131–147). https://doi.org/10.1093/ oxfordhb/9780195337228.013.0006

Kone, Z.L., & Özden, Ç. (2017). *Brain drain, gain and circulation*. KNOMAD Working Paper 19. Retrieved March 3, 2022, from https://www.knomad. org/sites/default/files/2017-04/KNOMAD%20WP19_Brain%20Drain%20 gain%20and%20circulation.pdf

Pienkowski, J. (2020). *The impact of labor migration on the Ukrainian economy*. DG EFIN Discussion Paper 123, EU, Brussels. https://doi. org/10.2765/450169

Strzelecki, P., Growiec, J., & Wyszynski, R. (2022). The contribution of immigration from Ukraine to economic growth in Poland. *Review of World Economics*, *158*, 365–399. https://doi.org/10.1007/s10290-021-00437-y

Temprano Arroyo, H. (2019). *Using EU aid to address the root causes of migration and refugee flows*. European University Institute. Retrieved March 3, 2022, from https://cadmus.eui.eu/bitstream/handle/1814/61108/EUaidMI gration_2019.pdf

UNHCR. (2022). Operational data portal. Ukraine refugee situation. Retrieved March 3, 2022, from https://data2.unhcr.org/en/situations/ukraine

Welfens, N. (2021). *Categories on the move. Governing refugees in transnational admission programs to Germany*. Ipskamp Printing.

Zimmermann, K. (2014). *Circular migration*. IZA World of Labor. Retrieved March 3, 2022, from https://doi.org/10.15185/izawol.1

CHAPTER 10

Key Ukraine-related Emigration Aspects and EU Enlargement Risks with Ukraine

Relations between Ukraine and the EU have been multifaceted ever since Ukraine emerged as an independent state in 1991 following the collapse of the Soviet Union—in a referendum on December 1, 1991, 90.3% of valid votes were in favor of independence. Ukraine, of course, had to regulate its relations with Russia in particular, but also with neighboring Eastern European countries and with the EU as a bloc, which in turn considered Ukraine an element of the EU's neighborhood policy. From relatively early on, there were Ukrainian guest workers who found work in Poland and other Eastern European EU countries. Since the Russian invasion in February 2022, there has been a great willingness in EU countries to allow immigration from Ukraine and to rapidly integrate refugees into the respective labor markets. At the same time, there is also broad political support in European Union countries to admit Ukraine to the EU; however, policymakers must proceed with caution—significant challenges and problems could arise in relation to migration and possible accession.

The 1922 Treaty on the Creation of the Union of Soviet Socialist Republics was abrogated by the Ukraine's parliament on December 5, 1991, and three days later the leadership of Ukraine together with that of Russia and Belarus agreed to establish the Commonwealth of Independent States (CIS). The recognition of the newly independent Ukraine by the new Russian Federation took place on December 2, 1991, with its borders with Russia firmly established in a Russian-Ukrainian Friendship Treaty in 1997. Further treaties and agreements also regulated the status of the city

© The Author(s), under exclusive license to Springer Nature Switzerland AG 2022
P. J. J. Welfens, *Russia's Invasion of Ukraine*,
https://doi.org/10.1007/978-3-031-19138-1_10

of Sevastopol in Crimea—and Ukraine's sovereignty over it—while at the same time, a guarantee was made that Russia would be granted the right to use a naval port there for at least two decades. The treaty had an initial term of one decade and, in the absence of termination, was automatically extended for ten additional years at a time.

Ukrainian attempts to conclude a free trade agreement with the EU initially led to political conflict among the country's leadership in November and December 2013, as it appeared that Russia was massively opposed to such a Ukraine-EU link. On November 21, President Viktor Yanukovych refused to sign the finalized association agreement with the EU which sparked the Maidan riots in late 2013. Ukraine's then president ultimately fled to Russia—but only following massive protests in Kyiv and violent clashes between police plus military units and protesters. In the run-up, Ukraine's parliament had restricted freedom of expression and assembly with very harsh laws. Protesters in the Ukrainian capital's Maidan Square set fire to barricades, and violent clashes broke out on the Maidan in February 2014, leaving up to 100 people dead. No sooner had Yanukovych fled to Russia, than the Russian occupation of Crimea began in February 2014 (in part by troops without insignia or any national markers), which had only been part of the Ukrainian Soviet Republic since 1954. Then, beginning in 2014, a civil war of sorts also erupted in parts of the Donbas region—with a predominantly Russian-speaking population—between pro-Russian local forces and the central government of Ukraine, with Russia providing military support to insurgent groups in the Donbas, near the border with Russia. Despite numerous attempts no real lasting cease-fire could be reached in the period from 2014 to 2022.

Even before the Russo-Ukrainian war, there was a significant level of emigration of Ukrainian male and female workers; migrating workers primarily went to Russia, Poland, and some other countries. Among the important findings is the analysis by Commander et al. (2013), based on a survey in Ukraine: Among emigrants, the well-educated and younger workers are over-represented. However, this is only partially reflected in the jobs they take up abroad; half of the emigrant group find themselves in jobs for which they are overqualified. This downskilling problem is due, among other reasons, to the fact that in Ukraine there is little correlation between qualification and job quality. Workers who experience downskilling in Ukraine will typically also experience it when emigrating in the destination countries. Such problems are comparatively strong in the EU when comparing the EU and other emigration destination countries.

Immigration to EU countries can change the demographics of individual member states in important ways; this also applies to refugee flows in the medium term, provided refugees integrate into the labor market and acquire the nationality of the host country. Among other things, population figures play an important role in weighted votes at the European Council—except in the areas of taxation and foreign policy, where the unanimity principle applies. At the European Council, weighted voting requires at least 55% of countries to be represented in the majority coalition, representing 65% of the EU's population. A conceivable eastward enlargement of the EU to include Ukraine would change the relative power positions, provided that the Banzhaf Index (or the Shapley value) is used to determine them. In the case of a an enlargement of the EU to include Ukraine, the corresponding figures were first calculated by Kirsch (2022), who shows that such an enlargement reduces the power of the large—existing EU countries—while the relative power position of the smaller countries increases (the Banzhaf Index is based on the proportion of conceivable losing coalitions that achieve a minimum majority of votes—according to the majority requirement—through the accession of a member country M). As for the longer-term emigration dynamics of Ukraine, Poland, and Germany, among others, will be able to increase their populations through immigration from Ukraine, with initial refugee flows in the context of the Russo-Ukrainian war likely to become immigration flows in the longer term.

One particularly important focus for analysis are potential emigration flows from Ukraine in the event that it indeed becomes an EU member country (see, e.g., Fertig & Kahanec, 2015). The two authors determine the migration potential toward the EU from their Eastern European neighbors plus Croatia: They conduct an analysis—an out-of-sample forecast—to estimate emigration potentials after the first EU enlargement round in Eastern Europe. The analysis illustrates that emigration numbers are determined by both migration costs and economic circumstances; the largest effects result from policy variables. After an initial increase in emigration—which is slightly higher with migration liberalization than without—emigration figures in the EU's Eastern European neighboring countries develop toward a long-term equilibrium. Ukraine is expected to have the highest emigration figures in absolute terms, while the highest immigration figures from the neighboring Eastern European EU countries are found in the simulation analysis for Germany, Italy, and Austria.

Relative to the population, the immigration intensities are highest in Ireland, Denmark, Finland, and Austria.

Even if one has to modify the Fertig-Kahanec analysis due to later the implementation of BREXIT—on January 1, 2021—valuable insights from the analysis remain:

- The integration of Ukrainian refugees or guest workers into EU societies and labor markets will not be an easy process—with the possible exceptions of Poland and some other Eastern European EU countries.
- There is a risk that large numbers of immigrants from Ukraine could focus on relatively few EU destination countries, which could politically destabilize some of these countries: the specter of another BREXIT case then looms.
- The EU's inclination to learn from previous mistakes and important political failures—such as the BREXIT—is noticeably low; it therefore seems implausible that a sensible political reform package will be adopted or implemented in the EU before Ukraine's accession.

Of course, the refugee flows from 2022 only partly follow normal emigration preferences; potential emigrants under normal circumstances are a random subset of the refugees. This does not exclude that in the medium term a share of the refugees may decide to work as guest workers in certain EU countries. Due to the close affinity between the Ukrainians and Polish, Poland is likely to be a preferred destination for many refugees. The economic logic of the so-called gravity equation suggests that refugees and emigrant groups from Ukraine will initially have a certain preference for countries a relatively short distance from Ukraine; in a second adjustment step, however, refugees and emigrants from Ukraine will—to a certain extent—select economically preferred destination countries.

The UK is likely an almost inaccessible destination for many of these people, and political resistance to refugees and worker immigration from Ukraine to the UK is high in that country. The issue of immigration has been the subject of much political criticism in the UK since around 2010. Before the BREXIT referendum in June 2016, the UK became home to almost half of all emigrants from Eastern European EU countries—which is one of the reasons why the issue of immigration became so politically prominent in the UK in the decade after 2004. The UK, Ireland, and Sweden were the only EU countries not to avail of the opportunity to implement a transitional period limiting the free movement of persons for Eastern European accession countries from 2004; unlike France and Germany—with a seven-year transition period—for example. Although ideological struggles in the UK were the main cause of the BREXIT majority, the overall uncoordinated EU immigration policy obviously played a role in the UK's EU exit; moreover, survey results in EU countries—with surveys regularly commissioned by the European Commission—were apparently not consistent in the run-up to the referendum (the European Commission did not change survey methodologies), and there was a lack of critical debate in Brussels (see Welfens, 2017a, 2017b).

A Ukraine Accession to the European Union

An enlargement of the EU to include Ukraine would leave the then enlarged European Union in a new situation of having a much longer (and probably still contentious) eastern border with Russia. For Russia, depending on the political tensions between Russia and the EU, an EU enlargement to the east to include Ukraine—with over 40 million inhabitants including a significant Russian-speaking minority population—could provide an incentive to destabilize Ukraine politically and economically in various ways. Within the framework of EU regional policy and EU cohesion policy, the European Union would then probably face considerable additional financial burdens. Moreover, a relatively unstable Ukraine would possibly also be a bone of contention within the EU itself, which could destabilize the European Union. Unreflective political enthusiasm in Brussels, and numerous EU member countries, for an expedited enlargement to include Ukraine is therefore neither appropriate nor responsible. In the event of an EU enlargement to include Ukraine, the EU would have to adopt a comprehensively altered policy toward Russia, which would bring its own political risks for the stability of EU integration.

An enlargement of the EU to include Ukraine brings opportunities for Ukraine and, under certain circumstances, also for the European Union. It brings conflicts in the field of enlargement policy more broadly insofar as the Western Balkan countries with aspirations to join the EU will fear being pushed back on the timeline. Austria is one of the few countries that would be in favor of a rapid enlargement to include the Western Balkans accession countries, if only for historical and economic-geographical reasons. However, an enlargement in the Balkans would create a problem for the EU as many small countries would be admitted to the EU—some of them are countries where Russia, Turkey, and Saudi Arabia also pursue politico-economic and religious interests. Many Eastern European EU countries, above all Poland and the Baltic countries, will be in favor of a rapid admission of Ukraine, as this will protect their own military security with regard to Russia; such considerations are also likely to apply to Finland, Sweden, and Denmark. A number of poorer countries in the south of the EU will tend not to vote for a quick admission of Ukraine, fearing that EU aid money will then be channeled relatively extensively in the direction of Ukraine; but then likely only aid money for Eastern European EU countries would remain. Ukraine as a political bone of contention in the EU or as a country that—even after a cease-fire—is likely to be in a kind of state of war with Russia (keywords: Donbas region; Crimea)—will make the military integration of the EU much more complicated than it appeared after BREXIT. The EU itself could come into a kind of permanent tension with Russia, which would be problematic for both sides.

EU enlargement to include Ukraine would bring a considerable potential immigration problem for a number of EU countries—and this would then also threaten the EU with the next "BREXIT case"; at least that is what can be assumed unless the political management in Brussels improves significantly or continues not to draw sensible conclusions from previous policy mistakes made in the matter of prior EU enlargements to the east (and indeed BREXIT itself). In particular, it should be ruled out for any EU country not to realize a transitional period for the free movement of persons. Otherwise, there is a risk that large emigration movements from Ukraine will be geographically concentrated in just a few EU countries, thus destabilizing the political system in at least some EU countries with high relative immigration or encourage radicalization and anti-EU attitudes there: This could bring about the next BREXIT.

Ukraine, as a relatively large country in terms of population and with a low per capita income, can expect to experience considerable levels of emigration to other EU countries for many years to come; with full freedom of movement for Ukraine, as an EU member state, there are considerable risks that high immigration figures in destination countries will destabilize those EU countries or the European Union as a whole in the medium term. The question of a sensible temporary restriction of immigration in the event of an EU enlargement should be reconsidered. There is also a danger that the topic of EU enlargement to include Ukraine will be discussed primarily on an emotional level in the public sphere and that an analytically reflective political debate will be largely absent with the result that the necessary risk-reducing flanking measures for a stable EU enlargement to the east not being initiated. Thus, in the end, the Russo-Ukrainian war could initiate the further disintegration of the European Union by creating more "BREXIT cases"; dynamics possibly supported in the political run-up to referendums by Russia's government and the Russian president. There is little doubt that President Putin and his government have supported BREXIT from the beginning in a variety of ways in the British political process—without any major public critical debate in the UK. In any case, further enlargement in Eastern Europe, in this case to include Ukraine, will be a complex challenge for the EU and its member states.

The process of EU enlargement could take about a decade in the case of Ukraine if one considers the accession process of Croatia as a benchmark for the timeline. However, Ukraine and the EU could argue that the existing Association Agreement and the Deep and Comprehensive Free Trade Area (DCFTA) agreement which had been signed in 2014 means that considerable progress in key fields relevant for an EU accession have already been achieved. As regards Western support for trade integration between the EU and Ukraine, one should recall that on April 6, 2016, there was a non-binding referendum on the Ukraine-European Union Association Agreement in the Netherlands. The required minimum turnout of 30% was achieved (32.28%) and the result was that 61% of Dutch voters voted against the Approval Act. In the Dutch Press it was argued that Russia's government had influenced the campaign in favor of a refusal of an association agreement (one may also recall that on June 23, 2016, there was the BREXIT referendum in the United Kingdom). The Dutch referendum shows that political support for an EU enlargement allows Ukrainian accession could be rather modest in some countries of the European Union; one may, however, assume that the Russo-Ukrainian war has reinforced political support for such an enlargement in many EU countries. The official request on the part of Ukraine for EU membership was submitted on February 28, 2022. As regards the position of Ukraine, President Zelenskyy argued in favor of a very fast membership procedure for Ukraine. However, at the Versailles summit in March 2022, EU countries dampened hopes that such an expedited procedure would be applied in the case of Ukraine.

As regards the fundamental requirements for EU membership, the "Copenhagen Criteria" of 1993 have to be fulfilled which means the ability of the country's economy to live with the competitive pressures of being part of the single market (including the four freedoms), firm state support for democracy and the protection of minority rights as well as the institutional and administrative capacity to effectively implement the *Acquis Communautaire*—the set of laws and rules relevant in the European Union; moreover the requirement that existing member countries must be able to absorb the new member countries. As the European Commission has stated in 2000, the critical criteria for membership are as follows (European Commission, 2022):

> *The accession criteria, or Copenhagen criteria (after the European Council in Copenhagen in 1993 which defined them), are the essential conditions all candidate countries must satisfy to become a member state. These are:*
>
> - *political criteria: stability of institutions guaranteeing democracy, the rule of law, human rights and respect for and protection of minorities;*
>
> - *economic criteria: a functioning market economy and the capacity to cope with competition and market forces;*
>
> - *administrative and institutional capacity to effectively implement the acquis (Communautaire—added by PJJW) and ability to take on the obligations of membership.*
>
> *The Union's capacity to absorb new members, while maintaining the momentum of European integration, is also an important consideration.*

The topics and chapters, respectively, which should be addressed in a timely manner for an EU accession are summarized in the following table which indicates the new clustering enlargement negotiation approach of the European Union: Since 2021, several chapters are grouped in certain clusters and negotiations for EU accession should follow the clusters emphasized in the EU's approach (see the subsequent Table 10.1 which consists of the topics under the headings of Fundamentals, Internal Markets, Competitiveness and inclusive growth, Green agenda and sustainability connectivity, Resources, agriculture and cohesion, External relations):

If one follows the CEPS analysis for early 2022 (Emerson et al., 2022), with the exception of anti-corruption policy and transport, none of the 26 chapters relevant for an EU accession have been rated by the authors with the weak rating of 1 ("some preparation") in 2021; 1.5 has been achieved

Table 10.1 Technical EU pillars: clusters of negotiating chapters for EU enlargement (European Commission, 2020)

1. Fundamentals	23—Judiciary and fundamental rights
	24—Justice, Freedom and Security Economic criteria
	Functioning of democratic institutions, Public administration reform
	5—Public procurement
	18—Statistics
	32—Financial control
2. Internal Market	1—Free movement of goods
	2—Freedom of movement for workers
	3—Right of establishment and freedom to provide services
	4—Free movement of capital
	6—Company law
	7—Intellectual property law
	8—Competition policy
	9—Financial services
	28—Consumer and health protection
3. Competitiveness and inclusive growth	10—Information society and media
	16—Taxation
	17—Economic and monetary policy
	19—Social policy and employment
	20—Enterprise and industrial policy
	25—Science and research
	26—Education and culture
	29—Customs union
4. Green agenda and sustainable connectivity	14—Transport policy
	15—Energy
	21—Trans-European networks
	27—Environment and climate change
5. Resources, agriculture and cohesion	11—Agriculture and rural development
	12—Food safety, veterinary and phytosanitary policy
	13—Fisheries
	22—Regional policy & coordination of structural instruments
	33—Financial & budgetary provisions
6. External relations	30—External relations
	31—Foreign, security & defence policy

Source: European Commission (2020)

in the field of intellectual property rights, macroeconomic policy, consumer protection, and company law. The only field where the EU's rating of Ukraine is 3 (a good rating in preparedness in relation to EU standards) concerns civil society; the other fields had been rated with 2 or 2.5 (see Table 10.2). Emerson et al. (2022) express clear support for a fast EU membership procedure; or more precisely: A quick start of the EU procedure for the Ukraine. Incidentally, the authors suggest that Ukraine should use frozen Russian assets abroad—read: foreign exchange reserves of the Russian central bank—to pay for the Ukraine's external debt of roughly $57 billion. This view is strange as this means that the authors are in favor of a kind of international bank robbery where the Ukraine would take $57 billion of Russian state property.

As regards the option of an expedited enlargement by the EU in relation to Ukraine, the authors do not consider the challenges of the four freedoms of the EU single market in general and of the free movement of labor in particular. One would witness considerable destabilization of the EU if the lessons from previous EU eastern enlargements—and of BREXIT—would not be carefully taken into account by the European Union. One can understand that many Western politicians, struck by strong emotions in the context of the tragic war between Ukraine and Russia, would be in favor of a faster than usual EU membership process for Ukraine; without taking into account the problems encountered in reality in an adequate way. Considering the experience of the EU eastern enlargement of 2004, which brought immediate freedom of labor mobility for the smaller states of Malta and Cyprus, but a general immediate freedom of movement for all accession countries was implemented only in the case of the UK, Sweden, and Ireland, it was remarkable that Germany, for example, opted for the maximum of a seven-year transition period and many other EU countries also opted to impose several years of a special transition regime without free labor mobility for the accession countries.

The resultant delays to the free migration of labor from Eastern European EU accession countries to older member states implied that a very strong immigration pressure would be faced by the United Kingdom where policymakers welcomed additional immigrants as those were assumed to help overcoming existing labor shortages; the situation in British labor markets, however, changed strongly following the Transatlantic Banking Crisis and the massive UK recession of 2008. The issue of excessive immigration to the United Kingdom became a prominent topic on the British political agenda. Prime Minister David Cameron

Table 10.2 Ukraine's implementation ratings of the main provisions of the association agreements and DCFTAs (as of early 2022)

Political principles, rule of law

Electoral democracy	2.5	Recent elections correct: President, Parliament, local
Human rights	2	Fundamental freedoms OK (except occupied Donbas and Crimea)
Rule of law	1.5	Judicial reform badly needed, not advancing consistently
Anti-corruption	1	Poor, only marginal improvement, inconsistent stance of leadership

DCFTA*

Market access	2	Shift in trade structure from Russia to EU and China
Customs services	2	Long resistance to reform; advances now being made
Technical product standards (TBT)	2	Good progress in implementing strategy
Food safety (SPS)	2	Strategy adopted; progress in implementation
Services	2.5	Ukraine more liberal than the EU for establishment
Public procurement	2.5	E-procurement system acclaimed; risks of backtracking
Intellectual property rights (IPR)	1.5	Limited progress in IPR protection and enforcement
Competition policy	2	Laws OK, but authority of government agency at risk
Statistics	2	Significant progress in adopting EU methodologies

Economic cooperation

Macroeconomic policy	1.5	Improved but still vulnerable; IMF/EU aid-dependent
Financial services	2	Proceeding with comprehensive alignment on EU laws
Transport	1	Road transport needs action by Ukraine (and EU)
Energy	2	Major challenges being addressed; joining Green Deal
Environment	2	Comprehensive, costly, long-term action engaged
Digital and cyber	2.5	Dynamic digital and cybersecurity sectors
Consumer protection	1.5	Progress in product safety, but much more outstanding
Company law	1.5	Legislative action, but uncertain enforcement
Employment and social policy	2	ILO conventions OK, but new Labour Code outstanding
Visa regime, movement of people	2.5	Successful implementation of visa-free travel
Education and culture	2.5	High educational standards, comparable to EU neighbours

(*continued*)

Table 10.2 (continued)

Gender equality	2.5	Comparable to EU neighbours
Civil society	3	Competent, independent civil society, forceful advocates of reform

Note: Ukraine's average rating 1.81 is rather average compared to the candidate states; the average ratings in the interpretation of the CEPS study are: Montenegro with 2.21, Serbia 2.11, North Macedonia 2.07, Albania 1.73, Bosnia and Herzegovina 1.55 and Kosovo 1.35

*DCFTA refers to the EU-Ukraine Deep and Comprehensive Free Trade Agreement

Source: Emerson et al. (2022), Table 2, p. 6

in turn had no idea how to really cope with the emergent problem or how to create a sufficient number of new jobs so that political populists (e.g., Nigel Farage) could exploit the new situation. Cameron's massive cuts to central government transfers to local communities—reaching 5% of national income within a few years—contributed to the perception of an under-provision of local public services which in the perception of the public then became largely associated with the problem of excessive immigration from Eastern Europe; anti-EU sentiments thus started growing especially after 2009. As regards Russian interference in the BREXIT campaign, it is unclear whether or not the Russian government supported in various ways the pro-BREXIT groups which in the end won the BREXIT referendum of 2016; little evidence of coordinated Russian interference via Twitter was found, for example, by Narayanan et al. (2017). However, Russian expatriates and oligarchs—with double nationality—living in London, have apparently been influential donators to the Conservative Party for many years (e.g., Parker, 2021).

If Russia's political leadership would follow Putin's aggressive policy attitude vis-à-vis the West in the long run, the EU should expect that Russia will invest significantly in the political and economic destabilization of Ukraine and the European Union, respectively. If the EU in the end would disintegrate, Putinism would have achieved success in Europe (this would possibly include new reinforced links between Russia and Serbia as well as other countries in the Balkans). As regards the cost of reconstruction of Ukraine, its government will most likely want to use Russia's foreign exchange reserves which have effectively been seized by the Western countries, Japan, and Australia within the sanction packages of March 2022. At the same time, it is clear that Russia would hardly accept such a procedure: With about $300 billion at stake—in the accounts of Western central banks—for Russia's central bank. The EU in turn might have to come up with considerable financial support for the reconstruction of Ukraine; at its summit of March 24/25, 2022, the European Council agreed to create a Ukrainian Solidarity Fund which is open for non-EU countries; if the EU were to follow the US Marshall Plan funding for Germany in 1948–1950, the European Union would have to put up about €16 billion.

If Russia should change its international policy course under Putin or Putin's successor in a way which is decisively more cooperative vis-à-vis the West, EU membership of the Ukraine would still be a formidable challenge. Geography cannot be changed and the EU cannot really have political stability in the long run if relations with both Ukraine and Russia are not based on clear principles, rules, and membership of functional international organizations such as the World Trade Organization, the Bank for International Settlements and the International Monetary Fund. Getting Russia back into the G8 could be considered in the long run. However, Western countries plus Japan should consider more seriously the political psychology of international cooperation in the future. For example, a repeat of the situation at the G8 Heiligendamm Summit of 2007 during Germany's G8 presidency—when Putin was visibly isolated among the other leaders and found himself alone at a table (while Chancellor Merkel, as the host, made no effort to avoid this situation which certainly was humiliating for President Putin)—should be avoided.

The idea of an energy import embargo vis-à-vis Russia is interesting, but a temporary special import tariff on Russian gas is more adequate from an economic perspective. In any case, there should be a clear signaling to Russia that a change in its military and foreign policy—toward peaceful cooperation in Europe—will make growing trade between the EU and Russia possible again. The regulatory and bureaucratic adjustment barriers to structural change toward a much higher share of renewable energy in many EU countries are still considerable. It often takes many years to start a new construction project or to get to begin construction on a new LNG terminal. Systemic reforms and deregulation would, to some extent, thus be adequate in many Western countries. As regards the expansion of solar electricity and heat production, one may point out that few EU countries could really push for a strong policy in favor of renewables in the household sector: There is a structural shortage of adequately skilled craftsmen in the renewable energy sector. Shifting from fossil fuels to CO_2-friendly renewable energy sources will therefore cost many years of adjustment time. The overall picture of challenges in the context of the Russo-Ukrainian war suggests that careful analysis is needed and a pragmatic medium-term adjustment approach should be useful.

LITERATURE

Commander, S., Nikolaychuk, O., & Vikhrov, D. (2013). Migration from Ukraine: Brawn or brain? New survey evidence. IZA Discussion Paper No. 7348, Institute for the Study of Labor, Bonn. https://docs.iza.org/dp7348.pdf

Emerson, M., Blockmans, S., Movchan, V., & Remizov, A. (2022). Opinion on Ukraine's application for membership of the European Union. CEPS Policy Insights, No. 2022-16. https://www.ceps.eu/download/publication/?id=36124&pdf=PI2022-16-Ukraines-EU-membership.pdf

European Commission. (2020). Communication from the Commission to the European Parliament, the Council, the European Economic and Social Committee and the Committee of the Regions, enhancing the accession process—A credible EU perspective for the Western Balkans. COM(2020) 57 final, Brussels.

European Commission. (2022). European Commission—enlargement—Accession criteria. Retrieved April 18, 2022, from https://ec.europa.eu/neighbourhood-enlargement/enlargement-policy/glossary/accession-criteria_en

Fertig, M., & Kahanec, M. (2015). Projections of potential flows to the enlarging EU from Ukraine, Croatia and other Eastern neighbors. *IZA Journal of Migration, 4*(6). https://doi.org/10.1186/s40176-015-0029-8

Kirsch, W. (2022). The distribution of power within the EU: Perspectives on a Ukrainian accession and a Turkish accession. *International Economics and Economic Policy, 19*(2). https://doi.org/10.1007/s10368-022-00541-w

Narayanan, V., Howard, P. N., Kollanyi, B., & Elswah, M. (2017). Russian involvement and junk news during Brexit. Oxford Internet Institute, Comprop Data Memo 2017.10. Published December 19. Retrieved April 20, 2022, from https://blogs.oii.ox.ac.uk/wp-content/uploads/sites/93/2017/12/Russia-and-Brexit-v27.pdf

Parker, S. (2021, April 21). Did donations to the conservatives buy a Kremlin Brexit. *West Country Voices.* Retrieved April 20, 2022, from https://westcountryvoices.co.uk/did-donations-to-the-conservatives-buy-a-kremlin-brexit/

Welfens, P. J. J. (2017a). *BREXIT aus Versehen* [transl. PJJW: An Accidental Brexit] (1st ed.). Springer. https://doi.org/10.1007/978-3-658-15875-0.

Welfens, P. J. J. (2017b). *An accidental BREXIT.* Palgrave Macmillan. https://doi.org/10.1007/978-3-319-58271-9

International Aid Pledges to Ukraine: Coverage, Effects, and Potential Challenges

The war between Russia and Ukraine, which entered a new phase on February 24, 2022, brought massive destruction to Ukraine, the deaths of thousands of civilians and Ukrainian and Russian military personnel, a great many injured, and about six million refugees fleeing Ukraine in the period of March–August 2022. Furthermore, the Western world, as well as Japan, the Republic of Korea, Australia, and several other countries, have pursued a policy of implementing successive waves of sanctions against Russian sectors, companies, and individuals. By August 2022, the Russian military had been only partially successful in capturing Ukrainian territory, particularly in eastern and southern Ukraine. Many countries have pledged aid to Ukraine, including military, economic, and humanitarian aid. Differentiated problem perspectives are developed here with regard to quantifying aid provided as well as considering the broader macroeconomic effects of refugee flows.

Ukraine has received significant military support from the US, the UK and some EU countries. The US and the UK have a long tradition of supporting allies through military aid, although in the case of the Ukraine, this aid is rather small relative to the respective national incomes of both countries; and the aid money from EU countries comes on top. Russia has entered into a hardly winnable military misadventure with its invasion of Ukraine, assuming sustained military resistance from Ukraine. Instead of going to war, Russia would have had the opportunity to instead consolidate its security through treaties with the West or NATO countries and to

P. J. J. Welfens, *Russia's Invasion of Ukraine*,
https://doi.org/10.1007/978-3-031-19138-1_11

promote innovation, structural change, and growth. President Putin did not seize this opportunity. However, it can be assumed that the increasing number of Western military advisors in Ukraine in the years after 2014 also aroused fears of military encirclement on the part of Russia and Putin. In any case, President Putin has given up non-military options for an understanding with Ukraine.

How much aid Ukraine will continue to receive from Western countries—including the assumption of accommodation and living costs for Ukrainian refugees in Europe—is an interesting question. Economic, humanitarian, and military aid to Ukraine must be presented and compared internationally; in this context, it makes most sense to relate aid payments to the national income or the gross domestic product of the respective donor country. From a European security-economic perspective, those EU countries that are geographically closest to the Russo-Ukrainian war, or where fears are relatively high that they will be Russia's next target of attack, are likely to make relatively high aid payments per unit of GDP. Poland and the Baltic countries are therefore likely to have high aid payment quotas. Particularly high aid payments will also be expected from Russia's global adversary, the US; for the Biden administration, this is about indirectly hitting back at Russia and clarifying the US leadership role in NATO.

Clearly, Russian aggression—relative to the apparent goal of a rapid defeat and occupation of—Ukraine has not been militarily successful; Western military support—including intelligence and other information from the United States and the United Kingdom has contributed to the success of Ukraine's military defense, which has nonetheless suffered the massive destruction of infrastructure and major cities and towns. As for the economic impact of the Russo-Ukrainian war, there are many aspects to consider (see, e.g., Welfens, 2022a, 2022b; Astrov et al., 2022; Roeger & Welfens, 2022).

Due to the war-related destruction and the loss of civilian and military lives, as well as Russia's blockade of Ukraine's main ports and export shipping facilities, Ukraine's economic output is expected to decline very sharply in 2022: The IMF (2022a, 2022b, 2022c) projects a decline in economic output of about 35%, leaving the Ukrainian government with the challenge of a serious government deficit and related problems. As a result, financial assistance—in addition to humanitarian and military aid—will be needed by Ukraine, with bilateral financial assistance and support from the IMF, World Bank, and the European Bank for Reconstruction and Development (EBRD) also critical. In order to provide some level of transparency on the activities and commitments of the main OECD donor countries, it would be useful to gather the relevant data as such data would allow for an international ranking of donor countries, which would provide useful information in a descriptive perspective, but which could also form a basis for an international debate on burden sharing with regard to assistance to Ukraine.

As far as publications which analyze the humanitarian, financial, and military aid to Ukraine are concerned, the Kiel Institute for the World Economy (IfW) has led the way with a paper by Antezza et al. (2022) covering the period from February 24 to March 27, 2022. However, this paper has a very biased approach and may be somewhat misleading when it comes to the international ranking of countries in terms of total aid—the sum of humanitarian, financial, and military aid as a share of GDP. The authors do not include pledges/spending on Ukrainian refugees, which is an inappropriate approach; in fact, the spending on Ukrainian refugees accounts for a high proportion of humanitarian aid and, in the case of many countries, total aid. While figures for the spending on Ukrainian refugees are not always easy to obtain on a country-by-country basis, this technical problem should not be an acceptable reason for publishing aid figures which do not include such spending. The Antezza et al. figures have been widely cited in both the national media in Germany and the international media. In May 2022, *The Economist* published the aid rankings for the top ten countries—with figures for aid given to Ukraine as a percentage of GDP; however, publishing the top ten aid table is a very dubious proposition, even when *The Economist* mentions that figures for refugee spending are not included in the IfW table. *The Economist* notes that the IfW figures show that the combined pledges of the EU27 countries are less than the aid-to-GDP ratio of the United States. The IfW publication has contributed to a lively international debate about why many EU countries' support for Ukraine appears to be rather modest. However, the rankings contained in the IfW working paper and published in *The Economist* are completely misleading, as will be shown here.

This affair not only shows that the well-known Kiel think-tank occasionally publishes very dubious analyses, it also testifies to an astounding lack of critical reflection on the part of *The Economist* and the many other journalists and politicians who blindly followed the rather misleading ranking. The IfW ranking of the top ten countries is as follows: Estonia, Poland, Lithuania, Slovakia, Sweden, the United States, Czechia, Croatia, the United Kingdom and France. However, the correct ranking—which also includes spending on Ukrainian refugees—looks quite different; for example, Croatia is far behind in the correct ranking, almost all countries have a different position in the corrected table, and the figures for the EU27 as a whole are in fact much higher than for the US.

Different types of aid are reflective of the different types of aid from government. Financial, humanitarian, and military aid play a crucial role when it comes to Western support for various countries in different regions of the world economy. The new rivalry between the US/EU and Russia—plus China—in Africa illustrates that the often relatively expensive infrastructure project offers and arms purchase options of the West are not very convincing politically in the addressee countries, and the higher price compared to offers from Russia or China is rarely outweighed by political advantages—such as access to the large markets of the EU and the US. Autocratic countries in Africa, by the way, naturally have no appreciation for the political curtain lectures of Western leaders on their various visits to Africa.

Incidentally, Western countries still appear to be attractive migration destinations, and balanced immigration policies have benefited many immigration countries: for decades, this was true for the US, Canada, and Australia, but also for France and Germany. However, since relatively poor countries with high population growth rates—especially in Africa and Asia—are a major source of emigration (current and potential), the US and EU countries are asking themselves how best to guard against excessive migratory pressure.

For the US, there is empirical evidence that the US actually achieves a containment of migratory pressure from potential emigration countries through a security partnership via military aid; other forms of aid show no such containment effects of emigration toward the US in recipient countries, which apparently can thus use military aid to hedge against a conceivable high emigration wave in many cases. Moreover, US military aid does not reduce migration pressure on other countries, nor does it reduce the levels of repression or other conflicts in recipient countries—as I learned from Laura Renner in a presentation entitled "A 'Good Deal'? U.S. Military Aid and Refugee Flows to the United States") who studied 161 countries over the period from 1988 to 2018 (Renner, 2022).

SUPPORT TO UKRAINE BY SELECTED OECD COUNTRIES

One could argue that an international comparison of government aid to Ukraine in the first few months of 2022 could be really useful; and that it could also be interesting to analyze the possible reasons for the large cross-country differences in terms of the aid-to-GDP ratios among OECD countries. Given the challenges of the Ukrainian refugee waves in early 2022, it is reasonable to assume that, for geographic and cultural reasons, but also simply because of the cost of international transportation, a relatively high proportion of Ukrainian refugees will attempt to reach neighboring Eastern European EU countries. One might also assume that geographic proximity matters not only for refugee numbers but also for military assistance to Ukraine: governments of countries geographically close to Russia tend to view Ukraine's attempts to doggedly defend itself against Russian aggression in part as an implicit reassurance against possible Russian military attacks on their own countries' territory in the near future. In terms of financial assistance, it is reasonable to assume that countries that have strong trade ties with Ukraine or are geographically close to Ukraine—and thus could face particularly strong immigration pressures if Ukraine's fight against Russia should prove unsuccessful—are more likely to make large donations relative to GDP.

Indeed, the Kiel Institute for the World Economy was a pioneer in the field of economic research when it published early insights into international data on humanitarian, financial, and military assistance to Ukraine; this look at individual countries included some indirect spending through memberships of major international organizations—but did not include private donations or donations to Ukrainian individuals. The summary of the Kiel IfW Discussion Paper 2218 (which argues, to some extent, that the paper provides useful data for the scientific community and the broader public and policymakers), published in April 2022, is as follows (p. 1):

> This paper introduces the "Ukraine Support Tracker", which lists and quantifies military, financial and humanitarian aid to Ukraine since Russia's invasion on February 24, 2022. We measure support from Western governments, namely by G7 and European Union member countries. Due to our focus on government-to-government commitments, we do not gather systematic data on private donations or aid by international organizations in this version of the database. To value in-kind support like military equipment or weapons, we use market prices and consider upper bounds to avoid underestimating the true extent of bilateral assistance. We find significant

differences in the scale of support across countries, both in absolute terms and as percent of donor GDP. In total amounts, by far the largest supporter of Ukraine is the United States, followed by Poland and the United Kingdom. In percent of donor GDP, small Eastern European countries stand out as particularly generous. Strikingly, the United States alone provides more support to Ukraine than all of the 27 EU member countries taken together, even after adding EU-level support. The gap is particularly large for military support, with the US committing more than twice as much weapons and military equipment than all other countries combined.

Interestingly, the summary provides the reader with some potentially very misleading results, which are of course related to the authors' somewhat strange approach of omitting expenditures on Ukrainian refugees. Tables 11.1, 11.2, and 11.3 provide the original figures from the Kiel IfW Discussion Paper 2218 by Antezza et al. (2022) in absolute terms and as relative indicators on a national basis (i.e., the ratio of obligations to the respective country's GDP). In addition, the tables, based in part on IfW figures, also include data on two EIIW estimates for total humanitarian, financial, and military aid—one "more generous" (MAX) and one "more conservative" (MIN) calculation; EIIW figures always include spending on refugees. While Table 11.1 provides information on the ratios themselves, Table 11.3 shows in a separate column the share of expenditures/ pledges for refugees based on certain assumptions, namely about both the number of refugees and the expenditures required to support, on average, one refugee from Ukraine.

As Table 11.2 shows, the pledges of EU countries (plus the pledge of the EU as a bloc)—including pledges for refugees in 2022—are almost five times higher than those of the United States in the period from February 24 to March 27. Moreover, the correct ranking for the sum of humanitarian, financial, and military aid (including pledges for Ukrainian refugees) in the EIIW approach differs significantly from the Kiel Institute for the World Economy ranking in most cases; interestingly, Germany's position is the same in both rankings, but the ranking for the United States in the comprehensive aid approach considered here shows a much weaker position than the work of Antezza et al. (2022) would suggest.

From a theoretical point of view, it should not be overstated that the table represents (only) a donor perspective, because many refugees will indeed integrate into the labor market of the respective host country; this process will take place within a relatively short period of time when

Table 11.1 Total pledges of assistance to Ukraine by selected European and other countries—Antezza et al./IfW Kiel expansion (2022): Plus pledges for refugees (in two scenarios), sorted by minimum total pledge in penultimate column

Rank[* is IfW Rank]	Country	Commitments in € billion (Antezza et al., 2022)		Number of registered refugees		Commitments per year for refugees in € billion[b,c]		Total commitments in € billion	
		Hum.	Total	Border crossings (million)	Target country (>10,000)	MIN[b]	MAX[b]	Min. total	Max. Total
1 [2]	Poland[a]	0.003	2.397	2.99	(2,205,795.7[a])	12.884	17.955	15.281	20.353
2 [1]	US[d]	4.482	10.314		100,000	1.000	1.000	11.314	11.314
3 [5]	Germany	0.472	1.815		379,123	4.549	4.549	6.364	6.364
4 [28]	Romania[a]	0.001	0.004	0.80	(590,742.6[a])	3.450	4.809	3.454	4.813
5 [3]	UK	0.495	2.096		27,100	0.325	0.325	2.421	2.421
6 [27]	Hungary[a]	0.007	0.007	0.51	(378,752.0[a])	2.212	3.083	2.220	3.090
7 [19]	Czechia	0.018	0.089		310,961	1.866	1.866	1.955	1.955
8 [4]	Canada	0.147	1.948		0	0.000	0.000	1.948	1.948
9 [13]	Slovakia[a]	0.005	0.201	0.37	(271,178.2[a])	1.584	2.207	1.785	2.409
10 [9]	Italy	0.005	0.265		102,654	1.232	1.232	1.497	1.497
11 [6]	France	0.116	0.567		48,776	0.585	0.585	1.152	1.152
12 [25]	Austria	0.001	0.011		64,400	0.773	0.773	0.784	0.784
13 [7]	Sweden	0.099	0.316		32,000	0.384	0.384	0.700	0.700
14 [15]	Denmark	0.018	0.124		30,000	0.360	0.360	0.484	0.484
15 [16]	Belgium	0.083	0.103		30,807	0.370	0.370	0.473	0.473
16 [12]	Estonia	0.002	0.222		39,500	0.237	0.237	0.459	0.459
17 [14]	Netherlands	0.018	0.149		21,000	0.252	0.252	0.401	0.401
18 [18]	Lithuania	0.040	0.093		49,300	0.296	0.296	0.388	0.388

(continued)

Table 11.1 (continued)

Rank[* is JfW Rank]	Country	Commitments in € billion (Antezza et al., 2022)		Number of registered refugees		Commitments per year for refugees in € billion[b,c]		Total commitments in € billion	
		Hum.	Total	Border crossings (million)	Target country (>10,000)	MIN[b]	MAX[b]	Min. total	Max. Total
19 [11]	Latvia	0.001	0.226		25,594	0.154	0.154	0.380	0.380
20 [17]	Ireland	0.065	0.098		23,000	0.276	0.276	0.374	0.374
21 [20]	Spain	0.042	0.046		51,957	0.312	0.312	0.358	0.358
22 [8]	Japan	0.000	0.276		0	0.000	0.000	0.276	0.276
23 [21]	Finland	0.014	0.025		20,396	0.245	0.245	0.269	0.269
24 [10]	Luxembourg	0.000	0.253		0	0.000	0.000	0.253	0.253
25 [26]	Portugal	0.000	0.010		33,106	0.199	0.199	0.209	0.209
26 [24]	Greece	0.000	0.014		21,230	0.127	0.127	0.141	0.141
27 [22]	Slovenia	0.002	0.020		18,415	0.110	0.110	0.131	0.131
28 [23]	Croatia	0.001	0.018		16,051	0.096	0.096	0.114	0.114
29 [29]	Cyprus	0.002	0.002		0	0.000	0.000	0.002	0.002
30 [30]	Malta	0.001	0.001		0	0.000	0.000	0.001	0.001
	EU(EC+EUCO)	1.015	2.215			32.553	40.477	41.844	49.768
	EU27 + EU[e]	2.034	9.291			2.649	1.952	1.952	2.649
	Moldova[a]			0.04	(325378.6[b])				
Total			23.925			35.779	44.451	59.703	68.376

Notes: Time period: data from Ukraine Tracker (Antezza et al., 2022), version 2, May 02, 2022; includes commitments through April 23, 2022. Data on refugees from April 27/28, 2022

[*] Ranked by Antezza et al. 2022, February 24, 2022 to March 27, 2022

Source: own representation and calculations; data from Antezza et al. (2022), UNHCR (2022), Wikipedia (2022, "2022 Ukrainian refugee crisis", compiled secondary data from figures reported by national governments); all figures as of April 27, 2022

[a]The numbers of registered refugees are published by UNHCR (2022) only for the border countries of Ukraine (marked in blue). Belarus and Russia are not included in this table, as it is unlikely that refugees registered in those countries first will continue their journey to Europe. Moldova is listed separately as it is not included in the list of Antezza et al. (2022)

[b]Own calculations based on the following two scenarios: (1) **MIN**: Assumed minimum number of refugees—each refugee registered in a country not bordering Ukraine is assumed to have already been counted once at the border. Due to the freedom of travel (in the Schengen area), individual movements within the EU cannot be tracked. Therefore, the numbers in the destination countries are deducted proportionally from the number of registered refugees in these border countries (figures in italics). This results in an additional minimum annual commitment of almost €35.8 billion.

(2) **MAX**: Maximum number of refugees assumed—each registered refugee from both border and destination countries is counted individually. This results in a maximum additional annual commitment of almost €44.5 billion

[c]Average pledges per refugee per month are assumed to be €1,000 in higher-income countries (United Kingdom, Germany, France, Italy, Sweden, Netherlands, Finland, Denmark, Belgium, Austria, and Ireland) and €500 in all other countries

[d]President Biden announced in March 2022 that the US would accept 100,000 Ukrainian refugees; assuming government spending of €10,000 per refugee per year, this translates into annual U.S. spending of €1 billion

[e]Sum of commitments of the EU27 countries and the EU (European Commission and European Council)

Table 11.2 Total pledges for aid to Ukraine by selected European and other countries—Antezza et al. expansion (2022): Plus pledges for refugees (in two scenarios) as a % of the donor country's GDP (2020), sorted by the minimum total pledge in the penultimate column

Antezza et al. ranking = *		Commitments as % of GDP (based on Antezza et al, 2022)		Number of registered refugees		Commitments per year for refugees as % of GDP b+f		Total commitments as % of GDP	
Rank[*]	Country	Hum.	Total	Border crossings (million)	Target country (>10,000)	MIN^b	MAX^b	Min. total	Max. Total
1 [3]	Poland[a]	0.00%	0.46%	2.99	$(2,205,795.7^b)$	2.50%	3.48%	2.96%	3.94%
2 [5]	Slovakia[a]	0.01%	0.22%	0.37	$(271,178.2^b)$	1.74%	2.43%	1.96%	2.65%
3 [1]	Estonia	0.01%	0.84%		39,500	0.89%	0.89%	1.73%	1.73%
4 [26]	Hungary[a]	0.01%	0.01%	0.51	$(378,752.0^b)$	1.64%	2.29%	1.65%	2.29%
5 [30]	Romania[a]	0.00%	0.00%	0.80	$(590,742.6^b)$	1.60%	2.23%	1.61%	2.24%
6 [2]	Latvia	0.00%	0.78%		25,594	0.53%	0.53%	1.30%	1.30%
7 [13]	Czechia	0.01%	0.04%		310,961	0.88%	0.88%	0.92%	0.92%
8 [6]	Lithuania	0.08%	0.19%		49,300	0.60%	0.60%	0.79%	0.79%
9 [4]	Luxembourg	0.00%	0.40%		0	0.00%	0.00%	0.40%	0.40%
10 [12]	Slovenia	0.00%	0.04%		18,415	0.24%	0.24%	0.28%	0.28%
11 [15]	Croatia	0.00%	0.04%		16,051	0.19%	0.19%	0.23%	0.23%
12 [29]	Austria	0.00%	0.00%		64,400	0.21%	0.21%	0.21%	0.21%
13 [11]	Germany	0.01%	0.05%		379,123	0.14%	0.14%	0.19%	0.19%
14 [14]	Denmark	0.01%	0.04%		30,000	0.12%	0.12%	0.16%	0.16%
15 [9]	Sweden	0.02%	0.07%		32,000	0.08%	0.08%	0.15%	0.15%
16 [7]	Canada	0.01%	0.14%		0	0.00%	0.00%	0.14%	0.14%
17 [21]	Finland	0.01%	0.01%		20,396	0.10%	0.10%	0.12%	0.12%
18 [27]	Portugal	0.00%	0.01%		33,106	0.10%	0.10%	0.11%	0.11%
19 [18]	Belgium	0.02%	0.02%		30,807	0.08%	0.08%	0.10%	0.10%

Rank[*]	Country	Hum.	Total	Border crossings (million)	Target country (>10,000)	MIN[b]	MAX[b]	Min. total	Max. Total
20 [16]	Ireland	0.02%	0.03%		23,000	0.07%	0.07%	0.10%	0.10%
21 [8]	UK	0.02%	0.09%		27,100	0.01%	0.01%	0.10%	0.10%
22 [20]	Italy	0.00%	0.02%		102,654	0.08%	0.08%	0.09%	0.09%
23 [24]	Greece	0.00%	0.01%		21,230	0.08%	0.08%	0.09%	0.09%
24 [10]	US[d]	0.02%	0.06%		100,000	0.01%	0.01%	0.06%	0.06%
25 [19]	Netherlands	0.00%	0.02%		21,000	0.03%	0.03%	0.05%	0.05%
26 [17]	France	0.01%	0.02%		48,776	0.03%	0.03%	0.05%	0.05%
27 [28]	Spain	0.00%	0.00%		51,957	0.03%	0.03%	0.03%	0.03%
28 [22]	Malta	0.01%	0.01%		0	0.00%	0.00%	0.01%	0.01%
29 [23]	Cyprus	0.01%	0.01%		0	0.00%	0.00%	0.01%	0.01%
30 [25]	Japan	0.00%	0.01%		0	0.00%	0.00%	0.01%	0.01%
	EU(EC+EUCO)								
	EU27 + EU[e]	0.01%	0.03%			0.25%	0.31%	0.32%	0.38%
	Moldova[a]			0.04	(325,378.6[b])	18.93%	25.69%	18.93%	25.69%

Note: Time period: data from Ukraine Tracker (Antezza et al., 2022), version 2, May 02, 2022; includes commitments through April 23, 2022. Data on refugees from April 27/28, 2022

Switzerland would, with <0.05% of GDP, take place 27 on the table behind France

[*] Ranking (with expenditures for refugees from Ukraine) according to Antezza et al. 2022, Kiel IfW Discussion Paper 2218

Source: own calculations; data from Antezza et al. (2022), UNHCR (2022), Wikipedia (2022, "2022 Ukrainian refugee crisis", compiled secondary data

(continued)

Table 11.2 (continued)

from figures reported by national governments); all figures as of April 27, 2022

[a]The numbers of registered refugees are published by UNHCR (2022) only for the border countries of Ukraine (marked in blue). Belarus and Russia are not included in this table, as it is unlikely that refugees registered in those countries first will continue their journey to Europe. Moldova is listed separately as it is not included in the list of Antezza et al. (2022)

[b]Own calculations based on the following two scenarios: (1) **MIN**: Assumed minimum number of refugees—each refugee registered in a country not bordering Ukraine is assumed to have already been counted once at the border. Due to the freedom of travel (in the Schengen area), individual movements within the EU cannot be tracked. Therefore, the numbers in the destination countries are deducted proportionally from the number of registered refugees in these border countries (figures in italics). This results in an additional minimum annual commitment of almost €35.8 billion

(2) **MAX**: Maximum number of refugees assumed—each registered refugee from both border and destination countries is counted individually. This results in a maximum additional commitment per year of almost €44.5 billion

[c]Average pledges per refugee per month are assumed to be €1,000 in higher-income countries (United Kingdom, Germany, France, Italy, Sweden, Netherlands, Finland, Denmark, Belgium, Austria, and Ireland) and €500 in all other countries

[d]President Biden announced in March 2022 that the U.S. would accept 100,000 Ukrainian refugees, which, assuming government spending of €10,000 per refugee per year, means an annual U.S. spending of €1 billion

[e]Sum of commitments of the EU27 countries and the EU (European Commission and European Council)

[f]The latest value of GDP is available for 2020 and was originally reported in current US dollars (World Bank: World Development Indicators, 2022). It is then converted to € based on an unweighted average of daily exchange rates between January 2, 2020 (year of GDP) and April 29, 2022 (most recent value, close to the date of data sourcing by Antezza et al.; ECB, 2022), resulting in an average exchange rate of $1 to €0.865

Table 11.3 Total pledges of aid to Ukraine by selected European and other countries—Antezza et al. expansion (2022): Plus pledges for refugees (in two scenarios) as a % of total pledges, sorted by share of refugee pledges

		Number of registered refugees		Commitments per year for refugees/total commitments [b,c]	Total commitments in € billion	
Rank	Country	Border crossings (million)	Target country (>10,000)	in % of total commitments	Min. total	Max. Total
1	Romania[a]	0.80	(590,742.6[b])	99.88%	3.454	4.813
2	Hungary[a]	0.51	(378,752.0[b])	99.67%	2.220	3.090
3	Austria		64,400	98.60%	0.784	0.784
4	Czechia		310,961	95.44%	1.955	1.955
5	Portugal		33,106	95.21%	0.209	0.209
6	Finland		20,396	90.84%	0.269	0.269
7	Greece		21,230	90.15%	0.141	0.141
8	Slovakia[a]	0.37	(271,178.2[b])	88.72%	1.785	2.409
9	Spain		51,957	87.08%	0.358	0.358
10	Slovenia		18,415	84.46%	0.131	0.131
11	Croatia		16,051	84.40%	0.114	0.114
12	Poland[a]	2.99	(2,205,795.7[b])	84.31%	15.281	20.353
13	Italy		102,654	82.31%	1.497	1.497
14	Belgium		30,807	78.18%	0.473	0.473
15	Lithuania		49,300	76.18%	0.388	0.388
16	Denmark		30,000	74.42%	0.484	0.484
17	Ireland		23,000	73.81%	0.374	0.374
18	Germany		379,123	71.49%	6.364	6.364
19	Netherlands		21,000	62.91%	0.401	0.401
20	Sweden		32,000	54.85%	0.700	0.700
21	Estonia		39,500	51.67%	0.459	0.459
22	France		48,776	50.80%	1.152	1.152
23	Latvia		25,594	40.42%	0.380	0.380
24	United Kingdom		27,100	13.43%	2.421	2.421
25	US[d]		100,000	8.84%	11.314	11.314
26	Canada		0	0.00%	1.948	1.948
27	Cyprus		0	0.00%	0.002	0.002
28	Japan		0	0.00%	0.276	0.276
29	Luxembourg		0	0.00%	0.253	0.253
30	Malta		0	0.00%	0.001	0.001
	EU(EC+EUCO)					

(continued)

Table 11.3 (continued)

		Number of registered refugees		Commitments per year for refugees/total commitments [b,c]	Total commitments in € billion	
Rank	Country	Border crossings (million)	Target country (>10,000)	in % of total commitments	Min. total	Max. Total
	EU27 + EU[e]			Min. 77.80% Max. 81.33%	41.844	49.768
	Moldova[a]	0.04	(325,378.6[b])	(100%)	1.952	2.649
Total				Min. 59.93% Max. 65.01%	59.703	68.376

Notes: Time period: data from Ukraine Tracker (Antezza et al., 2022), version 2, May 02, 2022; includes commitments through April 23, 2022. Data on refugees from April 27/28, 2022

Source: Own calculations; data from Antezza et al. (2022), UNHCR (2022), Wikipedia (2022, "2022 Ukrainian refugee crisis", compiled secondary data from figures reported by national governments); all figures as of April 27, 2022

[a]The numbers of registered refugees are published by UNHCR (2022) only for the border countries of Ukraine (marked in blue). Belarus and Russia are not included in this table, as it is unlikely that refugees registered in those countries first will continue their journey to Europe. Moldova is listed separately as it is not included in the list of Antezza et al. (2022)

[b]Own calculations based on the following two scenarios: (1) **MIN**: Assumed minimum number of refugees—each refugee registered in a country not bordering Ukraine is assumed to have already been counted once at the border. Due to the freedom of travel (in the Schengen area), individual movements within the EU cannot be tracked. Therefore, the numbers in the destination countries are deducted proportionally from the number of registered refugees in these border countries (figures in italics). This results in an additional annual commitment of almost €35.8 billion euros

(2) **MAX**: Maximum number of refugees assumed—each registered refugee from both border and destination countries is counted individually. This results in a maximum additional commitment per year of almost €44.5 billion

[c]Average pledges per refugee per month are assumed to be €1,000 in higher-income countries (United Kingdom, Germany, France, Italy, Sweden, Netherlands, Finland, Denmark, Belgium, Austria, and Ireland) and €500 in all other countries

[d]President Biden announced in March 2022 that the U.S. would accept 100,000 Ukrainian refugees; assuming government spending of €10,000 per refugee per year, this translates into annual US spending of €1 billion

[e]Sum of commitments of the EU27 countries and the EU (European Commission and European Council)

Ukrainian refugees arrive in countries that have a language largely similar to Ukrainian or where there are strong cultural and historical ties: here, Poland stands out among the EU's eastern neighbors. Of course, not every refugee will be integrated into the labor market of their host country in the medium term, but a large number of refugees are indeed likely to find some kind of work in the short term and work that better matches their respective skills and competencies in the medium term (work that is relatively better paid than previous jobs). With respect to Poland, Strzelecki et al. (2022) found in a growth accounting exercise that Ukrainian labor migrants in Poland contributed 0.5 percentage points per year to economic growth from 2013 to 2018.

Whereas the original Antezza et al. figures implied a country ranking (top ten) with Estonia in first place, followed by Poland, Lithuania, Slovakia, Sweden, the United States, Czechia, Croatia, the United Kingdom, and France, Table 11.2 shows a top ten led by Poland, with Slovakia, Estonia, Hungary, Romania, Czechia, Lithuania, Latvia, Slovenia, and Croatia (with large countries such as the United States, the United Kingdom, and France dropping out of the top ten to be replaced by smaller Central and Eastern European countries).

Table 11.3 shows that refugee spending for the top 23 countries accounts for between 51.68% and 99.96% of total commitments (including spending on Ukrainian refugees). In this context, the presentation by Antezza et al. (2022) could be considered quite misleading; the Kiel IfW data would only be really useful if data on commitments for refugees were included.

Comparing the IfW ratio and EIIW ratio figures—the latter including implicit pledges for refugees—in relation to aid to Ukraine, the two charts below, which refer to figures from the end of April 2022, show very different rankings (see Fig. 11.1). Such a ranking is politically sensitive and important; not least because a low-ranking position on the IfW chart could of course be used as an argument in public debates that, for example, Germany or Italy are not providing enough aid to Ukraine and that these countries should therefore increase both financial and military aid to Ukraine; incidentally, Germany's ranking position in both the IfW ranking and the EIIW ranking is—coincidentally—the same. However, it is reasonable to assume that both Germany and Italy are among the most important recipient countries of refugee flows from Ukraine in Western Europe, so that the approach of the EIIW which integrates refugees into the calculations paints a very different picture.

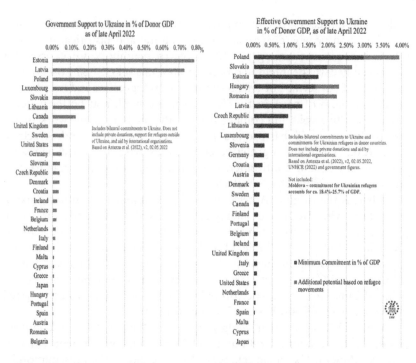

Fig. 11.1 Comparison of government aid to Ukraine as a percentage of GDP by Antezza et al. (IfW Kiel, 2022) and Welfens (see Welfens, 2022b)—the role of refugees. Source: Own presentation. Data from Ukraine Support Tracker, Antezza et al. (2022), version 2, May 2, 2022; UNHCR (2022); Wikipedia (2022, "2022 Ukrainian refugee crisis", compiled secondary data from figures reported by national governments); number of Ukrainian refugees in Germany: https://www.zdf.de/nachrichten/panorama/fluechtlinge-deutschland-bamf-ukraine-krieg-russland-100.html; other data through April 27, 2022

Comparing the IfW ranking with the EIIW approach, the latter suggests that the support of the UK, Canada, and the US—each a G7 country—is rather modest (given the Biden administration's announcement in early May 2022 of increased military support, while the UK in particular appears relatively weak in terms of the aid ratio to Ukraine). Prime Minister Boris Johnson's government appears unwilling to accept a significant number of Ukrainian refugees, which could be seen as an inappropriate free-riding position on Western Europe from the EU's perspective. The

EU should discuss the relatively modest British support for refugees from Ukraine in bilateral political talks. One can also point out that none of the rankings discussed here have taken into account the value of (military) intelligence support in kind to Ukraine—assessing the extent of such support would clearly be beyond the capabilities of economists; only in the future might historians be able to include this aspect

FURTHER INTERNATIONAL PERSPECTIVES ON REFUGEES

The economic prospects related to a high number of Ukrainian refugees in the EU for probably several years are quite interesting. A simplified analytical perspective looks as follows for the recipient countries:

- In the short term, the influx of refugees almost universally reflects a rather unskilled labor force, unless the refugees speak the language of the host country or at least a good level of English, for example. From this point of view, the temporary language barrier for refugees who want to work means that the number of jobs in construction, agriculture, and services (e.g., hotels and restaurants) will increase. Thus, after an initial very short period in which immigrants mainly boost aggregate demand, positive supply-side effects will become visible. In the short run, therefore, the output share of sectors that make intensive use of unskilled labor could increase, in line with the Heckscher-Ohlin theory.
- In the medium term—after many of the first cohorts of refugees have acquired sufficient knowledge of the host country's language or of English—a large share of immigrants (at some point even the majority of refugees) will find work, often in the tradable goods sector and sometimes in skill- or knowledge-intensive firms that pay relatively high wages. In the medium term, it is more likely that the skill- and knowledge-intensive sectors will increase their output shares in the overall economy.
- Since the language barrier for most Ukrainian refugees will be rather low in Poland and also in some other Eastern European EU countries, it can be assumed that economic growth in Eastern Europe will benefit in the medium term. In addition, qualified refugees with a knowledge of German, French, or English can be expected to work in Germany, the Netherlands, Belgium, France, and Italy as well as in some Scandinavian countries. In the long run, more "refugee

workers" from Ukraine will migrate westward to EU countries with relatively high wages (and also to Switzerland). Based on the wage differentials between immigrant men and women—compared to Swiss workers and employees with Swiss passports (Rochlitz & Wunsch, 2022)—it is reasonable to assume that skilled male immigrants can command a wage premium compared to native skilled workers. Such a premium could reflect an implicit international flexibility premium in international firms.

In the context of the Russo-Ukrainian war, there was a sharp increase in relative oil and gas prices in the first quarter of 2022: an international price shock that is exogenous. The fossil fuel sector can be considered production intensive, so we can apply the Stolper-Samuelson theorem: if the relative price of a tradable good i is exogenously increased in a neoclassical world with free trade, we can show that the relative factor price of that factor which is relatively intensively used in the production of that good is increased. Consequently, the wage rate of skilled workers (nominal wage of skilled workers relative to wage of unskilled workers) increases.

The wave of refugees from Ukraine to EU countries could also be understood with the help of the Rybczynski theorem: an exogenous increase in the endowment of production factor j (in this case labor) leads—for given relative goods prices—to higher production of the good that uses the abundant factor relatively intensively. The output of the other good falls in absolute terms. Example: assume that refugees arrive in Country I, then the output of those goods that are relatively labor intensive will increase (unskilled in the short run: construction, agriculture, hotels, and restaurants; in the medium run, the situation is different—when most refugees have gained some mastery of the language of the host country, then the skilled sector will expand, that is, the tradable goods sector, where a considerable share of the "refugee migrants" will find a job after a few years of integration into the domestic labor markets of the host countries). The assumption is that many Ukrainian refugees will actually stay in the EU27 countries for several years and that a considerable share of these refugees will eventually actually become labor migrants (to some extent, the implications of the Heckscher-Ohlin theorem and the Rybczynski theorem are equivalent, namely when it comes to the allocation of resources).

With respect to the Ukrainian refugee wave, however, the initial focus is on the expansion of the non-tradables sector—including care services provided, for example, by Ukrainian refugee women, who make up the majority of adult refugees. Since the imposition of martial law in response to Russia's invasion, most Ukrainian men aged 18 to 60 cannot leave Ukraine and must stand by for conscription into the military. In the medium term, the Heckscher-Ohlin theorem becomes particularly relevant, as the production share of the trade sector is expected to expand and international factor price equalization could play a significant role in the long run in the context of a rising trade intensity in the eastern EU countries.

Another conclusion is that Ukrainian refugees or migrant workers in the EU will contribute to increasing trade intensity within the EU in the medium term. To the extent that the expansion of the tradable goods sector in EU countries stimulates structural change in favor of an increasing share of high technology and "high knowledge" in production in the medium term, exports to high technology and high knowledge sectors in EU countries should gradually increase in the long term. To the extent that the Russo-Ukrainian war raises the risk premium for multinational companies' investments in Russia and China, the attention of Western investors could shift more toward Eastern Europe and the southwestern countries of the EU. This could—beyond the aforementioned trade effects—contribute to greater economic convergence within the EU in the long term. However, if Ukraine would remain a political bone of contention between the West and Russia for years to come, the risk premium for investments in Eastern European countries will rise.

It is reasonable to assume that the share of military spending in the total support provided to Ukraine will be relatively large in the EU countries that border Ukraine—or are at least geographically close to it. The logic behind this is that the governments of EU countries fear that a Russian victory in Ukraine would encourage the Russian military to attack other countries in Europe. It is also reasonable to assume that military assistance will play an important role in relation to the leading NATO members and Western countries, which are major arms exporters and have a positive comparative advantage in arms production. Humanitarian assistance as defined here—that is, including spending on refugees—will play a relatively large role in countries that are geographically close to Ukraine or have special cultural or historical ties to Ukraine, such as Poland or Austria. In the structural breakdown of German aid, it is expected that the share of military aid will be relatively small, given Germany's historical role in the twentieth century—in terms of the outbreak of World War I and World

War II—led to a particular political reluctance among post–World War II German governments to emphasize military options in international policy (for two decades after German reunification, Germany's military spending remained below 1.5% of GDP; revealing a major problem in the efficiency of the German military's procurement procedures).

CONCLUSIONS AND OPTIONS FOR FURTHER RESEARCH

An interesting area of research is to look closely at the combined humanitarian, financial, and military assistance provided by OECD countries to Ukraine. Such an analysis should definitely include recipient country spending on Ukrainian refugees. The Kiel IfW approach is therefore inadequate—this seems to be an unintended research pitfall (but surprising given the reputation of the IfW); the paper by Antezza et al. (2022) may be quite misleading as the authors omitted the commitments of the respective OECD countries to Ukrainian refugees. If one includes the relevant expenditures and commitments for 2022, the ranking of donor countries looks quite different from the ranking calculated by Antezza et al. in their IfW Discussion Paper 2218. Only the ranking of Germany remains unchanged.

It is also noteworthy that the press release of the Kiel Institute for the World Economy on the publication of the mentioned IfW Discussion Paper No. 2218 does not mention that the IfW sum indicator for assistance to Ukraine does not take into account expenditures for Ukrainian refugees, although it is noted within the paper itself; this was possibly an oversight in terms of the press release. Clearly, accurate figures on Ukrainian refugees are hard to come by, but difficult access to reliable statistics cannot be a ready excuse for omitting an important economic variable.

The IfW has stressed that its calculations show that US support for Ukraine significantly exceeds that of the EU in nominal terms. The Kiel IfW press release appears to be aimed at maximizing media attention, along the lines of "bad news is good news", which may be acceptable for newspapers and other media, but which undermines the goals of accuracy and thorough research in the field of economics. As shown in the reflections presented herein, pledges by EU countries (plus pledges by the EU as a bloc)—including pledges for refugees—were about five times higher than US pledges in the period from February 24 to March 27, 2022. Whether the combined Western aid to Ukraine will somehow help that country win the war or reach an acceptable compromise in peace negotiations with Russia remains to be seen. It cannot be ruled out that US aid pledges, especially in the military sphere, will once again place the US high in the aid table for Ukraine.

One specific element of assistance from EU countries concerns the exchange of cash balances on the part of Ukrainian refugees; the challenge is the willingness of national governments and the European Central Bank, as well as the national central banks of EU countries that are not members of the Eurozone, to offer Ukrainian refugees to exchange their Ukrainian currency—up to a critical limit—into local currency; for example, the Polish National Bank intends to offer Ukrainian refugees the exchange of Ukrainian Hryvnia (UAH) into Polish Zloty (the National Bank of Poland will also offer a $1 billion swap line to the Ukrainian central bank). The exchange rate is set bilaterally for this transaction, as stated in the NBP communiqué of March 31, 2022: "The exchange rate, set for this operation by the National Bank of Ukraine, is PLN 0.14 for one hryvnia. NBP will resell the purchased hryvnias to the National Bank of Ukraine at the same exchange rate. None of the participants involved in the operation charges fees for exchanging the Ukrainian hryvnia for the Polish zloty" (NBP, 2022). This amounts in part to a one-time transfer of Polish funds to refugees from Ukraine; the choice of bilateral exchange rate in EU countries should be coherent, so that bilateral negotiations would not take place with the establishment of a single bilateral exchange rate—rather, simultaneous negotiations by Ukraine with all 27 EU countries and the ECB seem appropriate.

The European Commission had proposed in early April that each refugee should have the right to exchange about 10,000 hryvnia for cash in the currencies of the respective EU host country, which is equivalent to about €310. If six million refugees arrive in the EU by the end of 2022, this would amount to about €2 billion for all refugees from Ukraine combined. It should be noted that the Ukrainian currency was only modestly convertible at the beginning of 2022.

Moreover, the correct ranking for the sum of humanitarian, financial, and military aid—including pledges for Ukrainian refugees—in the EIIW approach differs significantly in almost all cases from the ranking of the aid-to-GDP ratio of the Kiel IfW. In parts of the analytical discussion, Russo-Ukrainian war shocks are viewed through the lens of economic theorems: the Heckscher-Ohlin theorem, the Stolper-Samuelson theorem, and the Rybczynski theorem, respectively; it is argued that there is some equivalence between the Heckscher-Ohlin theorem and the Rybczynski theorem. One of the issues here is to understand the impact of the arrival of several million additional Ukrainian workers in the EU single market. How will this change production structures in EU countries in the medium and long term, and which export sectors will benefit relatively strongly?

Further research could include an empirical analysis of the structural division of Western support for Ukraine. With regard to the EU, it would also be interesting to analyze how the split between EU supranational support and EU member state support will evolve over time. Another interesting research question could be to analyze whether or not the support to Ukraine is efficient from Ukraine's perspective and to what extent the split between supranational and national support is economically optimal for Ukraine. Finally, it will be interesting to observe the relative relationship between EU and US support for Ukraine in the medium and long term.

LITERATURE

Antezza, A., Frank, A., Frank, P., Franz, L., Rebinskaya, E., & Trebesch, C. (2022). Which countries help Ukraine and how? Introducing the Ukraine Support Tracker. Kiel Working Paper No. 2218 April 2022, Kiel Institute for the World Economy.

Astrov, V., Ghodsi, M., Grieveson, R., Holzner, M., Kochnev, A., Landesmann, M., Pindyuk, O., Stehrer, R., Tverdostup, M., & Bykova, A. (2022). Russia's invasion of Ukraine: Assessment of the humanitarian, economic and financial impact in the short and medium term. *International Economics and Economic Policy, 19*(2). https://doi.org/10.1007/s10368-022-00546-5

IMF. (2022a). *IMF staff statement on the economic impact of war in Ukraine.* International Monetary Fund, Washington, DC. Retrieved March 30, 2022, from https://www.imf.org/en/News/Articles/2022/03/05/pr2261-imf-staff-statement-on-the-economic-impact-of-war-in-ukraine

IMF. (2022b). *World economic outlook: War sets back global recovery.* International Monetary Fund, April, Washington, DC.

IMF (2022c). Ukraine—IMF Country Report No. 22/74, March 2022, International Monetary Fund, Washington DC.

NBP. (2022). Communiqué of the National Bank of Poland. published March 31. Available on line (in English). Retrieved May 30, 2022, from https://www.nbp.pl/homen.aspx?f=/en/aktualnosci/2022/31.03.en.html

Renner, L. (2022). A 'Good Deal'? U.S. military aid and refugee flows to the United States, University of Freiburg. Presentation in the Brown Bag seminar series of the Schumpeter school of business and economics at the University of Wuppertal, May 17

Rochlitz, F., & Wunsch, C. (2022). Within-firm wage gaps between foreign and domestic workers, University of Basel. Paper presented at the Brown Bag Seminar of the Schumpeter School of Business and Economics, University of Wuppertal, May 3.

Roeger, W., & Welfens, P. J. J. (2022). EU gas import tariff under duopoly: A contribution to the energy sanctions debate on Russia. EIIW Discussion Paper No. 314. https://eiiw.wiwi.uni-wuppertal.de/fileadmin/eiiw/Daten/Publikationen/Gelbe_Reihe/disbei314.pdf

Strzelecki, P., Growiec, J., & Wyszynski, R. (2022). The contribution of immigration from Ukraine to economic growth in Poland. *Review of World Economics, 158*, 365–399. https://doi.org/10.1007/s10290-021-00437-y

UNHCR. (2022). Operational data portal. Ukraine Refugee Situation. Retrieved March 30, 2022, from https://data2.unhcr.org/en/situations/ukraine

Welfens, P. J. J. (2022a). Russia's attack on Ukraine: Economic challenges, Embargo issues & a new world order. EIIW Discussion Paper No. 312. https://eiiw.wiwi.uni-wuppertal.de/fileadmin/eiiw/Daten/Publikationen/Gelbe_Reihe/disbei312.pdf

Welfens, P. J. J. (2022b). Effective aid for Ukraine by OECD countries. EIIW Discussion Paper No. 315. https://eiiw.wiwi.uni-wuppertal.de/fileadmin/eiiw/Daten/Publikationen/Gelbe_Reihe/disbei315.pdf

Wikipedia. (2022). 2022 Ukraine refugee crisis. Retrieved May 05, 2022, from https://en.wikipedia.org/wiki/2022_Ukrainian_refugee_crisis

PART IV

The Implications for a New Global Economic Order

CHAPTER 12

Scenario Perspectives

It is, naturally, difficult to foresee a clear development of the further course of the war in Ukraine. Russia's war aims are relatively unclear; it cannot be ruled out that Russia wants to completely cut off Ukraine's access to the Black Sea, which would require the capture of Odesa, a city of over a million inhabitants, and further territorial gains by Russian forces. However, the Ukrainian military's successful defense over more than six months and Russia's overall modest territorial gains through the end of July 2022 show that Ukrainian national defenses have been quite successful to some extent. In any case, the Russian government will not be able to claim that its invasion forces outside the Donbas were greeted by cheering Ukrainians. It cannot be ruled out that Russia's invasion of Ukraine will be followed by further attempts to invade perhaps Moldova or the Central Asian republics plus Georgia. Depending on the duration of the war in Ukraine—and conceivable levels of escalation with regard to the West—various scenario perspectives for Europe and the wider world start to emerge.

With its war of aggression against Ukraine, Russia has become an international politico-economic destabilizing factor; normal economic and policy cooperative measures to improve relations between Russia and the West and between Russia and Ukraine have been set back many years. The fact that President Putin has chosen military force to enforce policy against Ukraine is completely unacceptable and ultimately probably not a reasonable course of action for Russia at all. Europe is likely to be marked by a new Cold War for a number of years, possibly with a militarily neutral

© The Author(s), under exclusive license to Springer Nature Switzerland AG 2022
P. J. J. Welfens, *Russia's Invasion of Ukraine*,
https://doi.org/10.1007/978-3-031-19138-1_12

Ukraine that loses part of its eastern territory to Russia. That Russia will aim to maintain control over Crimea at all costs is clear.

Whether Ukraine and Russia will succeed in resolving the relevant political rivalries and tension in the Donbas is unclear. A long-lasting war with both sides dug into fortified positions cannot be ruled out, and it is hard to imagine that Ukraine would quickly become an EU member, thus bringing the Russo-Ukrainian war into the European Union. The European Union would therefore be well advised to follow the proposal of French President Emmanuel Macron of May 9, 2022 (in his speech to the European Parliament; see Brzozowski et al., 2022) for a number of years, according to which one could create a kind of supplementary area of associated states alongside the EU: a sort of new European Political Community. Here, full EU membership would not apply then, but extensive access to the EU internal market should probably be possible, however, without full free movement of workers. The Macron proposal would only be feasible if there would be a broad majority of EU countries and candidate countries in favor. However, the EU would also have to have a clearly defined, gradual accession procedure from the outset so that a country could move up from the European Political Community to the EU.

The Russo-Ukrainian war has strengthened the cohesion of the NATO countries and also visibly illustrated the EU as a community of countries with a will to act internationally as a cohesive bloc. However, the question remains as to how this cohesion of EU countries or Eurozone countries will look in another phase of significantly rising interest rates in the medium term. With significantly higher nominal interest rates, the interest rate premiums for Italy, Portugal, Greece, and some other countries are likely to rise once again. In the medium term, a recession is also conceivable in the Eurozone and the US, and of course even more so in Russia and Ukraine.

A fundamental challenge for Russia is the question of which model the country really wants to move toward. It is hard to imagine that public policy debates in Russia will see a pronounced desire to maintain the previous model of a country with a strong focus on the natural resources sector—oil, gas, coal. The G7 is likely to have phased out coal as a fossil fuel by 2040, and oil and gas (not including so-called turquoise hydrogen, where CO_2 is captured from natural gas and injected into the ground, or blue gas, which comes from renewable energy resources) may have only a residual economic function from 2045 on: as input materials for the chemical sector, for example. It remains to be seen whether a New Russia will once again attempt to integrate itself into the major Western institutions with a more Western orientation. Such a modern Russia with a new Western orientation, which partly corresponds to its own historical orientation, would not necessarily be less attractive to China as a partner than it has been up to now. After all, China-Europe rail traffic passes over large parts of Russian territory, and Russia could therefore become an important economic and infrastructural bridge between the EU and China. Whether peace negotiations between Ukraine and Russia can be seriously conducted and concluded in the medium term remains to be seen. However, it is also conceivable that Moscow will not implement any viable reforms and will instead only strengthen its military resolve to conduct a static, war of attrition for the time being.

It is possible that the war in Ukraine will indeed drag on for many months as a war of attrition—with further destruction and many additional deaths. Under favorable circumstances, a peace agreement and a withdrawal of Russian troops as well as a phase of reconstruction of Ukraine would be conceivable, with the latter possibly choosing a neutral status; with political guarantees for Ukraine that are binding under international law.

The longer the war continues, the greater the media and political pressure in Germany and the EU will become to impose an energy import boycott on Russia in the short term. For Russia, this would be a high level of escalation in an international economic war, which will certainly lead to considerable countermeasures on the part of Russia. An energy boycott by Germany would be economically problematic, as the drop in real income is likely to be almost 6%—in year 1 of the boycott; the Bachmann et al. (2022) study has significant methodological problems, so the economic impact on Germany is certainly underestimated. Strong negative economic impulses on the Netherlands, France, and Belgium will emanate from Germany in the event of a German energy import boycott and a resulting severe recession; with negative repercussions from EU partner countries on Germany. Economic and digital retaliation (i.e., cyber-attacks from Russia) can be expected in the event of an energy import boycott.

Ukraine is certainly not served by an economic weakening of important EU countries. In addition, there are risks on the international financial markets that may arise in the context of instability impulses in the context of the Ukraine war and the economic war of the OECD countries against Russia.

The sanctions of the West, Japan, Australia, and so on against Russia probably result in a kind of encirclement fear in the Russian government, because economically more than half of the world economy is positioned against Russia in its war of aggression in Ukraine. Russia with its war of aggression against Ukraine is, however, responsible for Russia's own widespread international isolation. Instead of turning Russia's membership in the World Trade Organization—since 2012—into the starting point for Russia's long-term internationalization and modernization, the Russian economy has developed dynamically in only a few sectors; the share of Russia's high-tech exports has remained very low, even though Russia would have good chances to strengthen its export position in industrial goods, digital services, and also high-tech products if it had an innovation-friendly and internationally oriented economic policy. Putin's war in Ukraine threatens to damage three decades of Russian economic modernization, massively diminish Russia's international reputation, and reverse the modernization that has been successful in some sectors—including by foreign direct investors.

At the same time, it can be argued that the leading democracies across the world are acting together against Russia's war and that the Russo-Ukrainian war is a kind of political struggle of the democracy against authoritarianism as a political system; thus, in addition to Russia, China also indirectly comes into critical focus in some areas of the political system. However, based on the population figures of the countries that abstained from voting on the Ukraine resolution condemning Russia in the UN, it can be noted that around half of the world's population is not in favor of condemning and sanctioning Russia.

The risks of escalation in the Ukraine war are significant. President Putin's covert threat to use Russia's nuclear weapons against countries that interfere in the Russo-Ukrainian war has startled many Western countries. France, a nuclear power which usually has one of four nuclear-armed submarines operating in the world's oceans, decided in March 2022 to send three submarines on patrol; the vulnerability of the submarines appears too great if they are in port at the same time (Blegala, 2022). The risks of a military expansion of the Russo-Ukrainian war should be carefully considered in politics.

If the West rightly emphasizes the meaningful connections between democracy, market economies, and the rule of law, which secures freedom and prosperity, then it would be appropriate for the leading Western powers—including the US, the UK, France, Germany, Spain, and others—not to implement arbitrary political elements within the framework of the sanctions policy. The US ban on American citizens from accepting dividend and interest payments from Russia and Russian companies as of May 24, 2022, is a rather dubious measure if one takes the rule of law seriously. At the same time, it should be emphasized that the West should attach great importance to unity in a common, reasonable, effective sanctions policy toward Russia.

Even in the run-up to the Russo-Ukrainian war, the EU's international cooperation prospects were rather complicated and characterized by many areas of conflict with Russia. Within the framework of the EU's neighborhood policy, the European Union has a special commitment to cooperation in foreign and external economic policy. This involves sixteen countries, namely eight to the east of the EU and ten to the south. The Eastern EU Neighborhood Partner countries are Armenia, Azerbaijan, Belarus, Georgia, Moldova, and Ukraine. These are all former Soviet republics, and conflicts with Russia could arise with each country. For example, while Ukraine has been a politically disputed area of influence between the EU and Russia for many years, Russia is also active in an arbitration role between Armenia and Azerbaijan; with Belarus, Russia is a dominant partner, helping to use the country as a staging area for the Ukraine invasion. Meanwhile, Georgia was the target of a Russian military intervention in 2008, while Moldova has a serious challenge in Transnistria (or 'Pridnestrovian Moldavian Republic'), a strongly pro-Russia breakaway territory where the Russian military is stationed. Prior to the outbreak of war in 2022, the Russian list of demands (dated December 17, 2021) vis-à-vis NATO countries argued that Russia expects that the US and NATO would decide against integrating Ukraine and other former Soviet republics into NATO and that the West should withdraw weapons from, and end military exercises in, the region (ARD, 2021).

The US and NATO swiftly refuted these Russian demands and pointed out that each country was free to determine its own future. Russia also demanded that NATO troops be withdrawn from Eastern Europe which would amount to an effective cancellation of the previous accession of certain Eastern European states to NATO. On April 25, 2022, the Russian government declared that its war goals now included the establishment of a land-bridge between occupied regions in southern Ukraine and the breakaway Transnistria in Moldova which would indicate a Russian willingness to further escalate the war and indeed cause a spillover into another country (while a self-declared republic, Transnistria is not fully recognized as independent of Moldova). This, in turn, suggests that the EU/NATO member countries should undertake everything possible to support the Ukrainian government in driving out Russian forces from the southern parts of Ukraine and at least part of the Donbas region. If Putin should get a message that he can conquer neighboring countries on the basis of very strange arguments—bringing Europe back into the nineteenth century and creating a new form of expansionism, imperialism, and a form of international state-based terrorism—the Russian inclination to move militarily against yet more countries would grow over time. As a peaceful country, Russia could have a brilliant economic and political future as an internationally respected country, but as a war-prone system it is likely to face a decade of economic stagnation and decline (not the 5% real output growth as announced in a speech by President Putin) plus its possible disintegration sooner or later as the political consensus in the long run in Russia will decline very strongly. Russia as a war-prone regime is also likely to undermine economic stability in Asia/China and the world economy.

The EU seems to have chosen difficult countries for its neighborhood policy—the European Union can see this as a political goal, but the policy results so far are not encouraging. The EU's southern neighboring partners are Algeria, Egypt, Israel, Jordan, Lebanon, Libya, Morocco, Palestine, Syria, and Tunisia. In the case of Syria and Libya, this list of countries has a particular potential for conflict with Russia, and obviously Russia, as the successor to the Soviet Union, is a politically weighty actor in the Middle East; in Syria, Russia has militarily stabilized the Al-Assad regime for years and, in return, has a port base and military airport in its hands, which results in political influence for the Middle East and the Mediterranean. Relations with Israel are less problematic, but it is located in a region of tension and faces an unresolved peace problem with Palestine.

Spain has particular areas of conflict with Morocco because of the exclaves of Ceuta and Melilla in Morocco. The remaining countries on the southern list also face considerable economic and political challenges. Algeria, Lebanon, Morocco, and Tunisia are a particular focus of France's foreign policy, with EU-Maghreb country cooperation prospects including European gas use and the conceivable import of green hydrogen. Egypt is the most populous country in the Arab region, with the US, EU, and the UK rivals for influence. In African countries further south, the EU encounters economic and political influence from rivals China and Russia. The latter tends to offer particularly cheap weapons—compared with the US or EU countries—which ultimately brings political influence; China, on the other hand, has engaged in numerous infrastructure projects in African countries, with the EU appearing to be a relatively weak rival to China with more market-based approaches to infrastructure financing.

With regard to opportunities for shaping a new world order, the EU therefore has weak prospects. This makes closer cooperation with the United States all the more important for the EU. The United States, however, has been internally divided since at least the Trump presidency and can hardly be considered a reliable EU partner in the long term, especially since the EU countries will not automatically be active on the side of the US in conceivable US-China conflicts. In the area of defense policy, the US will demand greater commitment from the EU countries in the longer term—NATO is unlikely to be stable without increased defense spending by these countries.

One of the losers of the Russo-Ukrainian war seems to be, at least temporarily, climate protection policy. The readiness for international cooperation in the global economy has certainly been damaged with regard to important emitting countries of CO_2 in the context of this war. However, at least in the EU countries, a relevant problem has become clear, namely if one is heavily dependent on the import of fossil fuels on the energy production side. Incidentally, the sharp relative price increase for oil, gas, and coal is providing an impetus in many countries to invest more in renewable energies, at least in the medium term. The new geopolitical uncertainties and risks are likely to affect the financing of long-term climate protection projects worldwide. Special efforts will have to be made in the G20 countries—including Russia—to ensure successful international cooperation on climate protection policy.

As far as the prospects for a peace agreement are concerned, Ukraine will certainly want to emphasize the role of guarantor powers in the event that a neutral status is accepted, including Germany, France, the UK, and the US as well as Russia itself. One can only warn against Germany suddenly assuming a European leadership role here—in a new phase of hubris. First of all, the German government must ensure that Germany itself becomes defensible in the first place, that is, that years of underfunding and efficiency problems in the procurement area are sustainably overcome in the Bundeswehr. Solving this task in a meaningful way will take several years.

Ukraine's geographical situation is what it is, and the Ukrainian government itself should draw the right conclusions from this, including in negotiations with Russia. Years of negotiations between Russia and

Ukraine, which could keep the entire world economy in suspense for years, do not seem very desirable. It is certainly desirable that the EU countries support democracy, a market economy, and the rule of law in Ukraine. For the rest, it would make sense to try to keep Russia from going down a path of political autocracy or even dictatorship and to prevent, if possible, military interventions by Russia in other countries.

From the point of view of the global economy and, above all, the people in developing countries, a speedy conclusion to the Russo-Ukrainian war in the form of peace could help prevent the threat of a sharp rise in the price of wheat. If possible, both countries should be able to realize their usually relatively high grain exports. In principle, it would be desirable for both Russia and Ukraine to remain anchored in important international organizations so that conceivable conflicts of interest can be resolved within the framework of a rules-based legal system. The question remains why politicians and intelligence services in Western countries apparently fundamentally misjudged Putin's policy course on Ukraine for many years. The *Stiftung Wissenschaft und Politik* in Berlin, which is endowed with €15 million of state support per year, could have been expected to provide critical and competent analyses of Ukraine and Russia in the area of foreign policy earlier on.

As far as the twin challenges of the corona shock and the Russo-Ukrainian war shock in 2022 are concerned, innovative medium-sized and larger companies are likely to have an advantage in adapting. As always with shocks, efficient adaptation and sensible innovation dynamics are required for companies, for which a good positioning in the field of information and communication technology is important. In Germany, surveys of small and medium enterprises (SMEs) have shown that medium-sized and large companies are relatively advantageously positioned in ICT use and modernization: Larger SMEs have once again increasingly recognized the corona shock as an impetus for digital corporate modernization and the development of new procurement and sales channels (KfW Research, 2022a, 2022b).

For companies using gas in industrial processes, a gas supply embargo would be a major problem unless the embargo situation can be overcome within a few weeks. Sectors whose electricity intensity in production is relatively high will also be significantly negatively affected: Rising gas and coal prices will drive up electricity costs for private households and companies alike in the medium term. This is likely to apply to almost all EU countries, with the exception of France, whose high share of nuclear power generation should be an advantage in 2022. Sharply rising gasoline prices—which are an important market signal in terms of economic psychology—are likely to dampen household spending in all EU countries, which will act as a brake on the EU economy. The EU should be helped economically by the fact that the economic slowdown in the US is likely to be less severe than in Europe. In the United States in particular, gas prices are likely to rise much less than in the EU.

There will be need for broad EU support for the reconstruction of the Ukraine after the war. Such a reconstruction will take many years and should go along with institutional reforms which reinforce credibility of government and economic policy actors. One may doubt that it will be possible to rather quickly achieve the per capita income of Poland—as suggested by Becker et al. (2022)—which had better institutional modernization after the end of the socialist system and also a largely different privatization policy; to a considerable extent with a focus on enhancing economic competition. EU membership perspectives also helped Poland in the first 15 years of transition. The Ukraine of 2020 had a much larger corruption problem than Poland had around 2005 (see Chap. 13) and the Ukraine's privatization brought about a powerful group of oligarchs and big business with often rather modest competition in some sectors. The reconstruction of the Ukraine probably would take place in a rather destabilized global economic order.

Russia could declare a unilateral cease-fire in the relatively short term, which would presumably pose certain problems for Ukraine, as its leadership likes to recapture territories occupied by Russia; an outcome which is hardly possible without continuous and massive military aid from the West. The war could also drag on for years to come and cause a temporary destabilization of the world economy with considerable swings in (increased) commodity prices. From a Western perspective, it is important that Ukraine remains an independent state, which probably amounts to long-term economic and military support being provided. At the same time, the changed situation in Ukraine and Russia's invasion of the country have created a new regional conflict in Europe. Here, the EU, the UK, and US will be challenged, whereby the field of conflict represents many risks for all parties. In Washington DC, the originally apparent primary focus on China as a political opponent has thus become more complex. Russia, for its part, has little prospect of finding many economic or political heavyweight allies on the international stage. Brazil, Russia, India, China, and South Africa are working together in the framework of the

BRICS group of states, but this will hardly suffice for a close political alliance beyond the unequal pair of China and Russia. China and India have an ongoing territorial dispute including over parts of the Kashmir region; for Brazil good economic and political relations with the US, the UK, and the EU are more important—and more geographically relevant—than relations with Russia or China.

The logic of the economic gravity models for trade and direct investment, which emphasizes the distance of the respective country pairs or the negative role of transport and transaction costs in addition to the level of real income at home and in the respective partner country, will also have to be observed in the twenty-first century. In the field of climate protection policy, the Russo-Ukrainian war makes efficient cooperation between the G20 countries much more difficult for years to come. Russia, as an economically weak power, is likely to present itself even more strongly than before as a destructive, destabilizing power—promoting fake news dissemination—in Western countries if the conflict situation with the West continues. It would be all the more important that traditionally conservative parties in the US and the UK do not continue to themselves seek to gain influence and maintain power including via fake news, as was the case with Donald Trump in the United States and with Boris Johnson and his colleagues during and since the BREXIT campaign. Those who disregard the facts and the truth, and seek to manipulate them, tend to weaken overall progress in the fields of science and technology—and thus the economic and military strength of the respective country in the long term. For many years to come, global arms spending ratios will continue to increase unless a new, peaceful, and reformed Russia seeks sustainable cooperation with the West as a democracy and constitutional state in the medium and long term.

How strongly could the shutoff of Western countries from Russian gas supplies affect the Western world, in particular the EU (with gas prices in August 2022 about five or six times as high as the gas price in the US)? One should note, too, that as gas, coal, and oil are substitutes, fossil fuel prices of various resources are linked. One should keep in mind that the quadrupling of oil prices in the 1970s did occur in the context of a global supply cut of only 7% at that time, so that Russian cuts of fossil fuel exports could have a considerable shock effect in the world economy and certain crucial regions, including many EU countries in the case of gas cuts in particular. In a recent IMF paper (Lan et al., 2022) the authors have provided estimates which suggest—depending on two scenarios (integrated

EU energy markets vs. non-integrated markets)—that a stop of gas deliveries in the second half of 2022 could bring considerable negative real income effects for Germany: The cumulated negative output effect for 2022/2023 is -4.3% where this includes uncertainty effects plus the effects from the gas delivery cuts; a small negative output effect is also expected by the IMF for 2024, although the authors add that negative effects could be mitigated by adequate timely policy reforms. With simulations suggesting -2.7% output in 2022, -2.7% in 2023, and -0.4% in 2024, plus an additional 2 percentage points of inflation in that period, the potential negative welfare effect for Germany is considerable. One may add that there would be also negative German spillover effects (plus negative repercussion effects on Germany from partner countries) to major EU and non-EU trading partners. If the Russian gas cutoff would also apply to other EU countries—with the exception perhaps of Hungary which has agreed special contracts on gas imports with Russia—an output decline in the EU of close to 1.5% in 2022–2024 could occur whereby the main effects would be seen in 2023. This increases the risk of recession in the EU plus the UK where the latter is facing a strong recession risk in any case as the anti-inflation policy of the Bank of England has become rather strict during the course of 2022 (Bank of England, 2022). With the substitution effects of Germany and other EU countries' transitioning to liquid natural gas (LNG) imports to compensate for missing pipeline gas from Russia, international gas and oil prices would increase for some time worldwide which would further raise inflation rates; most notably in the South of the world economy (concerning energy importing countries) so that new balance of payments problems and other macroeconomic shock effects could affect many countries in the global system. The IMF could, under certain conditions varying across supported countries, offer additional loans for countries facing such adverse shocks and the World Bank, as well as regional development banks, could contribute to such stabilization efforts. Higher gas prices even are a strong concern for the Bank of England (2022, p. 13) in its Monetary Policy Report of the Monetary Policy Committee in August 2022:

> Russia's invasion of Ukraine is significantly adversely affecting world activity. The recent tightening in financial conditions also weighs on global activity over the forecast period, though to a much lesser extent (Section 2.1). As a result, in the MPC's baseline forecast, annual UK-weighted world GDP growth is projected to slow from 51/2% in 2021 to 21/2% in 2022, 1% in

2023 and 11/2% in 2024, below pre-pandemic rates.... This weighs materially on the demand for UK exports, in addition to the adverse direct impact on UK real incomes and spending from higher global energy and tradable goods prices.

There are considerable risks around the projections for global inflation and activity, which largely depend on how current geopolitical tensions evolve.

An upside risk to world prices is that the disruption to the supply of gas from Russia to Europe is even greater than embodied in the Committee's assumed path for gas prices in the baseline forecast.

An associated risk is that the available supply of other commodities, for example agricultural products and tradable goods, is hampered by more than assumed. That could stem from developments around Russia's invasion of Ukraine, or if new restrictions are introduced to contain Covid.

The compromise reached between Russia and Ukraine from August 2022 concerning exports of agricultural commodities from Ukraine's Black Sea ports might be a signal that Russia is seeking some first compromise with Western countries whose sanctions will strongly and negatively affect parts of the Russian economy in the medium term. Russia will want Western sanctions to be lifted in key fields, certainly in crucial international areas such as financial market transactions—also concerning the SWIFT agreement—and it will also have a strong interest in getting full access to its foreign currency reserves held abroad by various central banks in the West. It will be up to NATO and OECD countries to signal in an adequate way the requirements for a negotiation process; such an opportunity could be missed by both sides if there is no rising role of international diplomacy in the second half of 2022.

As the Ukrainian attacks on Crimea in August have shown, there is a considerable risk that the military conflict could intensify in the coming months or years. One cannot, of course, rule out that at some point the conflict could become frozen and a divided Ukraine would in principle face a situation similar to the division of Germany after World War II. Depending on the Western and Ukrainian policy in the medium term and the question of Putin's succession, there might emerge opportunities for achieving peace and restoring fruitful and stable economic relations between OECD countries and Russia. There is, however, as argued earlier in this study little hope for a new, cooperative regime between the West and Russia until the oligarchic nature of Russia's core economic system has not been changed; and it is unclear how this could come about. Even if this section of analysis contains several caveats, it might be useful for identifying some of the key issues with respect to Europe, Ukraine, and Russia in a medium-term perspective.

LITERATURE

ARD. (2021). *Osterweiterung; Russland veröffentlicht Forderungen an NATO* (transl. PJJW: 'Eastern Enlargement: Russia publishes demands on NATO'), version 17.12.2021 23:50 pm, available in German. Retrieved April 26, 2022, from https://www.tagesschau.de/ausland/europa/ukraine-konflikt-russland-ende-nato-osterweiterung-101.html

Bachmann, R., Baqaee, D., Bayer, C., Kuhn, M., Löschel, A., Moll, A., Peichl, A., Pittel, K., & Schularick, M. (2022). What if? The Economic Effects for Germany of a Stop of Energy Imports from Russia. ECONtribute Policy Brief Nr. 028. Retrieved May 24, 2022, from https://www.econtribute.de/RePEc/ajk/ajkpbs/ECONtribute_PB_028_2022.pdf

Bank of England. (2022). Monetary Policy Report, Monetary Policy Committee, August, London. Retrieved August 18, 2022, from https://www.bankofeng-land.co.uk/-/media/boe/files/monetary-policy-report/2022/august/monetary-policy-report-august-2022.pdf

Becker, T., Eichengreen, B., Gorodnichenko, Y., Guriev, S., Johnson, S., Mylovanov, T., Rogoff, K., & Weder di Mauro, B. (2022). *A blueprint for the reconstruction of Ukraine: A blueprint for the reconstruction of Ukraine*. CEPR Press. https://cepr.org/sites/default/files/news/BlueprintReconstruction Ukraine.pdf

Blegala, E. (2022). *La France renforce son niveau d'alerte et déploie trois sous-marins nucléaires en mer* [transl. PJJW: France raises its alert level and deploys three nuclear submarines to sea]. Retrieved March 30, 2022, from https://www.franceinter.fr/monde/la-france-renforce-son-niveau-d-alerte-et-deploie-trois-sous-marins-nucleaires-en-mer

Brzozowski, A., Basso, D., & Vasques, E. (2022). Macron teases alternative to EU enlargement, published by EURACTIV, dated May 9, updated May 10, 2022. Retrieved May 31, 2022, from https://www.euractiv.com/section/future-eu/news/macron-teases-alternative-to-eu-enlargement/?_ga=2.70936720.1061383478.1653987144-531813853.1653987144

KfW Research. (2022a). KfW digitization report for SMEs 2021. Retrieved April 04, 2022, from https://www.kfw.de/PDF/Download-Center/Konzern themen/Research/PDF-Dokumente-Digitalisierungsbericht-Mittelstand/KfW-Digitalisierungsbericht-2021.pdf

KfW Research. (2022b). Expected shift in demand toward digital offerings accelerates digitization in SMEs, No. 372. Published March 23. Retrieved April 04, 2022, from https://www.kfw.de/PDF/Download-Center/Konzernthemen/Research/PDF-Dokumente-Fokus-Volkswirtschaft/Fokus-2022/Fokus-Nr.-372-Maerz-2022-Digi-Nachfrage.pdf

Lan, T., Galen, S., & Jing, Z. (2022). The economic impacts on Germany of a potential Russian Gas Shutoff. IMF Working Paper No. 22/144 (July 2022), International Monetary Fund: Washington, DC.

CHAPTER 13

A New Global Economic Order

The global economic order will change permanently as a result of the Russo-Ukrainian war; in this context, the European Union already had to reckon with a less stable leading power in the United States since the 2016 election of Donald Trump. Under the Biden administration, the United States has emphasized a new confrontation between the West and political authoritarianism: Here, Russia—at least under President Putin—and China will then be seen as linked political opponents facing off against the West. Accordingly, Germany and other EU countries will partly turn away from China economically, and the German and European economy will have to seek much stronger cooperation with others in Asia, for example with the ASEAN group – standing for one-third of China's economic weight—than has been the case thus far. Even before the current phase of the war in Ukraine, in 2021, with negotiations on a trade and technology treaty with the EU, the US has begun to strengthen certain sectoral transatlantic cooperation ties, while at the same time insisting on joint security considerations, for example in the digital economy; this represents a visible US departure from multilateralism, that is, an emphasis on the important regulatory role of the World Trade Organization in favor of a more bilateral approach. This development has largely remained hidden from the public in Europe until now. At the same time, the US is trying to conclude a new cooperation treaty with Asia-Pacific countries with a similar approach under the Biden administration; that treaty was signed in 2022. For China, difficult questions arise, since an expansion of Sino-Russian economic

P. J. J. Welfens, *Russia's Invasion of Ukraine*, https://doi.org/10.1007/978-3-031-19138-1_13

relations is by no means a substitute for shrinking economic and techno-logical ties with the US, the EU, and the UK.

The Russo-Ukrainian war is a politico-economic shock that Russia, as the world's largest country in terms of area, has triggered with its invasion. Russia, with its Europe-Asia geographic span, is causing widespread inter-national shockwaves due to its own unilateral actions. Since Russia is in fact waging war directly on NATO's eastern border, thirty current NATO members are indirectly alarmed; moreover, the EU27 countries (the majority of which are also in NATO) and the United Kingdom plus the United States are particularly affected both politically and economically. In parts of Asia and in the NATO area, one wonders what the course and outcome of the Russo-Ukrainian war are likely to mean for possible China-Taiwan military conflict scenarios. Russia, as a major energy exporter, and Russia plus Ukraine as two of the 'big six' global grain producers are caus-ing prices to rise in key world markets—for energy and food; this is to the economic advantage of some energy exporting countries, for the global economy it has a dampening effect and for many energy and wheat import-ing countries in the global south it is an existential challenge, at least tem-porarily; here, new waves of emigration motivated by hunger and increased poverty could also become visible as a phenomenon: ultimately also as a North-South emigration phenomenon. In 2012, Russia had become the 156th country to join the World Trade Organization, bringing globaliza-tion to a temporary peak; and Russia is indeed likely to remain a member of the WTO. However, the Biden administration's inclination to contrib-ute significantly to a strengthening of the World Trade Organization, including through reform impulses, is further tempered by the Russo-Ukrainian war: from the US point of view, Russia's accession will be inter-preted in the future as another politically uncooperative great power now sitting at the table in the WTO alongside China; China and Russia are seen as authoritarian adversaries of the US (until perhaps the election of a pop-ulist US president in Washington DC once again leads to a change of view; precisely back to a kind of neo-great powers regime approach as in the late nineteenth century). The Russo-Ukrainian war has worldwide effects; in the course of the conceivable NATO accession of Sweden and Finland—assuming only temporary resistance to their accession on the part of Turkey—NATO will become larger and more militarily active; the global military expenditure ratio could increase by half a percentage point which, from an economic point of view, is hardly a permanent welfare gain, if one could make this military expenditure increase superfluous by way of an improved European and global security architecture instead. How could such a new security architecture be established within a few years is a big question—with no discernible answer.

Vladimir Putin's role in Russia in 1991, if one follows the book of Catherine Belton (Belton, 2020) titled "Putin's People" (the German edition, Belton (2022) "Putins Netz", p. 91), was initially still that of a defender of democracy in Russia. Putin, through his influence in his hometown of St. Petersburg, was able to halt the advance of tanks and troops under the de facto command of the hardliner faction of Russian intelligence in August of 1991. In Moscow, it was Boris Yeltsin who opposed the armored brigade ready to attack the White House (Russia's parliament building). Putin then found himself alongside Yeltsin in Moscow a few years later. It is not impossible that Putin, in addition to his basic nationalist political orientation that sought to restore Russia's economic-political-military greatness after 2000, was—for a time—willing to reach an understanding with the United States and the West. The details of covert disputes between the US and Russia are not known. However, some arguments in Belton's book are convincing, showing that after a temporary economic-political domination by the oligarchs, Russia's secret service (formerly the KGB, then mainly the FSB) gradually reclaimed economic power for the state—and often for the secret service itself; many privatizations and corporate governance episodes were probably not in accordance with the law, which made many oligarchs vulnerable to blackmail by politicians. Ownership was strangely and imprecisely defined under President Putin, since as a private part-owner one could not be sure that a dissatisfied state leadership would not demand the sale of company shares at artificially low prices to new owners or to the state or state-owned companies: company ownership in Russia can be seen as a kind of political feudal system, whereby many foreign investors were probably generally respected and only occasionally came under arbitrary political pressure (Western companies from strong mother countries have advantages here: one thinks, for example, of the US, Germany, France, and the United Kingdom).

At the same time, Putin allowed some oligarchs with strong political loyalty to invest in the UK on a large scale (large illegal capital outflows in excess of tens of billions of dollars annually were observed on top of this). In London, some oligarchs were able to acquire a prestigious position among the British public and also appeared as party donors to the Conservative Party, while in the US some oligarchs appeared in financing real estate projects of then developer, later President, Donald Trump. The old KGB, which in the early 1970s recognized the technological superiority of the West and in the years that followed focused heavily on illegal technology imports from the West on one hand and on political destabilization information campaigns in EU countries plus the US on the other, became a massive source of fake news—false reports contradicting reality, intended to stir up political discontent in the West. That in the UK in the run-up to BREXIT, leading Conservative politician Boris Johnson, for his part, knowingly and visibly used fake news in the BREXIT campaign—for example, by misstating the UK's financial contributions to the EU which, he claimed, would instead be available for the healthcare system in the event of BREXIT—can be considered surprising and a worrying decline in political quality standards in Anglo-American democracy. The same is apparently true with regard to the series of fake news, false reports, and allegations in the US during the 2016 presidential election campaign, namely by Republican Donald Trump, and then also immediately in the four subsequent years of the Trump administration and in the subsequent 2020 presidential election campaign. If the rules-based world order with a leadership of the West should be lost in the early twenty-first century, then it is not only the impulses from Moscow (or even China) that are important here.

Rather, a self-destabilization of the UK and the US is also relevant, a development, astonishingly, with a conservative political focus. After all, one would think that virtues such as honesty and adherence to contracts are classic building blocks of conservative ideologies of Western countries. There is a serious problem here, as the facts in the UK and US show, with the addition in the United States of the problem I have highlighted of a core political contradiction in the context of massively increased inequality, which amounts to a continuing internal rift and political voter dissatisfaction (Welfens, 2019, 2020). Economic inequality is unacceptably high in the United States, according to surveys of American voters; however, if one asks respondents who should be responsible for reducing this excessive inequality, the relative majority opinion is that big US firms should play the largest role. This is purely just wishful thinking, as profit-maximizing multinationals listed on US stock exchanges cannot be expected to do just raise costs.

One solution that is actually possible, namely for the state to solve the problem by changing the taxation system and broadening social policy (including the Europeanization of the health insurance system), does not find majority support in the US political system, while progressive digitalization continues to increase income inequality. This problem constellation creates broad political discontent in the US and strengthens the electoral chances of populist candidates, which in turn intensifies political polarization in the US and thus reduces its ability to be a leading Western power (which it has been able to do in part thanks to a broad internal US political consensus). From the EU perspective, this leads to critical questions about US leadership and, ultimately, the West's international power, especially in view of the Russo-Ukrainian war.

If one first assumes that US leadership will remain relatively undiminished for a number of years, or that the Biden administration and its successor will be able to maintain the NATO alliance as well as regional economic alliances under US leadership (e.g., with regard to Europe and Asia), then a Western economic slowdown strategy vis-à-vis China and Russia can be assumed. China will have greater problems in enforcing direct investment in Europe and North America as well as in ASEAN countries and will probably also experience problems with steel and electronics exports vis-à-vis the West+ (the West plus Japan, the Republic of Korea, Australia, and ASEAN countries). Russia is likely to experience major problems not only in energy exports vis-à-vis OECD countries for many years, but also in steel and aluminum exports, which in turn will strengthen the profitability of Western suppliers—unless there is a general international slowdown in economic growth. Russia's economic growth is likely to experience a long-term slowdown due to Western barriers and problems related to the import of technology-intensive goods and intermediate products. The fact that China will have to choose between close political cooperation with Russia and a broad partnership with the West+ is probably one of the new changes in the context of the war in Ukraine.

Even if China were to achieve only half the gross domestic product per capita (in purchasing power parity terms) of the US by 2040, that would still mean that China, with a population four times that of the US, is likely to be economically twice as strong as America in the long run. By contrast, the United States could introduce at least one important change (see Welfens, 2019, 2020): if the United States could reform health insurance in such a way that low-income mothers in particular experienced significantly reduced infant mortality, and if US infant mortality thus dropped to the level of Germany and France, the United States could see about 50 million additional residents within about 30 years (showing the enormous cost of the partly weak US healthcare system). However, this can probably only be expected if a new political consensus is reached in the US for a longer period of time and if the health insurance system would be Europeanized in a multi-stage reform process—presumably stimulated by an intensified transatlantic policy dialogue.

The changes brought about by the Russo-Ukrainian war and the rise of China can also be classified in a complementary and modified way, respectively (Gabriel & Hüther, 2022). According to the former German foreign minister and head of the German Economic Institute (*Institut der deutschen Wirtschaft*), the Atlantic is no longer the only center of gravity; it is now in strong competition with the Indo-Pacific region. However, as much as China's rise is impressive from an economic point of view—and Russia will probably be economically dominated by China—China's not very modern zero-Covid strategy (still with a massive focus on lockdowns even two years after the outbreak of the coronavirus pandemic) and also China's clear support for Russia stand for a double question mark with regard to China's strength. Whether China will succeed in the medium term in making the regional RCEP free trade agreement—under Chinese leadership—a reliable stimulus for more growth in China and Asia is uncertain; if China's economic and military expansion in Asia is perceived as being overly aggressive, the quality of regional cooperation in the China-dominated RCEP approach is likely to suffer a serious setback, or trade integration could be limited to only a limited group of classes of goods. China will also face the risk that, as the Russo-Ukrainian conflict continues, there will be the problem of the West gradually targeting its sanctions increasingly against China as well. This could happen, for example, if China realizes significantly increased oil and gas imports from Russia—in the wake of a partial or complete energy import embargo on Russia by the US and the EU.

A rapid military victory by a highly armed Russia against Ukraine has proved impossible in the spring of 2022. Russia's military advisers within President Putin's entourage have apparently not developed a realistic view on the question of the scale and determination of Ukraine's defense effort. Russia's war of aggression—without any real discernible reasoning—in February 2022 has destabilized the world's political and economic order:

- Western confidence and political trust in the promises made by President Putin and the Russian leadership will be significantly weakened for many years to come. Cooperation with Russia will become more difficult.

- Russia's economic modernization will suffer from reduced direct investment inflows from multinational companies from industrialized countries.
- Russia's political leadership—active as an autocracy (with Putin at times displaying dictatorial characteristics)—is seeking to close ranks with China, but this means assuming junior position for Russia in the long term; it will weaken over time due to China's increasing economic and military weight. A strong economic-political orientation of Russia toward China contradicts the historical orientation of Russia from before 1917—the year of the October Revolution—toward Western Europe. This then represents new contradictions in Russian society and its political system.
- Russia's economic growth is likely to be weakened in the medium term by new developments, especially since imports of high-tech products from the West will decline significantly for several years (even after an end to the war).
- After spring 2022, Eastern European EU countries will permanently experience an increased risk premium due to their geographical proximity to Russia as well as increased capital outflows—also because wealthy citizens buy real estate in Spain, France, and Italy. The conditions for economic convergence in the EU will thus deteriorate, and the EU will have to make more transfers (relative to national income) to Eastern European EU countries in the long term.
- Germany could benefit economically from increased emigration from Eastern European EU countries, but its growth prospects will be temporarily weakened by the dampening of German-Russian trade and the reduced attractiveness of Eastern European EU countries as suppliers of intermediate products for industry in Germany.
- By motivating Germany to significantly increase defense spending as a result of the Russo-Ukrainian war, Germany's military role within the EU will increase. However, Germany is likely to continue its efforts to realize a political-military anchoring in NATO.
- The EU's role in defense policy will increase in the medium term, although an efficient military industry in the European Union will only be visible in rudimentary form for years to come. Where Airbus, for example, encounters major international competition in civil aviation, the company generally develops excellent products; Airbus' defense division, on the other hand, has attracted attention, for example, due to enormous quality problems with military transport

aircraft. Behind this are apparently serious efficiency problems in government procurement in Germany and other EU countries.

- Germany's strong export- and direct investment–driven economic model is at risk of coming under massive pressure in the event of a disintegration of the world economy into an OECD-led bloc and a China-Russia bloc (Rürup, 2022). A rules-based world economic order without politically hostile blocs is also in the interest of global prosperity. How this order can be restored—after a peace agreement between Russia and Ukraine—is difficult to foresee for the time being. At least there is a chance, if the US and the EU are willing to invest in such a world economic order.

The Russo-Ukrainian war has weakened the rules-based international economic system that has existed since the end of World War II. Russia's participation in key international organizations was suspended in the spring of 2022, and the country will likely need several years to resume an active and credible role in these organizations. Presumably, there will also be new problems at the UN and G20 levels in reliably engaging with Russia as a player in the global climate change policy arena. To the extent that China's political leadership permanently sides with Russia, a new Cold War could emerge, placing China-Russia in political-economic conflict with the West plus Japan, the Republic of Korea, Australia, and some other countries; an important issue in Asia will concern the positioning of India, which has visible political ties with Russia through long-standing arms sales; but there is also latent India-China tension, especially as there are also border conflicts in the border regions—especially in Kashmir. In terms of security policy, as ASEAN countries see China's continued rise—and its growing military budget—as a long-term threat, these Asian countries may find themselves cooperating more politically with OECD countries in the early twenty-first century; even as the respective importance of China as a trading partner is likely to also increase over decades.

It cannot be ruled out that after decades of sustained globalization, a de-globalization phase will set in, with liberal principles losing influence in the global economic order. For the West, it appears to be a formidable challenge to promote Western values in a meaningful way in the dialogue of cultures and to develop starting points or policy areas for a new dialogue about important values. The influence of social media is likely to play a significant role in this context. Whether the US will present itself as a reliable partner of EU countries in security matters in the medium term, remains to be seen. The radicalization of the political fringes in the US—but also in Europe—is a serious challenge, which in turn is likely to be further encouraged by expansion of digital media. These are rather poor conditions for the West to successfully shape the new world order in the long term. Authoritarian regimes around the world will probably try to split what is actually a global Internet into regionally controlled Internet spheres.

A new lasting peace order in Europe is urgent. Realizing it will require special political and economic efforts. It is a question of a new safeguarding of life, security, prosperity, and trust. One might hope, following Böttcher (2022), that the common culture in the larger Europe, including Russia, will be effective as an active bridging and cooperation element for a common peaceful future after a Ukraine-Russia peace agreement.

Without international institutions—in which a peaceful Russia plays a lasting role—it will hardly be possible to achieve success here. In a transitional period, arms spending in Europe is likely to increase significantly; arms control will want to be meaningfully put back on the agenda. The EU should intensify its integration efforts and also cooperate more closely with other integration areas in the global economy. Within the European Union itself, it would be well advised to pay attention to innovation and competitive structures. An EU purchasing monopoly for gas, as proposed by the European Commission in 2022, is contradictory in view of this and, moreover, does not bode well after the experience with Covid-19 vaccine procurement. Procurement diversification in the energy sector will, however, be able to be strategically emphasized on the part of the EU.

Trade and direct investment networks must continue to be strengthened from a European perspective; and one should not allow a long-term weakening of international organizations in the context of the Russo-Ukrainian war. It will, however, take many years (following an assumed ultimate peace treaty between the Ukraine and Russia) to restore Russia's role in certain international organizations. Regular reviews of certain consistency aspects of national constitutions—for example by the Venice Commission of the Council of Europe—are worth considering.

As regards the EU, following a potential enlargement for the accession of Ukraine, there will be a change in the internal balance of power to the extent that one would want to analyze power dynamics via the Banzhaf Index; there would be an increase in terms of the power of smaller EU countries in decisions based on qualified majority voting in European Council meetings (Kirsch, 2022); it is not clear to what extent this could reduce political stability vis-à-vis EU integration—a potential remedy would be an adjustment in the EU's required critical percentages for qualified majority voting, namely a minimum of 55% of member countries and 65% of the EU population. There is some risk that accelerated EU enlargements also in the Western Balkans could undermine the economic and political stability in the European Union for some time as structural economic divergence would be raised.

It is in the interest of the West to reduce, in the short term, trade and investment relations with Russia under Putin. In a more long-term perspective, it is in the interest of the US, the EU and Japan to reinforce trade and two-way international investment with a new Russia (i.e., under a new president or a new government). Trade and international investment links are not a guarantee against war, but both trade and international investment create mutual interdependency; it gives the West and Japan an opportunity to influence Russia—and Russia has an opportunity to peacefully influence the Western world and Japan. As regards EU-China economic and political relations, the European Union and its member states should help to avoid a lasting impression that China is internationally isolated. International isolation could be a goal in an extreme situation, but if one is in favor of some trade and cooperation between the EU and China (or the US and China), one should indeed maintain mutually beneficial economic and political relations between the European Union and China. At the same time, the EU should point out to China that an active role in circumventing Western sanctions against Russia on its part is unacceptable in this critical situation of a war between the Ukraine and Russia. It would be wise if the US and the EU could encourage China to push Russia toward agreeing to a lasting peace settlement with the Ukraine quickly.

Following Kant's ideas on perpetual peace, the rule of law must be anchored in a sustainable manner both nationally and internationally. Global climate policy as a major international cooperation project should continue to be given high priority.

FUTURE PROSPECTS FOR THE EU PLUS THE UNITED KINGDOM AND RUSSIA

As for military developments in Ukraine, which in May 2022 was still largely successfully resisting Russia's invasion force, one can hope that a cease-fire could be reached soon; with Russia retaining Crimea and probably maintaining a massive influence in the Donbas region (and possibly even regions beyond). However, it cannot be ruled out that a protracted war (even more protracted if we consider the 2014 occupation of Crimea as the first phase of the war) will result, or even some kind of World War III. The risks associated with the Russo-Ukrainian war are difficult to quantify and even more difficult to control.

It is likely that the course of the Russo-Ukrainian war has been significantly impacted by behind-the-scenes assistance in various forms of (especially US) aid to Ukraine in 2022. In addition to US arms deliveries to Ukraine, US intelligence of a military nature was apparently essential to Ukraine's defense (presumably including the sinking of the Russian warship *Moskva*, its Black Sea flagship). In addition, in Europe there was significant support for Ukraine from the United Kingdom, although the government of Boris Johnson in 2021 was a far cry from the previous Cameron governments and the social democratic governments of Tony Blair in its orientation vis-à-vis its Russia policy. Under Prime Minister Blair, Vladimir Putin's visit to London in 2003 marked the first visit to the UK by a Russian (or indeed Soviet) head of government or state since 1874. One might have seen Putin's visit to London as a chance to renew relations and save Europe from reverting to the nineteenth century. Unfortunately, after a few years of halfway relaxed Anglo-Russian relations, London and Moscow seem to have fallen back into the times before 1874.

It is not easy to adequately describe Russia's international power position. First, Russia is the largest country in the world in terms of sheer geographic area, with a long western border with the EU at one end and an important eastern border—also with China—at the other; Russia is therefore relatively defensible militarily and has a basically European (traditional) policy perspective and also an Asian perspective. Second, Russia is one of the major exporters of oil and gas in the final phase of the fossil fuel era, which is not expected to end until the 2040s. Third, Russia is a nuclear power, an old European military power that is one of the five permanent members of the United Nations Security Council. Fourth, in the self-image of large segments of Russia's political leadership, it is an ancient superpower that has rightfully claimed substantial influence throughout Europe since the Congress of Vienna of 1814/15; Russia had repulsed Napoleon as well as, indirectly, Germany in World War I and, moreover, Nazi German armies in World War II. Fifth, Russia is a global religious center, as the Russian Orthodox Church—allied with the Tsars before the October Revolution of 1917—has once more become a pillar of the political system under President Putin. Sixth, Russia is a medium economic power whose real income (in purchasing power units) is about the same as that of Germany. Seventh, Russia is a country with a relatively large population, which could rise to 150 million by 2040. Eighth, Russia under Vladimir Putin has a state apparatus with low legitimacy and weak trust among the population, as evidenced by the low response of the Russian population to Putin's calls for widespread vaccinations in the context of the corona pandemic. Ninth, Russia is a leading international cyber-power, making it a key player in the global digital economy. Tenth, Russia is key to the fight against global warming and an important player in the G20.

There are certainly some parallels with the United States with regard to certain points. At the beginning of the twenty-first century, the US is conventionally superior to Russia in military terms and also tends to be economically superior, but the United States is internally divided by increased economic inequality and—as can be read in my book *The Global Trump* (Welfens, 2019)—has little prospect of overcoming this great inequality, which is not accepted by the majority of the US citizenry, in the medium term. Internal political polarization in the United States suggests that its ability to act has been weakened. One of the peculiarities of recent social developments is that the political party affiliation of citizens seemingly has a significant influence on the acceptance of scientific analyses: Republican Party voters have little confidence in science, while Democratic Party voters report a relatively high confidence in science.

As for Russia's relationship with the UK, apart from the period during World War II—and Russia's military alliance with the US and the UK (as well as the French government-in-exile and other allies)—there have been many decades of poor relations. Recent relations between Russia and the UK can be summarized as follows (Allan & Bond, 2022):

- The UK's 2021 Integrated Review of Security, Defense, Development and Foreign Policy classifies Russia as a threat to the UK.
- Russia's political leadership regards the UK as an adversary—thereby presenting it as a country weaker than Russia, with the UK rated weaker than Germany in Western Europe, and incidentally as a junior partner country of the US; BREXIT has weakened the UK's standing in the view of Russian observers.
- Anglo-Russian relations in a historical perspective offer four lessons: Since the UK and Russia share few common values and interests, the

basis of the relationship is not very stable; antagonism between the two countries is the historical norm. To a certain extent, both sides appear to possess an exaggerated self-image and their own countries positioning on the global stage. There are always external impulses beyond British control that have a dampening effect on UK-Russia relations.

- Larger international trends include the weakening of the Western-dominated international order; also, the rise of populism and growing resistance to economic globalization trends; finally, the spread of authoritarian rule globally.
- The UK can pursue its Russia-related interests through four priority points: Increasing UK flexibility, focusing defense resources in the Euro-Atlantic region; presenting itself as a trusted ally and acting as a partner.
- UK decision-makers should be guided by four propositions: Firstly, there must be a clear and well-thought-out policy orientation toward Russia. Secondly, antagonism between the two countries is not per se in Britain's interest. Thirdly, BREXIT makes it harder for both the UK and the EU to negotiate with Russia. Fourthly, an effective Russia policy requires that Britain make a realistic assessment of its own power. Following BREXIT, efforts are needed on the part of the UK to rebuild its reputation and strengthen cooperation with European partner countries.
- A meaningful Russia policy should focus on the defense of British territory and British citizens plus British institutions. A security policy anchored in the Euro-Atlantic area is necessary; the focus should also be on issues such as the non-proliferation of nuclear weapons, the development of economic relations, and contacts between citizens of both countries. Policy goals must be pursued with state power, but also with soft power and through international partnerships. Despite BREXIT, the EU remains an important international security partner for the UK.

Here, it can be noted that the development of economic relations will not be easy in the case of a de facto embargo on fossil fuel–based energy commodities; the question of to what extent they are ready to support Russia's economic modernization (i.e., overcoming the dominance of gas and oil in Russia's exports) would have to be put to both the UK and the EU.

It would be desirable that, in the event of a possible positive new beginning after the end of the Russo-Ukrainian war, political relations between the UK and Russia do not fall back into old patterns or long periods of inactivity. Regular political meetings at the highest levels and special EU/UK cooperation with Russia in the field of climate policy seem desirable. Such meetings would be relatively easy to organize if a new Russia could tend toward democracy, a market economy, and the rule of law. In this context, Russia itself can certainly take special positions, and of course its geographic location—and the further economic rise of China—will play an important role in Russia's foreign and economic policy. Russia, regardless of its form of government or style of governance, cannot readily be expected to simply accept NATO encirclement; unless Russia itself were a NATO member.

Perspectives on UK-Russia Political Relations

Relations between Russia and the UK have been almost consistently bad going all the way back to the Congress of Vienna in 1814/15, and neither side has been successful in overcoming this negative tradition in the recent past. Russia has not invested in improved relations with the UK and arguably assumed after the BREXIT majority in the EU referendum of June 23, 2016, that the UK was significantly weakened and that it would hardly be worth Russia's while to work toward improving relations. For its part, the United Kingdom also did little to improve relations with Russia, especially during the first 15 years after the breakup of the Soviet Union in 1991.

After several assassination attempts were made against fugitive Russian spies in Britain, apparently carried out by Russian intelligence operatives on Putin's orders, Anglo-Russian relations deteriorated significantly. Putin, who is poorly versed in foreign policy, apparently did not understand how politics in Britain works or simply overestimated Russia's power; the assassinations had a massively negative effect on the British public and in terms of British policy toward Russia, which became less and less cooperative over time. Incidentally, it is hard to understand why the UK did not give defected spies from Russia new identities to help protect them from the vengeance of Russia's intelligence services—as would have been the case in the Cold War. However, it also cannot be overlooked that Russia's seeming policy of killing prominent political opponents (and ex-spies) seems to have deliberately relied on a public spectacle as a political deterrence strategy: focusing inward, on Russia itself.

Regarding the UK's ability to influence Russia in three areas—military and economic power (hard power), soft power (e.g., media power), and cooperation with partners—Allan and Bond (2022) have indeed provided important considerations in their Chatham House research paper.

As far as the medium-term recovery prospects of the US, the UK, Germany, and France (plus other EU countries) are concerned, there is an overlay of negative corona impulses and the Russo-Ukrainian war shock which could have a negative impact for several years. It cannot be completely ruled out that Russia in essence loses the war against Ukraine and that change in the political system of Russia toward a modern democracy plus a constitutional state could then also take place. This prospect probably has only a low probability, but it should not be entirely ruled out either.

As far as the corona pandemic-related economic stimulus is concerned, negative demand effects are at work here, but also disruption effects in production—for example, because parts of the workforce were affected by Covid-19. After all, there were also temporary developments in terms of structural change in the corona shock years of 2020 and 2021 that led, for example, to labor productivity improvements in sub-sectors of the economy despite the economic downturn in Germany (Wilke & Welfens, 2022); similarly, this also applies to France, the UK, and the USA (de Vries et al. 2022), although here, as in Germany, attention must be paid in each case to the sectoral degree of home-office production contributions, which tend to favor productivity advances. Similarly, the focus on sectors with a high "digital production intensity", that is, where the use of ICT plays a significant role, is relevant.

International production chain disruptions should also be considered, with supplier problems affecting trade in computer chips, for example, being a serious problem at times in many sectors in the US and EU countries in 2021 and spring 2022. Supply problems also tend to weigh on the recovery in key sectors in industrialized countries. The European Central Bank (ECB XE "ECB" \t "see European Central Bank" , 2022) has pointed out in its Economic Bulletin 2022/2 that there was hardly any easing of problems with supply bottlenecks at the beginning of 2022; as also shown in Fig. 13.1 for four activity sectors (industry, services, nationwide problem sector, transport), with dark red boxes marking the highest intensity of supply problems, while dark blue boxes indicate an absence of such supply problems. A comparison of the Eurozone and the US shows that supply problems in 2021 were slightly more pronounced in Europe than in the United States (where commodity procurement problems are

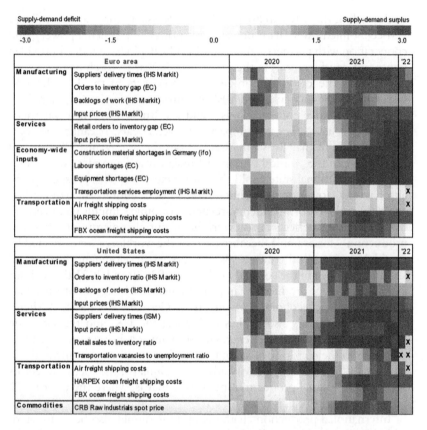

Fig. 13.1 Supply chain issues in the Eurozone and the US, 2020–2022 (January and February). Source: ECB (2022), Economic Bulletin 2022/2, p. 53

also considered, but countrywide problem areas are not captured as in the Eurozone). In the first quarter of 2022, the Eurozone continues to be more affected by supply problems than the United States.

As far as supplies for the Eurozone from China via rail traffic between China and Western Europe are concerned, the Russo-Ukrainian war is likely to have led to temporary disruptions in rail freight traffic to the Eurozone—and also from Europe to China—in the spring of 2022. After all, the relevant freight trains pass through Russia as a transit country. The problem is only relatively limited in its significance insofar as while the share of Europe-China rail freight traffic has increased over the longer term, the share of rail freight in total trade was still relatively low in 2020/21.

The Federal Reserve in the US and the ECB in the Eurozone had postponed planned interest rate increases at the beginning of 2022 due to increased inflation rates because of the negative economic effects of the Russo-Ukrainian war. However, the Federal Reserve indeed began with initial rate hikes in spring 2022. With over 7% inflation in the Eurozone in 2022 and around 10% inflation in the US, both the Federal Reserve and the European Central Bank will come under considerable pressure to raise central bank interest rates further in the medium term. Incidentally, the Biden administration attempted to counteract the rise in oil prices on world markets by releasing large quantities of oil from the US strategic reserve in March 2022; and indeed the oil price temporarily fell back below \$100/barrel at the beginning of April 2022. However, it can also be expected (based on informal conversations I have had with a small circle of energy experts) that existing political agreements between the USA and Saudi Arabia are continuing, and that informal political agreements between the US and Saudi Arabia should keep the oil price fluctuating in a price band of between \$80/barrel and \$130/barrel in the medium term.

In the EU, the increase in CO_2 emission certificate prices for suppliers from the energy sector and industry should be noted with regard to the medium-term economic dynamics, although this began before the Russo-Ukrainian war and brought certificate prices to over €90/ton CO_2 at times (see Fig. 13.2). The Russian invasion and campaign against Ukraine is causing price expectations for fossil fuel energies to rise in the medium term and this, in conjunction with rising CO_2 certificate prices, will accelerate the structural change toward renewable energies in the medium and long term.

This has an effect on suppliers in the energy and industrial sector in the EU as innovation impulses in the direction of an increased use of renewable energies or for investments that are energy-saving when using fossilized energies. It is true that governments in Germany and other EU countries have indeed initiated an accelerated promotion of renewable energies after spring 2022. However, in the process, old barriers to modernization—for example in Germany—in the area of reducing energy intensity in the real estate sector are not being addressed in a sensible way: Austria is one of the world's leading producer of passive houses; however, these Austrian house models cannot be built in Germany because 16

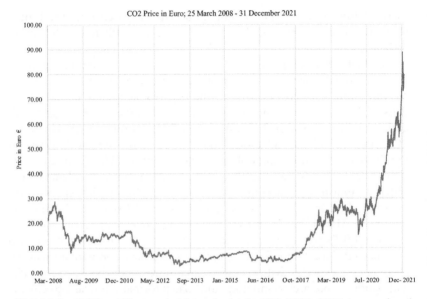

Fig. 13.2 CO2 certificate price dynamics in the EU, 2008–2022 (quarterly values). Source: Own representation of data available from https://icapcarbonaction.com/en/ets-prices

federal states with their regional building codes and over-regulation prevent this progress. This is an internal barrier in the EU market (one exists in most EU countries), but this obviously makes little sense either economically or ecologically.

If, in the medium term after 2022, global demand for solar and wind power deployment increases significantly, European and US producers in the solar power plant and wind power generation sectors will also see expansion momentum, in addition to suppliers from China and India. Suppliers from the US and the EU tend to specialize in large wind turbines—offshore and onshore—as well as high-tech solar products, while companies from China are well-positioned internationally in standard solar modules and mid-sized wind turbines. Some suppliers from India also have great potential for expansion in the field of photovoltaics or solar power plants.

Significant investment distortions arise in the US, the UK, and the Eurozone as a result of negative real interest rates for large companies over several years. Here, investment projects could have been realized that no longer prove profitable when real interest rates normalize. From an economic point of view, phases with negative real interest rates (the market interest rate minus inflation rate) are generally considered problematic when it comes to the efficiency of certain investment projects. In the case of the UK, the BREXIT decision in 2016 and the end of the UK's transition phase from January 1, 2021 (its de facto exit after having left the EU de jure on January 31, 2020) are also having a negative impact on foreign trade.

INTEGRATION AND DISINTEGRATION ASPECTS OF THE EU WITH REGARD TO THE UKRAINIAN ISSUE

Ukraine seemingly has a long-term interest in joining the European Union. As a country with a good 44 million inhabitants, Ukraine would be relatively influential—this is all the more true in the longer term as high economic growth would allow Ukraine to gradually approach the EU average income. Since 55% of the EU member countries (i.e., at least 15) representing 65% of the EU's population are required for qualified majority decisions in the European Council (at the ministerial level as well as at EU summits), Ukraine's large population would give the country a relatively large influence in such majority decisions.

At its Versailles summit in March 2022, the EU dampened the hopes of Ukraine's government and President Zelenskyy for Ukraine to be hastily admitted to the EU in a kind of fast-track procedure. Many accession countries have had to go through a methodical and multi-year preparation and adjustment process in the run-up to accession; Ukraine will hardly be any different. The IMF's Country Report on Ukraine (IMF XE "International Monetary Fund" , 2021) points to numerous economic, structural, and economic policy problems in Ukraine that are considered to remain in part unresolved: These include the large influence of state-owned enterprises, high levels of corruption, and insufficient modernization in parts of the country's infrastructure networks. One can add that Ukraine's economy is largely dominated by only a few "entrepreneurs", effectively oligarchs, which makes it difficult to clearly separate state tasks from the tasks of the economy. If Ukraine were to become an EU member—as the 28th EU member country—there would indeed be some changes with regard to the political balance of power in the EU based on any analysis using the Banzhaf Index.

The Banzhaf Index determines the power of countries in the case of certain majority requirements (e.g., X% of the population) according to the proportion of conceivable coalitions which country Y, by joining possible losing coalitions Z_i, would turn into a—minimal—winning coalition. Only in matters of defense and fiscal issues does a unanimity requirement apply in principle at the EU level. Thus, the question of changes in power in the EU based on the Banzhaf Index of different countries is of great interest in the case of Ukraine joining the EU (see Table 13.1). As regards the Banzhaf Index an EU enlargement to admit Ukraine as a member state would bring a considerable power loss for Poland (−13.55%) and Spain (−13.29%) as well as Italy, France, and Germany (−11.86%, −11.80%, and −10.41%, respectively) trailed by several other EU countries also facing a smaller loss of power. Thus, there may be a majority of members in favor of amending the Lisbon Treaty in order to raise the minimum percentage of the EU population which would have to be covered by a majority coalition (in qualified majority votes); for example, the winning coalition would have to stand for 70% of the population of the EU instead of the current 65%. Such a change would reverse some of the power losses for the larger countries mentioned, but also for many medium-sized and even some smaller countries.

In this context, Ukraine could well have the status of a neutral country in terms of military policy. Although this status would be more of a European exception in the case of Sweden and Finland joining NATO than it has been so far, if there are good reasons for such a militarily neutral position, this option can be seen as reasonable for Ukraine. Within the EU, the neutral member states are Austria and Malta, moreover Cyprus, which as a divided country cannot count on the agreement of the NATO country Turkey for it to join the alliance. Ireland, while not constitutionally neutral, has followed a traditional policy of neutrality for decades—initially following independence as Ireland wanted to differentiate itself from Britain, the former occupying country. There would likely be no majority found in Ireland to support its joining of NATO. Switzerland has also traditionally been neutral, and with this position it has weathered relatively unscathed both World War I and World War II, during which without a commitment to neutrality the country's general staff would likely have experienced an internal conflict with regard to the warring actors: Germany and France.

One of the important questions after the Russo-Ukrainian war is what conclusions Russia and China will draw with regard to integration into

Table 13.1 Distribution of political power in the EU27 and in an EU28 that Includes Ukraine (according to the Banzhaf Index), on the basis of Kirsch (2022)

Country	Pop. (mio.)	BI: EU27	BI: EU27+UA	Rel. Diff.
Germany	83.2	12.09%	10.83%	–10.41%
France	67.7	10.08%	8.89%	–11.80%
Italy	59.2	8.88%	7.83%	–11.86%
Spain	47.4	7.66%	6.65%	–13.29%
*Ukraine**	*41.4*		*5.96%*	
Poland	37.8	6.41%	5.54%	–13.55%
Romania	19.2	3.95%	3.73%	–5.49%
Netherlands	17.5	3.75%	3.56%	–5.11%
Belgium	11.6	3.05%	2.95%	–3.35%
Czechia	10.70	2.95%	2.86%	–3.01%
Greece	10.68	2.95%	2.86%	–3.00%
Sweden	10.4	2.91%	2.83%	–2.88%
Portugal	10.3	2.90%	2.82%	–2.84%
Hungary	9.7	2.83%	2.76%	–2.59%
Austria	8.9	2.74%	2.68%	–2.23%
Bulgaria	6.9	2.50%	2.47%	–1.12%
Denmark	5.8	2.37%	2.36%	–0.43%
Finland	5.53	2.33%	2.33%	–0.24%
Slovakia	5.46	2.32%	2.32%	–0.18%
Ireland	5.0	2.27%	2.27%	0.13%
Croatia	4.0	2.15%	2.17%	0.86%
Lithuania	2.8	2.00%	2.04%	1.98%
Slovenia	2.1	1.92%	1.97%	2.69%
Latvia	1.9	1.90%	1.95%	2.92%
Estonia	1.3	1.83%	1.89%	3.54%
Cyprus	0.90	1.77%	1.85%	4.06%
Luxembourg	0.63	1.74%	1.82%	4.39%
Malta	0.53	1.73%	1.81%	4.55%
Decision probability		13.2%	11.36%	

Note: Population figure for Ukraine is on the basis of Eurostat data with has removed the population figures for Crimea and the occupied territories in the Donbas region, lowering Ukraine's overall population by approx. 2.6 million.

Source: Own representation on the basis of Kirsch (2022), Table 1

Western payment systems. It is likely that both countries will try to establish their own international payment systems, which will lead to an increase in the international weight of the Chinese yuan in particular. The global market shares of the dollar and the euro in the world reserves of central banks are likely to decline in the long term. The not unproblematic seizure of a large share of Russia's foreign exchange reserves held abroad—for example, at foreign central banks—in March 2022 will certainly have the consequence that China, Russia, and a number of other countries will in the future hold at best only a small share of their respective foreign exchange reserves abroad. This development is one element of a temporary disintegration of the global economy. Less integration and less global foreign trade as well as reduced direct investment flows will dampen economic growth in the world economy for a number of years. This could contribute to political antagonism at the international level which could intensify significantly in the medium term.

Prospects for Developing Countries

Many developing countries suffered significant declines in terms of growth in 2020/21 due to the corona pandemic and yet had still expected positive economic development in the medium term at the beginning of 2022. The Russo-Ukrainian war has worsened the development prospects of many poorer countries, as transitory high oil price increases and rising wheat prices, as well as the important roles of both Russia and Ukraine as exporters of certain other agricultural products, pose new risks to developing countries. Before even dealing with comprehensive corona vaccination drives in most low- and middle-income countries, and thus containing the corona-related economic risks, a significant new challenge is coming to these countries in the form of the war. In March 2022, the World Bank (Indermit, 2022) and the UN's Food and Agriculture Organization (FAO XE "Food and Agriculture Organization" , 2022a) had already provided important analyses and policy considerations (FAO XE "Food and Agriculture Organization" , 2022b) in this regard. The FAO analyses point above all to aggravated hunger problems in relatively poor countries in the context of reduced wheat exports from Russia and Ukraine, among other things, and to sensible economic policy countermeasures.

Following a forthcoming World Bank analysis, a permanent 10% increase in oil prices leads to a 0.1% decline in economic growth (Indermit, 2022). Oil prices have doubled from mid-2021 to spring 2022, which, if the situation continues with such a significant increase in oil prices, will lead to a one percentage point loss in growth in oil importing countries such as China, Indonesia, Turkey, and South Africa. Prior to the outbreak of the war in Ukraine, real economic growth in South Africa was expected to be 2% in 2022 and 2023, 2% to 3% in Turkey, and 5% in China. This means that the loss of growth could reach half to one-fifth of the growth rates forecast before 2022.

However, in the event of a Western boycott of oil imports from Russia, oil prices outside the OECD countries could also be dampened, as Russia would only be able to sell surplus oil volumes on the world market at a discount to countries such as India, China, Indonesia, Turkey, and South Africa. The growth prospects of the important oil exporting countries could possibly improve in the medium term with an overall increase in oil prices; at least if higher oil prices do not lead to increased corruption and economic inefficiencies in the oil exporting countries outside group of industrialized countries.

RECONSTRUCTION PROSPECTS OF UKRAINE

In 1991, both Poland and Ukraine had similarly high per capita incomes at the beginning of the post-socialist transformation, but by 2021 Ukraine's per capita income was only about one-third that of Poland. Apparently, Poland has done a better job of getting institutional reforms off the ground and has also paid much more attention to anchoring competition in product markets during the privatization process than Ukraine (on Poland and important privatization issues, see Welfens & Jasinksi, 1994; Welfens, 1997). In Ukraine, on the other hand, similar problems have arisen in the course of privatization in the decade after 1991 as emerged in Russia during privatization, namely oligarchic structures. This meant that competitive dynamics became more weakly anchored in Ukraine than in Poland, as can also be seen from EBRD annual reports (see, e.g., EBRD, 2005, 2006). Poland's economic modernization has certainly benefited from that country's EU membership, and presumably also from its NATO membership, each of which is a positive signal of confidence from the perspective of foreign investors: in the case of the EU, it is a matter of legal security and unfettered access to the EU's internal market; in the case of NATO membership, the security perspective is important. In view of the different points of view, it is probably not realistic to expect that Ukraine could easily or rapidly catch up to Poland's per capita income in the medium term as part of a reconstruction program supported by the OECD countries. In addition, the problem of corruption in Ukraine is significantly greater than in Poland, as Table 13.2 shows.

In a CEPR analysis of reconstruction prospects from early April 2022, the authors develop some interesting considerations, according to which a

Table 13.2 Corruption Perception Index rankings for selected countries, 1995–2020

Country/Territory	Rank 2020	Rank 2015	Rank 2010	Rank 2005	Rank 2000	Rank 1995
Germany	9	11	15	16	17	13
Japan	19	18	17	21	23	20
France	23	23	25	18	21	18
United States of America	25	16	22	17	14	15
Poland	**45**	**29**	**45**	**70**	**43**	**N/A**
Italy	52	61	69	40	39	33
South Africa	69	61	56	46	34	21
China	78	83	78	78	63	40
India	86	76	91	88	69	35
Indonesia	102	88	116	137	85	41
Ukraine	**117**	**130**	**146**	**107**	**87**	**N/A**
Russia	129	119	154	126	82	N/A
No. of countries surveyed	180	168	178	159	90	41

Source: Own representation of data available from Transparency International Corruption Perceptions Index, 1995–2020; *in the field of corruption Russia is much worse than Poland while Poland, the Ukraine and Russia had rather similar indicator values in key institutional fields of systemic transformation; see the EBRD (2010), Annual Report, London.*

https://www.transparency.org/en/cpi/2021

politically independent agency in Ukraine should use Western (and probably also Japanese) aid money for efficient reconstruction (Becker et al., 2022). However, the authors' view that Ukraine could soon reach Poland's per capita income during a reconstruction phase—and after a reduction in corruption—is rather unrealistic: for the reasons given above.

What is also urgently needed is not only a reconstruction perspective for Ukraine, but also a meaningful policy approach toward Russia as a whole, which must include the question of how Russia's political leadership and policy trajectory can be anchored more firmly than before in ideas of the West and the Enlightenment. This involves not only leaving behind the ideas of communism, but also bringing about a critical examination of Stalin and Stalinism, as well as demystifying some of the right-wing philosophers which Putin has elevated as influential thinkers whose writings are shaping Russia's destiny (without Western intelligence agencies realizing the significance of these intellectuals and writings early on).

In 2014, for example, President Putin had 5000 copies of a book by the Russian philosopher Ivan Ilyin, *Our Tasks* distributed to senior officials and political friends in Russia. Ilyin's writings had been suppressed in the Soviet Union because he had supported the "Whites", or opponents of the revolution during the October Revolution and the immediate aftermath in the Russian Civil War. In addition, Putin's gift package contained two other books by Russian philosophers: *The Philosophy of Inequality* by Nikolai Berdyaev and *The Justification of the Good* by Vladimir Soloviev. The three philosophers were noted Russian thinkers of the nineteenth and early twentieth centuries.

Ilyin's thoughts on a unique Russian, guided form of democracy, which Ilyin, who had fled Russia to escape the communists, first wrote down in Germany in the 1920s and in Switzerland from 1938 on, were obviously very important to Putin from an ideological point of view: Ilyin, who was also a Slavophile philosopher, had been quoted by Putin in his major speeches in 2004 and 2005 as well as in 2014, whereby Ilyin was a critic of Western-style democracy with its, in his view, too frequent changes of government. By contrast, Ilyin called instead for a combination of Russian Orthodoxy—as a religious basis—and a kind of acclamatory democracy (echoing indeed part of the political program of Benito Mussolini in Fascist Italy). Incidentally, Ilyin also stressed that Ukraine is essentially an integral part of Russia, and he pointed out that one day the West, under pretexts such as securing freedom and democracy, might try to make Ukraine politically independent and dissolve the state of Russia, which could only end in chaos for Russia and the Russians. One wonders what reasoned assessment of Putin's behavior and policy course prevailed in, say, the Foreign Offices in Berlin, Paris, London, or in the upper echelons of the EU in Brussels over the period from 2015 to 2021: to what extent had the ideological changes in Putin's own ideology been recognized and sensibly reflected in analyses of both the man himself and of Russia—in part, apparently, changes that arose after it had apparently become clear from Putin's point of view that Russia was not really classified as a partner by the West.

Putin's new ideological course made the West appear as an active adversary opposing Russia's rightful claims to power; and this new ideology made Russian ideas from the 1920s influential once again, according to which Russia should increasingly turn to Asia rather than the West for preferred international cooperation (Eurasia approach). French philosopher Michel Eltchaninoff had already described important elements of the new ideology in his book on Putin's thinking which first appeared in French in 2015, but later appeared in both English and German also (Eltchaninoff, 2015, 2016, 2018). In 2018, the *Neue Zürcher Zeitung* (*NZZ*), a leading Swiss newspaper, published a brief summary analysis of Putin's evolving ideological approach and the obvious new influence by Ivan Ilyin, who died in Switzerland in 1954.

For centuries prior to the October Revolution of 1917, important historical influences in and on Russia came from the West (including Marx and Engels, who after all are two false prophets from the West). Czars and Czarinas allied themselves with conservative powers like Prussia and Austro-Hungarian Empire for centuries. From Putin's point of view—and that of some of the intellectuals in Russia and of some leading representatives of the Russian Orthodox Church—leading Western European countries in the modern world, such as Austria, Germany, and France, represent a decline in values when it comes to a tolerance of homosexuality or the role of human rights, for example. Moreover, temporarily high oil prices had allowed the Russian government to significantly increase its arms spending after 2000, increasing Russia's military power in the medium term, and arguably encouraging militaristic thinking among leading politicians.

EFFECTS OF THE UKRAINE-RUSSIA WAR ON COUNTRIES IN ASIA

Leaving China aside, there are a number of other countries in Asia that have been significantly or even massively affected by Russia's war of aggression. These are primarily those countries that are net importers of oil and gas, with the massive oil price hike in the spring of 2022 having macroeconomic dampening effects. Moreover, for a country like Cambodia, where oil and gas imports account for about 10% of GDP, this can also lead to a critically increased current account deficit or higher net imports of goods. Sri Lanka is also facing an energy supply crisis and Russia could in this context expand its political influence in Asia (later also in other emerging and developing countries) with loans to Sri Lanka and Cambodia.

Numerous countries in the Caucasus and Central Asia are dependent on Russia for foreign trade, in some cases significantly so, such that an economic slump in Russia in 2022 and 2023 will put a dampener on exports to Russia—Armenia and Kyrgyzstan, with exports to Russia of over 5% of GDP in 2021, are notable in this regard.

Guest worker remittances from Russia—and some other countries—have been of significant importance particularly in individual Caucasian and Central Asian countries in 2021 (more precisely: in the first three quarters): remittances from Russia accounted for more than 25% of GDP in the case of Kyrgyzstan and over 15% of GDP in Tajikistan (ADB, 2022)—see Fig. 13.3.

In the event of an economic collapse in Russia, many workers in the Russian construction industry and other sectors will lose their jobs, and this will primarily affect guest workers from the Caucasus and Central Asian republics. Countries such as Kyrgyzstan, Tajikistan, Uzbekistan, and Armenia will then have to cut their imports of goods considerably. Domestic political unrest may well then follow, as well as intensified international political conflicts between countries in Central Asia, for example. Western sanctions against Russia, which dampen the development of the Russian economy or cause a recession in Russia, thus have important destabilizing effects in countries in the Caucasus and Central Asia. If a Western

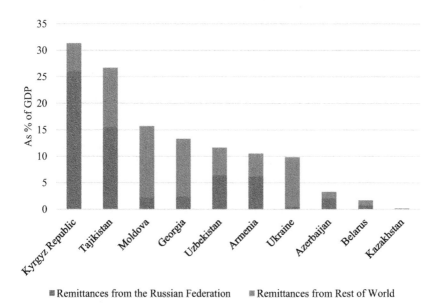

Fig. 13.3 Remittances in countries in Eastern Europe, the Caucasus, and Central Asia as a Percentage of GDP in 2020. Source: Own representation on the basis of data available in Ratha and Kim (2022), Table 1

energy import boycott against Russia is realized, causing a deepened recession and devaluation of the Russian ruble, guest worker remittances to the aforementioned countries will decrease significantly, and foreign trade of the affected countries (and of Russia itself) will also decrease. Incidentally, political instabilities can also come about through massively increased food prices—in the context of the Russo-Ukrainian war—and rising interest rates or risk premiums, as was already evident in Sri Lanka in the spring of 2022. The idea that economic sanctions can be used to induce Russia to call and end to its war against Ukraine may sound attractive from the political perspective of Western countries; but the expected serious side effects in other countries (outside Russia) should not be overlooked. A policy of harsh economic sanctions against Russia will not be a very unerring approach because of the international economic interdependencies.

If the border disputes which already exist in some cases, for example between certain Central Asian countries, should intensify in the course of a sharp recession in Russia, the Russian Federation will probably temporarily cease to be a traditional regional power of influence. The EU will hardly become involved as a regulatory power; at most, Turkey—already economically and politically active in these countries to some extent—could exert a conflict-reducing influence. It should be noted that the study by Bachmann et al. (2022) completely ignores the connections shown here.

Key Ukraine Emigration Aspects and EU Enlargement Risks with Ukraine

Even before the outbreak of the Russo-Ukrainian war, there were significantly high levels of emigration of both male and female Ukrainian workers, essentially to Russia, Poland, and some other countries. Among the important findings is the analysis of Commander et al. (2013), based on a survey in Ukraine: well-educated and younger workers are over-represented among emigrants. However, this is only partially reflected in the jobs they take up abroad—half of the emigrant group finds itself in jobs for which they are overqualified. This downskilling problem is due, among other things, to the fact that in Ukraine, personal qualifications and job quality exhibit little in the way of correlation. Emigrants who experience downskilling in Ukraine will typically also experience it in their destination countries. Such problems are comparatively serious in the EU when comparing the EU and other emigration destination countries.

One particularly important analysis focuses on potential emigration flows from Ukraine in the event that it would indeed become an EU member (Fertig & Kahanec, 2015). The authors determine the migration potential toward the EU from its neighboring countries in Eastern European plus Croatia: the two authors conduct an analysis—an out-of-sample forecast—to estimate emigration potential after the first round of EU enlargement to the east. The analysis illustrates that emigration numbers are determined by the costs of migration and economic circumstances; the largest effects arise from policy variables. After an initial increase in emigration—which is somewhat higher with migration liberalization than without—emigration figures from the EU's Eastern European neighboring states evolve toward reaching a long-term equilibrium. Ukraine is expected to have the highest emigration figures in absolute terms, while the highest immigration figures from the neighboring Eastern European EU countries are found in the simulation analysis for Germany, Italy, and Austria. Relative to the population, immigration intensity is highest in Ireland, Denmark, Finland, and Austria.

Even if one has to modify the Fertig-Kahanec analysis because of the implementation of BREXIT—taking full effect as of January 1, 2021—the insight from the above analyses remains:

- The integration of Ukrainian refugees and guest workers into the EU will not be an easy process, with the possible exception of Poland and some other Eastern European EU countries.
- There is a risk that large numbers of immigrants from Ukraine could focus on just a few EU countries, which could politically destabilize some of these countries: The next BREXIT-type disintegration case then looms.
- The EU's inclination to learn from mistakes and important political failures—such as BREXIT—is discernibly low; it therefore seems implausible that a sensible political reform package will be adopted or implemented in the EU before Ukraine's accession.

Of course, the outward refugee flows from Ukraine in 2022 only partially follow emigration preferences; possible emigrants, under normal circumstances, are a random subset of the refugees. This does not exclude the possibility that, in the medium term, a share of the refugees may indeed decide to work as guest workers in certain EU countries. Due to the close affinity between the Ukrainians and Polish, Poland is likely to be a preferred destination country for many refugees. The economic logic of the so-called gravity equation suggests that refugees and emigrants from Ukraine will initially have a certain preference for countries relatively close to Ukraine; in a second adjustment step, however, refugees and emigrants from Ukraine will select more economically preferable destination countries to a certain extent.

However, the UK is arguably an almost inaccessible destination for many of these people currently; before the BREXIT vote in June 2016, the UK had become home to almost half of all emigrants from Eastern European EU countries—one reason why the issue of immigration became so politically prominent in the UK in the decade after 2004. The UK, along with Ireland, and Sweden, had not taken advantage of the opportunity to implement a post-enlargement transition period with certain limitations on the free movement of persons from Eastern European accession countries; unlike Germany and France, for example. While ideological struggles within the UK were the primary cause for the BREXIT vote, the overall uncoordinated EU immigration policy obviously had a part to play in the UK's exit. Moreover, EU survey results in EU countries—regularly commissioned by the European Commission—were apparently not consistent in the run-up to the referendum (despite this, the European Commission did not change survey methodologies, and no critical debate took place in Brussels as to what lessons should have been learned; for more see Welfens, 2017a, 2017b, 2018).

A Ukrainian accession to the EU would put the then enlarged European Union in a new situation of having a long (and presumably contentious) eastern border with Russia. For Russia, depending on ongoing political tensions between Russia and the EU, an EU enlargement to the east to include Ukraine—with its over 44 million inhabitants (in 2020) and a Russian-speaking minority population—could provide an incentive to destabilize Ukraine politically and economically in various ways, thus acting as an external destabilizing force on the EU. In the context of EU regional policy and EU cohesion policy, the European Union would then likely face significant additional financial burdens. Moreover, a relatively unstable Ukraine would possibly also be a bone of contention within the EU, which could also destabilize the European Union from within. Unreflective political enthusiasm in Brussels, and numerous EU member countries, for an EU enlargement to include Ukraine is therefore neither appropriate nor responsible. In the event of an EU enlargement to include

Ukraine, the EU would have to adopt a modified, comprehensive Russia policy, which would bring its own political risks for the stability of EU integration.

An EU enlargement to include Ukraine will also bring a significant potential immigration problem for a number of EU countries—and this could then also precipitate the next case of an EU-EXIT; at least if the political management in Brussels does not improve significantly or does not draw sensible conclusions from the mistakes made during the last EU enlargement to the East (and indeed vis-à-vis BREXIT). In particular, it should be ruled out ex ante that some EU countries would not implement any kinds of transition period for the free movement of persons from Ukraine. Otherwise, there is a risk that large numbers of emigrants from Ukraine would focus on migrating to just a few EU countries and thus potentially destabilize the political system in at least some EU destination countries with high relative levels or immigration or even encourage radicalization and anti-EU attitudes there.

Ukraine, as a relatively large country in terms of population and with a low per capita income, can expect considerable levels of emigration to other EU countries for many years to come; with the full freedom of movement enjoyed by Ukraine as an EU member country, there are considerable risks that high immigration figures will destabilize other EU countries or the European Union as a whole in the medium term. The question of a reasonable—temporary—restriction on free movement in the event of EU enlargement should be reconsidered. There is also a danger that the topic of an EU enlargement to include Ukraine will be discussed primarily on an emotional level in the public arena with analytically reflective policy debates being marginalized or indeed entirely absent, and that the necessary risk-reducing flanking measures for a stable and sustainable enlargement of the EU to the east will not be initiated. Ultimately, the Russo-Ukrainian war could spark the further disintegration of the European Union by creating further "BREXIT"-type cases; possibly promoted and supported in the run-up by Russia's government and the Russian president. There is no doubt that President Putin and his government have supported BREXIT in a variety of ways in the British political process—without any major critical public debate about this in the UK. In any event, a further enlargement to the east, in this case to include Ukraine, will be a complex challenge for the EU and its member countries.

GLOBAL ECONOMIC OUTLOOK IN THE MEDIUM TERM

If the four economic fields of an aging society, ICT expansion, economic inequality, and globalization (trade and direct investment) are considered and related to the Russo-Ukrainian war, then certain important prospects emerge for Russia, the EU—plus the UK, Ukraine—as well as Japan and China.; Depending on the Russo-Ukrainian scenario, two alternative pictures emerge here in the medium term, with nominal interest rates expected to rise in the medium term and real interest rates in the long term. The Russo-Ukrainian war causes an international slowdown in economic development, which for China brings a dampening effect on real growth and a lower inflation rate than in the US, the Eurozone, and the UK.

In the UK, the Johnson government will push for the UK's agreement with the EU on Northern Ireland, namely the Northern Ireland Protocol, to be terminated in the slipstream of the war in Eastern Europe. However, according to Speaker Nancy Pelosi, the US will try to prevent that—there can be no US-UK free trade agreement, she said, if the UK would effectively undermine not only the Northern Ireland Protocol but also the Good Friday Agreement on Northern Ireland (in the negotiation of which the US had played a significant part). The post-BREXIT British approach, namely Global Britain, could then not be effective—that is, the claim of more global trade after the UK's exit from the EU will be dealt a serious blow. It will also hardly be feasible because the US has only partially reactivated the World Trade Organization under the Biden administration; difficulties with reform of the organization have prompted the Biden administration to organize international trade issues more strongly via the new US-EU institution called the Trade and Technology Council (TTC) which was established in 2021/22, and which entails a BREXIT-related disadvantage for the UK.

Ukraine will push for a quick accession to the EU after any peace agreement would be with Russia, but one can hardly advise the EU to act hastily, as the risk of the next BREXIT will then be relatively high, unless one develops a really well-thought-out admission strategy for Ukraine on the side of the EU. If the next EU enlargement to the East would be rushed, it should only accelerate further EU disintegration, Putin would probably have achieved his goal of weakening the West in various areas after all. From an EU perspective, US leadership should be viewed with a question mark in the medium term because the US itself is latently politically unstable because of the enormous levels of economic inequality that could be overcome with European-style social policies, while at the same time polls in the US show that the majority of the electorate does not want government to enact and be responsible for such social policies. Rather, a relative majority of respondents (Welfens, 2019, 2020) want large corporations to eliminate inequality by changing corporate wage structures: an illusory expectation in the US market economy, which in turn fosters the resurgence of US populism, that is, (a return to) Trumpism—along with the political polarization that is unlikely to reinforce Western leadership.

It is therefore up to the—already partly overstretched—European Union to contribute to the stabilization of the West through clever reforms and policy projects and, in the process, ultimately also to induce the US to switch more strongly to a social market economy as the economic order for the twenty-first century. A multi-year occupation of parts of Ukraine by Russia will create a relatively unstable situation in the middle of Europe. Overall, the present analysis shows how the terrible Russo-Ukrainian war could come about; political mistakes in parts of the West and certainly in Russia, as well as weaknesses in Western experts in and contributions to Russian studies, are two important explanatory pillars. Incidentally, there is little reason to believe that the US market economy is inherently stable—the 2007/08 Transatlantic Banking Crisis has already exposed enormous weaknesses in the Anglo-American model. However, the West's democracies have always remained capable of reform in important fields, which can make the combination of market economy, democracy, and rule of law attractive in the long term; perhaps one day it can bring about a rethink in China.

In Germany in particular, however, there is a contradiction in the area of energy policy, according to which the so-called "traffic light coalition" is calling for a rapid expansion of renewable energies, especially in 2022, so that Germany would be less dependent on energy imports from Russia. However, there are bureaucratic hurdles hindering a rapid expansion of renewable energies, and it is not clear how Germany and the EU intend to get through 2022/23 in terms of energy policy—given a hard winter. The parallel phase-out of coal and nuclear power has proven to be a risky policy for Germany; in the middle of the 2022 crisis, more fracked gas is now being imported from the US. The EU missed possibility of a gas import tariff vis-à-vis Russia in the first half of 2022, while Russia will presumably try to cause problems for many EU countries in the second half of the year via arbitrarily reduced gas supplies—while Russia will also presumably be able to increase its external surplus compared to the previous year as a result of increased gas prices (and increased oil prices). In the energy sector, the West's sanctions policy toward Russia seems ill-conceived to some extent, at least in the EU.

GLOBAL ECONOMIC AND POWER PERSPECTIVES ON THE TWENTY-FIRST CENTURY

From a US perspective, Russia's invasion of Ukraine—also against the backdrop of both China's rapid economic rise in the three decades after 1978 and its recognizable implicit support for Putin's positioning in the Russo-Ukrainian war—increases the pressure to position itself vigorously in international economic relations. After the failure to launch the Transatlantic Trade and Investment Partnership (TTIP)—a trade cooperation project with the EU—under President Obama and the scrapping of the finalized Trans-Pacific Partnership trade agreement with Japan and many other countries in Asia and the Pacific region by Obama's successor Donald Trump (who, incidentally, also made some changes to NAFTA, the US free trade agreement with Canada and Mexico), the United States is in a difficult position. The Obama administration's Trans-Pacific Partnership liberalization package eventually got off the ground without the US under the leadership of Japan (which itself came on board late in the negotiations), but the US has little ability to act on trade policy because the old compromise formula required of a Democrat US president plus a Republican-controlled US Senate no longer works: a free trade initiative launched by a Democrat president combined with the usually pro-free trade Republicans can yield a grand coalition for pro-trade liberalization—since the rise of the populist Trump, however, Republicans have swung to an anti-trade liberalization agenda as Trump has persuaded the Republican establishment that the US has fared poorly in free trade agreements and that the US has a structural trade and current account deficit problem. However, as the Roeger and Welfens (2022a) analysis shows—in a novel DSGE model with trade and direct investment relationships—Trump has not been able to gain any advantage in his trade war with China; moreover, an innovative DSGE model approach of Roeger and Welfens (2022b) has shown that the US current account deficit substantially reflects the influence of US multinationals and the so-called primary income balance, respectively (simplified here: the net profit position of US multinationals). This is therefore a misguided view on the part of the Trump administration.

How could the global economy be shaped in the long term? Before Trump, the US approach was to use economic power, trade networks, military alliances, and cooperation in important international organizations (under Trump, the alternative approach was "America First"—with a diminished role for international organizations and a weakening of rivals in the West, such as the European Union). In this contradictory starting position of US policy and with a view to new challenges, for example in the area of cyber warfare risks, the Biden administration sought a new international policy approach: with the EU, a politically speaking relatively non-binding new policy of security and trade policy of cooperation was launched under the heading TTC (Trade and Technology Council) in 2021. The agenda of the EU-US Trade and Technology Council has so far hardly been understood in Europe and the global economy.

The US has supplemented this transatlantic agenda with the new Indo-Pacific Economic Framework for Prosperity (IPEF) agreement—to be signed in Tokyo at the end of May 2022; the IPEF including the US represents 35.4% of world gross domestic product (excluding the US: circa 20%). In addition to Australia, the IPEF group primarily includes India—with a share of world gross domestic product (according to purchasing power parity) of around 7%—and also the majority of the ASEAN countries (the latter also comprise a good 6% of world gross domestic product). India is China's democratic rival and, according to UN population forecasts, will have a population around 2030 that slightly exceeds that of China.

India's per capita income in 2020 was considerably lower than China's, but with strong US-India-EU cooperation, India could probably close the per capita income gap with China in the long run. India is heavily dependent on Russia for arms, and that in turn makes India, China's old rival—both countries are nuclear powers—heavily dependent on Russian policies. India was one of the leading countries in the Non-Aligned Movement for decades during the Cold War and, as a large country, will not want to move into unilateral dependence on the United States. In terms of climate change policy, India is not an easy partner vis-à-vis cooperation with the West. The country was number 5 globally in terms of solar energy use in 2018 (Welfens, 2022), but at the same time is enormously coal-heavy—that is, with high CO_2 emissions—in power generation; and that, of all things, in conjunction with state-owned coal mines and coal-fired power plants, as well as a state-owned freight railroad networks where half of the ton-miles of transportation represented coal shipments.

From a New Political Economy perspective, it might be difficult for the West to win India over as an active partner for green economic growth. However, many EU countries (or OECD countries) must first face the challenge of overcoming their own inconsistencies in environmental and climate protection policy: if, for example, according to OECD data, Germany's eco-tax revenue amounted to 1.7% of GDP in 2020, while Denmark and the Netherlands stood at almost 4%, then this is an indication of the following:

- In Germany, the eco-tax revenue ratio is curiously about two percentage points below the optimal value; at least if one assumes that Denmark and the Netherlands were at about the optimal eco-tax revenue ratio.
- If a higher eco-tax revenue ratio had been achieved, it would also have been possible to increase funding for "green innovation projects" appropriately; in other words, to further internalize positive externalities, which would have brought a positive welfare effect (if the increased eco-tax revenue in Germany stood for a structural surplus—in the sense that a full internalization of positive externalities in—increased—research funding would have brought a budget surplus—it would also have been possible to reduce income tax rates; this would also be a possible welfare effect not yet realized).

Among the major global challenges that could also bring countries together through policy and economic cooperation are successes on green patent issues. Smart reforms of economic systems—plus a thoughtful political constitution—combined with smart economic policies can lead to higher innovation dynamics (including increased "green innovation dynamics"), as an analysis by Welfens et al. (2022) shows: an increase in direct investment stocks relative to the capital stock causes both green process innovation (cheaper manufacturing processes), green product innovation (new and improved goods and services) to increase and green patents. The authors conduct an empirical study on green product and process innovations, as well as firms that have both product and process innovations in Europe; the results when looking at both firms including innovations in industry (manufacturing) and firms without innovations in industry, respectively, are:

- A high score in the rule of law significantly or highly significantly strengthens green process innovations (with or without industry).
- Domestic direct investment rate (ratio of the inward foreign capital stock relative to the capital stock of the host country) has a highly significant positive effect on green product innovations—when both including and excluding industry. When one excludes industry, both the inward FDI stock intensities are also positively and significantly related to process innovations (at the 5% level). Here, process innovations are likely to benefit from international technology transfers.
- On green product innovation (excluding industry), outward foreign direct investment rates have a clearly negative effect; this could be explained by the fact that from a techno-globalization approach—multinationals have R&D for innovation in the headquarters country and in foreign subsidiaries—increased direct investment abroad leads to less investment in product innovation there in the headquarters country.
- There are some other significant influencing factors, with green international competitive advantage, represented by "Green RCA", having a positive effect: if countries have an advantage in terms of the relative export share of environmentally friendly products there or are positively specialized therein, respectively, product innovations increase significantly.

Thus, if the direct investments of multinational companies—as a partial element of globalization—can achieve settlement successes, this also brings an increase in sustainability-promoting innovation dynamics in the EU+ economic area (EU27, plus United Kingdom, Switzerland, Iceland, Norway, Turkey, Serbia, North Macedonia, and Montenegro). Whether these correlations also apply in a similar way in other world regions is not yet known; only further research could yield desirable findings here. Of course, multinational companies from the US, Europe, Japan, the Republic of Korea, China and other countries are part of global innovation and economic dynamics. Tendentially, the removal of trade barriers and international investment barriers means that international specialization gains in production, and thus real income gains, should result.

In addition, with more integrated markets, the fixed costs of companies in the area of research and development can be spread more easily over larger production or sales volumes, which means more innovation dynamics and thus welfare gains. Conversely, a conceivable de-globalization in the wake of the Russo-Ukrainian war means an international loss of welfare for many countries and the global economy as a whole. Whether or not a phase of de-globalization will indeed occur remains to be seen for the time being. Many influencing factors will play an important role. Among other things, it is conceivable that countries under strong structural adjustment pressure, such as the OPEC countries, will make a significant contribution to globalization in the course of efforts to achieve climate neutrality by 2050.

Individual countries can also improve their international income rankings significantly over the course of a few decades. Here, China itself is an important example. One could also consider the case of Poland or Ukraine, both of which have a roughly similar population, and yet real GDP in Poland was much higher than in Ukraine in 2020. This was largely due to the fact that Poland's transformation policies and constitutional reforms were more successful than Ukraine's in economic terms—with Poland also benefiting from EU membership. Of course, a country like South Africa could also catch up strongly internationally in the medium term with clever policy reforms.

ECONOMIC NETWORKING POWER PERSPECTIVES

How strong is the West, understood as the Western industrialized countries under US leadership in combination with influential countries in Latin America, Asia, and Africa? In 2020, the US itself stands for 16% of world income, the EU27 for 15%, the UK for 2%, and the Latin American Mercosur group for 3% of world income and South Africa for 0.6% (see Table 13.3).

China represented about 18% of world income in 2020 and could represent about 30% of global income by 2040. The West is still just about strong enough in 2020 that it can exert dominance in terms of setting technology standards in important fields; but hardly in communication technology. The poorer half of the global economy will have a propensity to want to rely on the relatively cheaper telecom infrastructure offerings from Chinese providers: even if there is some risk that, in a crisis situation, the Chinese state might gain access to the information held by the telecom networks and equipment by private and government customers of ordering countries. Neither the US nor the EU wants to take such a risk. Power in the twenty-first century is based on income, assets, military capabilities, data access, and knowledge. If the West had 50% of the world's

Table 13.3 Gross Domestic Product of selected countries and integration groups, Nominal and as a share of world GDP, 2020 (ranked by share of world GDP)

Country	2020 GDP PPP in 2017 US$	Share of 2020 World GDP
IPEF* countries	36,010,613.55	35.43%
China	23,020,463.49	18.32%
US	19,863,485.37	15.81%
EU27	18,666,106.83	14.86%
Eurozone	15,049,527.61	11.98%
India	8,508,757.58	6.77%
ASEAN	7,812,936.88	6.22%
Japan	5,062,661.21	4.03%
Germany	4,276,401.02	3.40%
Mercosur	4,046,361.18	3.22%
Russia	3,875,685.90	3.08%
Indonesia	3,130,467.09	2.49%
Brazil	2,989,431.81	2.38%
UK	2,868,465.20	2.28%
France	2,851,553.02	2.27%
Italy	2,322,896.05	1.85%
Mexico	2,301,753.89	1.83%
Rep. of Korea	2,194,532.03	1.75%
Canada	1,752,155.42	1.39%
Spain	1,715,070.84	1.36%
Poland	1,227,880.78	0.98%
South Africa	751,193.93	0.60%
Ukraine	516,637.61	0.41%
World	**125,653,507.41**	**100.00%**

Note: *IPEF: US, Japan, Australia, New Zealand, Republic of Korea, Singapore, Malaysia , Indonesia, Vietnam, Philippines, Thailand, Brunei, India

Source: Own presentation; data from the World Bank https://data.worldbank.org/indicator/NY.GDP. MKTP.PP.KD

income—at purchasing power parity—and (legally and illegally) 70% of global information, the West could still dominate the world economy in the twenty-first century. At the same time, "the West" as a grouping does not necessarily have to defer to the US as the leading power. Of course, it is hard to imagine that the United States could lose its Western and global leadership role, but if domestic political polarization in the US continues, destroying the broad policy consensus essential for global leadership, this new situation could very well occur. It is not credible that the United Kingdom—with its historically unprecedented BREXIT decision (which stands for economically irrational and politically self-centered behavior—to which, of course, a majority of the British population has every right)—will have a new leadership role in Western Europe or the West. Incidentally, it is not really conceivable that the EU27—after a Ukraine enlargement, an EU28—could be united under the leadership of France, which is the second nuclear power in Western Europe alongside the UK. For historical reasons, Germany as a nuclear power is also inconceivable.

If the US were to enter a downward spiral in terms of politics—or even a prolonged phase of political populism—then one could well imagine a new West as a New European Union. This would amount to a Political European Union with a social market economy, which at its core could be some kind of hybrid of the German and French political models and at the same time also represent an EU defense community including nuclear weapons. Many states would certainly try to prevent a New European Union from actually developing in such a direction; and over-confidence, a lack of political professionalism, or bad economic or defense policies could, on the one hand, also prove to be decisive obstacles. On the other hand, it should be borne in mind that, from an economic point of view, the Franco-German economic model is superior to the US economic model if the relevant ratios are carefully calculated:

- The level of figures for effective per capita income and effective per capita consumption are the same for Germany/France compared to the US; this is clearly shown by recent research, namely by correcting the US and the EU core figures (where EU core = Germany/France) for the structurally different health care expenditures on both sides of the Atlantic and by including the value of the higher leisure budget in Western Europe (Welfens, 2019, 2020. See this literature also for more on the following two points).
- Life expectancy in the EU is higher than in the US.
- Infant mortality in the EU is lower than in the US.

Of course, this should not obscure the fact that the United States is a global leader in military technology and civilian high technology. However, a politically unstable US will not be able to do much with its leading position in military technology. Incidentally, Western Europe is unlikely to be able to close its mind to the subject of the New European Union if around half a billion people in the EU28—after Ukraine is admitted to the EU—demand security, prosperity, and stability in the twenty-first century.

Europe has many decades of experience with EU reforms, and now that the United Kingdom, a country obviously politically insecure in European matters, has left the EU in an opportunistic political maneuver (Welfens, 2017a, 2017b, 2018), the EU will hardly want to wait for an alternative position of dependence on Russia or China.

Provided that one does not have to further discuss the concept of a New European Union, the question will immediately arise of what the "Old West"—still under US leadership in the twenty-first century—will be able to achieve. The West plus "democratic Asia" could represent 60% of the world economy in the long run, which is presumably sufficient in terms of economic weight to exert influence as a kind of balancing counterweight to China as an autocratic country.

As for the historical perspective for China in terms of democratization: China's historic opportunity to become a normal democracy—around 1911–1920—was missed by the US (and the leading countries of Europe). At that time, the US Congress was not prepared to support the democracy movement in China with even modest financial support. Therefore, for the West and democratic Asia, the question of how to secure security, stability, and democracy in a world with China will only arise anew in the twenty-first century; for the time being, this is an authoritarian China: with an autocratic Russia under the "young" Putin and then a totalitarian "older" Putin at its side. After China initially classified the United States as a role model and strong leader of the West following the country's economic opening up, Beijing's leadership reclassified the United States as representing a latently unstable market economy with the 2007/08 Transatlantic Banking Crisis. For a long time, US policymakers viewed China's economic rise with favor, especially since sustained US export growth and strong US direct investment in China, as well as high levels of cheap US imports from China, pointed to an economic win-win situation: Both sides could benefit simultaneously. However, the rising bilateral US trade deficit and the significant long-term increase in Chinese military spending, as well as China's expansion efforts in the Pacific region and Asia, have led to increasing political tensions between Washington and Beijing from around 2010.

China's new Silk Road project—the One Belt One Road—which sought land-based and maritime infrastructure modernization with an endpoint to transcontinental "pathways" in Western Europe, also showed that China's expansionist drive was aimed in the direction of Europe. China's leadership, however, was troubled under the Trump administration by the scale of the short-term US backlash: Trump was not only bent on a trade war, but also repeatedly accused China in particular of illegally acquiring US high technology on a large scale.

The early twenty-first century, however, will also be characterized by a gradual disintegration of the West, the starting point of which can probably be set at 2016: the year of the British EU referendum, or BREXIT. Autocratic Russia, which is also a nuclear power, could continue a policy of targeted needling against individual countries and the West, focusing on new destabilization points in Africa (e.g., in Mali, where Germany and France are being displaced as order-assisting powers; partly with the support of Wagner mercenaries financed by Russia) in addition to old geographic security impact regions such as Afghanistan and the Middle East (especially Syria). Latin America also offers certain destabilization hotspots for Russia, since with the often weak rule of law and populist governments there, a stable Western system is hardly likely to be realized in some countries in the long run: with a side effect that could become a major problem for the US, namely increased refugee flows or new high immigration pressure.

What could bring the West-Asian axis together with China and Russia would presumably be a common interest in achieving climate protection: in other words, achieving climate neutrality by 2050 through a cooperative policy approach. The Russo-Ukrainian war is therefore also about the question of the conditions under which future global cooperation can take place. It is doubtful that Russia will be able to achieve much in the long run through strong cooperation with China, because the economic size ratio of 6:1 in favor of China in 2020, and probably 10:1 in 2040, means that Russia will be in a relatively weak position. That Russia will receive broad recognition from China as a superpower of the twenty-fist century is unlikely. China's technological dynamism and China's self-interests are too great for that. If China, in turn, pushes itself to Russia's side, it would again place itself in an isolationist position in world politics, to its detriment. The question for China could be whether or not it wants to make moves toward a voluntary political decision to democratize in a Sino-Western model at a certain point in time.

China, for its part, has anchored a regional approach to trade integration with the 15-country Regional Comprehensive Economic Partnership agreement—effective from January 1, 2022 (RCEP); namely, with the countries of Australia, Brunei, Cambodia, Indonesia, Japan, the Republic of Korea, Laos, Malaysia, Myanmar, New Zealand, the Philippines,

Singapore, Thailand, and Vietnam. Here, China can try to positively present itself as a multilateral player in the Asian region. At the same time, however, China has the problem that the country is economically so much larger than all other countries—and will be even more so in the decades ahead until about 2060 at least—that even in the RCEP, it is not only political-ideological tensions on the one hand and trade advantages on the other that are invested. Rather, the US could also try to instigate certain disruptive maneuvers to undermine China's regional integration plans through its allies in the RCEP.

With the Russo-Ukrainian war, political tensions between the West and Russia are spilling over from Europe into all areas of integration. China, which, apart from its membership in the World Trade Organization since 2001, has had relatively little experience with multilateralism, has already had to learn from its experiences with President Trump that even an established international organization such as the WTO is by no means a stable space for action. Rather, Trump tried to block the functioning of the WTO, which is supposed to protect small countries as well as large countries from arbitrary trade policies by individual members, during the period 2016–2019. China also has limited experience with the multilateral Asian Infrastructure Investment Bank, headquartered in Beijing; that bank has been active since 2016 and has tremendous capacity to finance international infrastructure projects. Protectionist US policies under President Trump temporarily pushed China into a strange and unfamiliar role—when China's President Xi Jinping presented himself as a great defender of international free trade at the Davos World Economic Forum summit in 2017 (Parker, 2017).

In retrospect, one could get the impression here that a critical fork in the road of globalization was reached with the coinciding of a number of key events in a relatively short period of time—namely BREXIT, the Trump election in 2016, and the founding of the Asian Infrastructure Investment Bank (without the US as a founding country, while the UK, France, and Germany are co-founders along with China). It remains to be seen whether globalization—already temporarily disrupted by the corona pandemic and technical problems in international value chains in the context of zero-Covid actions in China (e.g., the lockdown of Shanghai in spring 2022)—can actually continue in the longer term as a model of internationalization in the twenty-first century. Incidentally, China's export ratio has already been declining over the 2014–2019 period, but this is not necessarily evidence of problematic de-globalization.

It is also conceivable that structural change in China or the increase in the share of the service sector in overall economic value added is an important explanatory factor here. However, it could also be expected that the increase in digital trade in services—including business process outsourcing—will also lead to a further rise in China's export ratio in the longer term, provided that trade globalization as a whole does not enter a crisis.

It is conceivable, however, that the existing leading regional integration areas of the EU, ASEAN, Mercosur (in Latin America), and ECOWAS (in Africa) could cooperate more closely with each other and include the US, Japan, and Australia. A kind of Hanseatic League comprising a group of countries could emerge, granting each other mutual trade and direct investment benefits and cooperating on defense.

It cannot be ruled out that after a number of years, the West's foreign trade with Russia will develop anew; however, Putin's invasion of Ukraine has clearly diminished Russia's economic prospects in the medium term—here, political trust on the part of Russia has been massively damaged vis-à-vis the West for decades to come. The fear of a military threat from China is likely to make many countries in Asia look to strengthen military cooperation with the UK and the US, as well as Australia; with the EU, only to a limited extent, as geography and also colonial history are likely to favor the US and the UK here. Within the EU, France's role as a military power and arms exporter is likely to increase in the direction of Asia. For Germany and the EU, respectively, the ASEAN group of countries is an important "fallback" partner with which economic relations could be expanded relatively easily. India also comes into focus here, to the extent that trade and investment relations with China can only grow at a subdued pace for some time from a Western perspective. In 2021, leading ASEAN countries already had achieved a per capita income (calculated according to purchasing power parity; World Bank data) similar to that of Eastern European EU countries, and the economic weight of the ASEAN countries as a bloc is still one third that of the global leader: China. In 2020, the US was about two percentage points behind China in an international comparison—calculated according to purchasing power parity figures. If China's export growth and economic growth were to slow, this could, in turn, lead to political and economic instability in China; China's interest in broad foreign economic cooperation with the EU and the US is therefore likely to be high in the medium term, although cooperation will probably become more difficult—all the more so, the more the US talks about a clash between democratic and authoritarian states.

Mid-term elections in the US in November 2022—that is, elections for the US Congress—could become a starting point for a change in US foreign policy, namely if the Republicans could win back the majority in the Senate. The US in any case will face new recession risks in the context of a necessary anti-inflation policy on the part of the US Federal Reserve which will want to avoid double-digit inflation and indeed to generate pressure for a strong decline of the US inflation rate in the medium term. As regards reducing economic exchange—including trade and foreign direct investment—with Russia and China, there seems to be a basic consensus among Democrats and Republicans. China as an economic partner is more important for the US than Russia, but Russia-US relations are critical in the field of nuclear armaments control; while many experts have suggested that China should also be included in new arms control treaties, the reduced political Sino-US cooperation in in the context of tensions over Taiwan in 2022 will make this rather difficult. The fact that China had already indicated during the summer of 2022 that it does not intend to continue climate policy cooperation with the United States will seriously undermine the G20's ability to come up with an efficient solution for achieving climate neutrality by 2050—and to come up with sufficient first-mover advantages in innovation and policy cooperation which would encourage other UN member countries (which represent 20% of global CO_2 emissions) to come on board for a global climate change policy approach. One cannot rule out that populist politicians in several EU countries, including Italy, will gain influence in the medium term—not least as part of the population in many countries is dissatisfied with low growth and rather high inflation (fueled partly by the Russo-Ukrainian war and Russia's energy policy, respectively); such a development would make cooperation among EU countries more difficult for many years to come. With Russia possibly continuing to act as a destabilizing influence in the Balkans, the EU will also come under pressure to proceed with an EU enlargement in the Western Balkans which will reinforce the economic heterogeneity of the European Union; the same would hold for an EU-Ukraine enlargement.

It should be noted here that some medium-term dynamics in the Russo-Ukrainian war—including developments emphasized in previous chapters (see, e.g., Chap. 9–11)—will have crucial long-term implications which are hard to anticipate at this point of time. However, one may still point out that the Western policy strategy after 1991 has been largely unsuccessful with respect to its support for systemic transformation in Russia. The consequences of the economic destabilization of Russia under

President Yeltsin have been of massive historical relevance and allowed Vladimir Putin come to power and to be perceived for almost a decade as having brought economic and political stability to Russia. With the invasion of Ukraine, Putin no longer will be able to quasi-guarantee such stability in the new Russia which has become much more authoritarian in 2022 than in previous years. The old historical insight that leaders in authoritarian countries with a flagging domestic economic performance have a rather strong tendency to engage in brinkmanship in foreign policy seems to be vindicated by Russia's aggression against Ukraine over the last decade and the invasion of 2022 in particular. At the bottom line, there is a risk that Russia's role in major international organizations, including the European Bank for Reconstruction and Development, the World Trade Organization and the Bank for International Settlements, for example, could strongly weaken over time which would extend bilateral conflict lines between Russia and Ukraine (plus part of the West) to the multilateral policy field. Common rules for the world economy would then be more difficult to develop and implement and the resultant decline in the growth of trade and foreign direct investment could undermine global economic growth in the long run.

References

ADB. (2022). Asian Development Outlook 2022, April, Asian Development Bank: Manila https://www.adb.org/sites/default/files/publication/784041/ado2022.pdf

Allan, D., & Bond, I. (2022). A new Russia policy for post-Brexit Britain, Research Paper, Russia and Eurasia Program, Chatham House, 27 January 2022. Retrieved May 25, 2022, from https://www.chathamhouse.org/sites/default/files/2022-01/2022-01-27-russia-policy-post-brexit-britain-allan-bond.pdf

Bachmann, R. et al. (2022). What if? The Economic Effects for Germany of a Stop of Energy Imports from Russia, ECONtribute Policy Brief Nr. 028. Retrieved May 24, 2022, from https://www.econtribute.de/RePEc/ajk/ajkpbs/ECONtribute_PB_028_2022.pdf.

Becker, T., et al. (2022). *A Blueprint for the Reconstruction of Ukraine*. CEPR Press. https://cepr.org/sites/default/files/news/BlueprintReconstructionUkraine.pdf

Belton, C. (2020). *Putin's People. How the KGB Took Back Russia and Then Took on the West*. William Collins.

Belton, C. (2022). *Putins Netz - Wie sich der KGB Russland zurückholte und dann den Westen ins Auge fasste*. HarperCollins Deutschland.

Böttcher, W. (2022). *Russland und der Westen.* Romeon-Verlag.

Commander, S., Nikolaychuk, O., & Vikhrov, D. (2013). Migration from Ukraine: Brawn or Brain? New Survey Evidence, IZA Discussion Paper No. 7348, Institute for the Study of Labor, Bonn https://docs.iza.org/dp7348.pdf

EBRD. (2005). Annual Report 2005, European Bank for Reconstruction and Development: London https://www.ebrd.com/downloads/research/annual/ar05a.pdf

EBRD. (2006). Annual Report 2006, European Bank for Reconstruction and Development: London https://www.ebrd.com/downloads/research/annual/ar06a.pdf

ECB. (2022). *Economic Bulletin 2022/2.* Frankfurt. https://www.ecb.europa.eu/pub/economic-bulletin/html/eb202202.en.html

Eltchaninoff, M. (2015). *Dans la tête de Vladimir Poutine.* Actes Sud.

Eltchaninoff, M. (2016). *In Putins Kopf. Die Philosophie eines Lupenreinen Demokraten.* Klett-Cotta.

Eltchaninoff, M. (2018). *Inside the Mind of Vladimir Putin.* Hurst & Co Publishers.

FAO. (2022a). Note on the impact of the war on food security in Ukraine, published 25 March 2022, Food and Agriculture Organization: Rome https://www.fao.org/3/cb9171en/cb9171en.pdf

FAO. (2022b). Impact of the Ukraine-Russia conflict on global food security and related matters under the mandate of the Food and Agriculture Organization of the United Nations, Hundred-and-sixty-ninth session, Council, dated 8th April 2022 https://www.fao.org/3/ni734en/ni734en.pdf

Fertig, M., & Kahanec, M. (2015). Projections of potential flows to the enlarging EU from Ukraine, Croatia and other Eastern neighbors. *IZA Journal of Migration, 4*(6), 1. https://doi.org/10.1186/s40176-015-0029-8

Gabriel, S., & Hüther, M. (2022). Europas Umgang mit China: Auf der Suche nach einer neuen Weltordnung [transl. PJJW: Europe's relations with China: Towards a new world order], published 8th June 2022, available in German online. Retrieved June 15, 2022, from https://www.handelsblatt.com/meinung/gastbeitraege/gastkommentar-europas-umgang-mit-china-auf-der-suche-nach-einer-neuen-weltordnung/28405834.html

IMF. (2021). Ukraine Staff Country Report No. 21/250, November 2021, International Monetary Fund: Washington DC

Indermit, G. (2022). Developing economies must act now to dampen the shocks from the Ukraine conflict, World Bank Blogs, published 9th March 2022, World Bank Group: Washington DC https://blogs.worldbank.org/voices/developing-economies-must-act-now-dampen-shocks-ukraine-conflict

Kirsch, W. (2022). The Distribution of Power within the EU: Perspectives on a Ukrainian Accession and a Turkish Accession. *International Economics and Economic Policy, 19*(2), 1. https://doi.org/10.1007/s10368-022-00541-w

Parker, C. (2017). China's Xi Jinping defends globalization from the Davos stage, World Economic Forum Agenda, 17th January 2017. Retrieved May 31, 2022, from https://www.weforum.org/agenda/2017/01/chinas-xi-jinping-defends-globalization-from-the-davos-stage/

Ratha, D., & Kim, E. J. (2022). Russia-Ukraine Conflict: Implications for Remittance flows to Ukraine and Central Asia, World Bank Blogs, published 4th March 2022, World Bank Group: Washington DC https://blogs.worldbank.org/peoplemove/russia-ukraine-conflict-implications-remittance-flows-ukraine-and-central-asia

Roeger, W., & Welfens, P. J. J. (2022a). The Macroeconomic Effects of Import Tariffs in a Model with Multinational Firms and Foreign Direct Investment, *International Economics and Economic Policy*, online first. https://doi.org/10.1007/s10368-022-00538-5

Roeger, W., & Welfens, P. J. J. (2022b). EU Gas Import Tariff Under Duopoly: A Contribution to the Energy Sanctions Debate on Russia, EIIW Discussion Paper No. 314, https://eiiw.wiwi.uni-wuppertal.de/fileadmin/eiiw/Daten/Publikationen/Gelbe_Reihe/disbei314.pdf

Rürup, B. (2022). Warum das Geschäftsmodell der deutschen Wirtschaft am Ende ist [transl. PJJW: Why the German business model is at an end], Handelsblatt, published 1st April 2022, available (in German only) at https://www.handelsblatt.com/meinung/kommentare/kommentar-der-chefoekonom-warum-das-geschaeftsmodell-der-deutschen-wirtschaft-am-ende-ist/28215714.html (last accessed 15.06.2022)

de Vries, K., Erumban, A., & van Ark, B. (2021). Productivity and the pandemic: Short-term disruptions and long-term implications. *International Economics and Economic Policy*, *18*, 541–570. https://doi.org/10.1007/s10368-021-00515-4

Welfens, P. J. J. (1997). Privatization, Structural Change and Productivity: Towards Convergence in Europe? In S. Black (Ed.), *Europe's Economy Looks East* (pp. 212–257). Cambridge University Press. https://doi.org/10.1017/CBO9780511551857.011

Welfens, P. J. J. (2017a). BREXIT aus Versehen [transl. PJJW: An Accidental Brexit] 1st Ed., Heidelberg: Springer. https://doi.org/10.1007/978-3-658-15875-0

Welfens, P. J. J. (2017b). *An Accidental BREXIT*. Palgrave. https://doi.org/10.1007/978-3-319-58271-9

Welfens, P. J. J. (2018). BREXIT aus Versehen, [transl. PJJW: An Accidental Brexit] 2nd extended and enlarged edition., Heidelberg: Springer. https://link.springer.com/book/10.1007/978-3-658-21458-6

Welfens, P. J. J. (2019). *The Global Trump – Structural US Populism and Economic Conflicts with Europe and Asia*. Palgrave Macmillan. https://doi.org/10.1007/978-3-030-21784-6

Welfens, P. J. J. (2020). *Trump global – Strukturellen US-Populismus und Wirtschaftskonflikte mit Europa und Asien.* Springer. https://doi.org/10.1007/978-3-658-30158-3

Welfens, P. J. J. (2022). *Global Climate Change Policy.* Palgrave Macmillan. https://doi.org/10.1007/978-3-030-94594-7

Welfens, P. J. J., & Jasinksi, P. (1994). *Privatization and Foreign Direct Investment in Trans-forming Economies.* Dartmouth Publishing Company.

Welfens, P. J. J., Xiong, T., & Hanrahan, D. (2022). An Analysis of the Determinants of Green Innovation Dynamics in Europe and Climate Neutrality-related Policy Options ICT, EIIW Discussion Paper No. 318 https://eiiw.wiwi.uni-wuppertal.de/de/publikationen/eiiw-diskussionsbeitraege/nr-318/

Wilke, A., & Welfens, P. J. J. (2022). An Analysis of Corona Pandemic-related Productivity Growth in Germany: Sectoral Aspects, Work-From-Home Perspectives and Digitalization Intensity, EIIW Discussion Paper No. 313, https://eiiw.wiwi.uni-wuppertal.de/fileadmin/eiiw/Daten/Publikationen/Gelbe_Reihe/disbei_313.pdf

CHAPTER 14

Free Trade, Freedom, the Rule of Law, and Democracy Belong Together

In the context of the Russo-Ukrainian war, a larger debate has emerged in the West and especially in Germany as to whether the idea of the 1970s to seek to achieve political rapprochement with, and change within, the Soviet Union and other Eastern European socialist countries in the Warsaw Pact through deeper economic relations was reasonable. Following Ricardo's historical arguments on the linkages between free trade and the (reduced) probability of war, there are indeed important arguments to support this approach. However, more trade is only a necessary condition for peace. The West has apparently failed to develop stable political relations with Russia in the three decades since the fall of the Soviet Union. Moreover, it can be shown that free trade, freedom, democracy, and the rule of law go together when it comes to peaceful and efficient international relations. Russia's shortcomings in the areas of democracy and the rule of law were difficult to overlook during the Putin years; the younger generation in Russia—with access to digital media—has had little political influence under his rule. This chapter explores the pillars required for a sustainable peace in Ukraine, and the full re-integration of Russia into the world economy.

NATO Secretary General Jens Stoltenberg announced at the 2022 World Economic Forum Summit in Davos, Switzerland, that in view of the Russo-Ukrainian war, there is a certain contradiction between free trade and freedom. What he apparently meant by this was that, on the part

P. J. J. Welfens, *Russia's Invasion of Ukraine*, https://doi.org/10.1007/978-3-031-19138-1_14

of the NATO countries at least, one should not simply refer to the rules of the traditional world trade order and multilateralism and rather be more circumspect when it comes to trade with Russia; and—if this logic should apply more generally—then there can be no trade with China either and ultimately perhaps no direct investment there. While it is true that there is no war between China and the West, China's leadership has shown a blatant disregard for human rights in part of its territory, and there are likely plans and blueprints in Beijing for a military attack on Taiwan in the near or distant future. However, the Stoltenberg thesis could sow confusion in the West and indeed around the world.

Jens Stoltenberg, the former Prime Minister of Norway, stood on the world stage of politics and capital (despite the exclusion of Russia in 2022), in Davos, Switzerland, at the end of May and propagated a misleading logic: displaying a certain lack of knowledge of the inter-relationships between freedom, free trade, per capita income, rule of law and democracy.

The old argument still holds that an increase in trade intensity leads to a decrease in incidents of war, as empirical conflict analysis shows; and as the British economist David Ricardo already formulated in his book *On the Principles of Political Economy and Taxation* as a hypothesis on the relationship between trade and the propensity for war as a necessary condition for peace. Of course, an increase in foreign trade alone is no guarantee of the absence of war. If Ricardo had had the time to formulate a second volume of his Principles, further insights could have been hoped for—perhaps a hypothesis that at the top level of foreign policy relations, the UK should not initiate a state visit by a foreign leader once every 129 years; even if the United Kingdom, as a major island power, could afford such behavior, which, with regard to Russia, naturally involves two heads of state or government. Here, we are talking about Vladimir Putin and his state visit to the UK in 2003.

The topic is the Russian president, who cannot currently claim much in the way of economic success, even though during his first two terms in office he stood for Russia's success in overcoming the economic crisis of 1998. In 1874, the then Czar, Alexander II, paid a visit to the United Kingdom, arriving from St. Petersburg on his yacht at the invitation of the Queen.

The collapse of the Soviet Union occurred in 1991, yet it was over a decade later that a Russian president first came to London. One can already understand the argument that after 2014 Anglo-Russian relations had to be downgraded from the British point of view. However, from

2003 to 2011, the UK had almost an entire decade to engage in high-level state visits. Of Prime Minister Blair's successors, only David Cameron visited Moscow in 2011 in an attempt to repair relations between both sides; other meetings with the Russian leader only took place when G7 (1998–2013), G8, or G20 summits made it quasi-inevitable on a larger scale. The G8 summit in 2006 took place in St. Petersburg. By then, Russia was already a de facto autocracy.

Boris Yeltsin's miserable economic policy and a fixed exchange rate of the Russian ruble against the US dollar were to blame for the historic economic crisis in Russia in 1998, which resulted in a loss of real income of about 6% of the gross domestic product. Every Western textbook on macroeconomics says that in a country with a clear export dominance of a very limited group of goods—in Russia's case: oil, gas, metals—flexible exchange rates are absolutely preferable to a fixed exchange rate regime, because this allows an early combination of fundamentally independent monetary policy with early impulses for necessary structural change.

The preliminary phase of the resulting economic disaster in Russia first emerged in the form of the Asian Crisis of 1997, where the starting point was Thailand—with a quasi-autocratic regime—in initially good economic weather; but with a partially corrupt system in which large political entrepreneurial friends could hope for large loans from politically influenced banks.

The Thai government in Bangkok, and those in other ASEAN countries, had implemented a tacit exchange rate pegging policy, thus inviting the business community for years to obtain cheap dollar-denominated loans in New York, often even short-term loans for long-term projects which posed a double risk: an interest rate risk and a devaluation risk. A mega-devaluation in Indonesia meant an enormous increase in the foreign debt of companies there—calculated in domestic currency—while the central bank raised the interest rate sharply, but did so in a manner which prompted a recession, for the purpose of exchange rate stabilization. Thus, Indonesia, an important oil exporting country at the time, was immediately dragged down. There was a regional aspect to the economic crisis in Asia on the one hand, but also international crisis transmission effects to Russia via Mexico.

A certain domino-effect meant that the crisis spread, resulting in an Asian recession and thus a massive drop in global oil demand. However, as countries such as Indonesia, but also Russia and Mexico, were reliant on increasing oil production and export volumes in the face of massively falling oil prices in 1998, the oil price quickly sank even lower and the three countries mentioned, whose national budgets were all heavily dependent on oil exports, quickly found themselves in deep trouble. Mexico was bailed out by the US and the IMF; Thailand and Indonesia and other countries in Asia by the Asian Development Bank (ADB), the IMF, Japan, and the US. In Europe, the European Bank for Reconstruction and Development did little to help Russia in 1998.

In the face of a large budget deficit and recession, President Yeltsin believed that the only way to save Russia from bankruptcy was through oligarchic privatization: more than half of the state's industrial assets were sold to some three dozen oligarchs within 18 months, thus avoiding Russia's plunge into state bankruptcy, while its path toward becoming a normal democracy was essentially now blocked. The gradual collapse of an unbelievably corrupt Soviet Union in the late 1980s was followed by the introduction of an oligarchic economic regime that, of course, had nothing to do with competition in goods and factor markets, with the passive exception of the fall of tradable goods or unavoidable import competition. There was barely any real competition in raw materials, but this was not very relevant economically speaking because of the low value added, if one disregards the otherwise enormous size of raw material exports relative to national income. And after all, about half of the state's revenues came from the energy/metals sectors. In terms of productivity, the energy sector was stabilized in the medium term thanks to high direct investment from Western countries and Japan.

One knows, of course, that even in the 200-year-old democracy the US, the United States Congress and the president have often only been able to offer a feeble defense against strong and coordinated industrial lobbying interests over the course of 200+ years of American democracy, including the military-industrial complex that Secretary of Defense Robert McNamara once famously referred to. That in the new Russia—as the primary successor state to the dissolved Soviet Union with its many republics—the state would hardly be able to meaningfully stand up to the few oligarch families was clear to Putin not only because of his certainly enormous knowledge of corruption in business and politics (gained during his time in the KGB and later its successor the Federal Security Service [or FSB]). As the former chief of the domestic intelligence service, Putin made clear on becoming president from 2000 on that politicians would interfere little in the economy if in return the oligarchs would keep out of the political competition.

Putin's quasi-ban on the economically powerful oligarchs entering the Russian political market—the Russian constitution did not contain a ban on political activity by wealthy business leaders—was, of course, also a de facto ban on competing parties from using Russian or foreign "financial capital" to better position themselves in the subsequent election campaigns. If, however, the president could in fact only ever be Putin, then of course there was no real democracy left in Russia at all; possibly not even the risk of the economic-political chaos in the country which Putin repeatedly invoked as a warning to his countrymen. With the annexation of Crimea in 2014 boosting Putin to high popularity ratings and with leading EU countries even lending explicit political approval to the Nord Stream 2 Russian-European Baltic Sea pipeline project the following year, the Russian president saw new opportunities for realizing his "project"— that of forcing Russia and "Little Russia" together, as he occasionally referred to Ukraine.

In terms of the development of democracy, Ukraine itself was also strongly influenced by oligarchic factors and massive corruption, but with his Russian point of view, Putin saw, among other things, the danger that what his esteemed Russian philosopher Ivan Ilyin—once a kind of intellectual advisor to the anti-Soviet "Whites" in the struggle for Russia after the October Revolution—had warned against in various writings could indeed come to pass: that the West, under the heading of securing democracy, would try to pull Ukraine, which in his mind is actually inseparable from Russia—see common history, culture, and language—out of the Soviet Union or away from its main successor state (the new Russia). The West would present such a maneuver as being pro-democracy, when in reality it would so only to try to weaken the Soviet Union or—if it exists— its successor state. It is certainly no coincidence that in 2014, Putin gave away 5000 copies of a book by Ilyin with such theses to high-level bureaucrats, various oligarchs, and close friends and, moreover, in 2003, 2004, and 2005 decorated his speeches to the Federation Council with Ilyin quotations.

Again, it is probably no coincidence that the ideological transformation of Vladimir Putin went largely unnoticed by the leading governments in the West without, for example, academics and Russian specialists or the generously endowed intelligence services becoming aware of Ilyin's growing influence over Putin's thinking nor the role of other Russian philosophers of the 1920s (including many Russian philosophers abroad, whose writings were not republished in Russia in book form until 1991) at an early stage—this should have been clear from 2015 at the latest, after Michel Eltchaninoff, a well-known French philosopher from Paris, published his book *Dans la tête de Vladimir Poutine* in 2015; which appeared a year later in German as *In Putins Kopf: Die Philosophie eines lupenreinen Demokraten* and in 2018 also in English as *Inside the Mind of Vladimir Putin*—but, if Google Scholar citation data is to be believed, his work in English has been cited over the four years since publication fewer than 25 times (Eltchaninoff, 2015, 2016, 2018).

One of the less convincing conclusions after a few months of the Russo-Ukrainian war is certainly the assertion that "change through trade" [*Wandel durch Handel*] has always been a false hypothesis—and, more recently, the idea free trade and freedom did not go together. From a reasonable economic analysis point of view, the connection is rather quite different: freedom emerges in an economically meaningful way from competition on domestic and foreign markets and with the ensuing rising per capita incomes, people can afford more than the basic needs—as recognized centuries ago by famed Scottish economist and philosopher Adam Smith. This leads to increased cultural needs, to individuals having the time for reflection, to think and engage in political arguments which thus gain in prominence in the public sphere.

With up-and-down cyclical pressures in key sectors of the economy for firms to monopolize or engage in mergers and acquisitions rising regularly during recessions, a powerful challenge arises for policymakers in a democracy: to defend competition in a sustainable way. If one wanted to follow the Chicago School in terms of competition policy, one should yield to the qualitatively new pressure with regard to size in the economy; monopolization is okay from an efficiency point of view. However, this is really a political misconception, because democracy cannot flourish in the case of the relocation of a market economy, with competition, large as well as small and medium-sized enterprises, to a digital monopolization space— but the democratic system is supposed to protect the rule of law.

Digital monopoly companies, possibly in the media market (or mega-companies with little competitive pressure), can—or indeed already do— extend the center of the political spectrum or its polar opposite ends, by, for example, moving the so-called Overton window. However, a polarization of politics also weakens the basic consensus required in a democracy and thus the democracy itself, since political consensus and compromise require an investment of the scarce political reputational capital on the part of the parties. The more of this capital that has to be invested in intra-party party profiling in a polarized society on both ends of the political spectrum, the more difficult it becomes to find political compromises and to nurture that domestic societal consensus which is an indispensable power base for leading global powers on the international political stage. The ICT sector is growing relatively strongly, especially in Western leading countries such as the US, the UK, and Germany, which in turn has caused income disparities, particularly in America and Britain, to increase enormously since about 2000; in some cases, especially in income positions abroad.

In Switzerland, too, the biggest driver of income inequality in the 15 years after 2000 was the growth in income from abroad—no wonder, since in the digital economy national borders play an increasingly minor role over time, while the size of digital companies increases disproportionately (think, for example, of Amazon, Alphabet, Microsoft, Meta). The US and the UK are doing little to counter rising income inequality, especially since government spending on further education and training has barely reached 0.1% of national income in the two decades after 2000. Switzerland, Germany, the Netherlands, Denmark, and some other EU countries are in a much better position.

In the US, on the other hand, there is a widespread political unwillingness to address what polls in the US show to be a major sources of political dissatisfaction among the American electorate, namely high income inequality, through sensible education, tax, and social policies; which is, however, unsurprising given the relative majority opinion of that same electorate, which acts as a kind of barrier to intervention by economic policymakers—the belief that large corporations should implement a wage policy across management and the broader workforce that reduces income inequality. However, in an economy of joint-stock companies, this is simply wishful thinking that requires policymakers to square an impossible circle.

The need for legal certainty increases with the accumulation of wealth, which initially indicates to an entrepreneurial minority that one has risen above the subsistence level. More legal certainty, however, is precisely a means of promoting markets, because only with confidence in contracts as a necessary part of market activity and their enforceability—if necessary before independent courts—can markets fully develop their productive potential: ideally in a politically, that is, democratically, determined framework that stimulates investment and education and ensures space for the diversity of individuals' ideas and of products and services in the competition of both minds and merchants. In terms of the rule of law, many countries in Europe and the United States can build upon great traditions and historical roots, something which Russia unfortunately cannot do. Apart from a brief period of local government known as Zemstvo in the early second half of the nineteenth century, few, if any, fully transparent and uncorrupted domestic political standards have emerged as a tradition in Russia either.

We know from modern development literature that opening up a country or economy to foreign trade and direct investors—see the Republic of Korea and Japan, for example—can change the domestic standards of political behavior in a meaningful way: toward less corruption, toward more competition in the political system, and ultimately toward a strengthened rule of law. A judiciary that, as in the US before 1880, was all too concerned with local power struggles and corruption as well as monopolization dynamics in the economy experienced little room for maneuver in terms of politics to reliably implement democratic reform policies in favor of the majority of the population. Until the early 1930s, the United States was a relatively consolidated constitutional state on which domestic investors could rely.

For foreign investors, conditions also improved, significantly so in the wake of the establishment of the World Trade Organization in the mid-1990s. TTIP, the project of an agreement establishing a Transatlantic Trade and Investment Partnership, could have been a happy completion of Western reform initiatives on the part of the US and the EU by 2015. By an institutional coincidence, however, the European Union had, from about 2001 on, been developing its own institutional and political reforms that would ultimately be passed in the form of the Lisbon Treaty (the quasi-constitution which entered into force from December 1, 2009) with responsibility for direct investment—as a complement to its supranational competence in EU foreign trade—largely residing with the European Commission. This not only put trade issues, such as non-tariff barriers, on the agenda of all things in terms of the transatlantic liberalization negotiations, rather, President Obama also had to push the issue of investment protection agreements onto the negotiating table vis-à-vis the then 28 EU member countries, a topic which was only there because, on the one hand, the EU had newly acquired competence in the area of investment protection agreements and, on the other, because nine Eastern European EU accession countries had already concluded bilateral investment protection agreements   with   the   US   prior   to   the   start   of   the   TTIP negotiations—naturally, out of an interest in attracting more US direct investment. By contrast, the UK, France, Germany, and Italy, for example, had never been linked to the US with an investment protection agreement.

However, since the focus of the European criticism of TTIP was precisely on investment protection issues which did not appear to have broad majority support at either the national or supranational levels—that is, in Brussels—the paradox arose that, in an unfortunate way, the Eastern European EU accession countries indirectly scuppered the potential TTIP agreement during the Obama presidency. With Trump, there was then a virtual stop on all free trade issues, especially since the populist Trump lacked support from competent advisors.

Free trade and freedom will not always mean a win-win situation for the countries involved in the short term, but it is no coincidence that the new Russia's economic heyday became visible as a phenomenon based on the main global institutional pillar of the world market economy thanks to positive anticipations in the run-up to Russia's 2012 accession to the global trade rulebook of the World Trade Organization. It is thus all the more tragic that in 2016, with the populist US President Trump, an opponent of the rules-based economic system came to power in Washington, of all places; while Russia's guest appearances at the important G8 round were already over again in 2013—the planned G8 summit in Sochi, Russia, never took place, instead a meeting in the G7-format was held in Brussels in 2014 (in 2014, Russia's annexation of Crimea took place).

There can be no doubt that a large, united coalition of the West plus Japan, the Republic of Korea, Australia, New Zealand, and others will support Ukraine's defensive struggle against Putin's Russia; Putin will not be able to achieve any real success. In the end, however, the West should not be without self-criticism—if there is a post-war chance for a new Russia in a peaceful European space, then this time the right lessons will hopefully have been learned from economic history. The ASEAN countries may yet form, both economically and politically, an important counterweight to China in Asia from an EU and US point of view. Particularly with regard to the ASEAN countries, the West and especially the EU would be well advised to develop long-term political and economic relations with a focus on freedom, free trade, the rule of law, and democracy; the EU should finally develop integration with the vast majority of ASEAN countries via a multilateral free trade agreement.

Since 2021, there may be a new institutional framework for transatlantic trade and security cooperation with the formation of the Trade and

Technology Council (TTC) after the failure of the TTIP integration project under the Obama administration; at its core, this is supposed to be about more digitalization, innovation, and digital security for both the EU and the US (Welfens & Hanrahan, 2022). In Asia, as part of its Indo-Pacific strategy, the US launched a trade deal with 12 Indo-Pacific countries in Japan on May 23, 2022, as a counter bloc to China (Indo-Pacific Economic Framework for Prosperity: IPEF). In addition to Japan, Australia, New Zealand, and the Republic of Korea, the expected participating countries in this treaty focused on trade integration and technological cooperation are India, Singapore, Malaysia, Indonesia, Vietnam, the Philippines, Thailand, and Brunei, which, including the US, account for about 40% of the world economy (White House, 2022). The pressure on China not to side with Russia thus continues to increase. The focus of the global economy could also shift in favor of the EU if it were able to push cooperation agreements with other regional integration areas such as Mercosur and ASEAN more strongly than in the past. This outlines the medium-term challenges for the US, the EU, Asia, and the global economy.

The Russo-Ukrainian war is an historic tragedy that has unexpectedly revealed new responses, behaviors, and reactions. It has also exposed significant unity on the part of the West. Difficult questions remain, however, such as how to bring Russia back into the community of nations as an accepted partner—with high credibility. The question of Ukraine's reconstruction and its financing will also arise, including the question of how Russia can be made to bear an appropriate share of the reconstruction costs in Ukraine. The West should be careful not to take arbitrary steps here. Rather, the dispute between the West and Russia is also about the West continuing to build on the three pillars of stability: the rule of law, democracy, and a market economy. Moreover, the analysis presented here has provided a number of new insights, including empirical evidence on the importance of the rule of law, especially for green innovation dynamics, as well as important considerations on the question of an energy embargo or an import tariff on Russian gas. The integration issues addressed—concerning both individuals as refugees and guest workers as well as Ukraine in terms of an enlargement of the EU—are of fundamental importance.

It is foreseeable that the world order will change significantly in the early twenty-first century in the context of the Russo-Ukrainian war (but not only from the side of this shock). As far as Brussels or the EU is concerned, it would be desirable to reflect with more self-criticism on its own earlier actions—from BREXIT to corona vaccine procurement; and to rely in the future on more competent analyses, also—and especially—from the scientific and academic fields. Within the policy debates about the Russo-Ukrainian war, strong emotions occasionally play a role, and not without good reason, but the yardstick for viable solutions in the medium and long term should be an appropriate and adequate, objective analysis of the associated problems and alternative solutions. There is no reason to be pessimistic. Germany and France in particular could do with increased cooperation and sensible reforms, as well as more self-confidence with regard to the effective lifetime per capita income situation in a transatlantic comparison would be entirely appropriate; for many EU countries, this is especially true in terms of a comparison with the US. As a matter of political common sense, it should be emphasized here that large countries such as Germany, France, Italy, and Spain would do well to take the political interests of the other countries in the EU or their interests more adequately into account.

The West won the Cold War at the end of the 1980s, but it was not a lasting victory with a continued stabilization of the US in its role of leading power. A fortiori, the West and the enlarged EU have not succeeded in developing an efficient, stable, and sustainable coexistence with Russia. The Russo-Ukrainian war is a turning point that has global significance and will shape the world economy for many years to come. Under less favorable conditions, the West, Japan, Russia, and China could regress to a situation akin to the nineteenth century; the West is recognizably trying to anticipate a new era of imperialism with its interventions against Russia. Weaknesses in important policy areas, in essential institutions, are clearly evident in the West; this applies to the United States, the United Kingdom, and the European Union. After a transitional period of a good ten years, the new Russia has appeared as a force that is often not particularly constructive in Europe, but the West for its part has also not developed a meaningful strategy for integrating the new Russia. Russia under Vladimir Putin has gone from being an autocratic to an almost totalitarian power that has yet to find a productive role in the community of states on a sustained basis.

Russia-centered research in large parts of the Western world—with a few notable exceptions—has been in a weak state for many years. It is not only necessary to provide more funds for national defense in EU countries, but above all to launch a more sustainable strategy in the field of

Russia research; simply put, more funds can not only be a useful avenue for cross-border exchanges, but more quality research through more competition in an internationally oriented research approach is also very important. A modernization of economic research in Russia—in a liberalized Russia—would certainly be desirable.

The Russo-Ukrainian war indirectly casts a new light on the West's relations with China. There is little in the way of continued dynamic economic development for China if the country would ally itself too closely with Russia. That the US and the West will not offer China the same easy cooperation after 2022 as in the years before is foreseeable for many reasons:

- The US is taking a more bilateral approach to cooperation with the European Union if one considers the EU-US Technology and Trade Council, in effect trying to avoid the need to upgrade the World Trade Organization or indeed to make it a globally effective organization; which is necessary since US President Trump nearly crippled the World Trade Organization toward the end of his term. In Asia, even during the Russo-Ukrainian war, the United States also embarked on a new pillar of cooperation with the new Indo-Pacific Economic Framework for Prosperity; with a prominent place for India.

- The human rights situation in parts of China is obviously problematic—at least worse than some actors in the Chinese leadership would have the West believe. Nevertheless, the notion that it would be best for OECD countries to simply end foreign trade with China tomorrow does not really make sense. Foreign trade increases per capita income in the OECD area and in China; higher real per capita income strengthens demand for the rule of law and reliable, international rules. From the West's perspective, the paradox of the twenty-first century is that you can digitally absorb the facts and debate almost anywhere; but determined government propaganda which creates a digital, parallel world cannot easily be countered by critical reflection in dialogue form. The reality is not a global, digital world; it is in fact a politically fragmented world, and this distorts the competition between political and economic systems. One assumption of the leadership of autocratic systems is recognizably that a politically and centrally controlled Internet increases political power both internally and externally. However, the massive theft of digital data in

China in the middle of 2022 shows that state-run data collection could possibly also be the basis for a loss of political reputation both internally and externally in the event of a successful hacker attack.

- Among the unpleasant findings in the West is the realization of how poorly developed the ability of the US and the UK, as well as the EU (and China in the matter of the Corona vaccine action), to embed early self-criticism as part of institutional learning actually is. The Asian Crisis had actually resulted in the creation of a voluntary basis to prevent the next crisis with the IMF's new Financial Sector Assessment Programme (FSAP) instrument. In fact, this was not the case, precisely because FSAPs were not routinely mandated, so that President George W. Bush could seriously conclude that an FSAP for the US would simply be a waste of money—a mistake that became obvious to everyone in 2008 and then only brought about a US FSAP in 2010, after President Bush had already left office. However, it is also the case that the IMF and its FSAP teams occasionally get the analysis badly wrong—and then it is not even always transparent or publicized, while corresponding analysis procedures are not routinely improved either: the FSAP report on Switzerland a few years before 2008 was one example of rather strange findings in the explanatory section, as the major bank UBS was certified to be in the best of health, while its actually quite obvious dangerous risk position later required the rescue of UBS by the Swiss central bank during the Transatlantic Banking Crisis. In 2006, shortly before that banking crisis, the IMF had also published an FSAP report on Ireland, according to which Ireland's banking sector was robust and healthy and that it was only in the area of reinsurance that there was some cause for concern in Ireland. At that time, it was already clear to any reasonably objective macroeconomic-financial auditing team that Ireland's main banks had huge exposure to risks in real estate markets on their books. In the Euro crisis, not only Greece but also Ireland and Portugal as well as Spain and Cyprus had to be rescued by a newly created EU bailout fund (most recently known as the European Stability Mechanism). Did the top IMF officials have to pay a price? Not really.

During a visit to the London School of Economics in the fall of 2008, the UK's Queen Elizabeth II asked why no one had seen the crisis coming. A few weeks later there came a somewhat confusing response from several economists—not a particularly convincing answer. The answer should have been that in 2005, Raghuram Rajan had indeed presented a working paper at the well-known central banking conference in Jackson Hole that had clearly highlighted that the risks at major Western banks were too great. The central bankers of the Western world who listened to Rajan's presentation in Jackson Hole found his presentation overly pessimistic—although the analysis, carefully read, must have seemed very sound in substance. With more learning ability on the part of the top central bankers of the Western world, the banking crisis could have been avoided relatively easily.

Why the leading political scientists and news media of the Western world did not adequately pick up the findings of Michel Eltchaninoff in his book *Dans le tête de Vladimir Poutine* in 2015, or at least in 2018—the year of publication of the English edition *Inside the Mind of Vladimir Putin*—is baffling: If they had taken adequate notice, then the heads of government and state would also have picked up on Russian developments in an appropriate way and should have called a G7 summit on the subject of Russia. If fundamental questions are not asked anew, very critically in Russia and also critically within the G7 countries, then the next X country-Russia war will possibly break out very soon.

That war is still a serious policy option was demonstrated by the West itself in the Kosovo War and Iraq wars. There is no easy way out of the contradictions of the UN system and security analysis; domestic policy is also a driver of foreign policy. The fact that Russia under Putin is apparently allowing the war in Ukraine to be waged in a particularly cruel manner raises the question of legal accountability for those actors who are responsible for any war crimes committed in Ukraine. The international legal system alone can provide only partial answers here. What remains at the end of the analysis is perhaps the hope that the global collective good of climate protection policy will bring the world's large and medium-sized countries together once again. This could be a great collective success project that could in the end have many sponsors. The creative and subversive nature of the Internet will hopefully be enough in the end to enable innovative solutions to problems to be worked out together in good time. "Old Europe" could contribute a lot to solving new problems. Before that can happen, however, Brussels should become a little more self-critical; it should formulate answers to questions such as why BREXIT came as such a surprise and why the corona vaccine procurement process went so poorly.

In such a way could the new challenges become a special opportunity for the EU?

The EU will still come under considerable adjustment pressure from the high inflation rates in the Eurozone. On June 9, 2022, the European Central Bank made its first central bank rate hike in 11 years—since the Transatlantic Banking Crisis—by 0.25 per cent. With this, the ECB follows the Federal Reserve in the US with a delay of a few months. The fact that the inflation rate in the Eurozone is historically high in the middle of 2022 (although having already been rising in 2021) leads to an artificial increase in employment in the medium term—in some years nominal wage increases are likely to be below the inflation rate; the Eurozone and the whole OECD are practically pushed back to a situation akin to the 1970s, when energy price increases and high inflation rates were significant problems. Whether there is also a stagflation problem, however, may be doubted. After all, there is every chance that the EU will continue to achieve economic growth; not least because of the high growth from almost all of Asia, which is not comparable to the situation in the 1970s.

Reconciliation of Interests of the US-Russia-Ukraine-EU and a New International Cities Network Policy

How can the Ukraine-Russia war be brought to a swift end? If the words of former US Secretary of State Henry Kissinger at the 2022 Davos World Economic Forum Summit are anything to go by, the West should try to stop the Russo-Ukrainian war through a reconciliation of interests; in doing so, Russia should pull back to its pre-February 24, 2022, borders—and that would mean that the West would be willing to recognize the Russian annexation of Crimea. In terms of a time horizon, Kissinger considered the next two months (apparently until the end of July 2022) critical to achieving a cease-fire. If border adjustments were to be discussed, wherein Russia would in effect be giving up portions of its previous gains in Crimea, that would in effect be a kind of new war against Russia. As reported in the *New York Times* (Bilefsky, 2022):

> Negotiations need to begin in the next two months before it creates upheavals and tensions that will not be easily overcome", he said. "Ideally, the dividing line should be a return to the status quo ante," he added, apparently referring to a restoration of Ukraine's borders as they were before the

war began in February. "Pursuing the war beyond that point would not be about the freedom of Ukraine, but a new war against Russia itself.

In a certain sense, France's President Macron also stands for the thesis that any peace reached between Ukraine and Russia should not amount to a humiliation of Russia. The Chancellery in Berlin appears to be thinking along the same lines. The US and the UK are more likely to stand for a different view, according to which the Russo-Ukrainian war should go in the direction of weakening Russia in the long term. From the US point of view, this should also serve as a message to China—with regard to the Taiwan issue.

Obviously, what is needed are negotiations between Russia, Ukraine, the US and the UK, as well as the EU and presumably also China. In this context, China and the EU (representing significantly more than France and Germany) would be a new diplomatic player at the table, if one considers the situation in light of the negotiations in Versailles after the First World War. It is in fact remarkable that such a reconciliation of interests is more conceivable in a political-architectural context of the Treaty of Versailles than in the final phase of the Second World War. But this also brings one closer to the nineteenth century as an imperialist phase. Nevertheless, it is conceivable that the UN could play an important role in a Russo-Ukrainian peace settlement. From the point of view of the EU and the US, an important purpose of a reconciliation of interests would include the following:

- Firstly, that the war would be over.
- Secondly, that Russia would have to pay a significant price for taking over Crimea, with a referendum to be held in the region—by the people living there in the spring of 2022—after five years, and under international supervision;
- Thirdly, Russia would have to strive to become a member of the OECD, that is, it would ultimately have to prove that Russia is a democracy—the OSCE would have to be substantially involved in this;
- Fourthly, that the EBRD in London should provide analytical and practical support for a process of normalization in a market economy that would lead Russia within a decade to a comprehensive new privatization process with increased competition, reduced oligarchic tendencies, and a massive reduction in corruption. Without massive reform of the political system, that is, however, unlikely to transpire.

Such a reconciliation of interests is likely to reflect relatively little of the Ukrainian view—the Ukrainian people ultimately want a decisive military victory against Russia; with Western military assistance, of course. Many Eastern European EU member countries may think relatively little of a diplomatic resolution in terms of rapid peace negotiations with a great balance of interests. Their main interest, from an economic and geographic point of view, is to permanently weaken Russia as a military power. In this context, Russia can certainly cooperate with China and India—Russia could be an important supplier of military technology to both countries; more so for India than for China which is itself an emerging high-tech power. For both countries, Russia could also be a major supplier of both fossil fuels and nuclear power, which would matter little if renewables would rapidly gain global importance. In fact, the steps toward more renewables will be relatively difficult. Russia itself probably has little interest in seeing the global economy take quick steps toward climate neutrality. There is only one caveat here: namely, the relatively large capabilities of Russia's nuclear industry to build nuclear power plants of conventional design and new types of small nuclear power plants.

The alternative would likely be a war between Russia and Ukraine that would drag on for many years and which could destabilize Europe in the long term, including the EU countries, which would have to keep supplying Ukraine with new armaments and financial aid. Russia, for its part, could try to cut back on oil and gas production and specifically reduce exports to Western Europe. In doing so, a secondary goal of Russia could be to destabilize EU countries through stoking ever-new internal conflicts over the Russian war of aggression against Ukraine and also to contribute to political conflicts through a persistently high inflation rate. Incidentally, a multi-year Russo-Ukrainian war could also buy time from Russia's perspective to strengthen the role of right-wing parties across Europe in the shadow of expanding nationalism. One can assume that the populist Putin is strategically counting on a new Europe in the mold of the nineteenth century, in which Russia would then represent an important imperialist power—enriched by the US and China and possibly India.

A fundamentally new approach at the end of a cease-fire might be to seek to entrench a new market economy—along with democracy and the rule of law—in Russia. This will be more likely to happen if Russia experiences a significant defeat in Ukraine; and if the US and the EU, together with international organizations including the EBRD, would support a thoughtful modernization policy in Russia for decades to come. Whether there is sufficient willingness to do so on the part of Western countries may be doubted. The tendency to demonize Russia in some media portrayals is not very appropriate, and it certainly does not provide a basis for achieving Russia's integration into the world economy in the long term. One of the first intermediate goals should be to rebuild economic relations with Russia; however, not as before with a main focus on the energy sectors, but with a clear focus instead on industrial and digital modernization in Russia. It will be difficult to anchor more sustainable competition in markets in both Ukraine and Russia and to push back the role of the oligarchs.

Building a stable and modern civil society in Russia (and Ukraine) will be a major challenge for many decades to come—a task that is feasible, but which requires a very special commitment and will probably only be possible if, in addition to top-down politics driven by leaders, but also if, for example, city networks and twinning projects are established to promote a constructive spirit of bottom-up cooperation.

The old idea of the Hanseatic League, which dates back to 1200, was revived in Old Europe in 1980—with an idea originating in the Dutch city of Zwolle; by 2022, there were more than 190 Hanseatic cities in more than 20 countries working together on joint projects, including 16 Russian cities. Municipal networks can, of course, not replace high-level politics. But active urban networks in Europe could well be an important element for a peaceful and prosperous future in a real and digital world economy. Here, there are new opportunities for peaceful and market-based cooperation that could secure more foreign trade and direct investment in Europe and Asia; the admission of countries from Asia could take place indirectly in a first step through existing city partnerships and quite possibly directly in a second step—so that, for example, in the long term, existing city partnerships of German cities with cities in China could also become an expanded Hanseatic-type network. Such a European city network could not only be open to Asia, but also have the chance to expand to the US and other regions of the world, whereby existing city twinning connections would be an important starting point. A peaceful and economically prosperous world economy must therefore be developed both by "big politics" from above and by the pragmatic networking politics of cities and communities from below, which could be a new perspective for the twenty-first century. The long-term experiences of Hanseatic cities in Europe should be the core foundation here, whereby, in addition to continental European cities, the historically important city of London should certainly also play its old pillar role once again—also with a view to being an overcoming element in relation to BREXIT. Thus, a meaningful review of European history would result in institutional innovations and positive impulses for a prosperous and peaceful twenty-first century. In early September 2022, the Ukrainian military launched a successful counteroffensive against Russian forces in the country. Such a development—combined with the rising political resistance against Vladimir Putin in St. Petersburg, Moscow and other major Russian cities—could bring about a defeat of Russia's military in Ukraine in the medium term. If Russia would choose a new, pro-democratic president and if a lasting peace between Ukraine and Russia could be achieved, this would be a historical event for Europe, Asia and the whole world. It remains to be seen, however, how the conflict will develop on the ground in late 2022, into 2023 and beyond.

LITERATURE

Bilefsky, D. (2022, May 24). Kissinger suggests that Ukraine give up territory to Russia, drawing a backlash. *New York Times*. Retrieved June 07, 2022, from https://www.nytimes.com/2022/05/25/world/europe/henry-kissinger-ukraine-russia-davos.html

Eltchaninoff, M. (2015). *Dans la tête de Vladimir Poutine*. Actes Sud.

Eltchaninoff, M. (2016). *In Putins Kopf: Die Philosophie eines Lupenreinen Demokraten*. Klett-Cotta.

Eltchaninoff, M. (2018). *Inside the mind of Vladimir Putin*. Hurst & Co Publishers.

Welfens, P. J. J., & Hanrahan, D. (2022). The EU-US Trade and Technology Council: Developments, key issues and policy options. EIIW Discussion Paper No. 316. https://eiiw.wiwi.uni-wuppertal.de/fileadmin/eiiw/Daten/Publikationen/Gelbe_Reihe/disbei316.pdf

White House. (2022). FACT SHEET: In Asia, President Biden and a Dozen Indo-Pacific partners launch the Indo-Pacific economic framework for prosperity. White House Briefing Room, Statements and Releases, May 23. Retrieved May 27, 2022, from https://www.whitehouse.gov/briefing-room/statements-releases/2022/05/23/fact-sheet-in-asia-president-biden-and-a-dozen-indo-pacific-partners-launch-the-indo-pacific-economic-framework-for-prosperity/

Annex A: German-Russian Economic Relations in 2021 (Federal Statistical Office of Germany, 24/2/2022)

Reproduced here (in an English translation) is Press Release No. N 010, dated February 24, 2022:

Foreign Trade with Russia Up 34% Year-on-Year in 2021

Due to Higher Energy Prices, Imports in Particular Increase Significantly (+54%)

Crude Oil and Natural Gas Account for Around 59% of All Imports from Russia

WIESBADEN—Despite growing political tensions, trade between Germany and Russia increased significantly again in 2021 compared with the first pandemic year 2020. As reported by the Federal Statistical Office (Destatis), goods worth around 59.8 billion euros were traded between the two countries in 2021—34.1% more than in the previous year. Goods worth 33.1 billion euros were imported from the Russian Federation, while exports worth a good 26.6 billion euros went there. Foreign trade turnover between Germany and Russia was thus 3.4% higher than the pre-crisis level in 2019.

Imports Exceed Exports Again in 2021: In Contrast to 2020

Imports from Russia in particular grew strongly in 2021, rising by +54.2% compared with 2020. The value of goods exported to Russia also increased in the same period—but at a much more moderate rate of +15.4%. Thus, in contrast to the previous year, the value of German imports from Russia in 2021 again exceeded the value of exports to Russia. In 2020, Germany had achieved an export surplus for the first time since 1993. One reason for this: In the first Corona year, the value of crude oil and natural gas imports in particular had fallen significantly.

Crude Oil and Natural Gas Account for 59% of All Imports from Russia

The primary commodities traded between Russia and Germany are raw materials, vehicles and machinery. Germany imported mainly crude oil and natural gas worth €19.4 billion in 2021—this was an increase of 49.5% and accounted for 59% of all imports from Russia. Russia also supplied metals in particular (€4.5 billion, +72.1% compared to 2020), petroleum and coke products (2.8 billion euros, +23.0%), and coal (2.2 billion euros, +153.0%) to Germany.

By contrast, Germany's exports to Russia in 2021 were mainly machinery (5.8 billion euros, +5.7%), motor vehicles and parts (4.4 billion euros, +31.8%) and chemical products (3.0 billion euros, +19.7%).

With a share of 2.3% of Germany's total foreign trade, Russia was one of the country's 15 most important trading partners in 2021. Outside the European Union, Russia was Germany's fourth most important import partner and fifth most important buyer of German goods in 2021. By way of comparison, the Federal Republic of Germany conducts most of its trade outside the EU with the People's Republic of China (9.5%) followed by the USA (7.5%). However, Russia's importance for German foreign trade has declined over the past decade: In the record year 2012, which was also characterized by high energy prices, goods traded to and from Russia still accounted for 4.1% of German foreign trade.

Russian-managed Companies in Germany Generated Almost 32 Billion Euros

The linkages between German and Russian companies are at a similar level to foreign trade. 1.9% of the sales of all foreign-controlled companies in Germany in 2019 were generated by those headquartered in Russia. By comparison, companies headquartered in the United States accounted for 17.9% of sales. There were 164 Russian-headquartered companies in Germany in 2019. They employed a good 8,100 people and generated sales of €31.6 billion in the process.

Conversely, according to the Deutsche Bundesbank, 472 companies in Russia were controlled by German investors in 2019. These employed just under 129,000 people and generated annual sales of a good 38.1 billion euros. This corresponds to a share of 1.5% of global annual sales generated abroad by companies of German investors in 2019. By way of comparison, 21.1% of this global turnover by companies of German investors was generated in the USA (545.4 billion euros).

Methodological Notes

The statistics on companies under foreign control include companies domiciled in Germany that are controlled by a parent company based abroad. Control exists when a company directly or indirectly owns more than 50% of the shares of another company.

Source: DeStatis (2022), Facts on Trade with Russia, Federal Statistical Office of Germany, Press release February 24, 2022, available at https://www.destatis.de/EN/Press/2022/02/PE22_N010_51.html;jsessionid=BE99A7ABE55B771D0E1A17DCECCE1117.live732 (last accessed 25.05.2022)

Annex B: NATO Aircraft for Ukraine?

Russia has apparently achieved clear air superiority in the first two weeks of the war against Ukraine—mainly by destroying airports in Ukraine. Ukraine's government has called for the delivery of weapons from Western countries. A critical issue in mid-March included the possible delivery of 29 Soviet-made aircraft in service with the Air Force in Poland. News reports in Germany on March 8th said that Poland's government, initially reluctant, was willing to deliver the said aircraft to the US (to be flown to Ramstein US Air Force Base in Germany); Poland's government was said to have demanded that other NATO countries also cooperate here, with the air forces in Bulgaria and Slovakia also still using Soviet-made aircraft. Poland's government did not want to deliver the requested aircraft to Ukraine from Polish airports under any circumstances, as it feared that otherwise it would be classified as a warring party in the Ukraine war from the point of view of Russia's political leadership. Incidentally, the US is said to have promised that Poland would receive modern aircraft from the US to fill the emerging defense gap. Such a promise, however, can only be kept after several months, even if the US Air Force were willing to supply Poland with used US aircraft—F16s, for example. After all, Polish military pilots would first have to be trained on the new US aircraft. Incidentally, Poland's government has demanded that its aircraft could only be transferred to Ukraine with a unanimous NATO decision.

P. J. J. Welfens, *Russia's Invasion of Ukraine*,
https://doi.org/10.1007/978-3-031-19138-1

In principle, a transfer of aircraft from NATO countries to Ukraine could result in little countering of the then "new Ukrainian air force" against Russian air superiority. With some 40 aircraft that would be hard to ship to Ukraine under Russian radar and space-based satellite reconnaissance, little is likely to be accomplished in terms of strengthening Ukrainian defenses in the Ukraine war, while Russia is likely to point out that such Ukrainian aircraft could also attack targets in Russia: NATO countries could quickly become an active part of the Russo-Ukrainian war against this backdrop, something NATO had said in the early days of the war should be avoided at all costs. Finally, there would then be the danger of a nuclear war between Russia and the US as well as the UK plus France as soon as an escalation within the framework of conventional warfare should have exceeded a critical threshold.

It is therefore not surprising that Germany did not agree to the transfer of the 29 Polish military jets to Ramstein. In the end, the US also rejected Poland's proposal. The problem is too obvious: Bringing Ukrainian pilots to Ramstein so that they can take off from there for military action in Ukraine's airspace would draw Germany and NATO into the crosshairs of the Russian military. Ukraine, Poland, and the US could have raised questions about strengthening Ukraine's air force as early as spring 2021, when Russia's armed forces launched their maneuvers on Ukraine's borders.

Annex C: Ukraine's Neo-Nazi Problem— Cohen (2018), Published on REUTERS on March 19th, 2018

Commentary: Ukraine's Neo-Nazi Problem

"As Ukraine's struggle against Russia and its proxies continues [PJJW: referring in 2018 to the regional military conflicts in eastern Ukraine between the two self-proclaimed independent people's republics in the Donbas region—with a Russian-speaking majority—namely, Donetsk and Luhansk—and Ukraine's military], Kiev must also contend with a growing problem behind the front lines: far-right vigilantes who are willing to use intimidation and even violence to advance their agendas, and who often do so with the tacit approval of law enforcement agencies."

Josh Cohen is a former USAID project officer involved in managing economic reform projects in the former Soviet Union.

Source: Cohen, J. (2018), Ukraine's Neo-Nazi Problem, published by Reuters on March 19th, 2018, available https://www.reuters.com/article/us-cohen-ukraine-commentary-idUSKBN1GV2TY (last accessed 24.05.2022)

Annex D: EU Sanctions Against Russia (from EU Ukraine Support Website, March 2022)

"The sanctions include:

- financial sanctions that make it more difficult for Russia to access EU capital markets, freeze assets and prevent transactions with three Russian banks, and disconnect key banks from the SWIFT system
- Sanctions in the energy sector to make it harder and more expensive for Russia to expand its oil refineries
- Prohibition of export, sale and supply of aircraft and related equipment to Russian air carriers, as well as of all related repair, maintenance or financial services
- Closure of EU airspace to all Russian-owned, Russian-registered or Russian-controlled aircraft. These aircraft will no longer be able to land on the territory of the EU, take off from the territory of the Union or fly over the territory of the Union.
- Expand export controls on dual-use items to limit Russia's access to key technologies such as semiconductors or cutting-edge software
- EU entry restrictions for Russian diplomats and similar groups and for business people
- EU-wide suspension of broadcasting rights for state media Russia Today and Sputnik and their affiliates."

P. J. J. Welfens, *Russia's Invasion of Ukraine*,
https://doi.org/10.1007/978-3-031-19138-1

Source: European Commission (2022b), EU Solidarity with Ukraine, available online at

https://ec.europa.eu/info/strategy/priorities-2019-2024/stronger-europe-world/eu-solidarity-ukraine_en (last accessed 27.05.2022)

Annex E: OECD Interim Economic Outlook, March 2022 (Economic Model Analysis of the Russo-Ukrainian War/ Main Assumptions and Selected Results)

"The main text incorporates simulations of the potential economic impact of the Russia-Ukraine conflict using the NiGEM global macroeconomic model. The simulations consider the impact of the shocks to commodity and financial markets seen in the first two weeks since the invasion by Russia, and large up-front declines in domestic demand in Russia and Ukraine.

The commodity price shocks are the percentage difference in the average price of selected commodities over February 24 to March 9 from the average price in January 2022. Translating these into the global commodity price aggregates included in NiGEM:

- World oil prices are increased by 33% and coal prices by 80%.
- Gas prices are raised by 85% in Europe, 10% in North America and 20% in the rest of the world.
- World metals prices are increased by 11%, based on a weighted average of changes in prices for copper, gold, zinc, iron ore, nickel, aluminum, palladium and platinum.
- World food prices are raised by a weighted average of 6%, with wheat prices up by 90%, corn prices by 40% and all other index components assumed to remain unchanged.
- Fertiliser prices are assumed to be 30% higher.

© The Author(s), under exclusive license to Springer Nature Switzerland AG 2022
P. J. J. Welfens, *Russia's Invasion of Ukraine*,
https://doi.org/10.1007/978-3-031-19138-1

The financial market shocks are also calibrated on the average changes seen since the start of the war relative to January 2022. They include:

- A 50% depreciation of the rouble against the US dollar, and an initial increase of 10.5 percentage points in Russian policy interest rates, with smaller bilateral US dollar currency depreciations of 5% in the Czech Republic, Hungary, Poland, Romania and Turkey. These shocks imply small effective exchange rate appreciations in the major advanced economies.
- Greater financial market uncertainty and diminished risk appetite has pushed up investment risk premia by around 1000 basis points in Russia, 500 basis points in Ukraine, 100 basis points in Turkey, 50 basis points in Bulgaria, Czech Republic, Hungary, Poland and Romania, and 25 basis points in all other emerging-market economies.

The potential scale of the likely hit to domestic demand in Russia and Ukraine is extremely uncertain, but is likely to be large. Past episodes in Russia, such as the financial crisis in 1998 and the aftermath of the annexation of Crimea in 2014 were accompanied by sizeable domestic demand declines of between 10–15 per cent. The stronger sanctions applied following the invasion of Ukraine suggest that the downturn in Russia could be even larger than these past episodes. Sharp downturns have also occurred in other countries subject to international sanctions, including Iran. In Ukraine, the scale of the damage caused by the war is likely to be greater still. Other conflicts have resulted in annual GDP declines of between 25–40% in some countries, including Iraq, Syria and Yemen.

The simulations incorporate ex-ante domestic demand declines of 15% in Russia and 40% in Ukraine. Domestic demand is left endogenous to reflect other factors that are adjusting in the simulation.

All shocks are assumed to last for at least one year. The simulations are undertaken on the NiGEM model in backward-looking mode. This means that consumers and companies do not make their current spending choices with certainty about the future evolution of the conflict. Policy interest rates are endogenous and adjust according to the balance of the shocks to growth and inflation.

The fiscal scenario considers the impact of an increase in final government spending of 0.5% of GDP in all OECD economies. In practice, the measures taken could vary across countries, reflecting a combination of stronger investment and defense spending and cash transfers targeted on lower income households or refugees with a high marginal propensity to consume. In countries less directly affected by the conflict, the additional spending could also reflect temporary delays in some previously-planned discretionary consolidation."

Source: OECD (2022), p. 13

Annex F: Joint Statement by the Leaders of International Financial Organizations with Programs for Ukraine and Neighboring Countries (World Bank, 2022a)

An unusual joint statement of the leaderships of international financial organizations expresses a special cooperation of these organizations in the assistance to Ukraine in the spring of 2022.

Joint Statement of Heads of International Financial Institutions with programs in Ukraine and neighboring countries

Statement from Odile Renaud-Basso, President of the European Bank for Reconstruction and Development (EBRD), Werner Hoyer, President of the European Investment Bank (EIB), Carlo Monticelli, Governor of the Council of Europe Development Bank (CEB), Kristalina Georgieva, Managing Director of the International Monetary Fund (IMF), and David Malpass, President of the World Bank Group (WBG).

We, the heads of the EBRD, EIB, CEB, IMF, and WBG, met today to discuss impacts on the global economy of the ongoing war in Ukraine and our respective and collective response to this crisis. We are horrified and deeply concerned about the Russian invasion of Ukraine and the ensuing crisis. The attacks on civilians and civilian infrastructure are causing tremendous suffering, creating massive population displacements, threatening international peace and security, and endangering basic social and economic needs for people around the world.

© The Author(s), under exclusive license to Springer Nature Switzerland AG 2022
P. J. J. Welfens, *Russia's Invasion of Ukraine*,
https://doi.org/10.1007/978-3-031-19138-1

In addition to the devastating human catastrophe unfolding in Ukraine, the war is disrupting livelihoods throughout the region and beyond. The impacts will be extensive-from reduced energy and food supplies, to increases in prices and poverty and a massive undertaking of Ukraine's reconstruction, all of which will hamper the post-pandemic recovery around the world.

The entire global economy will feel the effects of the crisis through slower growth, trade disruptions, and steeper inflation, harming especially the poorest and most vulnerable. Higher prices for commodities like food and energy will push inflation up further. Countries, particularly those neighboring Ukraine will suffer disruptions in trade, supply chains and remittances as well as surges in refugee flows. Reduced confidence and higher investor uncertainty will impact asset prices, tighten financial conditions, and could even generate capital outflows from emerging markets.

Our institutions have responded with emergency support to Ukraine and its neighbors.

The **EBRD** has approved a "War on Ukraine - EBRD Resilience Package", initially sized at EUR 2 billion, to respond to the immediate needs of the people affected by the war and - when conditions permit - support the substantial reconstruction of Ukraine. The EBRD's package comprises an immediate Resilience and Livelihoods program covering the areas of energy security, nuclear safety, municipal services, trade finance support and liquidity for SMEs in Ukraine and in neighboring affected countries. Once conditions permit, the EBRD will also be prepared to take part in a reconstruction program for Ukraine, to rebuild livelihoods and businesses; restore vital infrastructure; support good governance; and enable access to services. It envisages working with international partners including the EU and U.S., as well as bilateral donors and other international financial institutions.

The **EIB** has prepared an emergency solidarity package for Ukraine of EUR 2 billion, including the provision of EUR 668 million in immediate liquidity assistance to the Ukrainian authorities. This has been developed in close collaboration with the European Commission. As part of this package, the Bank is also accelerating the delivery of an additional EUR 1.3 billion of commitments made for infrastructure projects. Of the emergency liquidity assistance, EUR 329 million has been disbursed in the past week. An additional EUR 329 million will be disbursed over the coming days. In parallel, the Bank is developing a multi-billion euro package for the EU Eastern and Southern Neighborhood, the EU Enlargement

Region and Central Asia to mitigate the consequences of the refugee crisis, and help address the social and economic fallout caused by the war. Within the EU, EIB will work closely with Member States, National Promotional Banks and the European Commission to prepare an action plan to help alleviate the impact of the refugee crisis on EU countries hosting refugees.

The **CEB**, according to its membership and special social mandate, has provided emergency grants to Ukraine's neighboring countries to cover immediate needs of refugees, including transportation and orientation. The CEB stands ready to also provide flexible, fast-disbursing loans to address the significant financial needs of neighboring and other countries hosting large inflow of refugees, while remaining focused on the social sector.

The **IMF** disbursed emergency assistance of US$1.4 billion to Ukraine on March 9 under the https://www.imf.org/en/About/Factsheets/Sheets/2016/08/02/19/55/Rapid-Financing-Instrument the war. IMF staff remains closely engaged with the authorities to provide policy support as they continue to design and implement effective crisis mitigation measures. The IMF is also currently working with Moldova, which has requested an augmentation of its existing IMF-supported program. The Fund stands ready to support neighboring and other countries affected by the spillovers of the war through all its relevant instruments.

The **World Bank Group** has already mobilized more than US$925 million for Ukraine, including fast-disbursing budget support to help the government provide critical services to Ukrainian people, of which US$350 million has been disbursed. This financing is part of a US$3 billion package of support planned for Ukraine in the coming months. The World Bank also set up a multi-donor trust fund (MDTF) that is among the most rapid, targeted, and secure mechanisms to facilitate channeling grant resources from donors to Ukraine, with contributions of US$145 million thus far. The World Bank Group is also working on options to assist neighboring countries, including to support refugee populations, and will continue to provide trade finance to support the private sector.

We acknowledge the importance of working together to coordinate our respective responses to support Ukraine and neighbors on the financing and policy fronts and maximize impact on the ground. We are committed to strengthening international cooperation and solidarity in the face of this enormous challenge.

Source: World Bank (2022a), Joint Statement of Heads of International Financial Institutions with Programs in Ukraine and Neighboring Countries, published 17th March 2022, available online at https://www.worldbank.org/en/news/statement/2022/03/17/joint-statement-of-heads-of-international-financial-institutions-with-programs-in-ukraine-and-neighboring-countries (accessed 24.05.2022)

Annex G: Intra-EU Solidarity Requirements of Member Countries under the EU Gas Supply Emergency Directive (Excerpts: 2017)

The directive refers directly, amongst other things, to supply problems from Russia in 2009; it is probably unclear what solidarity requirements apply in a case where EU member states—individually or collectively—implement a gas import boycott. Nevertheless, Germany, for example, is likely to have a special obligation to help within the EU if the EU decides to impose a gas import boycott on Russia.

The following are excerpts from the EU Directive:

"([1]) Commission Regulation (EU) No 312/2014 of 26 March 2014 establishing a network code for gas balancing in transmission systems (OJ L 91, 27.3.2014, p. 15).

28.10.2017

Official Journal of the European Union L 280/7 (Official Journal of the European Union 28.10.2017)

This Regulation establishes sufficiently harmonized standards for security of supply to deal with at least a situation such as that which occurred in January 2009, when gas supplies from Russia were interrupted. These standards take into account the differences between Member States as well as public service obligations and customer protection as set out in Article 3 of Directive 2009/73/EC. The security of supply standards should be stable to ensure the necessary legal certainty, they should be clearly defined and they should not impose an unreasonable and disproportionate burden

P. J. J. Welfens, *Russia's Invasion of Ukraine*, https://doi.org/10.1007/978-3-031-19138-1

on natural gas undertakings. They should also ensure equal access of Union natural gas undertakings to national customers. Member States should establish measures to ensure in an effective and proportionate manner that natural gas undertakings comply with those standards, including the possibility of imposing financial penalties on suppliers where they deem it appropriate.

The roles and responsibilities of all natural gas undertakings and Competent Authorities should be clearly defined in order to maintain a properly functioning internal gas market, in particular in the event of supply disruptions and crises. The definition of roles and responsibilities should be such as to ensure that a three-level approach is followed, with action being taken in a first step by the natural gas undertakings and industry concerned, in a second step by the Member States at national or regional level and in a third step by the Union. This Regulation should enable natural gas undertakings and customers to rely on market mechanisms for as long as possible in the event of supply disruptions. However, it should also provide for mechanisms to be resorted to in the event that markets alone can no longer adequately deal with a gas supply disruption.

In the event of a gas supply disruption, market participants should be given sufficient opportunity to respond to the situation with market-based measures. Where market measures have been exhausted and are still not sufficient, Member States and their competent authorities should take measures to remedy or mitigate the effects of the gas supply disruption.

Where Member States intend to adopt non-market based measures, the introduction of the measures should be accompanied by a description of the economic consequences. This will ensure that customers receive the information they need on the costs of such measures and that the measures are transparent, in particular as regards their impact on the gas price.

The Commission should be empowered to ensure that new non-market-based preventive measures do not jeopardize the security of gas supply of other Member States or of the Union. Since such measures may be highly detrimental to the security of gas supply, it is appropriate that they enter into force only if they have been approved by the Commission or amended in accordance with a Commission decision.

Demand-side measures such as fuel switching or reducing gas supplies to large industrial customers in an economically efficient sequence can make a valuable contribution to securing gas supplies, provided they can be implemented quickly in response to a gas supply disruption and reduce demand appreciably. More should be done to encourage efficient energy use, especially when demand-side measures are necessary. The environmental impacts of proposed demand-side and supply-side measures should be adequately considered, and preference should be given as much as possible to those measures that have the least impact on the environment. At the same time, the considerations of security of gas supply and preservation of competition should be taken into account.

It is necessary to ensure the predictability of the actions to be taken in an emergency so that all market participants have sufficient opportunity to respond and prepare for such circumstances. In principle, therefore, the competent authorities should act in accordance with their emergency plans. However, in duly justified special circumstances, they should be allowed to take measures that deviate from those plans. It is also important to make the way in which emergencies are announced more transparent and predictable. In this respect, information on the network balancing status (the overall status of the transmission network)—the relevant framework is set out in Commission Regulation (EU) No 312/2014 (¹)—can play an important role. This information should be available in real time to the competent authorities and to the national regulatory authorities where they are not the competent authorities.

As was made clear in the context of the October 2014 stress test on the short-term resilience of the European gas system, solidarity is needed to ensure security of gas supply in the Union. This will spread the impact more evenly and mitigate the overall impact of a severe disruption. The solidarity mechanism is designed to deal with extreme situations where the supply of customers protected by solidarity is at stake as an essential necessity and indispensable priority in a Member State. Solidarity ensures cooperation with the more vulnerable Member States. Solidarity is also a last resort, used only in an emergency and under limited conditions. Therefore, when an emergency is declared in a Member State, a graduated and proportionate approach should be taken to ensure security of gas supply. In particular, the Member State which has declared the emergency should first take all the emergency measures provided for in its emergency plan in order to ensure gas supply to its customers protected by solidarity. At the same time, all Member States that have implemented an increased supply standard should temporarily lower it to the normal supply standard in order to increase the liquidity of the gas market if the Member State declaring the emergency declares that cross-border measures are necessary. If these two sets of measures do not result in the necessary supply, solidarity measures should be taken by the directly connected Member

States to ensure gas supply to customers protected by solidarity in the Member State where the emergency has occurred, upon its request. Such solidarity measures should ensure that gas supplies to customers not protected by solidarity are reduced or withdrawn in the territory of the Member State providing solidarity in order to make gas quantities available to the extent needed and for the period during which the gas needs of customers protected by solidarity are not met in the Member State requesting solidarity. Under no circumstances should this Regulation be understood as requiring or allowing a Member State to exercise sovereign authority in another Member State.

39. Solidarity measures should also apply as a last resort where a Member State is connected to another Member State through a third country, provided that the flow through that third country is not restricted and subject to the agreement of the Member States concerned, which should include, where appropriate, the third country through which they are connected.

40. Where solidarity measures are applied as a last resort, the curtailment or withdrawal of gas supply in the Member State providing solidarity should affect all customers not protected by solidarity where this is necessary to meet its solidarity obligations and to avoid discriminatory treatment, irrespective of whether the customers receive gas in the form of heat directly or through district heating facilities protected by solidarity. The same should be ensured in reverse for customers who are not solidarity-protected customers in the Member State purchasing gas through the solidarity mechanism.

41. Where solidarity measures are taken as a last resort, preference should first be given to reducing gas consumption in the Member State providing solidarity on a voluntary basis, through market-based measures such as voluntary demand-side measures or reverse auctions where certain consumers, such as industrial consumers, notify the transmission system operator or other competent authority of the price at which they would reduce or stop their gas consumption. If market-based measures prove insufficient to remove the congestion in the necessary gas supply, and given the importance of solidarity as a last resort, the Member State providing solidarity should be able to apply non-market-based measures, including supply cuts for certain groups of consumers, as a second step to meet its solidarity obligations.

42. Compensation should be provided for solidarity measures as a last resort. The Member State providing solidarity should receive adequate compensation without delay from the Member State benefiting from solidarity, including for gas delivered to its territory and for any other relevant reasonable costs incurred in providing solidarity. Solidarity measures as a last resort should be conditional on the commitment of the Member State requesting solidarity to provide adequate and prompt compensation. This Regulation does not harmonize all aspects of adequate compensation. The Member States concerned should take the necessary measures—in particular technical, legal and financial arrangements—to implement the provisions on prompt and adequate compensation between them.

43. Member States, when taking measures under the provisions of this Regulation on solidarity, implement Union law and are therefore required to respect fundamental rights guaranteed by Union law. Such measures may therefore lead to an obligation for a Member State to provide compensation to those affected by its measures. Member States should therefore ensure that there are national provisions on compensation that are compatible with Union law and in particular with fundamental rights. In addition, it should be ensured that the Member State benefiting from solidarity ultimately bears any reasonable costs incurred by the Member State providing solidarity as a result of the aforementioned obligation to provide compensation, as well as any further reasonable costs incurred as a result of providing compensation under the aforementioned national compensation schemes.

Since more than one Member State may provide solidarity support to a requesting Member State, there should be a burden-sharing mechanism. Under this mechanism, the Member State requesting solidarity should, after consulting all Member States concerned, select the most advantageous offer in terms of cost, speed of delivery, reliability and diversification of gas supply from different Member States. Member States should, as far and as long as possible, make such offers on the basis of voluntary demand-side measures before resorting to non-market-based measures.

This Regulation introduces for the first time such a solidarity mechanism between Member States as a tool to mitigate the effects of a severe emergency within the Union—including a burden-sharing mechanism. The Commission should therefore review the burden-sharing mechanism and the solidarity mechanism in general in the light of future experience with their functioning and propose amendments to them as appropriate.

Member States should adopt the necessary measures to implement the provisions on the solidarity mechanism, including that the Member States concerned agree on technical, legal and financial arrangements. Member States should describe the details of these arrangements in their contingency plans. The Commission should provide non-legally binding guidance on the main elements to be included in these arrangements.

As long as a Member State is able to cover the gas consumption of customers protected by solidarity from its own production and therefore does not need to request solidarity, it should be exempted from the obligation to establish technical, legal and financial arrangements with other Member States to obtain a solidarity payment. This should not affect the obligation of the Member State concerned to provide a solidarity benefit to other Member States.

There should be a safeguard clause for cases where the Union bears the costs of measures which Member States are required to take under the solidarity mechanism provisions of this Regulation, on the basis of liability other than for unlawful acts or conduct within the meaning of Article 340(2) TFEU. In such cases, it is appropriate that the Member State benefiting from solidarity should reimburse the costs incurred by the Union.

Where necessary, solidarity should also be exercised through assistance provided by the Union and its Member States in the framework of civil protection. Such assistance should be facilitated and coordinated through the Union Civil Protection Mechanism established by Decision No 1313/2013/EU, which aims to strengthen cooperation between the Union and the Member States and facilitate coordination in the field of civil protection in order to improve the effectiveness of systems for preventing, preparing for and responding to natural and man-made disasters.

Access to relevant information is essential for assessing the security of gas supply of a Member State, part of the Union or the Union as a whole. In particular, Member States and the Commission need regular access to information from natural gas undertakings on the main parameters of gas supply, including precise measurements of available storage reserves, as a basic starting point for designing strategies to safeguard gas supply. Independent of the declaration of an emergency, access to additional information needed to assess the overall gas supply situation should also be possible in justified cases. Such additional information would typically be non-price gas supply information, e.g., on minimum and maximum gas volumes, delivery points, or gas supply suspension conditions.

An efficient and targeted mechanism for Member States' and the Commission's access to key gas supply contracts should ensure a comprehensive assessment of the relevant risks that may lead to a disruption of gas supply or affect the necessary mitigation measures in case a crisis nevertheless occurs. Under this mechanism, certain major gas supply contracts should be automatically notified to the competent authorities of the Member States most affected, whether the gas originates in the Union or in third countries. New contracts or modifications should be notified immediately after their conclusion. In order to ensure transparency and reliability, existing contracts should also be notified. The notification obligation should also apply to all commercial agreements relevant to the performance of the gas supply contract, including relevant agreements which may be related to infrastructure, storage and other aspects important for the security of gas supply.

Any obligation to automatically notify a contract to the competent authority must be proportionate. Applying this obligation to contracts between a supplier and a buyer representing at least 28% of the national market is balanced in terms of administrative efficiency and transparency and imposes clear obligations on market participants. The Competent Authority should assess the contract from the point of view of ensuring the security of gas supply and send the results of the assessment to the Commission. If the Competent Authority has doubts as to whether a particular contract is a risk to the security of gas supply in a Member State or region, it should notify that contract to the Commission for assessment. This does not mean that other gas supply contracts are not relevant for the security of gas supply. Where the competent authority of the Member State most concerned or the Commission considers that a gas supply contract which is not subject to the automatic notification requirement under this Regulation could, due to its specificities, the group of customers supplied or its importance for security of gas supply, pose a risk to security of gas supply in a Member State, in a region of the Union or in the Union, the competent authority or the Commission should be able to request the contract in order to assess its impact on security of gas supply. This information could be requested, for example, if there is a change in the pattern of past gas supplies to one or more customers in a Member State which would not be expected under normal market conditions and which could have an impact on the gas supply to the Union or parts of the Union. This mechanism will ensure that access to other important gas supply contracts relevant to security of supply is guaranteed. Such a requirement should be duly justified and should take into account the need to minimize the administrative burden of this measure."

Source: OJEU (2017), Official Journal of the European Union L 280/7,   28.10.2017,   https://eur-lex.europa.eu/legal-content/EN/ TXT/PDF/?uri=OJ:L:2017:280:FULL&from=ES   (last   accessed 25.05.2022)

ANNEX H: LARGEST EXPORTERS OF CRUDE OIL AND COAL

Table A1 Top 15 Exporting Countries of Crude Petroleum Oil in 2020, Exported Value in Thousand US$

Ranking	Country	Exported value in 2020 (thousand US$)	Share of world exports
	World	*607,279,930*	*100.00%*
1	United Arab Emirates	105,123,365	17.31%
2	Russian Federation	72,564,294	11.95%
3	Iraq	50,907,809	8.38%
4	United States of America	49,507,575	8.15%
5	Canada	47,605,672	7.84%
6	Kuwait	28,629,492	4.71%
7	Nigeria	25,161,351	4.14%
8	Kazakhstan	23,703,746	3.90%
9	Norway	22,671,605	3.73%
10	Angola	20,227,206	3.33%
11	Brazil	19,613,858	3.23%
12	United Kingdom	16,096,917	2.65%
13	Oman	15,023,520	2.47%
14	Mexico	14,683,691	2.42%
15	Iran	10,034,998	1.65%
Total			**85.88%**

Note: Product Code 2709—Petroleum oils and oils obtained from bituminous minerals, crude
Source: Own calculations (IV); data are ITC calculations based on UN Comtrade and ITC statistics (2022)

© The Author(s), under exclusive license to Springer Nature Switzerland AG 2022
P. J. J. Welfens, *Russia's Invasion of Ukraine*,
https://doi.org/10.1007/978-3-031-19138-1

Table A2 Top 15 Exporting Countries of Liquified Natural Gas in 2020, Exported Value in Thousand US$

Ranking	Country	Exported value in 2020 (thousand US$)	Share of world exports
	World	77,923,928	100.00%
1	Australia	26,312,442	33.77%
2	United States of America	13,045,788	16.74%
3	Malaysia	6,865,068	8.81%
4	Russian Federation	6,745,828	8.66%
5	Nigeria	3,748,842	4.81%
6	Oman	3,677,245	4.72%
7	Indonesia	3,609,514	4.63%
8	Papua New Guinea	3,310,233	4.25%
9	Trinidad and Tobago	2,341,485	3.00%
10	Brunei Darussalam	2,161,184	2.77%
11	Algeria	2,099,697	2.69%
12	Angola	1,016,229	1.30%
13	Peru	520,027	0.67%
14	Equatorial Guinea	505,253	0.65%
15	Norway	466,569	0.60%
Total			**98.08%**

Note: Product Code 271111—Natural gas, liquefied

Source: Own calculations (IV); data are ITC calculations based on UN Comtrade and ITC statistics (2022)

Table A3 Top 15 Exporting Countries of Coal in 2020, Exported Value in Thousand US$

Ranking	Country	Exported value in 2020 (thousand US$)	Share of world exports
	World	82,636,102	100.00%
1	Australia	32,725,103	39.60%
2	Indonesia	14,547,621	17.60%
3	Russian Federation	12,388,244	14.99%
4	United States of America	6,072,849	7.35%
5	South Africa	3,910,237	4.73%
6	Colombia	3,542,690	4.29%
7	Canada	3,396,095	4.11%
8	Mongolia	2,123,670	2.57%
9	Mozambique	590,789	0.71%
10	Poland	507,316	0.61%

(*continued*)

Table A3   (continued)

Ranking	Country	Exported value in 2020 (thousand US$)	Share of world exports
	World	82,636,102	100.00%
11	Netherlands	437,116	0.53%
12	China	435,278	0.53%
13	Kazakhstan	339,784	0.41%
14	Philippines	231,103	0.28%
15	United Kingdom	180,464	0.22%
Total			98.54%

Note: Product Code 2701—Coal; briquettes, ovoids, and similar solid fuels manufactured from coal

Source: Own calculations (IV); data are ITC calculations based on UN Comtrade and ITC statistics (2022)

Table A4   Top 15 Exporting Countries of Natural Gas in 2017, Estimated Volumes in Cubic Meters

Ranking	Country	Gas exports (in millions of cubic meters), 2017	Share of world exports
	World[a]	1,166,342	100.00%
1	Russian Federation	210,200	18.02%
2	Qatar	126,500	10.85%
3	Norway	120,200	10.31%
4	United States of America	89,700	7.69%
5	Canada	83,960	7.20%
6	Australia	67,960	5.83%
7	Algeria	53,880	4.62%
8	Netherlands	51,250	4.39%
9	Malaysia	38,230	3.28%
10	Turkmenistan	38,140	3.27%
11	Germany	34,610	2.97%
12	Indonesia	29,780	2.55%
13	Nigeria	27,210	2.33%
14	Trinidad and Tobago	15,490	1.33%
15	Bolivia	15,460	1.33%
Total		1,002,570	85.96%

Note: [a]World sum is calculated as the sum of all 215 countries and territories included in the dataset, of which 56 have a gas export quantity of zero

Source: Own calculations (IV); data are ITC calculations based on UN Comtrade and ITC statistics (2022)

Annex I: On Important Sectors with High Electricity Intensity of Production (Expert Opinion for the German Federal Ministry of Economic Affairs and Energy, 2015)

The use of gas—and also coal—from Russia is important for power generation in Germany, but also in Poland (where coal imports from Russia are particularly significant) and other countries. Power generation from gas-fired power plants is relatively flexible and increased output can be realized at short notice, while the ramp-up of coal-fired power plants takes more than a day and is less favorable than power generation from gas-fired power plants in terms of climate policy because of the relatively high CO_2 emissions. In the event of an energy import embargo on gas and coal supplies from Russia, sharply rising gas and coal prices in the EU are to be expected—and therefore electricity prices for private households and industry will also rise. Electricity price increases will only affect companies and private households with a time lag of several months or quarters. The Fraunhofer Institute ISI, together with partner institutes (ISI et al., 2015), has presented an analysis of what role rising energy or electricity prices would have for the economy in Germany; and how the policy in Germany should be classified in comparison to other industrialized countries. In Germany, relatively electricity-intensive companies have special (regulated) electricity price concessions—from an economic perspective, this is relatively problematic.

Executive Summary

© The Author(s), under exclusive license to Springer Nature Switzerland AG 2022
P. J. J. Welfens, *Russia's Invasion of Ukraine*,
https://doi.org/10.1007/978-3-031-19138-1

"Energy prices are a key factor for the competitiveness of many German companies. To finance the energy transition, the costs of promoting renewable energy technologies in Germany are passed onto the consumer, predominantly via energy prices (i.e., electricity prices). A large number of levies as well as the electricity tax are currently raising the price of electricity and thereby the electricity costs of industries. To limit the burden, especially for energy-intensive industries, the German government has designed various rules regarding exemptions and rebates (privileges). For the same economic considerations, competing national economies have also introduced special regulations for industrial electricity consumers. The present study examines in detail, the composition of electricity prices in Germany and ten other countries: the Netherlands, the United Kingdom, France, Italy, Denmark, Canada, the United States, China, Korea and Japan. It assesses the effects of the special regulations on the competitiveness of industrial companies in Germany on four levels. The analysis divides electricity price components into three categories:

Electricity purchase prices include the costs of purchasing electricity on the wholesale market and the margins of the utilities. Their value is determined by the composition and technical characteristics of the power plant fleet, the fuel costs, the development of demand, and the framework regulation of the electricity market.

Network charges distribute the costs of transmission and distribution system operators for their services to end users.

State-regulated components finance the cost of energy policy instruments or channel revenues to the state budget. These components include taxes and levies, as well as the costs of meeting established quotas.

The analysis of national electricity markets shows the different regulatory approaches in the examined countries. While European regulators in Germany, the Netherlands, France, Italy and Denmark distribute the costs of energy policy measures through levies and taxes with defined privileging criteria for individual customers, the British and North American governments employ quota systems for the distribution of costs, thereby leaving the question of burden sharing largely to market players. In none of three Asian countries under consideration was it transparent how the costs of political interventions in the power system are distributed.

In the context of this study, the electricity purchase prices, network charges, and privileging criteria on taxes and levies determined are applied to case study examples from six energy-intensive industries: chemicals, paper, steel, aluminium, copper and textiles. The power consumption of these industries accounts for 70% of electricity consumption in the manu-facturing sector and about 27% of total electricity consumption in Germany.

Aluminium and copper producers, steel production in electric arc fur-naces, and chemical reduction processes meet almost all of the privileging criteria that are applied by countries to relieve businesses with high inter-national competition from state-regulated electricity tariff components. These privileging criteria include:

Absolute consumption: The rates of many state-regulated electricity tariff components are graded or contain fixed base amounts. Thus compa-nies with high consumption pay, on aver- age, less per unit of energy. For example, in Germany all companies in the special equalisation scheme (BesAR) pay the full EEG surcharge for the first Gigawatt hour of consumption.

Energy intensity: The total electricity costs compared to sales or gross value added shows which company's competitiveness might be put at risk as a result of high electricity prices. In various regulations, companies that exceed a certain threshold of energy intensity are privileged. In the German special equalisation scheme, this threshold is 16% of gross value added in 2015.

Sector affiliation: Some industries are more exposed to international competition than others, so exemptions are often tied to sector affiliation. The revision of the special equalisation scheme is also an example thereof: Depending on the sector affiliation, companies must reach different thresholds of energy intensity to be privileged.

Processes used: Some industrial processes are power-intensive by nature. The power consumption of defined processes is therefore often exempt from taxes and levies. An example is electricity consumption in metallurgical processes, for which no electricity tax is paid in Germany.

Energy efficiency measures: Some regulators reward energy efficient companies with lower electricity prices by reducing taxes and levies. An example of this is the special equalisation scheme in Germany, which requires companies to install energy management systems.

Costs cap: Some regulators set a relative or absolute cost cap to limit the total expenditures per company for a policy measure. For example, the newly regulated special equalisation scheme in Germany limits the pay-ments for the EEG surcharge to a maximum of 4%, or 0.5% of the gross value added of a company.

Autoproduction: Energy-intensive companies sometimes produce their own power to save costs. Self-consumption is often exempt from taxes and levies. The special equalisation scheme in 2014, for instance, provides that companies are charged 15% of the EEG surcharge for self-consumption

As the example of the German special equalisation scheme shows, criteria are combined in many cases to limit the number of privileged end consumers.

Compared to the other countries studied, Germany raises quite a few and rather high taxes and levies. Without the German privileges, electricity prices for some companies would be almost 8 ct/kWh higher in 2014. The special equalisation scheme on its own accounted for up to 6.2 ct/kWh difference in electricity prices for Germany companies in 2014. Without the special equalisation scheme in Germany, electricity prices for households, commercial consumers, and less energy-intensive industrial companies would be about 1.6 ct/kWh lower in 2014.

To investigate the effects of the German exemptions on the competitiveness of industrial companies, the share of electricity costs to production costs of different products is determined. This share displays how strongly electricity prices, hence the exemptions impact the competitiveness at product level. The findings underpin that in particular, aluminium producers and chlorine manufacturers are sensitive to rising electricity costs. Without the special equalisation scheme, the production of these goods would not be profitable in Germany and production facilities would be forced to shut down sooner or later. This also applies to many paper and steel producers.

At the second stage, the importance of energy costs on the competitiveness at company level is investigated. An analysis of profit and loss accounts of exemplary companies shows what effects can be expected when rising electricity costs cannot be passed on to customers. This analysis also demonstrates the importance of exemptions for metal producers and papermakers that produce electricity-intensive products. In contrast, diversified companies, such as integrated chemical companies, generate a large share of their income from non-energy-intensive products. These cases show that increased energy costs affect the division's earnings, but have little impact on the company's overall results.

Additional interviews underline the importance of market proximity as well as of qualification of workers for the competitiveness of companies in Germany. These location-specific factors can only compensate rising electricity cost to a certain extent. The case analysis shows that especially companies with a limited, electricity-intensive product portfolio could probably not compensate cost increases.

The analysis of the importance of electricity costs for competitiveness at sectoral level determines the short-term impact on product prices, demand, and production in case increased electricity costs in the value chain are fully passed on. It is shown how current prices and total production changes if a single sector is excluded from the special equalisation scheme and the increase in electricity prices is fully passed on product prices. The results show that product prices in the paper industry and in the non-ferrous metal industry would increase substantially. The average increase would be at about 5%. Exports in the metal and paper industry sector would decline by 16% to 18% because of the increased prices. Calculations show that in the short-term, the production of these industries would decrease by 11 to 18%. However, it should be noted that the analyses are based on statistical electricity cost shares and estimated price elasticities of demand. The effects of shut-downs of single companies or the end of production in parts of the supply chain cannot be mapped on sectoral level. This analysis therefore underestimates the effects of electricity cost increases, especially in industries with long and complex supply chains like the chemical industry.

Lastly, in the fourth stage, the long-term macroeconomic effects of the exemptions in Germany are investigated by applying a macro-econometric model. It is estimated how the total economic situation would change if privileges were abolished for all sectors. Ex-ante and ex-post scenarios for the timeframe of 2007 to 2020 are used to determine the impact of changes in the exemptions in Germany on production, added value, employment, investment and foreign trade. For the sectors of the non-privileged industries, commerce, trade, services and households in Germany, the average prices with and without exception are calculated. Electricity prices in other countries stay unchanged in these scenarios.

In the ex-ante scenario (2020) of the complete elimination of the special equalisation scheme, average production prices rise up to 3.5%. For individual companies, the increase of production costs is significantly higher. Compared to the reference, which is the retention of the current regime, German exports in 2020 would be up to 0.3% or EUR 4.7 billion lower. In the calculations, the total negative effect on the gross domestic product amounts to 4 billion Euros or 0.15% in 2020. On the labour market, total employment losses after abolishing the special equalisation scheme would be up to 45,000. If all privileges of the current tax and levies model were to be abolished, calculations show a loss of up to 104,000 jobs by 2020, of which more than 70,000 in the manufacturing sector.

Abolishing the special equalisation scheme would reduce levies for non-privileged sectors and thus lift the cost burden for these sectors. Cost savings for households could amount to two billion Euros annually. In addition, parts of the other industries (approximately 0.5 billion euros) and the commerce, trade, and service sectors (about 2 billion Euros) would be relieved. This results in higher private consumption. Over time, however, consumption growth is weakening as the real income is decreasing. The negative effects in the privileged companies with the change of current regulations outweigh the slightly positive effects of unprivileged consumers that are then charged slightly lower rates, mainly due to lower international competitiveness in price.

The modelling approach has limitations: decisions on the relocation of production are taken at corporate level and depend on company-specific factors, intra-industry integration, and product-related aspects. This cannot be mapped comprehensively using industry statistics. Additional qualitative analyses lead to the suggestion that the effects reported here are probably underestimated at sectoral and macroeconomic levels.

Even with these limitations, all analyses at the different levels lead to the same result: existing exemptions for energy-intensive companies support the competitiveness of the industry and have positive macroeconomic effects."

Source: Fraunhofer ISI/Ecofys (2015), Electricity Costs of Energy Intensive Industries An International Comparison, Report for the German Ministry of Economic Affairs and Energy, July 2015, available at https://www.isi.fraunhofer.de/content/dam/isi/dokumente/ccx/2015/Electricity-Costs-of-Energy-Intensive-Industries.pdf   (last   accessed 25.05.2022)

Annex J: Sanctions Against Russia (According to Spisak [2020], Tony Blair Institute)

An Overview of Sanctions against Russia (as of 22 March, Non-comprehensive List)

Restrictions on the Central Bank of Russia and the Russian Government

- Freezing of the foreign reserves of the Central Bank of Russia (UK, US, EU and Canada)
- Ban on transactions with the Central Bank of Russia (UK, US, EU and Canada), and with the National Wealth Fund and Ministry of Finance (UK and US)

Financial Sanctions

- Exclusion from SWIFT, the global financial messaging system, for several large Russian financial institutions (UK, US, EU and Canada), including SberBank and VTB (US and UK), and several Belarusian banks, including Bank Dabrabyt, Development Bank and Belagroprombank (EU)
- Freezing of the assets of leading Russian banks and other financial institutions, and blocking sanctions, including on: VTB Bank (US and UK); SberBank (US); Alfa-Bank, Otkritie (EU and US); Bank

Rossiya (EU, UK, US and Japan); Promsvyazbank (EU, UK, Switzerland, Japan and Canada); Sovcombank, Novikombank, Russian Agricultural Bank, Central Bank of Moscow, Gazprombank (US); Is Bank, GenBank, Black Sea Bank for Development and Reconstruction (UK); VEB.RF (EU, UK, US, Switzerland, Japan and Canada); and others.

- Freezing of assets of state-owned Belarusian banks, including Belinvestbank and Bank Dabrabyt (US)
- A ban on Russian deposits above €100,000 in EU banks, on Russian accounts held by EU central-securities depositories and on selling euro-denominated securities to Russian clients (EU)
- A ban on listing the shares of Russian state-owned entities (EU); on the issuance of new Russian sovereign bonds (Japan); on sterling clearing through UK and Russian companies from the issuing of transferable securities and money-market instruments (UK); and on the dollar clearing for Russian financial institutions (US)

Economic and Trade Restrictions

- A ban on commercial activities with selected Russian companies, particularly in the aerospace, defense and energy sectors, and with most publicly owned and controlled Russian companies (UK, US, EU, Switzerland, Canada and Australia)
- Export ban on an array of goods and technologies aimed at the transport, telecoms, energy and commodities sectors, and wider sectors (UK, US, EU, Switzerland and Australia)
- Ban on dual-use items and high-end technologies, covering key sectors such as defense, aerospace and maritime (US, EU, UK and Japan). Limited exemptions for international organizations, pandemic-related supplies, overflight and emergency landings, and energy
- Restrictions on providing certain services that relate to some sanctioned goods and activities, including technical assistance and engineering services related to selected sectors and the supply of tourism services (UK, US, EU, Switzerland and Australia)
- A wide range of import restrictions, including a ban on Russian crude oil imports (US, Canada and Australia); the phasing out of gas by the end of 2022 (UK); and a ban on natural gas and coal, and other raw materials (US)

- A ban on the import of targeted goods from Russia, such as agri-food products and raw materials including steel (EU, US and Canada); plus all goods originating from Russia (Australia)
- Withdrawal of the "most favored nation" status for Russia and Belarus from the World Trade Organization (UK, US, EU, South Korea, Canada, Australia, Japan and eight other WTO members)

Restrictions on Persons

- Restrictions on providing assets to designated persons and on dealing with the assets of designated persons (asset freezes), covering the Russian elite and including members of the government, the State Duma and businesspeople (UK, US, EU, Switzerland, Australia and Canada); plus lists of designated persons that varies country by country
- Travel bans on designated persons (UK, US, EU, Switzerland, Australia and Canada)

Other
Source: TBI

- Territorial sanctions already imposed on Crimea extended to Donetsk and Luhansk (UK and EU)
- Ban on Russian planes using airspace (UK, US, EU and Switzerland)
- Ban on Russian ships using ports (UK, EU and Canada)

Source: Based on Spisak (2020), Fig. 1

Annex K: Extract from the Emergency Plan for Gas for the Federal Republic of Germany (2019); (Transl: PJJW)

"Residential" is considered a priority over industrial firms when it comes to a secure gas supply. Gas supply issues with industry are considered in parallel with gas use issues in the electric power industry, where appropriate. A three-stage crisis scheme is used in the emergency plan: Early Warning Stage (declared in Germany on March 30th, 2022), Alert Stage and Emergency Stage. As important points, the gas emergency plan states:

"3.1 Requirements pursuant to Art. 10 of the SoS Regulation

The required content of the national Emergency Plans is defined in Art. 10 of the SoS Regulation. According to this provision, the Emergency Plans must meet the following criteria:

a) They are built on three main crisis levels:

- Early warning level (early warning)
- Alert level (alert)
- Emergency level (emergency)

b) they define the role and responsibilities of natural gas undertakings and of industrial gas customers including relevant electricity producers, taking account of the different extents to which they are affected in the event of gas supply disruptions, and their interaction with the Competent Authorities and where appropriate with the national regulatory authorities at each of the crisis levels;

© The Author(s), under exclusive license to Springer Nature Switzerland AG 2022
P. J. J. Welfens, *Russia's Invasion of Ukraine*,
https://doi.org/10.1007/978-3-031-19138-1

c) they define the role and responsibilities of the Competent Authorities and of the other bodies to which tasks have been delegated (...) at each of the crisis levels defined;

d) they ensure that natural gas undertakings and industrial gas customers are given sufficient opportunity to respond at each crisis level;

e) they identify, if appropriate, the measures and actions to be taken to mitigate the potential impact of a gas supply disruption on district heating and the supply of electricity generated from gas, including through an integrated view of energy systems operations across electricity and gas if relevant;

f) they establish detailed procedures and measures to be followed for each crisis level, including the corresponding schemes on information flows;

g) they designate a crisis manager or team and define its role;

h) they identify the contribution of market-based measures for coping with the situation at alert level and mitigating the situation at emergency level.

i) they identify the contribution of non-market-based measures planned or to be implemented for the emergency level, and assess the degree to which the use of such non-market-based measures is necessary to cope with a crisis. The effects of the non-market-based measures shall be assessed and procedures for their implementation defined. Non-market-based measures are to be used only when market-based mechanisms alone can no longer ensure supplies, in particular to protected customers, or for the application of Article 13;

j) they describe the mechanisms used to cooperate with other Member States for each crisis level;

k) they detail the reporting obligations imposed on natural gas undertakings at alert and emergency levels;

l) they describe the technical or legal arrangements in place to prevent undue gas consumption of customers who are connected to a gas distribution or transmission network but not protected customers;

m) they describe the technical, legal and financial arrangements in place to apply the solidarity obligations laid down in Article 13;

n) they estimate the gas volumes that could be consumed by solidarity protected customers covering at least the cases described in Article 6(1);

o) they establish a list of predefined actions to make gas available in the event of an emergency, including commercial agreements between the parties involved in such actions and the compensation mechanisms for natural gas undertakings where appropriate, taking due account of the confidentiality of sensitive data. Such actions may involve cross-border agreements between Member States and/or natural gas undertakings. Such actions may involve cross border agreements between Member States and/or natural gas undertakings."

Source: Federal Ministry for Economic Affairs and Energy (2019), Emergency Plan for Gas for the Federal Republic of Germany, available in English at https://www.bmwk.de/Redaktion/EN/Downloads/E/emergency-plan-gas-germany.pdf?__blob=publicationFile&v=5 (last accessed 25.05.2022)

Annex L: Indirect Job Effects of Major Sectors in Germany (per 100 Direct Job Effects in the Respective Sector; Based on Input Output Analysis)

Germany: Indirect jobs created by 100 direct jobs in industry

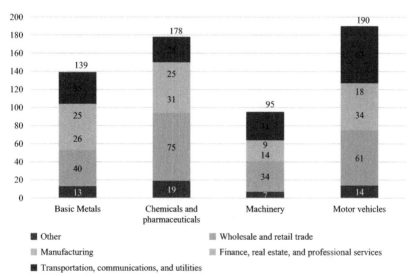

Fig. A1 Indirect Job Effects of Major Sectors in Germany (per 100 Direct Job Effects in the Respective Sector). Source: Own representation of data from IHS Markit

Annex M: Conceptual Framework—Key Quantities in the Bachmann et al. (2022) Model

Note: The subsequent equations come from the presentation by David Baqaee and Ben Moll on April 7, 2022 in the Princeton Webinar of Markus Brunnermeier

Subsequently C denotes consumption in real terms, p denotes price, w nominal wage rate, m import quantity of energy (e.g., gas), x is export quantity, L is labor input: The subsequent equation is a second-order Taylor approximation for the consumption effects where relevant terms concern in the first line expenditures shares and changes in import quantity, export quantity and sectoral labor input, respectively (and other inputs); the second term refers to the impact of changes in the expenditure shares of imports, exports and labor input (and also other inputs) as well as the changes in import quantity, export quantity, and sectoral labor input, respectively (and other inputs):

$$
\Delta \log C \approx \sum_{j \in \text{imports}} \frac{p_j m_j}{GNE} \Delta \log m_j - \sum_{i \in \text{exports}} \frac{p_i x_i^X}{GNE} \Delta \log x_i^X + \sum_{f \in \text{factor}} \frac{w_f L_f}{GNE} \Delta \log L_f
$$
$$
+ \frac{1}{2} \left[\sum_{j \notin D} \Delta \frac{p_j m_j}{GNE} \Delta \log m_j - \sum_{i \in D} \Delta \frac{p_i x_i^X}{GNE} \Delta \log x_i^X + \sum_{f \in F} \Delta \frac{p_f L_f}{GNE} \Delta \log L_f \right]
$$

© The Author(s), under exclusive license to Springer Nature
Switzerland AG 2022
P. J. J. Welfens, *Russia's Invasion of Ukraine*,
https://doi.org/10.1007/978-3-031-19138-1

Key uncertainty:

$\Delta \log m$: size of the shock – reduction in energy imports.

How big will the volume of short-term energy import reduction be? This refers to the decision of the German government on whether it decides to impose a boycott on Russian energy imports—and the associated short-term reallocation of the use of various energy forms plus changes in overall imports (e.g., Germany's additional gas and oil imports from other countries).

Order of Magnitudes: Basic Calculation in the Bachmann et al. Paper
Assumption is a reduction in gas availability: $\Delta \log m$ is -30 percent;
The share of gas in GNE/GDP is 1.2 percent;
It is assumed that the expenditure share quadruples (roughly comparable to the oil crisis in the 1970s); then

$$\Delta \log C \approx \frac{p_j m_j}{GNE} \Delta \log m_j + \frac{1}{2} \Delta \frac{p_j m_j}{GNE} \Delta \log m_j$$

$$= 1.2\% \times \log(0.7) + \frac{1}{2} \times 3.6\% \times \log(0.7) \approx -1\%$$

going further, the authors use a series of structural models (basically 40 countries with 30 industrial sectors for each country)

$\Delta \dfrac{p_j m_j}{GNE}$: change in expenditures – complementarities / essentialness.

ANNEX N: ON INTERNATIONAL CITATIONS OF THE ELTCHANINOFF BOOK ON PUTIN (ENGLISH EDITION: *INSIDE THE MIND OF PUTIN*)

One would have expected that the excellent book of Michel Eltchaninoff could find many readers in the English, or indeed French, version in the Western world and India/Australia/New Zealand etc. This, however, does not seem to be the case if one considers the number of citations—according to Google Scholar—in the period 2018–2021; and this could indicate barriers preventing the diffusion of knowledge in the social sciences—an inadequate and peculiar situation which could even lead to significant risk and dangers.

Below one can find a list of the works in English citing the 2018 translated version of the book of Michel Eltchaninoff (a number of which are master's theses). Only one contribution has a clear direct military/policy background—a 2019 technical note by US Army Major Francesca Graham titled "Putin's Political Philosophy: Implications for Future Russian Military Activity" published by the US Army School of Advanced Military Studies—who came to the conclusion Putin would *not* seek further military escalation against Ukraine (quite contrary to what the contents of the book actually indicate).

There were two more contributions in either Russian/Ukrainian and a paper in Portuguese which cited the English edition of the book. This, in turn, could point to some crucial and actually dangerous inefficiencies of the strong Anglo-Saxon emphasis on journal publications—and a lack of

© The Author(s), under exclusive license to Springer Nature Switzerland AG 2022
P. J. J. Welfens, *Russia's Invasion of Ukraine*,
https://doi.org/10.1007/978-3-031-19138-1

appreciation of scientific books—the latter point a finding one could contemplate when considering the collective intelligence of the West.

2021

Cronin, G. (2021), Disenchanted Wanderer: The Apocalyptic Vision of Konstantin Leontiev, Cornell University Press, https://muse.jhu.edu/book/94427

Oskanian, K. (2021), Hybrid Exceptionalism in Contemporary Russia, in: Russian Exceptionalism between East and West. Palgrave Macmillan, Cham. https://doi.org/10.1007/978-3-030-69713-6_5

Pynnöniemi, K., (2021), Ivan Ilyin and the Kremlin's strategic communication of threats: Evil, worthy and hidden enemies, in: Pynnöniemi, K. (Ed.), Nexus of patriotism and militarism in Russia: A quest for internal cohesion. Helsinki University Press, Helsinki. https://doi.org/10.33134/HUP-9-4

van der Zweerde, E. (2021), Russian Political Philosophy: Between Autocracy and Revolution. In: Bykova, M.F., Forster, M.N., Steiner, L. (eds) The Palgrave Handbook of Russian Thought. Palgrave Macmillan, Cham. https://doi.org/10.1007/978-3-030-62982-3_4

2020

Beck, C. (2020), The rise of Strongmen leaders: a threat to global security, submitted as Master Thesis for a Degree in Political Science at Stellenbosch University, 2020, https://scholar.sun.ac.za/handle/10019.1/108215

Langdon, K.C., Tismaneanu, V. (2020), The Intellectual Origins of Putinism. In: Putin's Totalitarian Democracy. Palgrave Macmillan, Cham. https://doi.org/10.1007/978-3-030-20579-9_4

Löhlein, A. (2020), Biopolitical Conservatism: Identity-Making Projects in Poland and Russia vis-à-vis gender and sexuality, Master Thesis submitted for Degree in Development and International Relations at Aalborg University, https://projekter.aau.dk/projekter/files/334968282/Master_Thesis_Alena_Lohlein.pdf

Sakwa, R. (2020), Russian Politics and Society, 5th Edition, Routledge, London https://doi.org/10.4324/9781003053569

Sakwa, R. (2020), The Putin Paradox, IB Taurus/Bloomsbury Publishing, London https://kar.kent.ac.uk/80013/1/9781788318303_Final_Revised_Proofs.pdf

2019

Berezovenko, A. (2019). CULT OF PERSONALITY OF VLADIMIR PUTIN IN POST-MODERN CONTEXT. *Strategic Priorities,*

49(1), 117–132 https://niss-priority.com/index.php/journal/article/view/245 (paper in Ukrainian, abstract in English)

Graham, F.A. (2019), Putins Political Philosophy: Implications for Future Russian Military Activity, US Army School of Advanced Military Studies, https://apps.dtic.mil/sti/pdfs/AD1083386.pdf

O'Meara, P. (2019), The Russian Nobility in the Age of Alexander I, Bloomsbury Publishing, London (paperback edition 2021)

Pilkington, M. (2015–2019), The Political Economy of the Russian Religious Renaissance—The Place of Putinism Between Spirituality and Modernity (last revised 17 December 2019) https://doi.org/10.2139/ssrn.2659422

Syrovátka, J. (2019), Taylor, Brian D.: The Code of Putinism, *Czech Journal of Political Science*, Issue 3, 217–219 https://www.politologicky-casopis.cz/userfiles/file/2019/3/Polcas_2019_3_pp_217-219.pdf   (a review of Taylor's 2018 book The Code of Putinism—see below)

Worth, O. (2019), Morbid Symptoms: The Global Rise of the Far-Right, Zed Books Ltd., London

2018

Taylor, Brian D. (2018), The Code of Putinism, Oxford University Press, Oxford

Annex O: IMF World Economic Outlook Projections, April 2022

(Percent change, unless noted otherwise)

	2021	Projections 2022	Projections 2023	Difference from January 2022 WEO Update[1] 2022	Difference from January 2022 WEO Update[1] 2023	Difference from October 2021 WEO[1] 2022	Difference from October 2021 WEO[1] 2023
World Output	**6.1**	**3.6**	**3.6**	**–0.8**	**–0.2**	**–1.3**	**0.0**
Advanced Economies	**5.2**	**3.3**	**2.4**	**–0.6**	**–0.2**	**–1.2**	**0.2**
United States	5.7	3.7	2.3	–0.3	–0.3	–1.5	0.1
Euro Area	5.3	2.8	2.3	–1.1	–0.2	–1.5	0.3
Germany	2.8	2.1	2.7	–1.7	0.2	–2.5	1.1
France	7.0	2.9	1.4	–0.6	–0.4	–1.0	–0.4
Italy	6.6	2.3	1.7	–1.5	–0.5	–1.9	0.1
Spain	5.1	4.8	3.3	–1.0	–0.5	–1.6	0.7
Japan	1.6	2.4	2.3	–0.9	0.5	–0.8	0.9
United Kingdom	7.4	3.7	1.2	–1.0	–1.1	–1.3	–0.7
Canada	4.6	3.9	2.8	–0.2	0.0	–1.0	0.2
Other Advanced Economies[2]	5.0	3.1	3.0	–0.5	0.1	–0.6	0.1
Emerging Market and Developing Economies	**6.8**	**3.8**	**4.4**	**–1.0**	**–0.3**	**–1.3**	**–0.2**
Emerging and Developing Asia	7.3	5.4	5.6	–0.5	–0.2	–0.9	–0.1
China	8.1	4.4	5.1	–0.4	–0.1	–1.2	–0.2
India[3]	8.9	8.2	6.9	–0.8	–0.2	–0.3	0.3
ASEAN-5[4]	3.4	5.3	5.9	–0.3	–0.1	–0.5	–0.1
Emerging and Developing Europe	6.7	–2.9	1.3	–6.4	–1.6	–6.5	–1.6
Russia	4.7	–8.5	–2.3	–11.3	–4.4	–11.4	–4.3
Latin America and the Caribbean	6.8	2.5	2.5	0.1	–0.1	–0.5	0.0
Brazil	4.6	0.8	1.4	0.5	–0.2	–0.7	–0.6
Mexico	4.8	2.0	2.5	–0.8	–0.2	–2.0	0.3
Middle East and Central Asia	5.7	4.6	3.7	0.3	0.1	0.5	–0.1
Saudi Arabia	3.2	7.6	3.6	2.8	0.8	2.8	0.8
Sub-Saharan Africa	4.5	3.8	4.0	0.1	0.0	0.0	–0.1
Nigeria	3.6	3.4	3.1	0.7	0.4	0.7	0.5
South Africa	4.9	1.9	1.4	0.0	0.0	–0.3	0.0
Memorandum							
World Growth Based on Market Exchange Rates	5.8	3.5	3.1	–0.7	–0.3	–1.2	0.0
European Union	5.4	2.9	2.5	–1.1	–0.3	–1.5	0.2
Middle East and North Africa	5.8	5.0	3.6	0.6	0.2	0.9	0.1
Emerging Market and Middle-Income Economies	7.0	3.8	4.3	–1.0	–0.3	–1.3	–0.3
Low-Income Developing Countries	4.0	4.6	5.4	–0.7	–0.1	–0.7	–0.1
World Trade Volume (goods and services)	**10.1**	**5.0**	**4.4**	**–1.0**	**–0.5**	**–1.7**	**–0.1**
Imports							
Advanced Economies	9.5	6.1	4.5	–0.2	0.0	–1.2	0.4
Emerging Market and Developing Economies	11.8	3.9	4.8	–1.7	–0.9	–3.2	–0.9
Exports							
Advanced Economies	8.6	5.0	4.7	–1.1	0.0	–1.6	0.7
Emerging Market and Developing Economies	12.3	4.1	3.6	–1.7	–1.5	–1.7	–1.4
Commodity Prices (US dollars)							
Oil[5]	67.3	54.7	–13.3	42.8	–5.5	56.5	–8.3
Nonfuel (average based on world commodity import weights)	26.8	11.4	–2.5	8.3	–0.6	12.3	–1.0
Consumer Prices							
Advanced Economies	3.1	5.7	2.5	1.8	0.4	3.4	0.6
Emerging Market and Developing Economies[6]	5.9	8.7	6.5	2.8	1.8	3.8	2.2

Source: IMF staff estimates.

Note: Real effective exchange rates are assumed to remain constant at the levels prevailing during February 7, 2022–March 7, 2022. Economies are listed on the basis of economic size. The aggregated quarterly data are seasonally adjusted. WEO = *World Economic Outlook*.

[1]Difference based on rounded figures for the current, January 2022 WEO *Update*, and October 2021 WEO forecasts.

[2]Excludes the Group of Seven (Canada, France, Germany, Italy, Japan, United Kingdom, United States) and euro area countries.

[3]For India, data and forecasts are presented on a fiscal year basis, and GDP from 2011 onward is based on GDP at market prices with fiscal year 2011/12 as a base year.

Fig. A2 Overview of the World Economic Outlook Projections (IMF, 2022b). Source: IMF (2022b), Table 1.1, p. 6f

(Percent change, unless noted otherwise)

	Year over Year				Q4 over Q4[8]			
			Projections				Projections	
	2020	2021	2022	2023	2020	2021	2022	2023
World Output	−3.1	6.1	3.6	3.6	−0.3	4.6	2.5	3.5
Advanced Economies	−4.5	5.2	3.3	2.4	−2.7	4.7	2.5	2.0
United States	−3.4	5.7	3.7	2.3	−2.3	5.6	2.8	1.7
Euro Area	−6.4	5.3	2.8	2.3	−4.3	4.6	1.8	2.3
Germany	−4.6	2.8	2.1	2.7	−2.9	1.8	2.4	2.5
France	−8.0	7.0	2.9	1.4	−4.3	5.4	0.9	1.5
Italy	−9.0	6.6	2.3	1.7	−6.1	6.2	0.5	2.2
Spain	−10.8	5.1	4.8	3.3	−8.8	5.5	2.3	4.0
Japan	−4.5	1.6	2.4	2.3	−0.8	0.4	3.5	0.8
United Kingdom	−9.3	7.4	3.7	1.2	−6.3	6.6	1.1	1.5
Canada	−5.2	4.6	3.9	2.8	−3.1	3.3	3.5	2.2
Other Advanced Economies[2]	−1.8	5.0	3.1	3.0	−0.4	4.5	2.5	2.8
Emerging Market and Developing Economies	−2.0	6.8	3.8	4.4	1.7	4.4	2.5	4.9
Emerging and Developing Asia	−0.8	7.3	5.4	5.6	3.7	4.2	4.4	5.8
China	2.2	8.1	4.4	5.1	6.4	3.5	4.8	4.7
India[3]	−6.6	8.9	8.2	6.9	1.5	5.6	2.7	9.0
ASEAN-5[4]	−3.4	3.4	5.3	5.9	−2.5	4.5	5.1	5.3
Emerging and Developing Europe	−1.8	6.7	−2.9	1.3	0.0	6.3	−6.0	3.3
Russia	−2.7	4.7	−8.5	−2.3	−1.7	5.0	−14.1	3.3
Latin America and the Caribbean	−7.0	6.8	2.5	2.5	−3.2	3.8	1.6	2.5
Brazil	−3.9	4.6	0.8	1.4	−1.0	1.6	0.8	1.9
Mexico	−8.2	4.8	2.0	2.5	−4.4	1.1	3.3	1.9
Middle East and Central Asia	−2.9	5.7	4.6	3.7	...	...	...	...
Saudi Arabia	−4.1	3.2	7.6	3.6	−3.8	6.7	6.9	3.6
Sub-Saharan Africa	−1.7	4.5	3.8	4.0	...	...	...	...
Nigeria	−1.8	3.6	3.4	3.1	−0.2	2.4	2.1	2.3
South Africa	−6.4	4.9	1.9	1.4	−3.4	1.8	2.3	1.1
Memorandum								
World Growth Based on Market Exchange Rates	−3.5	5.8	3.5	3.1	−0.9	4.5	2.6	2.9
European Union	−5.9	5.4	2.9	2.5	−4.1	5.0	1.8	2.7
Middle East and North Africa	−3.3	5.8	5.0	3.6	...	...	...	...
Emerging Market and Middle-Income Economies	−2.2	7.0	3.8	4.3	1.8	4.5	2.4	4.9
Low-Income Developing Countries	0.2	4.0	4.6	5.4	...	...	...	...
World Trade Volume (goods and services)	−7.9	10.1	5.0	4.4	...	...	...	...
Imports								
Advanced Economies	−8.7	9.5	6.1	4.5	...	...	...	...
Emerging Market and Developing Economies	−7.9	11.8	3.9	4.8	...	...	...	...
Exports								
Advanced Economies	−9.1	8.6	5.0	4.7	...	...	...	...
Emerging Market and Developing Economies	−4.8	12.3	4.1	3.6	...	...	...	...
Commodity Prices (US dollars)								
Oil[5]	−32.7	67.3	54.7	−13.3	−27.6	79.2	28.6	−11.6
Nonfuel (average based on world commodity import weights)	6.8	26.8	11.4	−2.5	15.4	17.3	9.4	−2.5
Consumer Prices								
Advanced Economies[6]	0.7	3.1	5.7	2.5	0.4	4.9	4.8	2.2
Emerging Market and Developing Economies[7]	5.2	5.9	8.7	6.5	3.3	6.0	8.8	5.3

[4]Indonesia, Malaysia, Philippines, Thailand, Vietnam.

[5]Simple average of prices of UK Brent, Dubai Fateh, and West Texas Intermediate crude oil. The average price of oil in US dollars a barrel was $69.07 in 2021; the assumed price, based on futures markets, is $106.83 in 2022 and $92.63 in 2023.

[6]The inflation rates for 2022 and 2023, respectively, are as follows: 5.3 percent and 2.3 percent for the euro area, 1.0 percent and 0.8 percent for Japan, and 7.7 percent and 2.9 percent for the United States.

[7]Excludes Venezuela. See the country-specific note for Venezuela in the "Country Notes" section of the Statistical Appendix.

[8]For world output, the quarterly estimates and projections account for approximately 90 percent of annual world output at purchasing-power-parity weights. For Emerging Market and Developing Economies, the quarterly estimates and projections account for approximately 80 percent of annual emerging market and developing economies' output at purchasing-power-parity weights.

(Percent change)

	2021	Projections		Difference from January 2022 WEO *Update*[1]		Difference from October 2021 WEO[1]	
		2022	2023	2022	2023	2022	2023
World Output	5.8	**3.5**	**3.1**	−0.7	−0.3	−1.2	0.0
Advanced Economies	5.1	**3.3**	**2.3**	−0.6	−0.2	−1.2	0.2
Emerging Market and Developing Economies	6.8	**3.8**	**4.2**	−0.8	−0.3	−1.2	−0.3
Emerging and Developing Asia	7.4	5.0	5.4	−0.5	−0.2	−1.0	−0.1
Emerging and Developing Europe	6.4	−2.1	0.8	−5.6	−2.1	−5.8	−2.1
Latin America and the Caribbean	6.6	2.4	2.4	0.2	−0.1	−0.6	−0.1
Middle East and Central Asia	5.1	4.6	3.4	0.5	0.2	0.7	0.0
Sub-Saharan Africa	4.5	3.8	3.9	0.2	0.1	0.1	0.0
Memorandum							
European Union	5.3	2.8	2.4	−1.1	−0.2	−1.5	0.2
Middle East and North Africa	5.0	4.8	3.2	0.7	0.2	0.9	0.1
Emerging Market and Middle-Income Economies	7.0	3.7	4.2	−0.8	−0.3	−1.3	−0.3
Low-Income Developing Countries	4.0	4.6	5.3	−0.6	−0.1	−0.6	−0.1

Source: IMF staff estimates.
Note: The aggregate growth rates are calculated as a weighted average, in which a moving average of nominal GDP in US dollars for the preceding three years is used as the weight. WEO = *World Economic Outlook*.
[1]Difference based on rounded figures for the current, January 2022 WEO *Update*, and October 2021 WEO forecasts.

Fig. A3 Overview of the World Economic Outlook Projections at Market Exchange Rate Weights (IMF, 2022b). Source: IMF (2022b), Table 1.2, p. 8

Annex P: Traditional Gas Market Perspective in the EU and New Approach

The following graph (Fig. A4) shows the standard economic perspective on the EU Gas Market (with DD denoting the EU demand for gas; k'* is the supply curve of Gazprom and other firms). If the EU would impose an import tariff on Russian gas, the standard result is that the net price—the offer price without the tariff—will fall, while the gross price p' will rise (p_1 >p_0). The assumption here is that firms are profit maximizing. However, in the situation with the Russo-Ukrainian war, Gazprom is not maximizing profits, but rather acting as an instrument of the Kremlin trying to create high economic damage in the EU. Gazprom might decide to raise the offer price of gas by as much as the import tariff of the EU is (see the reduced quantity q_2).

P. J. J. Welfens, *Russia's Invasion of Ukraine*,
https://doi.org/10.1007/978-3-031-19138-1

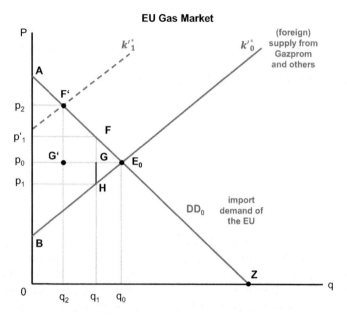

Fig. A4   EU Gas Market and EU Import Tariff. Source: Own representation

As regards inflation pressure in the context of rising expected oil and gas prices in 2022, one may point out the paradoxical possibility that rising central bank interest rates in the course of 2022 (e.g., in the Eurozone and the US plus the UK) could stimulate oil production which in turn could dampen the inflation dynamics in the context of a modified Hotelling pricing rule of natural resources.

A Modified Hotelling Approach

Let i, P" and P"^{E} denote the nominal interest rate, the oil price and the expected oil price, respectively; H is the unit cost of resource extraction (t is the time index). The Hotelling rule says that the marginal profit for taking an extra resource unit from the ground in time t should be equal to the expected marginal profit for an extra unit of production in the next period. The marginal profit from an extra unit produced in period t is the cash flow (P" minus unit costs H) times the nominal interest rate. Subsequently r is the real interest rate and the inflation rate is denoted by π where π" is the oil price inflation rate and π' is the inflation rate for non-oil goods (v is the share of non-oil goods in the consumption basket); q^s is the quantity of oil offered, π^E is the expected inflation rate.

(1) $i(P''-H) = dP''^E/dt$ (t is time index); divide by P''
(2) $i(1 - H/P'')= \pi''^E$; if $H=H'q$ ($H'>0$), q quantity

Taking logs on both sides gives (assuming that H/P'' is close to zero)

(3) $\ln i - H'q/P'' = \ln\pi''^E$; H' is a cost parameter
(4) Hence quantity supplied $q^s= \ln(i/\pi''^E)P''/H'$ and with $i = r + \pi^E$ and $\pi := v\pi' +(1-v) \pi''$ ($0<v<1$) for case $\pi'=\pi''$ (constant relative price) and with $\ln(1+x)\approx x$ (small r/π''^E)
(5) $q= (r/\pi''^E)P''/H'$

Hence we get:

(6) $P''=H'(\pi''^E/r)q$

Assuming that global oil demand depends on the real income and—negatively—on P''/P (P is the general price level; V' and V'' are positive parameters):

(7) $q^d=V'Y-V''P''/P$

Considering the supply side and the demand side we get the equilibrium price P'':

(8) Equilibrium $P'' = V'Y/((r/\pi''^E)/H' + V''/P)$; $V'>0$; $V''>0$
(9) $\ln P''= \ln V' + \ln Y - \ln((r/\pi''^E)/H' +V''/P)$

The equilibrium price is a positive function of real income and a negative function of r/π''^E and a negative function of the price level P. For an expected inflation rate, the equilibrium oil price is a negative function of the real interest rate. If the real interest rate is falling in the US, the Eurozone, and the UK—in 2019–2021—the equilibrium price of oil is rising. If, however, the real interest rate is rising (possibly in 2022–2024) in the world economy, then the equilibrium price of oil will fall. In a second stage this could bring about a fall of the expected inflation rate.

ANNEX Q: EU TRADE RELATIONS WITH UKRAINE. FACTS, FIGURES, AND LATEST DEVELOPMENTS (EUROPEAN COMMISSION, 2020B)

Negotiations and Agreements

- The Association Agreement, including a Deep and Comprehensive Free Trade Area (DCFTA) between the EU and Ukraine was negotiated between 2007 and 2011, and signed on 21 March and 27 June 2014.
- The DCFTA has been provisionally applied since 1 January 2016. The Association Agreement formally entered into force on 1 September 2017 following ratification by all EU Member States.
- The Association Agreement is the main tool for bringing Ukraine and the EU closer together: it promotes deeper political ties, stronger economic links and the respect for common values.
- The EU granted Autonomous Trade Measures (ATMs) for Ukraine, topping up the concessions included in the Association Agreement/DCFTA for several industrial goods and agricultural products from October 2017 for a period of three years.

Trade Topics

- The EU is Ukraine's largest trading partner, accounting for more than 40% of its trade in 2019. Ukraine is the 18th trading of the EU accounting for around 1.1% of EU's total trade. Total trade between EU and Ukraine reached €43.3 bn in 2019.

- Ukraine exports to the EU amounted to €19.1 bn in 2019. The main Ukraine exports are raw materials (iron, steel, mining products, agricultural products), chemical products and machinery. This is a considerably increase of 48.5% since 2016.
- The EU exports to Ukraine amounted to over €24.2 bn in 2019. The main EU exports to Ukraine include machinery and transport equipment, chemicals, and manufactured goods. EU exports to Ukraine have been subject to a similar impressive increase since 2016 of 48.8%.
- The number of Ukrainian companies exporting to the EU has increased at an impressive rate, from approximately 11,700 in 2015 to over 14,500 in 2019.

The EU and Ukraine

- The AA/DCFTA aims to boost trade in goods and services between the EU and Ukraine by gradually cutting tariffs and bringing Ukraine's rules in line with the EU's in certain industrial sectors and agricultural products.
- To better integrate with the EU market, Ukraine is harmonising many of its norms and standards in industrial and agricultural products. Ukraine is also aligning its legislation to the EU's in trade-related areas such as:
- Competition
- Technical barriers to trade (TBT)
- Sanitary and phytosanitary (SPS)
- Customs and trade facilitation
- Protection of intellectual property rights

The EU has banned the import of goods originating in Crimea and Sevastopol, as well as investments and a number of directly related services there until at least 23 June 2020. This is in line with its policy of not recognising the Russian Federation's illegal annexation of Crimea and Sevastopol.

Export Ban on Unprocessed Wood

- The EU-Ukraine Association Agreement prohibits any form of export restrictions.
- The EU considers therefore that keeping in place since 2005 a permanent ban on exports of sawn wood violates the terms of the agreement.

Committees and Dialogues

- The EU and Ukraine meet regularly to discuss issues and best practices and oversee the proper functioning of the Agreement.

Source: European Commission (2020b), Ukraine—EU trade relations with Ukraine. Facts, figures and latest developments, available at https://policy.trade.ec.europa.eu/eu-trade-relationships-country-and-region/countries-and-regions/ukraine_en (last accessed 25.05.2022)

Annex R: House of Commons Foreign Affairs Committee (2017)

"The bilateral relationship between the United Kingdom and Russia is at its most strained point since the end of the Cold war. This is because Russia and the UK have fundamentally different perceptions of recent history and the current international order. UK foreign policy is predicated on the maintenance of the rules-based international order and of international law, self-determination for sovereign nation states and the promotion of human rights and freedom of expression. Russia's post-Soviet experience and the apparent self-interest of the governing elite has led to a Russian foreign policy which more or less explicitly rejects and undermines that order and the principles on which it relies.

Refusal to engage with the Russian Government is, however, not a viable long-term foreign policy option for the UK, because Russia is a European nuclear-armed United Nations Security Council member state. The UK can communicate with the Russian Government without ceding moral and legal legitimacy or sacrificing its values and standards. Such conversations might well prove uncomfortable, but they would at least allow the clarification of specific points of agreement and points of difference on issues such as counter-terrorism and provide a basis for progress towards improving relations, if and when the time is right. To that end, we recommend the commitment of increased FCO resources to enhance analytical and policymaking capacity and the appointment of an FCO Minister with more specific responsibility for Russia.

© The Author(s), under exclusive license to Springer Nature
Switzerland AG 2022
P. J. J. Welfens, *Russia's Invasion of Ukraine*,
https://doi.org/10.1007/978-3-031-19138-1

Russia's actions in Ukraine and Syria constitute the two most urgent foreign policy challenges to the UK-Russia relationship. Ukraine must choose its own future. The UK and its allies should support Ukraine in developing resilience to further Russian encroachment and in building its social, political and physical infrastructure, which will facilitate further engagement with the West and allow Ukraine to engage with Russia on a more level playing field. While it may be increasingly difficult to sustain a unified western position on Ukraine-related sanctions, unilateral sanctions targeted on individuals, as set out in the Criminal Finances Bill, would enable the Government more effectively to hold to account people associated with the Putin regime who are responsible for gross human rights violations or abuses.

In Syria, UK Government officials have accused Russia of committing war crimes but have not published evidence to support their claims. The Government is right to call out the Russian military for actions that potentially violate International Humanitarian Law. However, if the Government continues to allege that Russia has committed war crimes in Syria without providing a basis for its charge, it risks bolstering the Kremlin's narrative that Russia is held to unfair double standards by hostile and hypocritical western powers.

The British and Russian people have healthy cultural relations despite the ongoing political difficulties. Bearing that point in mind, the Government must look beyond President Putin and reach out to the Russian people through mechanisms such as educational exchanges and support for small businesses in Russia in non-sanctioned sectors. A people-to-people strategy building bridges with the next generation of Russian political and economic leaders could underpin improved UK-Russia relations in the future."

House of Commons Foreign Affairs Committee (2017), The United Kingdom's relations with Russia, Seventh Report of Session 2016–2017, https://publications.parliament.uk/pa/cm201617/cmselect/cmfaff/120/120.pdf (last accessed 25.05.2022)

Annex S: Simplified Regression Analysis for the Russian Real Gross Domestic Product, 2005–2021

Looking for a simple explanation of the development of Russia's real GDP 2005–2021—based on annual data—the coefficient for the industrial power consumption is highly significant in the subsequent simple regression; the adjusted R^2 is 0.8. The elasticity of real GDP with respect to industrial electricity consumption is 1.86 so that a 1% increase of the real GDP of Russia goes along with a rise of electricity consumption of 1.86%. The basic idea here is that all value-added (except for a large part of the shadow economy) is linked to industrial electricity consumption. Thus, if one has some doubts about official Russian statistics one could replace real GDP figures by industrial power consumption to have a rather simple estimation of the true real output development (a procedure used, for example, more than a decade ago by Evgeny Gavrilenkov). Such a procedure would then be adequate to estimate for example the real GDP in Russia in 2022. Rosstat issued a statement in August 2022 claiming that real GDP in the second quarter of 2022 had declined by 4% on an annual basis, i.e., compared to the second quarter of 2021.

In principle it is possible to consider a longer time period for the subsequent analysis than just 2005–2021. It is assumed here that the Russian government may have influenced the preparation of non-accurate real GDP numbers in some publications of Rosstat, while the figures on electricity consumption are more accurate. The subsequent graphs on real GDP growth (Fig. A5) and industrial electricity consumption (Fig. A6)

© The Author(s), under exclusive license to Springer Nature Switzerland AG 2022
P. J. J. Welfens, *Russia's Invasion of Ukraine*,
https://doi.org/10.1007/978-3-031-19138-1

show some crucial developments and implicit linkages between real income growth and the growth of electricity consumption (Fig. A7).

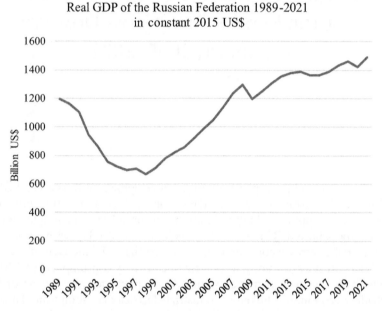

Fig. A5 Real GDP of Russia in billions of constant 2015 US$, 1989–2021. Source: Own representation of data from World Bank (World Development Indicators, Indicator Code *NY.GDP.MKTP.KD*)

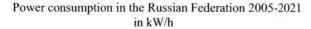

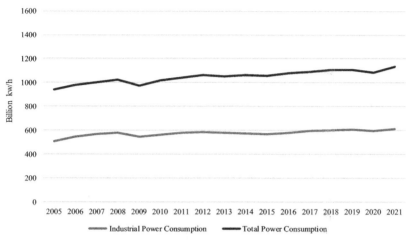

Fig. A6 Industrial and total power consumption in Russia 2005–2021 in kW/h. Notes: Industrial energy consumption is comprised of (1) Mining, manufacturing, electricity, gas and water production and distribution; (2) Construction; (3) ICT activities (from 2017). Total energy consumption further includes (1) Agriculture, hunting and forestry production; (2) Wholesale and retail trade (from 2012) and repair of motor vehicles and motorbikes (from 2017); (3) Transport and communications (2005–2016) / Transport and storage (from 2017); (4) Other economic activities; (5) [Urban and rural] population; (6) Power grid losses. Source: Rosstat (2022), updated 26.05.2022

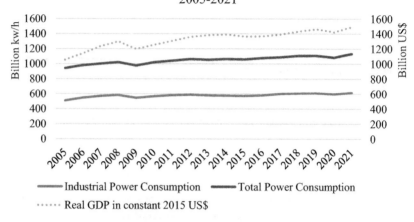

Fig. A7 Industrial and total power consumption in Russia in kW/h and real GDP in constant 2015 US$, 2005–2021. Notes: Industrial energy consumption is comprised of (1) Mining, manufacturing, electricity, gas and water production and distribution; (2) Construction; (3) ICT activities (from 2017). Total energy consumption further includes (1) Agriculture, hunting and forestry production; (2) Wholesale and retail trade (from 2012) and repair of motor vehicles and motorbikes (from 2017); (3) Transport and communications (2005–2016) / Transport and storage (from 2017); (4) Other economic activities; (5) [Urban and rural] population; (6) Power grid losses. Source: Own calculations and representation of energy data from Rosstat (2022), updated 26.05.2022, and own representation of GDP data from World Bank (World Development Indicators, Indicator Code *NY. GDP.MKTP.KD*)

A group of researchers led by a team from the Yale Chief Executive Leadership Institute at the Yale School of Management have published a paper (Sonnenfeld et al., 2022) which argues that the effects of sanctions on Russia, and firms withdrawing from the Russian market, are "nothing short of catastrophic, eroding the Russian economy's competitiveness while exacerbating internal structural weaknesses" (p. 57). The Yale research group—with its very negative outlook on the Russian economic development in 2022—has not considered this approach so that considerable doubts remain about the conjectures in the Yale group's report on the negative effects of the war and the response of other countries and firms, respectively, on the Russian economy.

Simplified Regression Approach for Russia (where Y_{real} is real gross domestic product)

$ln(Y_{real}) = \alpha_0 + \alpha_1 * ln(\text{industrial power consumption})$

Y_{real} : real GDP (of the Russian Federation from 2005-2021)

Industrial power consumption: industrial power consumption (of the Russian Federation from 2005-2021)

Data Sources:

Real GDP: World Bank (World Development Indicators, Indicator Code NY.GDP.MKTP.KD).

Industrial power consumption: Rosstat (2022)

Regression output:

lm(formula = lngdp ~ lnpower)

Information on Russian Power System Operator, accessed August 16, 2022

Based on the figures of the leading Power Systems Operator's monthly electricity production information, one can derive a rough estimate of the real GDP growth in Russia. There is one specific caveat with respect to 2022 as Russia's gas exports have considerably declined which itself could amount to a real GDP decline of about 1%—if gas export volumes in the first half of the year and the second half of the year have dropped by about 50%; the direct output decline effect on real GDP could be only about

Table A5 Residuals of a Simplified Regression Approach

Min	1Q	Median	3Q	Max
–0.047312	–0.021093	0.001309	0.014978	0.058723

Table A6 Coefficients of Simplified Regression Approach

	Estimate	Std. Error	t value	Pr(>|t|)
(Intercept)	–22.4615	4.6053	–4.877	0.000201***
lnpower	1.8601	0.1701	10.937	1.52e-08***

Level of statistical significance: 0 '***' 0.001 '**' 0.01 '*' 0.05 '.' 0.1 ' ' 1

Residual standard error: 0.03217 on 15 degrees of freedom

Multiple R-squared: 0.8886; Adjusted R-squared: 0.8812; F-statistic: 119.6 on 1 and 15 DF, p-value: 1.518e-08

0.5% if one assumes that excess gas produced in the first half of Russia is used for filling storage capacity in 2022—this argument will hardly still be valid in 2023 when gas storage capacities are rather limited in Russia. To the extent that Gazprom supplies additional gas deliveries (compared to 2021) within Russia at a relative price discount, there would be an incentive for output expansion in gas-consuming sectors. As the export volume of gas has declined particularly in 2022, the above regression might have to be modified in order take into consideration that gas production and distribution could be more electricity-intensive than the average value-added in Russia. Subsequently, information is used from the regional Russian Power System Operator which publishes monthly production data on electricity production.

The Russian Power System Operator (*Системный Оператор Единой Энергетической Системы*; SO-UPS, 2022a) is a specialized organization solely responsible for centralized operational and dispatch management in the Unified Power System (UPS) of Russia (*ЕЭС России*) which consists of seven large unified energy system covering 71 regional power systems. It covers a large part of the Russian territory and energy use (see map of the unified energy systems below (Fig. A8)—the grey area encompasses independent power systems).

Fig. A8   Map of the Russian Power System Operator and Seven Regional Power Systems. Source: SO-UPS (2022b), available online at https://www.so-ups.ru/functioning/ees/ups2022/

Table A7 Implied annual growth rate of Russia's real GDP[b] on the basis of changing power consumption

	Jan.	Feb.	March	April	May	June
Power consumption in the UPS in billion kW/h	106.9	95.0	101.5	89.0	84.9	78.9
Power consumption in Russia in billion kW/h	108.6	96.5	103.1	90.5	86.3	80.1
Change in power consumption in the UPS[a]	3.8%	−0.2%	2.9%	2.2%	3.7%	0.5%
Annual change in power consumption in Russia	3.7%	−0.2%	3.0%	2.3%	3.8%	0.5%
Implied annual growth rate of Russia's real GDP[b]	**6.88%**	**−0.37%**	**5.58%**	**4.28%**	**7.07%**	**0.93%**

Notes: [a]Compared to the same month of the previous year; [b]Change in power consumption in Russia (%) multiplied by 1.86. Real GDP is measured in constant 2015 US$

Source: Own calculations using data from SO-UPS (2022c, 2022d, 2022e, 2022f, 2022g, 2022h)

Change in power consumption in Russia (last line based on the regression above)

In February 2022, the real GDP growth rate (actually a decline of output) was close to zero, and in July this figure was slightly less than 1%. Based on the percentage change of power consumption in the first six months of 2022, there is little evidence for a very strong reduction of real GDP growth. Industrial output and GDP seem, however, to have become rather volatile; a real decline of real GDP is likely for the second half of 2022 and also for 2023.

Sources:

Sonnenfeld, J. et al. (2022), Business Retreats and Sanctions Are Crippling the Russian Economy, August 2022 update, available at https://papers.ssrn.com/sol3/papers.cfm?abstract_id=4167193 (last accessed 18.08.2022)

SO-UPS (2022a), About the Company, online: https://www.so-ups.ru/about/.

SO-UPS (2022b), Unified Power System of Russia, online: https://www.so-ups.ru/functioning/ees/ups2022/.

SO-UPS (2022c), Press Release: *Потребление электроэнергии в ЕЭС России в январе 2022 года увеличилось на 3,8 % по сравнению с январем 2021 года*, 01.02.2022, online: https://www.so-ups.ru/news/press-release/press-release-view/news/17676/

SO-UPS (2022d), Press Release: *Потребление электроэнергии в ЕЭС России в феврале 2022 года уменьшилось на 0,2 % по сравнению с февралем 2021 года*, 02.03.2022, online: https://www.so-ups.ru/news/press-release/press-release-view/news/17816/

SO-UPS (2022e), Press Release: *Потребление электроэнергии в ЕЭС России в марте 2022 года увеличилось на 2,9 % по сравнению с мартом 2021 года*, 05.04.2022, online: https://www.so-ups.ru/news/press-release/press-release-view/news/17973/

SO-UPS (2022f), Press Release: *Потребление электроэнергии в ЕЭС России в апреле 2022 года увеличилось на 2,2 % по сравнению с апрелем 2021 года*, 05.05.2022, online: https://www.so-ups.ru/news/press-release/press-release-view/news/18177/

SO-UPS (2022g), Press Release: *Потребление электроэнергии в ЕЭС России в мае 2022 года увеличилось на 3,7 % по сравнению с маем 2021 года*, 02.06.2022, online: https://www.so-ups.ru/news/press-release/press-release-view/news/18435/

SO-UPS (2022h), Press Release: *Потребление электроэнергии в ЕЭС России в июне 2022 года увеличилось на 0,5 % по сравнению с июнем 2021 года*, 04.07.2022, online: https://www.so-ups.ru/news/press-release/press-release-view/news/18740/

Annex T: Analytical Approach for the Economic Effects of a Gas Cut-off in Germany in the Second Half of 2022, According to Lan et al. (2022, p. 25)

The Lan et al. (2022) analysis of the effects of a Russian gas shutoff for Germany is built on a clear modeling approach which is reproduced here from the Appendix I of the authors (p. 25):

Nested Production Model and Extensions

"Assume that a representative firm in sector k operates a constant return to scale production function

$$Y_k = Z_k E_k^{\alpha_{E_k}} \Pi_{j=1}^{J} X_{jk}^{\alpha_{jk}}, \tag{1}$$

where $\alpha_E > 0$ parameterizes the importance of energy input in production; X_{jk} is the intermediate input from sector j used in the production of sector k and α_{jk} reflects the relative importance of intermediate goods from sector j in the production of output in sector k; and E_k is an aggregation of gas and other energy inputs, such as coal, oil, and renewables,

$$E_k = \left(\omega e_{gas_k}^{\frac{\epsilon-1}{\epsilon}} + (1-\omega) e_{oth_k}^{\frac{\epsilon-1}{\epsilon}} \right)^{\frac{\epsilon}{\epsilon-1}}, \tag{2}$$

where $\omega > 0$ captures the importance of gas in total energy inputs and ϵ is the elasticity of substitution between gas and other energy inputs.

© The Author(s), under exclusive license to Springer Nature Switzerland AG 2022
P. J. J. Welfens, *Russia's Invasion of Ukraine*,
https://doi.org/10.1007/978-3-031-19138-1

Following Kmenta (1967), the CES production function of energy inputs could be approximated by a function of the form

$$E_k \approx e_{gas_k}^{\omega} e_{oth_k}^{1-\omega} \left(\frac{e_{gas_k}}{e_{oth_k}} \right)^{\frac{1}{2}\left(1-\frac{1}{\epsilon}\right)\omega(1-\omega)\ln\left(\frac{e_{gas_k}}{e_{oth_k}}\right)}, \tag{3}$$

and a second-order approximation gives

$$d \ln E_k = \omega d \ln e_{gas_k} + \frac{1}{2}\left(1-\frac{1}{\epsilon}\right)\omega(1-\omega)d \ln e_{gas_k} d \ln e_{gas_k}. \tag{4}$$

The constant return to scale production function for a representative firm in sector k can be approximated by

$$d \ln Y_k \approx \alpha_{E_k} d \ln E_k + \sum_j \alpha_{jk} d \ln X_{jk} \tag{5}$$

Plugging equation (4) into equation (5) allows us to obtain the relationship between changes in gross output and gas usage, which summarizes the direct impact of gas shocks on gross output,

$$d\ln Y_k^d \approx \alpha_{E_k}\left(\omega \ln e_{gas_k} + \frac{1}{2}\left(1-\frac{1}{\epsilon}\right)\omega(1-\omega) d\ln e_{gas_k} d\ln e_{gas_k} \right), \tag{6}$$

where $d \ln Y_k^d$ is denoted as the direct impact on gross output.

Direct impact

Given that the distribution parameters α_E and ω reflect the importance of energy inputs in production and the importance of gas in energy inputs respectively, we calibrate α_E to energy expenditure share $\frac{P_E E_K}{P_k Y_k}$ in total output and ω to the gas share in energy inputs $\frac{P_{gas} e_{gas_k}}{P_E E_K}$. Equation (6) can be rewritten as

$$d \ln Y_k^d \approx \frac{P_{gas} e_{gas_k}}{P_k Y_k} d \ln e_{gas_k} + \frac{1}{2}\Delta \frac{P_{gas} e_{gas_k}}{P_k Y_k} d \ln e_{gas_k}, \tag{7}$$

where changes in gas expenditure shares

$$\Delta \frac{p_{gas} e_{gas_k}}{P_k Y_k} = \alpha_E \left(1 - \frac{1}{\epsilon}\right) \omega (1 - \omega) d \ln e_{gas_k}.$$ ϵ reflects how easy it is to substi-

tute gas with other inputs in production. A higher elasticity of substitution means that firms can switch from gas to alternative resources with greater ease, meaning that a smaller increase in the price of natural gas is needed to bring about the fall in demand to clear the market, and thus with smaller implied changes in gas expenditure shares."

The authors also cover second-round effects for which the interested reader is referred to the working paper of Lan, T.; Sher, G.; Zhou, J. (2022), The Economic Impacts on Germany of a Potential Russian Gas Shutoff. IMF Working Paper No. WP/22/144. Washington DC

Index

© The Author(s), under exclusive license to Springer Nature Switzerland AG 2022
P. J. J. Welfens, *Russia's Invasion of Ukraine*,
https://doi.org/10.1007/978-3-031-19138-1

Printed by Printforce, the Netherlands